Lecture Notes in Computer Science 7498

Commenced Publication in 1973
Founding and Former Series Editors:
Gerhard Goos, Juris Hartmanis, and Jan van Leeuwen

Lecture Notes in Computer Science 7405

Commenced Publication in 1973
Founding and former Series Editors:
Gerhard Goos, Juris Hartmanis, and Jan van Leeuwen

Editorial Board

David Hutchison
    Lancaster University, UK
Takeo Kanade
    Carnegie Mellon University, Pittsburgh, PA, USA
Josef Kittler
    University of Surrey, Guildford, UK
Jon M. Kleinberg
    Cornell University, Ithaca, NY, USA
Alfred Kobsa
    University of California, Irvine, CA, USA
Friedemann Mattern
    ETH Zurich, Switzerland
John C. Mitchell
    Stanford University, CA, USA
Moni Naor
    Weizmann Institute of Science, Rehovot, Israel
Oscar Nierstrasz
    University of Bern, Switzerland
C. Pandu Rangan
    Indian Institute of Technology, Madras, India
Bernhard Steffen
    TU Dortmund University, Germany
Madhu Sudan
    Microsoft Research, Cambridge, MA, USA
Demetri Terzopoulos
    University of California, Los Angeles, CA, USA
Doug Tygar
    University of California, Berkeley, CA, USA
Gerhard Weikum
    Max Planck Institute for Informatics, Saarbruecken, Germany

Rohit Gheyi   David Naumann (Eds.)

Formal Methods: Foundations and Applications

15th Brazilian Symposium, SBMF 2012
Natal, Brazil, September 23-28, 2012
Proceedings

 Springer

Volume Editors

Rohit Gheyi
Universidade Federal de Campina Grande
Departamento de Sistemas e Computação
Aprigio Veloso, 882
Campina Grande 58429 900, PB, Brazil
E-mail: rohit@dsc.ufcg.edu.br

David Naumann
Stevens Institute of Technology
Department of Computer Science
Hoboken, NJ 07030, USA
E-mail: naumann@cs.stevens.edu

ISSN 0302-9743   e-ISSN 1611-3349
ISBN 978-3-642-33295-1   e-ISBN 978-3-642-33296-8
DOI 10.1007/978-3-642-33296-8
Springer Heidelberg Dordrecht London New York

Library of Congress Control Number: 2012946266

CR Subject Classification (1998): D.2.4-5, D.2, F.3.1, F.4.1-2, D.3, K.6

LNCS Sublibrary: SL 2 – Programming and Software Engineering

Typesetting: Camera-ready by author, data conversion by Scientific Publishing Services, Chennai, India

Printed on acid-free paper

Springer is part of Springer Science+Business Media (www.springer.com)

Preface

This volume contains the papers presented at SBMF 2012: the 15th Brazilian Symposium on Formal Methods. The conference was held in the city of Natal, Brazil, colocated with CBSoft 2012, the Third Brazilian Conference on Software: Theory and Practice.

The conference program included two invited talks, given by John Rushby (SRI International, USA) and Wolfram Schulte (Microsoft Research, USA).

A total of 14 research papers were presented at the conference and are included in this volume; they were selected from 29 submissions. The submissions came from 12 countries: Argentina, Brazil, Canada, China, France, Germany, Morroco, Portugal, Swiss, Uruguay, the UK, and the USA. There was also a special track for short papers, which are published as a technical report.

The deliberations of the Program Committee and the preparation of these proceedings were handled by EasyChair, which indeed made our lives much easier.

We are grateful to the Program Committee, and the additional reviewers, for their hard work in evaluating submissions and suggesting improvements. SBMF 2012 was organized by Departamento de Informática e Matemática Aplicada da Universidade Federal do Rio Grande do Norte (DIMAP/UFRN) under the auspices of the Brazilian Computer Society (SBC). We are very thankful of the organizer of this year's conference, David Deharbe (UFRN), and we are specially thankful to CBSoft2012 organizers Nélio Cacho (DIMAP/UFRN), Frederico Lopes (DIMAP/UFRN), and Gibeon Aquino (DIMAP/UFRN), who arranged everything and made the conference run smoothly.

The conference was sponsored by the following organizations, which we thank for their generous support:

- CNPq, the Brazilian Scientific and Technological Research Council
- CAPES, the Brazilian Higher Education Funding Council
- Microsoft Research
- Universidade Federal do Rio Grande do Norte

July 2012

Rohit Gheyi
David Naumann

Organization

Steering Committee

Jim Davies	University of Oxford, UK
Rohit Gheyi	UFCG, Brazil (Co-chair)
Juliano Iyoda	UFPE, Brazil
Carroll Morgan	University of New South Wales, UK
David Naumann	Stevens Institute of Technology, USA (Co-chair)
Marcel Oliveira	UFRN, Brazil
Adenilso Simao	ICMC/USP, Brazil
Jim Woodcock	University of York, UK

Program Chairs

Rohit Gheyi	UFCG, Brazil
David Naumann	Stevens Institute of Technology, USA

Program Committee

Aline Andrade	UFBA, Brazil
Luis Barbosa	Universidade do Minho, Portugal
Roberto Bigonha	UFMG, Brazil
Christiano Braga	UFF, Brazil
Michael Butler	University of Southampton, UK
Andrew Butterfield	Trinity College Dublin, Ireland
Ana Cavalcanti	University of York, UK
Márcio Cornélio	UFPE, Brazil
Andrea Corradini	Università di Pisa, Italy
Jim Davies	University of Oxford, UK
David Deharbe	UFRN, Brazil
Ewen Denney	SGT/NASA Ames, USA
Clare Dixon	University of Liverpool, UK
Jorge Figueiredo	UFCG, Brazil
Rohit Gheyi	UFCG, Brazil
John Harrison	Intel Corporation, USA
Rolf Hennicker	Ludwig-Maximilians-Universität München, Germany
Juliano Iyoda	UFPE, Brazil
Zhiming Liu	UNU-IIST, China
Gerald Luettgen	University of Bamberg, Germany

Patricia Machado	UFCG, Brazil
Tiago Massoni	UFCG, Brazil
Ana Melo	USP, Brazil
Stephan Merz	INRIA Lorraine, France
Alvaro Moreira	UFRGS, Brazil
Anamaria Moreira	UFRN, Brazil
Carroll Morgan	University of New South Wales, UK
Alexandre Mota	UFPE, Brazil
Arnaldo Moura	Unicamp, Brazil
David Naumann	Stevens Institute of Technology, USA
Daltro Nunes	UFRGS, Brazil
Jose Oliveira	Universidade do Minho, Portugal
Marcel Oliveira	UFRN, Brazil
Alberto Pardo	Universidad de la República, Uruguay
Alexandre Petrenko	CRIM, Canada
Leila Ribeiro	UFRGS, Brazil
Augusto Sampaio	UFPE, Brazil
Leila Silva	UFS, Brazil
Adenilso Simao	ICMC/USP, Brazil
Heike Wehrheim	University of Paderborn, Germany

Additional Reviewers

Almeida, José	Rosa, Cristián
Barbosa, Paulo	Sierra, Luis
Costa, Umberto	Silva, Paulo
de Vink, Erik	Sun, Meng
Duarte, Lucio	Wang, Hao
Dury, Arnaud	

Table of Contents

The Versatile Synchronous Observer

John Rushby

Computer Science Laboratory, SRI International, USA
rushby@csl.sri.com

Abstract. A synchronous observer is an adjunct to a system model that monitors its state variables and raises a signal when some condition is satisfied. Synchronous observers provide an alternative to temporal logic as a means to specify safety properties but have the benefit that they are expressed in the same notation as the system model. Model checkers that do use temporal logic can nonetheless employ synchronous observers by checking for properties such as "never (signal raised)."

The use of synchronous observers to specify properties is well-known; rather less well-known is that they can be used to specify assumptions and axioms, to constrain models, and to specify test cases. The idea underlying all these applications is that the basic model generates more behaviors than are desired, the synchronous observer recognizes those that are interesting, and the model checker is constrained to just the interesting cases. The value in this approach is that it is usually much easier to write recognizers than generators. The approach is best exploited in languages such as SAL that provide explicit first class operators for synchronous and asynchronous composition.

The paper describes and illustrates these applications of synchronous observers.

R. Gheyi and D. Naumann (Eds.): SBMF 2012, LNCS 7498, p. 1, 2012.

Thirteen Years of Automated Code Analysis at Microsoft

Wolfram Schulte

Microsoft Research, Redmond, USA
schulte@microsoft.com

Abstract. Modern program analysis and model-based tools are increasingly complex and multi-faceted software systems. They analyze models and programs using advanced type systems, model checking or model finding, abstract interpretation, symbolic verification or a combination thereof. In this talk I will discuss and compare 10 program analysis tools, which MSR build during the last 10 years. They include theorem provers, program verifiers, bug finders, malware scanners, and test case generators. I will describe the need for their development, their innovation, and application. These tools had both had considerable impact on the research community, as well as being shipped in Microsoft products such as the Static Driver Verifier or as part of Visual Studio and other, widely-used internal software development tools. I highlight that many of these analyzers build on generic infrastructure, most of which is available outside of Microsoft as well. With every analyzer build there is a new opportunity, and with every solution there is a new challenge problem. Thus, I will conclude with 10 challenges in program analysis which hopefully triggers new aspiring directions in our joint quest of delivering predictable software that is free from defect and vulnerabilities.

R. Gheyi and D. Naumann (Eds.): SBMF 2012, LNCS 7498, p. 2, 2012.
© Springer-Verlag Berlin Heidelberg 2012

Model Checking Propositional Deontic Temporal Logic via a μ-Calculus Characterization

Araceli Acosta[1], Cecilia Kilmurray[2],
Pablo F. Castro[2,3], and Nazareno M. Aguirre[2,3]

[1] Facultad de Matemática, Astronomía y Física, Universidad Nacional de Córdoba,
Córdoba, Argentina
aacosta@famaf.unc.edu.ar
[2] Departamento de Computación, FCEFQyN, Universidad Nacional de Río Cuarto,
Río Cuarto, Argentina
{ckilmurray,pcastro,naguirre}@dc.exa.unrc.edu.ar
[3] Consejo Nacional de Investigaciones Científicas y Técnicas (CONICET)

Abstract. In this paper, we present a characterization of a propositional deontic temporal logic into μ-calculus. This logic has been proposed to specify and reason about fault tolerant systems, and even though is known to be decidable, no tool realizing its corresponding decision procedure has been developed. A main motivation for our work is enabling for the use of model checking, for analyzing specifications in this deontic temporal logic.

We present the technical details involved in the characterization, and prove that the model checking problem on the deontic temporal logic is correctly reduced to μ-calculus model checking. We also show that counterexamples are preserved, which is crucial for our model checking purposes. Finally, we illustrate our approach via a case study, including the verification of some properties using a μ-calculus model checker.

1 Introduction

With the increasing demand for highly dependable and constantly available systems, being able to reason about computer systems behavior in order to provide strong guarantees for software correctness, has gained considerable attention, especially for safety critical systems. In this context, a problem that deserves attention is that of capturing *faults*, understood as unexpected events that affect a system, as well as expressing and reasoning about the properties of systems in the presence of such faults.

Various researchers have been concerned with formally expressing fault tolerant behavior, and some formalisms and tools associated with this problem have been proposed [1,20,18,7,9,12,16,15,14,13]. A particular trend in formal methods for fault tolerance, that concerns the work in this paper, is based on the observation that normal vs. abnormal behaviors can be treated as behaviors "obeying" and "violating" the rules of correct system conduct, respectively. From a logical point of view, this calls for a *deontic* approach, since deontic operators are especially well suited to express permission, obligation and prohibition, and thus

R. Gheyi and D. Naumann (Eds.): SBMF 2012, LNCS 7498, pp. 3–18, 2012.

to describe fault tolerant systems and their properties [6]. This idea has been exploited by various researchers in different ways (see for instance [6,17,8,5]). In this paper, we are concerned with the approach taken in [5], where a propositional deontic logic (PDL) is introduced, and then extended with temporal logic features to express temporal behavior with a distinction between normative (i.e., non faulty) and non normative (i.e., faulty) behaviors, with straightforward applications to fault tolerance.

In the context of formal approaches to software development, it is generally recognized that powerful (semi-)automated analysis techniques are essential for a method to be effectively used in practice. In particular, the possibility of algorithmically checking whether a PDL formula, or a formula in its temporal extension DTL, holds for a given system is of great relevance for the take up of these logics as part of a formal method for fault tolerance. Fortunately, both PDL and its temporal extension DTL are known to be decidable [5]: a decision procedure for the logic DTL, based on a tableaux calculus, is proposed in [4]. However, the proposed decision procedure had a theoretical motivation, namely, proving that the logic was decidable; in fact, this tableaux calculus proved useful for investigating decidability and the logic's complexity, but was not devised as part of a tool for formal verification. Because of this fact, no practical considerations were taken in the definition of this decision procedure, and it has not been implemented in a tool for the analysis of fault tolerant specifications.

In this paper, we are concerned with the definition of a decision procedure for PDL and its extension DTL, with the purpose of being used for automated verification. Our approach consists of characterizing PDL/DTL in μ-calculus, and then use a μ-calculus model checker in order to verify whether a given system satisfies a fault tolerance property expressed in PDL/DTL. We thoroughly present our characterization of PDL/DTL in μ-calculus, and show how a fault tolerant system, captured by a deontic structure, can be analyzed for the satisfaction of PDL/DTL formulas, describing fault tolerant properties of the system. Moreover, we show that our translation from PDL/DTL into μ-calculus is correct, in the sense that the model checking problem in PDL/DTL is soundly reduced to model checking in μ-calculus. Moreover, we also show that counterexamples are maintained, meaning that every μ-calculus counterexample, resulting from the verification of a translated property on a translated model, can be mechanically traced back to a counterexample of the original deontic temporal specification. Finally, we provide some experimental results using the Mucke μ-calculus model checker [2], on a small case study illustrating how deontic structures capture systems with faults, and also illustrating our approach, as well as the details of our translation.

The paper proceeds as follows. In section 2 we present some preliminaries, including the syntax and semantics of PDL, as well as those of the μ-calculus. Section 3 introduces our translation from the core logic PDL to μ-calculus, and a proof of the correctness of the translation. Section 4 introduces DTL, consisting of PDL extended with CTL temporal operators, and Section 5 deals with the translation from DTL to μ-calculus, including a proof of the correctness of this characterization. The fact that counterexamples are preserved is also studied in this section. Section 6 presents an example, consisting of a simple system with faults, and various sample properties regarding this faulty system and its fault tolerance mechanism. Finally, in Section 7 we draw some conclusions and discuss our current lines of work.

2 Preliminaries

2.1 A Propositional Deontic Logic (PDL)

We start this section with an introduction to the logic presented in [5], with some remarks. This logic is a propositional deontic action logic with boolean operators over actions, which comprises *vocabularies* and *actions*.

Definition 1 (Language). *A language or vocabulary is a tuple* $\langle \Phi, \Delta \rangle$, *where* Φ *is a finite set of propositional variables and* Δ *is a finite set of primitive actions.*

Primitive actions are used for describing the events that may occur during the execution of the system. Intuitively, events are identified with state changes. Primitive actions can be composed using the action operators $\emptyset$ (the abort action), $\mathbf{U}$ (the execution of any action of the system), $\sqcup$ (nondeterministic choice of two actions) and $\sqcap$ (parallel execution of two actions). Also, given an action α, $\neg \alpha$ denotes the execution of an alternative action to α (complementation). Given a set Δ_0 of primitive actions, the set Δ of action terms is defined as the closure of Δ_0 using the above action operators. From now on, Greek letters are used as action variables, and lowercase Roman letters are used as propositional variables.

Given a language $\langle \Phi_0, \Delta_0 \rangle$ [1], the set Φ of *formulas* over this language is defined as the minimal set satisfying the following:

- $\Phi_0 \subseteq \Phi$,
- $\top, \bot \in \Phi$,
- if $\alpha, \beta \in \Delta$, then $\alpha =_{act} \beta \in \Phi$,
- if $\varphi, \psi \in \Phi$, then $\varphi \wedge \psi \in \Phi$ and $\neg \varphi \in \Phi$,
- if $\varphi \in \Phi$ and $\alpha \in \Delta$, then $\langle \alpha \rangle \varphi \in \Phi$,
- if $\alpha \in \Delta$, then $P(\alpha) \in \Phi$, $P_w(\alpha) \in \Phi$.

The models of PDL are given by deontic structures, which essentially consist of standard Kripke structures where each arc is colored with one of two colors: green, intuitively corresponding to allowed transitions, or red, intuitively denoting forbidden transitions (representing faults). Formally, given a language $\langle \Phi_0, \Delta_0 \rangle$, a deontic structure M over it is a tuple $\langle \mathcal{W}, \mathcal{R}, \mathcal{E}, \mathcal{I}, \mathcal{P} \rangle$, where:

- $\mathcal{W}$ is a set of states,

---

[1] We will use the 0 subscript when referring to languages for deontic formulas (in PDL or DTL).

- $\mathcal{R} : \mathcal{E} \to \mathcal{W} \to \mathcal{W}$ is a function that for each $e \in \mathcal{E}$ returns a function $\mathcal{R}(e) : \mathcal{W} \to \mathcal{W}$. We say that $w \xrightarrow{e} w'$ when $(\mathcal{R}(e))(w) = w'$.
- $\mathcal{E}$ is a non-empty set of events.
- $\mathcal{I}$ is an interpretation function, such that:
  - for each $p \in \Phi_0 : \mathcal{I}(p) \subseteq \mathcal{W}$,
  - for each $\alpha \in \Delta_0 : \mathcal{I}(\alpha) \subseteq \mathcal{E}$;

  function $\mathcal{I}$ must also satisfy the following:

  I.1 for each $\alpha_i \in \Delta_0 :\mid \mathcal{I}(\alpha_i) - \bigcup \{\mathcal{I}(\alpha_j) \mid \alpha_j \in (\Delta_0 - \alpha_i)\} \mid \leq 1$;

  I.2 for each $e \in \mathcal{E}$: if $e \in \mathcal{I}(\alpha_i) \cap \mathcal{I}(\alpha_j)$ where $\alpha_i \neq \alpha_j \in \Delta_0$, then

  $$\bigcap \{\mathcal{I}(\alpha_k) \mid \alpha_k \in \Delta_0 \wedge e \in \mathcal{I}(\alpha_k)\} = \{e\};$$

  I.3 $\mathcal{E} = \bigcup_{\alpha_i \in \Delta_0} \mathcal{I}(\alpha_i)$.
- $\mathcal{P} \subseteq \mathcal{W} \times \mathcal{E}$ is a relationship indicating, for every state, the events that are allowed in it.

Due to space restrictions, we are unable to provide a thorough explanation of the intuitions behind the conditions on $\mathcal{I}$. We refer the reader to [5] for a more detailed explanation. It is worth remarking that the conditions on $\mathcal{I}$ imply that there is a one-to-one mapping between events and subsets of actions; basically, we can identify every subset of actions as the event that the parallel execution of these actions produces.

The interpretation mapping $\mathcal{I}$ can be extended to action terms, as follows:

- $\mathcal{I}(\neg \varphi) = \mathcal{W} - \mathcal{I}(\varphi)$,
- $\mathcal{I}(\varphi \wedge \psi) = \mathcal{I}(\varphi) \cap \mathcal{I}(\psi)$,
- $\mathcal{I}(\alpha \sqcup \beta) = \mathcal{I}(\alpha) \cup \mathcal{I}(\beta)$,
- $\mathcal{I}(\alpha \sqcap \beta) = \mathcal{I}(\alpha) \cap \mathcal{I}(\beta)$,
- $\mathcal{I}(\neg \alpha) = \mathcal{E} - \mathcal{I}(\alpha)$,
- $\mathcal{I}(\emptyset) = \emptyset$,
- $\mathcal{I}(\mathbf{U}) = \mathcal{E}$.

Satisfaction of formulas in a deontic structure is defined, given a deontic structure $M = \langle \mathcal{W}, \mathcal{R}, \mathcal{E}, \mathcal{I}, \mathcal{P} \rangle$ and a state $w \in \mathcal{W}$, as follows:

- $w, M \models_{PDL} p \iff w \in \mathcal{I}(p)$ with $p \in \Phi_0$,
- $w, M \models_{PDL} \alpha =_{act} \beta \iff \mathcal{I}(\alpha) = \mathcal{I}(\beta)$,
- $w, M \models_{PDL} \neg \varphi \iff$ not $w, M \models_{PDL} \varphi$,
- $w, M \models_{PDL} \varphi_1 \wedge \varphi_2 \iff w, M \models_{PDL} \varphi_1$ and $w, M \models_{PDL} \varphi_2$,
- $w, M \models_{PDL} \langle \alpha \rangle \varphi \iff$ there exists some $w' \in \mathcal{W}$ and $e \in \mathcal{I}(\alpha)$ such that $w \xrightarrow{e} w'$ and $w', M \models_{PDL} \varphi$,
- $w, M \models_{PDL} P(\alpha) \iff$ for all $e \in \mathcal{I}(\alpha)$, we have $\mathcal{P}(w, e)$,
- $w, M \models_{PDL} P_w(\alpha) \iff$ there exists some $e \in \mathcal{I}(\alpha)$ such that $\mathcal{P}(w, e)$.

From this definition, it becomes apparent that the "color" of arcs given by a deontic structure is captured by the relation $\mathcal{P}$. We have two deontic operators for permission, the standard one and "weak" permission. Obligation is defined in terms of these two, as follows:

$$O(\alpha) = P(\alpha) \wedge \neg P_w(\neg \alpha).$$

2.2 The μ-Calculus

The μ-calculus, as other logics with fixed point operators, is an expressive formalism useful for investigating the expressiveness and algorithmic complexity of temporal and modal logics. A detailed introduction to μ-calculus can be found in [19]. In this section, we briefly recall the basic definitions regarding this formalism, since we use it as a target framework for interpreting the logic PDL, and its extension DTL, introduced in Section 4.

Given a language $\langle \Phi_1, \Delta_1 \rangle^2$ and a set V of variables, the set Φ_μ of $\mu-$calculus formulas is defined as follows:

- $\Phi_1 \subseteq \Phi_\mu$
- $V \subseteq \Phi_\mu$
- if $\varphi, \varphi_1, \varphi_2 \in \Phi_\mu$, then $\varphi_1 \wedge \varphi_2 \in \Phi_\mu$ and $\neg\varphi \in \Phi_\mu$
- if $\varphi \in \Phi_\mu$ and $\alpha \in \Delta_1$, then $\langle\alpha\rangle\varphi \in \Phi_\mu$ and $[\alpha]\varphi \in \Phi_\mu$
- if $\varphi \in \Phi_\mu$, then $\mu R.\varphi \in \Phi_\mu$ and $\nu R.\varphi \in \Phi_\mu$.

It is required that bound variables appear under an even number of negations.

Models of μ-calculus formulas are Kripke structures. More precisely, given a language $\langle \Phi_1, \Delta_1 \rangle$, a model for it is a tuple $M_\mu = \langle S, T, L \rangle$, where:

- S is a set of states.
- L is a function $L : \Phi_1 \to \wp(S)$ assigning to each proposition the set of states where it is true.
- T is a function $T : \Delta_1 \to \wp(S \times S)$ which, given an action, returns a binary relation whose domain and codomain is S. We say that $s \xrightarrow{a} s'$ if $(s, s') \in T(a)$.

Satisfaction in μ-calculus is defined as follows. Given a model M_μ, a state $s \in S$ and a formula φ without free variables, $s, M \models_\mu \varphi$ holds if and only if $s \in [\![\varphi]\!]_{M_\mu}\rho$, where ρ is a variable assignment (a mapping assigning values to variables). The interpretation $[\![\varphi]\!]_{M_\mu}\rho$ is recursively defined in the following way:

- $[\![p]\!]_{M_\mu}\rho = L(p)$ for $p \in \Phi_1$,
- $[\![R]\!]_{M_\mu}\rho = \rho(R)$ for $R \in V$,
- $[\![\neg\varphi]\!]_{M_\mu}\rho = S - [\![\varphi]\!]_{M_\mu}\rho$,
- $[\![\varphi \wedge \psi]\!]_{M_\mu}\rho = [\![\psi]\!]_{M_\mu}\rho \cap [\![\varphi]\!]_{M_\mu}\rho$,
- $[\![\langle a\rangle\varphi]\!]_{M_\mu}\rho = \{s \in S \mid \exists t[s \xrightarrow{a} t \wedge t \in [\![\varphi]\!]_{M_\mu}\rho]\}$,
- $[\![[a]\varphi]\!]_{M_\mu}\rho = \{s \in S \mid \forall t[s \xrightarrow{a} t \wedge t \in [\![\varphi]\!]_{M_\mu}\rho]\}$,
- $[\![\mu R.\varphi]\!]_{M_\mu}\rho$ is the least fixed point of the function $\tau : \wp(S) \to \wp(S)$, defined as:

$$\tau(T) = [\![\varphi]\!]_{M_\mu}\rho[R \mapsto T]^3,$$

- $[\![\nu R.\varphi]\!]_{M_\mu}\rho$ is defined in the same way, but using the greatest fixed point,

We will use $[\![\varphi]\!]_M$ instead of $[\![\varphi]\!]_{M_\mu}$ when no confusion is possible.

---

[2] We will use the 1 subscript when referring to languages for μ-calculus formulas, to distinguish these from those for the deontic logics.

[3] $(\rho[R \mapsto T])$ is the assignment ρ "updated" with the mapping $R \mapsto T$, i.e., it maps all elements as ρ, except for R which is mapped to T.

3 A μ-Calculus Characterization of PDL

In this section, we start with our characterization of deontic temporal logic in terms of μ-calculus, by first dealing with the deontic logic PDL. As we explained in section 1, the purpose of this characterization, which we materialize via a translation Tr, is to be able to use μ-calculus model checkers for the verification of fault tolerance properties of systems, specified in PDL and its temporal extension DTL.

In what concerns this section, we expect to reduce PDL model checking to μ-calculus model checking, via Tr; that is, whenever we obtain that

$$Tr^m(w, M) \not\models_\mu Tr(\varphi)$$

then we must have that

$$w, M \not\models_{DPL} \varphi$$

and vice versa. Thus, we need the translation from PDL to μ-calculus to satisfy the following:

$$w, M \models_{PDL} \varphi \iff Tr^m(w, M) \models_\mu Tr(\varphi).$$

Theoretically, translations between logics satisfying this property are called *forward morphisms* [11]. As we will show later on, this property allows us to guarantee that the model checking problem is preserved by translation.

Let us start by formally defining our translation.

Definition 2. *Let $\langle \Phi_0, \Delta_0 \rangle$ be a language, and $M = \langle \mathcal{W}, \mathcal{R}, \mathcal{E}, \mathcal{I}, \mathcal{P} \rangle$ be a deontic structure over that language. The mapping $Gen : \mathcal{E} \to \wp(\Delta_0)$ is defined as:*

$$Gen(e) = \{\alpha \mid \alpha \in \Delta_0 \wedge e \in \mathcal{I}(\alpha)\}$$

Given an event e, $Gen(e)$ corresponds to the set of actions whose parallel execution yield event e.

Lemma 1. *Gen is injective.*
Proof: *Let $e, e' \in \mathcal{E}$ be events such that $Gen(e) = Gen(e') = \{\alpha_1, \alpha_2, \ldots, \alpha_n\}$. First, notice that because of I.3, $n \neq 0$.*

If $n = 1$, we have that $e, e' \in \mathcal{I}(\alpha_1)$, and $\forall \alpha \in \Delta_0 - \{\alpha_1\} : e \notin \mathcal{I}(\alpha) \wedge e' \notin \mathcal{I}(\alpha)$. Then, $\{e, e'\} \subseteq \mathcal{I}(\alpha_1) - \bigcup\{\mathcal{I}(\alpha_i) \mid \alpha_i \in (\Delta_0 - \alpha_1)\}$, and because of I.1[4], it must be the case that $e = e'$.

If, on the other hand, $n > 1$, then there exist $\alpha_i, \alpha_j \in \Delta_0$ such that $\alpha_i \neq \alpha_j$, $\{e, e'\} \subseteq \mathcal{I}(\alpha_i)$ and $\{e, e'\} \subseteq \mathcal{I}(\alpha_j)$. But because of I.2[5], it must be the case that $e = e'$.

Let us now define the translation of PDL models into corresponding μ-calculus structures. This is, in fact, the first part of translation Tr.

---

[4] For each $\alpha_i \in \Delta_0 : \mid \mathcal{I}(\alpha_i) - \bigcup\{\mathcal{I}(\alpha_j) \mid \alpha_j \in (\Delta_0 - \alpha_i)\} \mid \leq 1$.
[5] For each $e \in \mathcal{E}$: if $e \in \mathcal{I}(\alpha_i) \cap \mathcal{I}(\alpha_j)$ where $\alpha_i \neq \alpha_j \in \Delta_0$, then $\bigcap\{\mathcal{I}(\alpha_k) \mid \alpha_k \in \Delta_0 \wedge e \in \mathcal{I}(\alpha_k)\} = \{e\}$.

Definition 3. *Let* $\langle \Phi_0, \Delta_0 \rangle$ *be a language, and* $M = \langle \mathcal{W}, \mathcal{R}, \mathcal{E}, \mathcal{I}, \mathcal{P} \rangle$ *and* $w \in \mathcal{W}$ *be a deontic structure. The mapping* Tr^m *is defined as:*

$$Tr^m(w, M) = w, M_\mu,$$

where $M_\mu = \langle S, T, L \rangle$ *is a model of the language* $\langle \Phi_1, \Delta_1 \rangle$ *such that:*

- $\Delta_1 = \wp(\Delta_0)$,
- $\Phi_1 = \Phi_0 \cup \{P_a \mid a \in \Delta_1\} \cup \{E_a \mid a \in \Delta_1\}$,
- $S = \mathcal{W}$,
- $T = \{w \xrightarrow{Gen(e)} w' \mid w \xrightarrow{e} w' \in \mathcal{R}\}$,
- $L(p) = I(p)$, *for every* $p \in \Phi_0$,
- $L(P_a) = \{w \mid \exists e \in \mathcal{E} : (w, e) \in \mathcal{P} \wedge Gen(e) = a\}$, *for every* $a \in \Delta_1$,
- $L(E_a) = \{s \mid \exists s' : s \xrightarrow{a} s' \in T\}$.

It is worth noting that, in the above model translation, and since each event is the result of the parallel execution of a set of actions, we capture each event as the set of actions whose parallel execution produces it.

Now let us start dealing with the translation of formulas. First, notice that PDL formulas use action letters from Δ_0, whereas μ-calculus formulas use names coming from Δ_1 (i.e., subsets of Δ_0). So, our translation must relate both sets. In order to do so, we define the mapping *Set*, as follows.

Definition 4. *The mapping* $Set : \Delta_0 \to \wp(\Delta_1)$ *is defined as*

$$Set(\alpha) = \{a \mid a \in \Delta_1 \wedge \alpha \in a\}.$$

This mapping is extended recursively to action terms, in the following way:

- $Set(\emptyset) = \emptyset$,
- $Set(U) = \Delta_1$,
- $Set(\neg \alpha) = \Delta_1 - Set(\alpha)$,
- $Set(\alpha \sqcup \beta) = Set(\alpha) \cup Set(\beta)$,
- $Set(\alpha \sqcap \beta) = Set(\alpha) \cap Set(\beta)$.

Finally, we are ready to define function Tr, that translates PDL formulas to μ-calculus formulas.

Definition 5. *The translation* Tr, *mapping PDL formulas to* μ-*calculus formulas, is defined as follows:*

- $Tr(p) = p$, *for every* $p \in \Phi_0$,
- $Tr(\top) = \top$,
- $Tr(\bot) = \bot$,
- $Tr(\neg \varphi) = \neg Tr(\varphi)$,
- $Tr(\varphi_1 \wedge \varphi_2) = Tr(\varphi_1) \wedge Tr(\varphi_2)$,
- $Tr(\alpha =_{act} \beta) = \bigwedge_{a \in (Set(\alpha) \cup Set(\beta)) - (Set(\alpha) \cap Set(\beta))} \neg E_a$,
- $Tr(\langle \alpha \rangle \varphi) = \bigvee_{a \in Set(\alpha)} \langle a \rangle Tr(\varphi)$,
- $Tr([\alpha] \varphi) = \bigwedge_{a \in Set(\alpha)} (E_a \to [a] Tr(\varphi))$,
- $Tr(P(\alpha)) = \bigwedge_{a \in Set(\alpha)} (E_a \to P_a)$,
- $Tr(P_w(\alpha)) = \bigvee_{a \in Set(\alpha)} P_a$.

3.1 On the Correctness of Tr

Let us briefly discuss some characteristics of the defined translation. Translations between logical systems have been extensively studied by the community of Institutions [10,11]. In this context, logical systems are captured in abstract terms. The most usual kinds of translations between logical systems are the so called *morphisms* and *comorphisms* (or representations). In both of these cases, translations of models and formulas go in opposite directions. More precisely, a morphism between logical systems L and L' translates models of L into models of L', and formulas of L' into formulas of L, in a property-preserving way. Comorphisms, on the other hand, behave in the opposite way. Both cases then have the characteristics of Galois connections.

Our translation differs from morphisms and comorphisms, in the sense that it maps models and formulas "in the same direction". This kind of translation is called *forward morphism* [11]. Fortunately, this is the kind of morphism that we need, since forward morphisms are well suited for model checking reduction (the purpose of our translation). In section 5, we show that traces of a translated model can be traced back to the traces of the original model. Intuitively, this means that our translation preserves counterexamples, a crucial property for our model checking purposes.

The following theorem establishes that our translation is sound with respect to model checking reduction. It is proved straightforwardly by induction on the structure of PDL formulas, and resorting to their semantics and the definition of translation Tr. Due to space restrictions, the proof is not reproduced here.

Theorem 1. *Given a language* $\langle \Phi_0, \Delta_0 \rangle$*, a structure* $M = \langle \mathcal{W}, \mathcal{R}, \mathcal{E}, \mathcal{I}, \mathcal{P} \rangle$ *and a state* $w \in \mathcal{W}$*, we have:*

$$w, M \models \phi \Leftrightarrow Tr^m(w, M) \models_\mu Tr(\phi).$$

4 A Temporal Extension of PDL

The propositional deontic logic PDL that we introduced previously involves deontic operators for permission and obligation. In order to be able to express fault tolerance system properties, these deontic operators are combined with temporal ones, so that we can predicate about system executions. The temporal component of the resulting logic, that we call DTL, is a CTL-like logic. Besides the traditional CTL operators, this logic features an operator called *Done*, which enables one to talk about the immediate past. Intuitively, $Done(\alpha)$ is true when α was the last action executed in the system. Let us formally define this logic.

Definition 6. *Given a PDL language* (Φ_0, Δ_0)*, the set of temporal formulas over it is defined as the minimal set* Φ_T *satisfying the following:*

- $\Phi \subseteq \Phi_T$,
- *if* $\alpha \in \Delta$*, then* $Done(\alpha) \in \Phi_T$,
- *if* $\varphi, \psi \in \Phi_T$*, then* $\varphi \wedge \psi \in \Phi_T$ *and* $\neg\varphi \in \Phi_T$,

- if $\varphi, \psi \in \Phi_T$, then $AG\varphi \in \Phi_T, AN\varphi \in \Phi_T, A(\varphi\mathcal{U}\psi) \in \Phi_T, E(\varphi\mathcal{U}\psi) \in \Phi_T$.

Note that Φ represents the set of PDL formulas and Δ the set of actions terms as defined on page 3.

Other CTL operators can be defined from the basic ones in the above definition, in the usual way. The temporal operators enable us to reason about execution traces. Let us define these traces formally.

Definition 7. *Given a structure $M = \langle \mathcal{W}, \mathcal{R}, \mathcal{E}, \mathcal{I}, \mathcal{P} \rangle$ and an initial state w_0, a trace or path is a labeled sequence $s_0 \xrightarrow{e_0} s_1 \xrightarrow{e_1} s_2 \xrightarrow{e_2} \dots$ of states and events, such that for every i: $s_i \xrightarrow{e_i} s_{i+1} \in \mathcal{R}$ and $s_0 = w$.*
The set of all the traces starting in w is denoted by $\Sigma(w_0)$.

Given a trace π, we use the following notation to refer to states and events in a trace, to refer to subtraces, and to state that a trace is a prefix of another one:

- $\pi.i = s_i$,
- $\pi^{\rightarrow}.i = e_i$,
- $\pi[i,j]$ (where $i \leq j$) is the subpath $s_i \xrightarrow{e_i} \dots \xrightarrow{e_{j-1}} s_j$,
- we say that $\pi' \preceq \pi$, if π' is an initial subpath of π; i.e. $s_0 \xrightarrow{e_0'} s_1' \xrightarrow{e_1'} s_2' \xrightarrow{e_2'}$ $\dots s_k' \preceq s_0 \xrightarrow{e_0} s_1 \xrightarrow{e_1} s_2 \xrightarrow{e_2} \dots$ iff $s_i' = s_i$ for all $i \leq k$ and $e_i' = e_i$ for all $i < k$.

Let us define satisfaction for our deontic temporal logic (DTL). This definition extends the definition of satisfaction for PDL.

Definition 8. *Given a structure $M = \langle \mathcal{W}, \mathcal{R}, \mathcal{E}, \mathcal{I}, \mathcal{P} \rangle$, an initial state $w_0 \in \mathcal{W}$ and a path $\pi \in \Sigma(w_0)$, the relation $\models_{DTL}$ is defined as follows:*

- $\pi, i, M \models_{DTL} \varphi \Longleftrightarrow \pi.i, M \models_{PDL}$, if $\varphi \in \Phi$,
- $\pi, i, M \models_{DTL} \neg\varphi \Longleftrightarrow not\ \pi, i, M \models_{DTL} \varphi$,
- $\pi, i, M \models_{DTL} \varphi \wedge \psi \Longleftrightarrow \pi, i, M \models_{DTL} \varphi$ and $\pi, i, M \models_{DTL} \psi$,
- $\pi, i, M \models_{DTL} Done(\alpha) \Longleftrightarrow i > 0$ and $\pi^{\rightarrow}.(i-1) \in \mathcal{I}(\alpha)$,
- $\pi, i, M \models_{DTL} AN\varphi \Longleftrightarrow$ for every $\pi' \in \Sigma(\pi.0)$ such that $\pi[0,i] \preceq \pi'$ we have that $\pi', i+1, M \models_{DTL} \varphi$,
- $\pi, i, M \models_{DTL} AG\varphi \Longleftrightarrow$ for every $\pi' \in \Sigma(\pi.0)$ such that $\pi[0,i] \preceq \pi'$ we have that $\forall j \geq i : \pi', j, M \models_{DTL} \varphi$,
- $\pi, i, M \models_{DTL} A(\varphi U \psi) \Longleftrightarrow$ for every $\pi' \in \Sigma(\pi.0)$ such that $\pi[0,i] \preceq \pi'$ we have that $\exists j \geq i : \pi', j, M \models_{DTL} \psi$ and $\forall k : i \leq k < j : \pi', k, M \models_{DTL} \varphi$,
- $\pi, i, M \models_{DTL} E(\varphi U \psi) \Longleftrightarrow$ there exists $\pi' \in \Sigma(\pi.0)$ such that $\pi[0,i] \preceq \pi'$ we have that $\exists j \geq i : \pi', j, M \models_{DTL} \psi$ and $\forall k : i \leq k < j : \pi', k, M \models_{DTL} \varphi$.

Given a structure $M = \langle \mathcal{W}, \mathcal{R}, \mathcal{E}, \mathcal{I}, \mathcal{P} \rangle$, an initial state $w_0 \in \mathcal{W}$ and a formula φ, we say that

$$M, w_0 \models \varphi$$

if and only if

$$\forall \pi \in \Sigma(w_0) : \pi, 0, M \models_{DTL} \varphi.$$

5   Translating DTL Formulas to μ-Calculus

Now that we have extended PDL with temporal operators, obtaining the logic DTL, we need also to extend the definition of Tr, to cope with temporal formulas. Let us first deal with the translation of models, via a translation that we refer to as Tr^{tm}. This involves explicitly identifying the initial states, which we achieve via a function called Tr^s in the definition below.

Definition 9. *Let (Φ_0, Δ_0) be a language, $M = \langle W, \mathcal{R}, \mathcal{E}, \mathcal{I}, \mathcal{P} \rangle$ a structure over that language, and $w_0 \in W$ an initial state in M. The functions Tr^{tm} and Tr^s are defined as follows:*

$$Tr^{tm}(M) = M_\mu$$
$$Tr^s(w) = s_\emptyset^w$$

where $M_\mu = \langle S, T, L \rangle$, a μ-calculus model for the language $\langle \Phi_1, \Delta_1 \rangle$, and $s_\emptyset^w \in S$ are obtained in the following way:

- $\Delta_1 = \wp(\Delta_0)$,
- $\Phi_1 = \Phi_0 \cup \{P_a \mid a \in \Delta_1\} \cup \{E_a \mid a \in \Delta_1\} \cup \{D_a \mid a \in \Delta_1\}$,
- $S = \{s_a^w \mid w \in W \land a \in (Im(Gen) \cup \{\emptyset\})\}$,[6]
- $T = \{s_a^w \overset{Gen(e)}{\longrightarrow} s_{Gen(e)}^{w'} \mid w \overset{e}{\longrightarrow} w' \in \mathcal{R} \land a \in (Im(Gen) \cup \{\emptyset\})\}$,
- $L(p) = \mathcal{I}(p)$ *for every* $p \in \Phi_0$,
- $L(P_a) = \{w \mid \exists e \in \mathcal{E} : (w, e) \in \mathcal{P} \land Gen(e) = a\}$ *for every* $a \in \Delta_1$,
- $L(E_a) = \{s \mid \exists s' : s \overset{a}{\longrightarrow} s' \in T\}$,
- $L(D_a) = \{s_a^w \mid w \in W\}$.

Let us now deal with the translation of DTL formulas into μ-calculus. Because of the operator *Done*, this translation requires characterizing the last executed action, as it can be seen in the next definition.

Definition 10. *The translation Tr from PDL to μ-calculus is extended to DTL formulas in the following way:*

- *for* $\varphi \in \Phi$, $Tr(\varphi)$ *is defined as described in Definition 5,*
- $Tr(\neg\varphi) = \neg Tr(\varphi)$,
- $Tr(\varphi \land \psi) = Tr(\varphi) \land Tr(\psi)$,
- $Tr(Done(\alpha)) = \bigvee_{a \in Set(\alpha)} D_a$,
- $Tr(AN\varphi) = Tr([U]\varphi)$,
- $Tr(EN\varphi) = Tr(\langle U \rangle \varphi)$,
- $Tr(AG\varphi) = \nu R.(Tr(\varphi) \land \bigwedge_{a \in \Delta_1} [a]R)$,
- $A(\varphi U \psi) = \mu R.(Tr(\psi) \lor (Tr(\varphi) \land \bigwedge_{a \in \Delta_1} [a]R))$,
- $E(\varphi U \psi) = \mu R.(Tr(\psi) \lor (Tr(\varphi) \land \bigvee_{a \in \Delta_1} \langle a \rangle R))$.

---

[6] $Im(f)$ denotes the image of f.

5.1   On the Correctness of the Extended Tr

The correctness of the translation extended to DTL is proved by generalizing the theorem regarding the correctness of the translation on PDL. Let us first define the translation of paths.

Definition 11. *The mapping Tr^p is defined as follows:*

$$Tr^p(w_0 \overset{e_0}{\to} w_1 \overset{e_1}{\to} w_2 \overset{e_2}{\to} \ldots) = s_\emptyset^{w_0} \overset{Gen(e_0)}{\to} s_{Gen(e_0)}^{w_1} \overset{Gen(e_1)}{\to} s_{Gen(e_1)}^{w_2} \overset{Gen(e_2)}{\to} \ldots .$$

Notice that, since Gen is injective, given a translated trace π in the target model, we have a unique trace π' in the original model, such that $Tr^p(\pi') = \pi$. In other words, the translation of traces is invertible. On the other hand, Tr^p is surjective by construction, and therefore we obtain the following Lemma.

Lemma 2. *Tr^p is a bijection.*

The following theorem enables us to relate validities in μ-calculus with validities in the deontic-temporal logic DTL.

Theorem 2. *Given a language $\langle \Phi_0, \Delta_0 \rangle$, a structure $M = \langle \mathcal{W}, \mathcal{R}, \mathcal{E}, \mathcal{I}, \mathcal{P} \rangle$, an initial state $w_0 \in \mathcal{W}$, and a formula ϕ, $s_a^w \in [\![Tr(\phi)]\!]_{Tr^{tm}(M)}$ if and only if $\forall \pi, i \cdot \pi, i, M \models_{DTL} \phi$ when $s_a^w = Tr^p(\pi).i$.*

This theorem implies the correctness of the translation of DTL formulas, in a straightforward way.

Corollary 1. *Given a language $\langle \Phi_0, \Delta_0 \rangle$, a structure $M = \langle \mathcal{W}, \mathcal{R}, \mathcal{E}, \mathcal{I}, \mathcal{P} \rangle$, an initial state $w_0 \in \mathcal{W}$ and a formula φ, the following holds:*

$$w_0, M \models_{DTL} \varphi \leftrightarrow s_\emptyset^{w_0}, Tr^{tm}(M) \models_\mu Tr(\varphi)$$

It is worthwhile remarking that, since there is a bijection between paths (and states and translated states maintain equivalent properties), for every path in a translated model that is a counterexample of a given translated property, a trace in the original model can be systematically constructed, which is guaranteed to be a counterexample of the original property. In other words, counterexamples that are obtained using μ-calculus model checkers can be systematically translated into counterexamples of the original DTL specification.

6   An Example

In this section, we describe a small example illustrating our translation. Moreover, we will use the Mucke model checker [2] in order to verify fault tolerance properties over this example. Our example consists of a simple communication scenario, composed of a producer, a consumer, and a channel used for communicating these two. The structures in Figure 1 graphically depict these components. In order to incorporate faults, and as a consequence the need for fault tolerance,

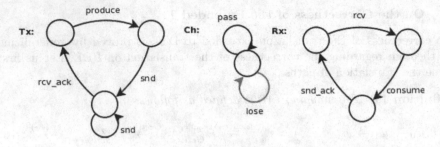

Fig. 1. A producer, a consumer, and a faulty channel

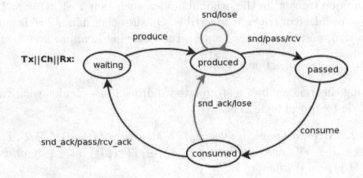

Fig. 2. Composition of the producer, consumer and faulty channel

the channel is assumed to have "noise", and therefore some messages might be lost. In order to cope with this fault, the producer and consumer communicate using a typical protocol that forces the sender to resend the last message until an acknowledgement is received. The only forbidden action is the one corresponding to "losing" a message held in the channel. The deontic operators will allow us to indirectly refer to executions exercising normal (permitted) and faulty (forbidden) transitions.

In this paper, we do not deal in detail with the way components are synchronized. But basically, if an action, normal or faulty, is synchronized with a faulty action, the composite action is also considered faulty. Therefore, and since the use of the channel (sending a message) can be synchronized with the correct "passing" of the message and with the unfortunate event of "losing" it, the latter will be considered faulty. For this reason, in the system resulting of the composition of the producer, the consumer, and the channel (see Figure 2), the faulty actions are snd/lose and snd_ack/lose.

In this example, the language of the deontic structure is given by the following sets of propositional variables and actions:

$$\Phi_0 = \{\texttt{waiting, produced, passed, consumed}\}$$
$$\Delta_0 = \{\texttt{produce, consume, snd, rcv, snd\_ack, rcv\_ack, pass, lose}\}$$

The deontic structure for the example is formally the following:

- the set of states $\mathcal{W}$ and the transition system R are defined as in Figure 2,
- the set of events is the following:

$$\mathcal{E} = \{\text{produce, consume, snd/lose, snd/pass/rcv,}$$
$$\text{snd\_ack/lose, snd\_ack/pass/rcv\_ack}\},$$

- the interpretation of the propositional variables is described in Figure 2, and the interpretation of actions is given by
  - $\mathcal{I}(\text{produce}) = \{\text{produce}\}$,
  - $\mathcal{I}(\text{consume}) = \{\text{consume}\}$,
  - $\mathcal{I}(\text{snd}) = \{\text{snd/lose, snd/pass/rcv}\}$,
  - $\mathcal{I}(\text{rcv}) = \{\text{snd/pass/rcv}\}$,
  - $\mathcal{I}(\text{lose}) = \{\text{snd/lose, snd\_ack/lose}\}$,
  - $\mathcal{I}(\text{pass}) = \{\text{ snd/pass/rcv, snd\_ack/pass/rcv\_ack}\}$,
  - $\mathcal{I}(\text{rcv\_ack}) = \{\text{snd\_ack/pass/rcv\_ack}\}$,
  - $\mathcal{I}(\text{snd\_ack}) = \{\text{snd\_ack/lose, snd\_ack/pass/rcv\_ack}\}$.
- Allowed events are all the arrows in Figure 2, except for those labeled with snd/lose and snd_ack/lose.

Now let us describe the resulting μ-calculus model, obtained by translating the above deontic structure. Following our description of the translation, the resulting model is composed of the following ingredients:

- $\Delta_1 = \{\text{produce, consume, snd/lose, snd/pass/rcv,}$
       $\text{snd\_ack/lose, snd\_ack/pass/rcv\_ack }\}$,
- $\Phi_1 = \Phi_0 \cup \{P_a \mid a \in \Delta_1\}$,
- $S = \mathcal{W} = \{waiting, produced, passed, consumed\}$,
- T is as described in Figure 2,
- $L(p)$ is as described in Figure 2,
- $L(P_a)$ is true in those states in which we have a transition labeled with a, other of the two faulty ones,
- $L(E_a)$ is true in those states in which we have a transition labeled with a.

6.1 Expressing Properties of Producer-Consumer

Now that the model has been fully described, we may start specifying intended properties of this model. Some interesting sample properties are the following:

- Whenever the system is in the waiting state, it is obliged to produce an item.
- After the production of an item, and if no fault occurs, then the system is obliged to consume.
- If an item has been produced, then no new item can be produced until the current item has been consumed.
- When a item has been consumed, then no additional items are consumed until some new item is produced.
- When an item is produced, all possible ways of performing the send action are allowed.

These properties are captured using DTL rather straightforwardly, thanks to the deontic component of this logic:

P1 $waiting \rightarrow O(produce)$
P2 $[\,produce\,]\,[\,\neg lose\,]\,O(consume)$
P3 $produced \rightarrow \mathbf{A}(\,O(\neg produce)\,\mathbf{U}\,consumed\,)$
P4 $consumed \rightarrow \mathbf{ANA}(\,\neg consumed\,\mathbf{W}\,produced\,)$
P5 $[\,produce\,]\,P(snd)$

In order to model check these properties for the above described model, we have to use our translation Tr from DTL to μ-calculus. This translation gives us the following μ-calculus formulas for the above DTL properties:

TP1 $waiting \rightarrow P_{\mathsf{produce}} \wedge \bigwedge_{a \in \delta} \neg P_a$,where:

$\delta = \{\mathsf{consume,\ snd/lose,\ snd/pass/rcv,\ snd\_ack/lose,}$
$\mathsf{snd\_ack/pass/rcv\_ack}\,\}$

TP2 $[\,\mathsf{produce}\,]\,(\bigwedge_{a \in \delta}[\,a\,]\,(P_{\mathsf{consume}} \wedge \bigwedge_{a \in \delta'} \neg P_a))$, where:

$\delta = \{\mathsf{produce,\ consume,\ snd/pass/rcv,\ snd\_ack/pass/rcv\_ack}\,\}$
$\delta' = \{\mathsf{produce,\ snd/lose,\ snd/pass/rcv,\ snd\_ack/lose,}$
$\mathsf{snd\_ack/pass/rcv\_ack}\,\}$.

TP3 $produced \rightarrow$
$\mu R.\left(consumed \vee \left(\bigwedge_{a \in \delta}(E_a \rightarrow P_a) \wedge \neg P_{\mathsf{produce}} \wedge \bigwedge_{a \in \Delta_1}[\,a\,]\,R\right)\right)$,
where

$\delta = \{\mathsf{consume,\ snd/lose,\ snd/pass/rcv,\ snd\_ack/lose,}$
$\mathsf{snd\_ack/pass/rcv\_ack}\,\}$

TP4 $consumed \rightarrow \bigwedge_{a \in \Delta_1}[\,a\,]\,((\mu R.\,(produced \vee (\neg consumed$
$\wedge\ \bigwedge_{a \in \Delta_1}[\,a\,]\,R)) \vee \nu R.\,(\neg consumed \wedge \bigwedge_{a \in \Delta_1}[\,a\,]\,R))$
TP5 $[\,\mathsf{produce}\,]\,\bigwedge_{a \in \delta}(E_a \rightarrow P_a)$, where:

$\delta = \{\ \mathsf{snd/lose,\ snd/pass/rcv,\ snd\_ack/lose,\ snd\_ack/pass/rcv\_ack}\,\}$

The careful reader might notice that, technically, formula **TP4** is not a valid μ-calculus formula, since an odd number of negations appear under the scope of fix point operators. However, our use of negation in this case is simply as a shorthand: $\neg consumed$ can be positively described as the disjunction of all states different from $consumed$.

We employed the Mucke model checker to verify these formulas. Properties **P1**, **P2**, **P4** were found to hold in the presented model, whereas **P3** and **P5** are invalid. The invalidity of **P3** could seem surprising at first sight; the counterexample found by the model checker is the following:

$$produced \overset{snd/lose}{\rightarrow} produced \overset{snd/pass/rcv}{\rightarrow} passed \overset{consume}{\rightarrow} consumed$$

Notice that the transition labelled by $snd/lose$ is not allowed, and therefore it is not obligatory, falsifying $O(\neg produce)$.

7   Conclusions and Future Work

We have presented an approach for model checking a propositional temporal-deontic logic, with applications to fault tolerance verification, based on a characterization of this logic into the μ-calculus. This characterization is materialized via two translations, one capturing deontic structures as Kripke structures for μ-calculus, and the other translating formulas in the deontic temporal logic into μ-calculus. This translation is shown to be correct, in the sense that the model checking problem in the deontic-temporal logic is reduced to model checking in μ-calculus. Moreover, we also show that counterexamples are also maintained, meaning that every μ-calculus counterexample, resulting from the verification of a translated property on a translated model, can be mechanically traced back to a counterexample of the original deontic temporal specification. Although the deontic temporal logic subject of study in this paper was known to be decidable, the decision procedure for it was not originally conceived for model checking purposes, and therefore none of the practical considerations we had in our approach were previously taken. In our opinion, this justifies the relevance of our work, aiming at automated verification of fault tolerance models.

We also provided a simple example illustrating various points. First, it illustrates the use of deontic structures for capturing systems with faults; second, it allows us to show how fault tolerance properties are straightforwardly captured by the combination of deontic and temporal operators; and third, it allowed us to illustrate the translation from deontic temporal logic into μ-calculus. Moreover, we employed the Mucke model checker in order to verify some sample properties on the presented model, and found a nontrivial counterexample on a property that was supposed to hold in the model.

As work in progress, we are developing a tool for fault tolerance system description and verification, which this work is part of. We are also studying the complexity of the model checking problem for PDL/DTL in relation to our translation. It is known that SAT for PDL is in PSPACE [3], but we do not have yet results regarding DTL, nor the complexity of these logics' model checking. Other concerns we are currently investigating are compositional reasoning on the presented temporal deontic logic, and integrating the presented model checking approach with the deductive mechanisms for verification presented in [3].

Acknowledgements. The authors would like to thank Pedro D'Argenio and the anonymous referees for their helpful comments. This work was partially supported by the Argentinian Agency for Scientific and Technological Promotion (ANPCyT), through grants PICT PAE 2007 No. 2772, PICT 2010 No. 1690 and PICT 2010 No. 2611, and by the MEALS project (EU FP7 programme, grant agreement No. 295261).

References

1. Bernardeschi, C., Fantechi, A., Gnesi, S.: Model checking fault tolerant systems. Softw. Test., Verif. Reliab. 12(4), 251–275 (2002)
2. Biere, A.: μcke - Efficient μ-Calculus Model Checking. In: Grumberg, O. (ed.) CAV 1997. LNCS, vol. 1254, pp. 468–471. Springer, Heidelberg (1997)
3. Castro, P.F.: Deontic Action Logics for the Specification and Analysis of Fault-Tolerance. PhD thesis, McMaster University, Department of Computing and Software (2009)
4. Castro, P.F., Maibaum, T.S.E.: A Tableaux System for Deontic Action Logic. In: van der Meyden, R., van der Torre, L. (eds.) DEON 2008. LNCS (LNAI), vol. 5076, pp. 34–48. Springer, Heidelberg (2008)
5. Castro, P.F., Maibaum, T.S.E.: Deontic action logic, atomic boolean algebra and fault-tolerance. Journal of Applied Logic 7(4), 441–466 (2009)
6. Coenen, J.: Formalisms for Program Reification and Fault Tolerance. PhD thesis, Tenische Universiteit Eindhoven (1994)
7. Cristian, F.: A rigorous approach to fault-tolerant programming. IEEE Trans. Software Eng. 11, 23–31 (1985)
8. French, T., Mc Cabe-Dansted, J.C., Reynolds, M.: A Temporal Logic of Robustness. In: Konev, B., Wolter, F. (eds.) FroCos 2007. LNCS (LNAI), vol. 4720, pp. 193–205. Springer, Heidelberg (2007)
9. Gärtner, F.: Specification for fault-tolerance: A comedy of failures. Technical report, Darmstadt University of Technology (1998)
10. Goguen, J.A., Burstall, R.M.: Institutions: Abstract model theory for specification and programming. Journal of the Association of Computing Machinery (1992)
11. Goguen, J.A., Rosu, G.: Institution morphisms. Formal Asp. Comput. 13(3-5), 274–307 (2002)
12. Janowski, T.: On Bisimulation, Fault-Monotonicity and Provable Fault-tolerance. In: Johnson, M. (ed.) AMAST 1997. LNCS, vol. 1349, pp. 292–306. Springer, Heidelberg (1997)
13. Lamport, L., Merz, S.: Specifying and Verifying Fault-Tolerant Systems. In: Langmaack, H., de Roever, W.-P., Vytopil, J. (eds.) FTRTFT 1994 and ProCoS 1994. LNCS, vol. 863, pp. 41–76. Springer, Heidelberg (1994)
14. Laranjeira, L.A., Malek, M., Jenevein, R.M.: Nest: A nested-predicate scheme for fault tolerance. IEEE Trans. Computers 42, 1303–1324 (1993)
15. Liu, Z., Joseph, M.: Specification and verification of fault-tolerance, timing, and scheduling. ACM Trans. Program. Lang. Syst. 21(1), 46–89 (1999)
16. Lomuscio, A., Sergot, M.J.: A formalisation of violation, error recovery, and enforcement in the bit transmission problem. Journal of Applied Logic 2, 93–116 (2004)
17. Magee, J., Maibaum, T.S.E.: Towards specification, modelling and analysis of fault tolerance in self managed systems. In: Proceeding of the 2006 International Workshop on Self-Adaptation and Self-Managing Systems (2006)
18. Schneider, F., Easterbrook, S.M., Callahan, J.R., Holzmann, G.J.: Validating requirements for fault tolerant systems using model checking. In: 3rd International Conference on Requirements Engineering, ICRE 1998 (1998)
19. Schneider, K.: Verification of Reactive Systems, Formal Methods and Algorithms. Springer (2004)
20. Yokogawa, T., Tsuchiya, T., Kikuno, T.: Automatic verification of fault tolerance using model checking. In: Pacific Rim International Symposium on Dependable Computing (2001)

An Approach Using the B Method
to Formal Verification of PLC Programs
in an Industrial Setting*

Haniel Barbosa and David Déharbe

Departamento de Informática e Matemática Aplicada, UFRN, Brazil
hanielbbarbosa@gmail.com, deharbe@dimap.ufrn.br

Abstract. This paper presents an approach to verify PLCs, a common platform to control systems in the industry. We automatically translate PLC programs written in the languages of the IEC 61131-3 standard to B models, amenable to formal analysis of safety constraints and general structural properties of the application. This approach thus integrates formal methods into existing industrial processes, increasing the confidence in PLC applications, nowadays validated mostly through testing and simulation. The transformation from the PLC programs to the B models is described in detail in the paper. We also evaluate the approach's potential with a case study in a real railway application.

Keywords: B method, PLC, IEC 61131-3, safety critical systems, formal methods.

1 Introduction

Programmable Logic Controllers (from now on, PLCs) perform control operations in a system, running in *execution cycles*: they receive information from the environment as *inputs*, process them and affect this environment with the resulting *outputs*.

In many industries, such as mass transport and energy, it is very common to use PLCs in control applications. Those applications are mostly programmed according to IEC 61131-3 [1], an international standard that specifies the five standard PLC programming languages, namely: LD (Ladder Diagram) and FBD (Function Block Diagram), graphical languages; IL (Instruction List) and ST (Structured Text), textual languages; and SFC (Sequential Function Chart), that shows the structure and internal organization of a PLC. It is not rare that a variation of such languages is employed too.

As the complexity of the PLC applications increases, and as various are safety critical, it is important to ensure their reliability [2]. Since testing and simulation, the *de-facto* method in many branches to perform verification, can leave flaws

---

* Project supported by ANP. CNPq grants 560014/2010-4 and 573964/2008-4 (National Institute of Science and Technology for Software Engineering—INES, www.ines.org.br).

R. Gheyi and D. Naumann (Eds.): SBMF 2012, LNCS 7498, pp. 19–34, 2012.

undiscovered, something intolerable in safety-critical systems, another strategy is necessary. A mean to fulfill this requirement is with formal methods. However, they are difficult to integrate with the industrial process [3], since most control engineers are not familiarized with formal verification [4].

Some recent works have been trying to integrate formal methods and PLC programs verification, using different approaches. In [5], the authors created a new language combining ST and Linear Temporal Logic, ST-LTL, to ease the use of formal verification by control engineers. A method is presented in [6] to verify applications using Safety Function Blocks with timed-automata through model-checking and simulation. A model-driven engineering approach is used in [7] to generate models in a FIACRE language from LD programs. To this date, these approaches are concerned only with parts of the IEC 61131-3 standard.

Our approach consists of developing a tool that receives a PLC program based in the IEC 61131-3 standard and builds an intermediary model from it. This model is automatically translated to a formal model in the B notation [8]. Additional *safety constraints* requirements are then manually inserted and verified using theorem proving, thus avoiding state-explosion problems. We can also specify and verify dynamic properties, such as *deadlock freedom*, performing *model checking* in the model using the tool ProB[1], which also supports the definition and verification of new constraints in Linear Temporal Logic. Our approach is thus able to verify that the PLC is presenting the expected behavior in its *execution cycle*.

We chose the B Method because it is used successfully in safety-critical applications, e.g. in the railway industry [12]. Besides, it has a strong support of tools and the B language can handle decomposition, refinement and generation of verified code. It is better discussed in 2.2.

In order to include all the IEC 61131-1 languages, we based our intermediary model (from now on called "PLC model") in the PLCopen [9] standard, which provides an interface representing all such languages in an XML-based format, working also as *documentation*. This PLC model stands between the PLC programs and the formal models to be generated, then reducing the semantic gap between PLC and B and defining a unique semantics for different PLC languages [7]. The process also involves a customizable parser, so we can treat PLC programs that are not *strictly* following the IEC standard; as numerous legacy systems deviate from the standard, still our approach would thus be able to handle them.

Thus, as the generation of the formal model is automatic and as it makes correctness, according to the specification, a realistic and achievable goal, we facilitate the use of formal methods in industry and increase confidence in the PLC applications.

We also present a case study in a real safety-critical railway system: the Central Door Controller (from now on, CDC) of the doors subsystem of a train. We show the step by step automatic generation of the formal specification from its PLC program and, after defining the safety constraints, perform a full formal verification in the application, at the end exhibiting the results.

---

[1] http://www.stups.uni-duesseldorf.de/ProB

This paper presents the continuation of the work in [10] and [11]. A new definition of the formal model generated, as well as improvements on *how* it is generated and an evaluation of the whole method in a real case study are the main contributions of this new paper.

Structure of the paper. Section 2 presents in more detail PLCs and the B method. In section 3 we have the description of the different phases of our method, and in section 4 we present our case study. Section 5 concludes the paper and presents future work.

2 Context and Techniques

2.1 Programmable Logic Controllers

We base our work with PLCs on the PLCopen standard. This standard is an effort to gather all the information of the five different languages of the IEC standard and provide an interface with their supporting tools, as well as the ability to transfer information between different platforms. It is an XML- based standard able to store not just the textual, but also the graphical information of a project, allowing complete translation from a representation to another.

The PLCopen standard structures PLCs in three specific parts: the *Headers* structures, containing information such as the project name, the company associated, etc.; the *Instance* specific part, representing the configurations of the environment in which the PLC may operate; and the *Type* specific part, where we have the *Program Organization Units* (POUs) and the defined *Data Types*. In our approach we will consider only the elements of *Type*.

The Data Types are either *elementary* (Bool, Integer, etc.), *derived* (Enumeration, Array, Structure, etc.) or *extended* (Pointers); generic data types can also be defined. They are used to type the variables used in the POUs.

The POUs represent the PLC programs, being divided in three categories: *functions, function blocks* and *programs*:

- The POU *functions*, when executed, produce exactly *one* data statement – a variable typed according to one of the possible data types in the standard –, the function result, and arbitrarily many additional output variables. These POUs are stateless: they contain no state information, i.e., invocation of a function with the *same arguments* shall always produce the *same result*.
- The POU *function blocks* produce *one or more* data statements as result. The state of a function block persists from one execution to the next – they are stateful – , therefore invocation with the the *same arguments* may produce *different results*.
- The POU *programs* are defined as a "logical assembly of all the programming language elements and constructs necessary for the intended signal processing required for the control of a machine or process by a programmable controller system". Their declaration and usage is equivalent to the *function blocks*. It also may use the previous two POU types as auxiliary elements.

The three POU elements have an *interface* with its several kinds of variables: input, local, output, inout, etc. They also have a *body*, composed by IL (Instruction List), ST (Structured Text), LD (Ladder Diagram), FBD (Function Block Diagram) or SFC (Sequential Function Chart) elements, according to the language of the POU. In figure 1 we can see an example of a POU *program* in LD that makes use of an instantiation of a POU *function block* in FBD. In section 4 bits of PLC programs in SFC and ST are shown as part of our case study. For more details, see [1] and [9].

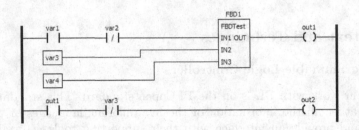

Fig. 1. LD program with rungs executed from left to right, sequentially. Boolean variables and a function block are evaluated in the execution.

2.2   B Method

The B Method [8] is a formal approach for the specification and development of software. It includes a first-order logic with integers and sets, substitutions and refinement rules. It is based on the Abstract Machine Notation (AMN), which provides a unique language for the construction of machines, refinements and implementations, thus representing the different levels of abstraction that a specification of a system may take. Besides, the language supports decomposition, since it is based around the concept of layered development and the construction of larger components from collections of smaller ones.

The B Method provides a unified pragmatic and usable development methodology based on the concept of refinement, requiring the consistency verification for each transformation of the specification from the abstract level towards the concrete one. This, along with the generation and verification of proof obligations to guarantee the consistency of the initial model, makes correctness according to the specification a realistic and achievable goal throughout system development.

3   The Method

The method we are proposing consists of three main phases:

1. translate the information in the PLC programs into an intermediary model, either from a standard or hybrid PLC program, or from an XML file in the PLCopen standard;

2. generate from it a B model that makes possible to check the structural and safety properties of the project;
3. and at last complete the formal model with such safety properties, derived from the project requirements (manually, for now).

Figure 2 illustrates the method. A case study covering all the phases of this method is shown in section 4.

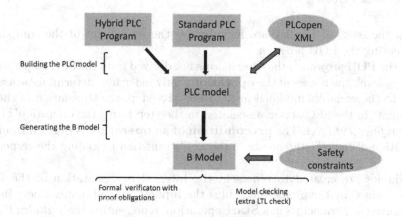

Fig. 2. Illustration of the complete method

3.1   Towards the PLC Model

The PLC model may be generated either directly from an PLCopen XML-based representation, from the programs in the standard languages or from programs in some hybrid language, presenting differences from the IEC 61131-3 standard. Such languages are common, as adaptations to specific domain PLCs may be necessary.

We projected a parser to analyze the programs; it deals with the elements of the standard languages and may be customized to specified differences, to accommodate new languages. This way we can deal with legacy programs that are not strictly standard compliant. To handle XML, we developed a reader module along with the default parser to load the PLC model.

Once the PLC model is constructed, we are able to work independently from the PLC programs to generate the B specification. It is also possible to generate a PLCopen XML, as documentation, to the PLCs that were not in this format.

3.2   Generation of the B Model

A good architecture is essential to generate a good model, as well as to define which information from the PLC model will be responsible for which elements of the B model. The architecture of this model is depicted in figure 3. It represents a POU *program* and the auxiliary POU *functions* or *function blocks* that it may

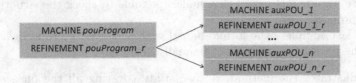

Fig. 3. B model representing a POU *program* and its use of auxiliary *function* and *function block* POUs

use; in the sense of B, they are included by the refinement of the component representing the POU *program*.

For the POU *program*[2], the **operations** are derived from the SFC steps. At the *machine* level, the bodies of the **operations** only make non-deterministic assignments to the variables modified in the respective step; the translation of the ST statements in the SFC action associated to the step forms the operation's body at the *refinement* level. The **precondition** of an **operation** is derived from the translation of the ST statements in the SFC transition preceding the respective step.

Variables are created to represent the internal representation of the POU inputs, named by the prefix "int_" plus the input's original name. These inputs are received as parameters in a **Start** operation, representing the *initialization* of the POU in each *execution cycle*. In the body of this operation, at the *refinement* level, each internal variable receives the value of its corresponding input.

The POU *outputs* are treated as local variables; it is no loss of generality to deal with them like that since we are dealing with the POUs only as independent components. The safety constraints will concern mostly these *outputs*.

To emulate the *execution cycle* of the POU, non-existent in B, a boolean variable is created for each step, named by the step's original name plus the suffix "_done". It is stated true as the respective **operation** is performed and falsified as the correspondent next **operation** in the *execution cycle* is reached. These variables will be part of the **operations**' preconditions: the predecessors step variables must be valid so that a step can be reached.

A variable *beginning* is also created, stated true in the **INITIALISATION** clause of the *refinement*, and is part of the precondition of the **Start** operation. It marks the first *execution cycle*, when **Start** must always be available. In its body *beginning* will be falsified.

In the *auxPOU_n* components, the **operations** are constructed with the translated statements from the auxiliary POUs, *functions* or *function blocks*, either in ST, IL, LD or FBD. In the POU *program*'s *machine* and *refinement* are created and typed variables according to the return type of these **operations**' outputs; they are used whenever one of them is invoked.

Further refinements may be performed to optimize the model, like adding invariants or changing its structure to facilitate automated proof.

---

[2] Due to space limitations and to the fact that our case study in this paper deals particulary with SFC and ST, this explanation covers only the elements of these languages.

3.3   Inserting the Safety Constraints

The next phase is to add safety constraints. Since PLC programs do not represent such constraints explicitly, they have to be manually extracted from the project requirements and modeled to be used in the formal models. This is a hard task and still an open issue in the industry [13], and we have not decided yet which methodology to adopt to tackle this problem. However, some promising approaches as [14] and [15] may be suited for our purpose; the latter was used in our case study.

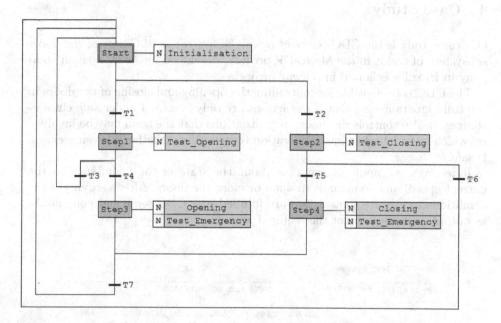

Fig. 4. SFC program for CDC. Execution goes from the initial step to sequential ones according to the validation of the transitions; the actions performed in each step are implemented in ST.

Once the safety constraints are defined, they are inserted into the model as **invariants** in the POU components, conditions that must always hold as the PLC actions are performed. Tools such as Atelier B[3] can perform automatic verification of their consistency and point out where lies any problem, guiding its treatment.

To guarantee that the PLC performs the expected behavior of its *execution cycle* we may create LTL formulas over the variables representing the **operations'** execution, verifying, e.g., if a given **operation** is ever reached from a predecessor one.

---

[3] http://www.atelierb.eu/

We may also verify properties that cannot be modeled with regular first order logic, requiring modalities found in LTL: one example is the condition that *whenever* a given variable has a given value, there must be *some* state reached by the PLC where another certain variable receives another certain value. This can be modeled with the operators □, meaning "it will *always* be the case that..."; and ◇, meaning "it will *eventually* be the case that...".

ProB is an animator and LTL model checker capable of handling B machines. It also provides support to verify structural properties such as *deadlock-freedom*.

4   Case Study

Our case study is the CDC (*Central Door Controller*), a PLC part of the doors subsystem of trains in the Metro-DF project, developed by AeS[4], a small company in Brazil specialized in railway projects.

The CDC is responsible for controlling the opening and closing of the doors in the train, guaranteeing that these actions are only executed under *safe* circumstances. It also controls the emergency situations that the train may be involved in, which must be taken in consideration to determine whether a given scenario is safe.

It receives, as input, information about the state of the train, such as the current speed, and commands to open or close the doors. After verifying if the conditions to execute some action are fulfilled, the CDC sends out commands, as outputs, allowing or not the required actions.

```
CDC-Test_Opening

ok_opening := NOT isHigher_op(train_speed) AND
              (
                  (train_stopped AND train_in_platform AND
                    (train_mode = MCS OR train_mode = ATO)
                  )
              OR
                  (train_mode = MAN)
              );
```

Fig. 5. ST action associated to the SFC program of CDC. Tests if the conditions to open the doors of the train are satisfied.

A simplified PLC representing the CDC is shown in figure 4, with a POU *program* in SFC, and its *transitions* and *actions* written in ST – they are not all presented due to space limitations, but in figure 5 we have the action *Test_Opening* in detail. The CDC interface is shown in table 1. Associated with the CDC is also a POU *function*, *isHigher_op*, which receives an integer as input and returns a boolean result indicating whether the input is higher than 6. This function is used to check the speed of the train.

---

[4] http://www.grupo-aes.com.br/site/home/

Table 1. Interface of CDC

Name	Class		Type
train_stopped	Input		BOOL
train_in_platform	Input		BOOL
train_speed	Input		INT
train_mode	Input	OPERATION_MODES	
mech_emg_actuated	Input		BOOL
close_from_ATC	Input		BOOL
close_from_cabin	Input		BOOL
doors_closed	InOut		BOOL
ok_opening	Local		BOOL
ok_closing	Local		BOOL
emergency_evaluated	Local		BOOL
control_mech_emg_actuated	Output		BOOL
authorize_emergency	Output		BOOL
cab_emg_sound	Output		BOOL
interlock_doors_traction	Output		BOOL
apply_emg_breaks	Output		BOOL

– **Inputs**: environment state and commands.
– **Locals**: CDC operational variables.
– **Outputs**: Results of the CDC operations.

The execution begins at the step **Start**: the PLC reads the inputs of the external system and initialize its local variables. The transitions **T1** and **T2** will test if an opening or closing operation, respectively, was requested, then directing the execution to **Step1**, where the CDC tests if the conditions to *open* the doors are satisfied; or to **Step2**, where the CDC tests if the conditions to *close* the doors are satisfied. If the conditions either to open or to close the doors were satisfied, situation controlled respectively by the local variables *ok_opening* and *ok_closing*, the execution continues; otherwise it goes back to **Start**, where the CDC will wait until the next reading of inputs. In **Step3** or **Step4**, responsible respectively for opening and closing operations, the outputs controlling the state of the doors are modified, corresponding to the kind of action performed – opening or closing; the emergency circumstances are evaluated in these steps; the corresponding controlling outputs are also modified here.

4.1   Applying the Method

We use the tool Beremiz[5] to create the PLC program and obtain a PLCopen XML document representing the CDC. We translate the information in it into our PLC model, then generate a B model representing the CDC. The architecture of the generated model is presented in figure 6. This process is fully automatic.

The variables with the prefix "int_" are the internal variables created to represent the inputs received by the PLC. The local and the output variables are created with the same names as the ones shown in table 1. The auxiliary variable *aux_bool* is created to be used when the operation **isHigher_op** is invoked in *CDC_r*. The others are the step variables, used to represent the *execution cycle*, plus *beginning*, signaling the first execution.

In figure 7, we can see part of the B operation produced by the translation of **Start**. The precondition types the inputs and specify the conditions when **Start** can be executed: the first execution cycle – *beginning* = **TRUE**; the condition of transition **T3** is satisfied and the execution is in **Step1**; the condition of transition **T6** is satisfied and the execution is in **Step2**; or the condition of transition **T7** is satisfied and the execution is in **Step3** or **Step4**.

---

[5] http://www.beremiz.org/

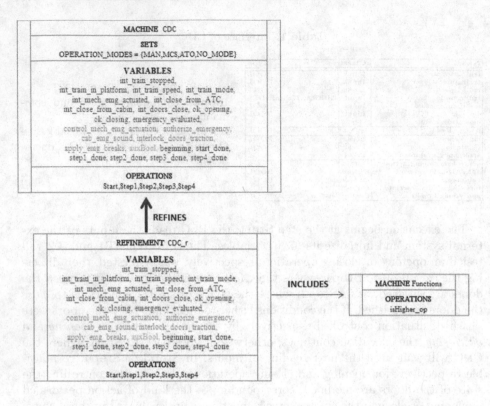

Fig. 6. Architecture of the B model generated representing the CDC

$Start(train\_stopped, train\_in\_platform, train\_speed, train\_mode, mech\_emg\_actuated,$
$close\_from\_ATC, close\_from\_cabin, doors\_closed) =$
   PRE
      $train\_stopped :$ **BOOL** & $train\_in\_platform :$ **BOOL** & $train\_speed : \{0, 5, 10\}$
      & $mech\_emg\_actuated :$ **BOOL** & $close\_from\_ATC :$ **BOOL** &
      $close\_from\_cabin :$ **BOOL** & $train\_mode : OPERATION\_MODES$ &
      $doors\_closed :$ **BOOL** & $(beginning =$ **TRUE** or $(($**not**$(ok\_opening =$ **TRUE**$)$
      & $step1\_done =$ **TRUE**$)$ or $($**not**$(ok\_closing =$ **TRUE**$)$ & $step2\_done =$ **TRUE**$)$
      or $(emergency\_evaluated =$ **TRUE** & $(step3\_done =$ **TRUE** or
      $step4\_done =$ **TRUE**$))))$
   $(...)$

Fig. 7. Start operation in the CDC *machine*. Only the precondition is exhibited.

The body of the **Start** operation at the *refinement* level, shown in 8, consists of the translation of the statements in the ST action—the initialization of the local variables—, plus the generated initialization of the variables representing the outputs; then the assignments of the inputs to its internal variables; and finally the initialization of the step variables, marking the active step as **Start** – $start\_done :=$ **TRUE**.

$Start(train\_stopped, train\_in\_platform, train\_speed, train\_mode, mech\_emg\_actuated,$
$close\_from\_ATC, close\_from\_cabin, doors\_closed) =$
    BEGIN
       $ok\_opening :=$ **FALSE**; $ok\_closing :=$ **TRUE**; $emergency\_evaluated :=$ **FALSE**;

       $control\_mech\_emg\_actuation :=$ **FALSE**; $authorize\_emergency :=$ **FALSE**;
       $cab\_emg\_sound :=$ **FALSE**; $interlock\_doors\_traction :=$ **FALSE**;
       $apply\_emg\_breaks :=$ **FALSE**;

       $int\_train\_stopped := train\_stopped$; $int\_train\_in\_platform := train\_in\_platform$;
       $int\_train\_speed := train\_speed$; $int\_mech\_emg\_actuated := mech\_emg\_actuated$;
       $int\_close\_from\_ATC := close\_from\_ATC$;
       $int\_close\_from\_cabin := close\_from\_cabin$;
       $beginning :=$ **FALSE**; $start\_done :=$ **TRUE**; $step1\_done :=$ **FALSE**;
       $step2\_done :=$ **FALSE**; $step3\_done :=$ **FALSE**; $step4\_done :=$ **FALSE**
    END

Fig. 8. Start operation in the CDC_r *refinement*

$Step1 =$
    PRE
       not$(int\_close\_from\_ATC =$ **TRUE or** $int\_close\_from\_cabin =$ **TRUE**$)^{T1}$
       & $start\_done =$ **TRUE**
    THEN
       $start\_done :=$ **FALSE**; $auxBool < - -$ $isHigher\_op(int\_train\_speed)$;
       IF $auxBool =$ **TRUE THEN**
       /*block opening*/
       $ok\_opening :=$ **FALSE**
       ELSE IF $((int\_train\_mode =$ MAN$)$ **or** $((int\_train\_mode =$ MCS **or**
       $int\_train\_mode =$ ATO$)$ & $(int\_train\_stopped =$ **TRUE**$)$
       & $(int\_train\_in\_platform =$ **TRUE**$)))$
       THEN
         /*Opening allowed*/
         $ok\_opening :=$ **TRUE**
       ELSE
         /*block opening*/
         $ok\_opening :=$ **FALSE**
       END
       END;
       $step1\_done :=$ **TRUE**
    END

Fig. 9. Operation representing **Step1** (The precondition of the *machine* operation is
exhibited together with the *refinement* operation due to space limitations

The B operation resulting from the translation of **Step1** is shown in figure 9.
In its precondition we have **T1** and the obligation that **Step1**'s predecessor step

INVARIANT
((*ok_opening* = **TRUE**) =>
  ((*int_train_speed* <=6) & (((*int_train_mode* = MCS **or** *int_train_mode* = ATO)
  & (*int_train_stopped* = **TRUE**) & (*int_train_in_platform* = **TRUE**))
  or (*int_train_mode* = MAN))
)
) &
((*ok_closing* = **FALSE**) =>
  (*int_train_mode* = ATO & *int_close_from_cabin* = **TRUE**)
)

Fig. 10. Invariants concerning opening and closing safety

variable, *start_done*, must be valid. Its body statements are the translation of the ST statements in the step's associated action, *Test_Opening*, shown in figure 5.

The other operations are generated according to the same guidelines. Once the B model is ready, the next phase in our method is to insert, manually, the *safety constraints* of the project as *invariants*. We used the ProR approach [15] to define the formal constraints from the natural language requirements, easing the process and assuring reliable traceability; the whole effort is in [16]. We present here only the results to the following requirements, concerning the opening and closing operations:

1. The doors shall open only when the train's speed is lower than or equal to 6km/h.
2. The conditions to open all the doors located in one or in the other side of the train, when in the operation mode ATO or MCS, are the train be stopped and in the platform.
3. The condition to open all the doors located in one or in the other side of the train, when in the operation mode MAN, is the train's speed be lower than or equal to 6km/h.
4. In ATO mode, the Central Door Controller must not close the doors while receiving the command to open them from the driver push buttons.

We have the resulting B invariants in figure 10. The first invariant, referring to the situations where opening is *allowed*, covers the items 1, 2 and 3. The second invariant, referring to the situation where closing is *prohibited*, covers the item 4. The model is then ready to formally verify them.

The last phase of the process is to create the LTL formulas to check if the PLC program's behavior is as expected. Concerning the *execution cycle*, the conditions to be verified and the respective formulas are shown below:

1: **Start** is reachable :

1: $\diamond\ start\_done$

2: **Step2** must be reachable from **Start** when **Step1** is not :

2: $\Box((start\_done \land \neg \diamond step1\_done)$ $\Rightarrow \diamond step2\_done)$

3: **Step1** must be reachable from **Start** when **Step2** is not :

3: $\Box((start\_done \land \neg \diamond step2\_done)$ $\Rightarrow \diamond step1\_done)$

4: **Step3** must be reachable from **Step1** when **Start** is not :

4: $\Box((step1\_done \land \neg \diamond start\_done)$ $\Rightarrow \diamond step3\_done)$

5: **Start** must be reachable from **Step1** when **Step3** is not :

5: $\Box((step1\_done \land \neg \diamond step3\_done)$ $\Rightarrow \diamond start\_done)$

6: **Step4** must be reachable from **Step2** when **Start** is not :

6: $\Box((step2\_done \land \neg \diamond start\_done)$ $\Rightarrow \diamond step4\_done)$

7: **Start** must be reachable from **Step2** when **Step4** is not :

7: $\Box((step2\_done \land \neg \diamond step4\_done)$ $\Rightarrow \diamond start\_done)$

8: **Start** must be reachable from **Step3** or **Step4** :

8: $\Box((step3\_done \lor step4\_done)$ $\Rightarrow \diamond start\_done)$

We also verify constraints non-expressible through the invariants, such as:

9: Always when the CDC attests that the conditions to open are satisfied, then the doors must open at some point of its execution :

9: $\Box(ok\_opening \Rightarrow$ $\diamond \neg int\_doors\_closed)$

10: Always when the CDC attests that the conditions to close are satisfied, then the doors must close at some point of its execution :

10: $\Box(ok\_closing \Rightarrow$ $\diamond int\_doors\_closed)$

4.2   Results

Once the model is complemented with the invariants representing the safety constraints and the LTL formulas to verify the program's behavior are defined, we are in position to carry on formal verification through theorem proving of proof obligations, model checking and LTL formulas check.

Ten proof obligations were generated to verify the invariants inserted in the model: 6 in the operation **Step1**, related to the invariant concerning the opening conditions; and 3 in the operation **Step4**, associated with the invariants representing the emergency conditions, not exhibited here due to space limitations. The Atelier B theorem prover was able to prove them all automatically, without any user interaction. The operation **Step2** does not generate proof obligations because its statements are strictly equal to the invariant concerning the closing conditions, and the operation **Step3**, as it opens the doors, directly satisfies all the invariants concerning emergency conditions, by vacuity.

Next, we model check the model for the properties not covered by the proof obligations, such as *deadlock-freedom* and *liveness*. As a result we had 4969 states, all free from deadlock, and a total of 1792080 transitions were necessary to cover them all. An important observation is that in order to avoid a state-explosion problem we restricted, *only* for the model checking phase, the values of the **INT** variables - *train_speed* and *int_train_speed* - to {0, 5, 10}; there is no loss of generality, since the chosen values represent the three possible states of the train: *"stopped"*, *"in movement and with its speed lower than 6km/h"* and *"in movement and with its speed not lower than 6km/h"*. Without this restriction an infinite number of states would have be generated by the model checker to cover the possible values of the **INT** variables.

We can see in table 2 that most of the operations performed in the model checking phase were at **Start**, where the inputs are received and the *execution cycle* of the PLC is initiated. The computing time was of ten minutes.

Table 2. Total of transitions covered

Operation	Number of visits
Initialisation	1536
Start	1787904
Step1	384
Step2	1152
Step3	48
Step4	1056

The final step was to check the LTL formulas to verify if the PLC was presenting the expected behavior. All the formulas were proven correct, so the CDC was indeed executing as planned. The computing time was of less than one minute per formula.

5   Conclusions and Future Work

We have overviewed a method to carry out formal verification of PLC programs, according to the IEC 61131-3 standard, through the automatic generation of a B specification. Safety constraints are inserted in the formal model and then verified through theorem proving; we also verify structural properties and if the PLC presents the expected behavior performing model checking and using LTL formulas. Thus we increase the reliability of the application, having correctness according to the specification as a realistic and achievable goal.

Another key point of our approach is that, as it allows the users to generate the B models automatically from the PLC programs, only lacking the safety properties, it boosts the process of formal verification of such programs, skipping all the hard work to design and construct the model that prevents formal methods from being easily inserted in industrial projects.

We also presented a case study in a real railway application where our approach was applied with success. We were able to attest the efficacy of the automatic provers and verify the safety constraints of the project.

Future work lies mostly in expanding and adjusting the generation of the B models, improving the way the method deals with some issues, such as multi-dimensional arrays, loops and data types supported, for instance. Scalability is also an issue, since the bigger and more complex the generated models are, the harder it is to verify them; we plan to tackle this exploiting the decomposition support of B, splitting the complexity of the application in several components and verifying them independently.

The results obtained from the model and LTL checking can be used to improve the PLC, but we have not defined yet an appropriate methodology on how to perform this improvement; that is in our future works as well. We are also studying the automatization of the process of deriving the safety constraints from the requirements.

To improve the confidence in our translation method, another future work is to make the inverse process: generate the former PLC programs from the B models, so that we can apply testing technique to validate our approach.

As we expand the scope of our method, we also intend to perform more case studies. We are about to start one with the company ClearSy[6], strongly involved with the B method and safety critical systems engineering, in a real project also in the railway field, to execute problem diagnosis in high speed trains.

References

1. IEC (2003): IEC 61131-3 - Programmable controllers. International Electrotechnical Comission Standards (2003)
2. Kron, H.: On the evaluation of risk acceptance principles. In: 19th Dresden Conference on Traffic and Transportation Science (2003)
3. Amey, P.: Dear sir, yours faithfully: an everyday story of formality. IN Proc. 12th Safety-Critical Systems Symposium, p. 318 (2004)
4. Parnas, D.: Really rethinking 'formal methods'. Computer (January 2010), http://portal.acm.org/citation.cfm?id=1724964.1724987
5. Ljungkrantz, O., Åkesson, K., Fabian, M., Yuan, C.: A Formal Specification language for PLC-based Control Logic. In: Proc. of 8th IEEE International Conference on Industrial Informatics, pp. 1067–1072 (2010)
6. Soliman, D., Frey, G.: Verification and Validation of Safety Applications based on PLcopen Safety Function Blocks using Timed Automata in Uppaal. In: Proceedings of the Second IDAC Workshop on Dependable Control of Discrete Systems (DCDS), pp. 39–44 (2009)
7. Farines, J., de Queiroz, M.H., da Rocha, V.G., Carpes, A.A.M., Vernadat, F., Crégut, X.: A model-driven engineering approach to formal verification of PLC programs. In: IEEE EFTA (2011)
8. Abrial, J.R.: The B-book: assigning programs to meanings. Cambridge University Press, Cambridge (2005)
9. PLCopen : XML Formats for IEC 61131-3. PLCopen Technical Committee, 6 (2009)
10. Barbosa, H., Déharbe, D.: Towards formal verification of PLC programs. In: 14th Brazilian Symposium on Formal Methods: Short Papers, São Paulo- SP (2011)

---

[6] http://www.clearsy.com/

34   H. Barbosa and D. Déharbe

11. Barbosa, H., Déharbe, D.: Formal Verification of PLC Programs Using the B Method. In: Derrick, J., Fitzgerald, J., Gnesi, S., Khurshid, S., Leuschel, M., Reeves, S., Riccobene, E. (eds.) ABZ 2012. LNCS, vol. 7316, pp. 353–356. Springer, Heidelberg (2012)
12. Lecomte, T., Servat, T., Pouzancre, G.: Formal methods in safety-critical railway systems. In: Proc. Brazilian Symposium on Formal Methods: SMBF (January 2007)
13. Abrial, J.R.: Formal methods in industry: achievements, problems, future. In: Proceedings of the 28th International Conference on Software Engineering, pp. 761–768 (2006)
14. Cabral, G., Sampaio, A.: Formal Specification Generation from Requirement Documents. In: SBMF (2006)
15. Ladenberger, L., Jastram, M.: Requirements Traceability between Textual Requirements and Formal Models Using ProR
16. Barbosa, H.: Desenvolvendo um sistema crítico através de formalização de requisitos utilizando o método B. B.Sc. Thesis, UFRN, DIMAp, Natal, Brazil (2010)

Palytoxin Inhibits the Sodium-Potassium Pump – An Investigation of an Electrophysiological Model Using Probabilistic Model Checking

Fernando A.F. Braz[1], Jader S. Cruz[2],
Alessandra C. Faria-Campos[1], and Sérgio V.A. Campos[1]

[1] Department of Computer Science, Federal University of Minas Gerais,
[2] Biochemistry and Immunology Department, Federal University of Minas Gerais,
Av. Antônio Carlos, 6627, Pampulha, 30123-970 Belo Horizonte, Brazil
fbraz@dcc.ufmg.br,jcruz@icb.ufmg.br,{alessa,scampos}@dcc.ufmg.br

Abstract. Automatic verification techniques such as Probabilistic Model Checking (PMC) have been successfully applied in the specification and analysis of stochastic systems. Some biological systems show these characteristics, allowing PMC usage in unexpected fields. We present and analyze a probabilistic model for palytoxin toxin (PTX) effects on cell transport systems, structures which exchange ions across the plasma membrane. Several diseases are linked to their irregular behavior and their study could help drug development. The model developed in this work shows that as sodium concentration increases, PTX action enhances, suggesting that individuals with diets high in sodium are more vulnerable to PTX. An opposite effect is observed when the potassium concentration increases. PMC can help significantly in the understanding of how cell transport systems behave, suggesting novel experiments which otherwise might be overlooked by biologists.

Keywords: Probabilistic Model Checking, Systems Biology, Sodium-Potassium Pump, Palytoxin, Ion Channels Blockers and Openers.

1 Introduction

Probabilistic model checking (PMC) is an automatic procedure to model and analyze non-deterministic, stochastic and dynamical systems. PMC completely explores a probabilistic model, establishing if given properties in special types of logics are satisfied by the model. Different properties can be expressed, such as "What is the probability of an event happening?", which offers important information about the model [7,20,16].

PMC can be used to study biological systems, which show some of the characteristics of PMC models. The PMC approach can obtain a better understanding of these systems than others methods are able to, such as simulations, which present local minima problems that PMC avoids [9,15,14,8,4].

We present and analyze a PMC model of the sodium-potassium pump (or Na^+/K^+-ATPase), a transmembrane ionic transport system that is a

R. Gheyi and D. Naumann (Eds.): SBMF 2012, LNCS 7498, pp. 35–50, 2012.

fundamental part of all animal cells and plays an important role in several biological functions such as cell volume control and heart muscle contraction. The Na^+/K^+-ATPase is one of the main targets of toxins and drugs and it is related to several diseases and syndromes [3]. In this work we present a model where the pump was exposed to a deadly toxin called palytoxin (PTX) — which completely alters the behavior of the pump — in order to understand PTX effects on the pump [22].

The model has shown that high doses of sodium could enhance PTX effects. For example, when the sodium concentration is increased by 10 times its normal values, the probability of being in PTX related states is increased by 17,46%. This suggests that individuals with electrolyte disturbances (changes in normal sodium or potassium levels caused by diseases or syndromes) are more susceptible to the toxin.

The opposite behavior is observed regarding high doses of potassium – when the potassium concentration is increased by 10 times its normal values, PTX effects are reduced by 23,17%. Both results suggest that sodium and potassium levels could be changed to reduce PTX effects on the pump by decreasing sodium and increasing potassium. Since electrolyte levels in the blood can be manipulated up to a certain degree, the study of their role and capability to change Na^+/K^+-ATPase behavior is important.

Our results show that PMC can improve the understanding of cell transport systems and its behavior and may help in the development of new drugs.

This paper is part of an ongoing effort to better understand transmembrane ionic transport systems. The PMC model of the pump was described in [9], where the dynamics of the pump were studied. The toxin palytoxin was included in the model in [4], where different scenarios for the pump disturbances caused by the toxin in cell energy related reactions were studied.

Outline. In Section 2 we describe ionic pumps. The related work of the analysis of these systems and PMC usage are covered in Section 3. Our model is presented in Section 4 and 5, while our experiments, properties and results are shown in Section 6. Finally, our conclusions and future works are in Section 7.

2   Transmembrane Ionic Transport Systems

Every animal cell contains structures named transmembrane ionic transport systems, which exchange ions from the intra to the extracellular medium. An electrochemical gradient is created due to charge and concentration differences between ions in both sides. Gradient maintenance is conducted by cell transport systems, and without it the cells would not perform their functions properly [2].

Transmembrane transport systems are divided in two types: ion channels (passive transport) which do not consume energy; and ionic pumps (active transport) which consume cell energy (Adenosine Triphosphate or ATP).

The behavior of an ion channel depends on transported ion concentration gradients and moves ions in favor of their gradient. Ionic pumps move ions against their electrical charge, concentration gradient, or both [17].

Only specific ions such as sodium, potassium and calcium can pass through ion channels and ionic pumps. Ionic pumps can be viewed as two gates, one internal and another external, that open or close based on chemical and electrical signals, and other different factors [2].

The sodium-potassium pump (Na^+/K^+-ATPase), exchanges three sodium ions from the intracellular medium for two potassium ions from the extracellular medium (Figure 1). This pump can be in two different states: open to either its internal or external side. When the pump is open to its internal side, three sodium ions can bind to it. An ATP molecule binds to the pump, which is followed by its hydrolysis (or energy consumption), releasing the sodium ions to the external side. An Adenosine Diphosphate (ADP) molecule is released while a phosphate molecule remains bound to the pump. Two potassium ions in the external side bind to the pump, which are released in the internal side. The phosphate is also released. The pump is ready now to repeat the cycle [2].

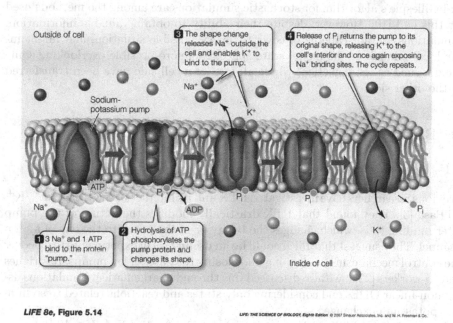

LIFE 8e, Figure 5.14

LIFE: THE SCIENCE OF BIOLOGY, Eighth Edition © 2007 Sinauer Associates, Inc. and W. H. Freeman & Co.

Fig. 1. The Na^+/K^+-ATPase cycle. Adapted from [24].

Ion channels and ionic pumps play an important role in cellular volume control, nerve impulse, coordination of heart muscle contraction, release of accumulated calcium in the sarcoplasmic reticulum for performance of muscle contraction, and several other biological processes [2]. Their irregular behavior is associated with several diseases, such as hypertension and Parkinson's disease. This makes cell transport systems one of the main targets in research for discovery and development of new drugs [2].

Due to their major role in nervous functions, ion channels and ionic pumps are the main targets of neurotoxins [2]. Palytoxin (PTX), a deadly toxin from the coral *Palythoa toxica*, is an example of a toxin that can affect ionic pumps. PTX changes the behavior of the Na^+/K^+-ATPase, essentially turning it into an ion channel, which means that the pump transfers ions based on their concentration gradient, instead of exchanging ions slowly against their concentration gradient [3].

Despite the discovery of ion channels and ionic pumps over 50 years ago, they are not yet completely understood [2]. However, recent studies about PTX effects on the Na^+/K^+-ATPase are changing how these structures are viewed by the scientific community, helping to understand better how they work [3].

Cell transport systems usually are investigated through expensive and time-consuming experimental procedures in laboratories. Different types of simulations, mathematical and computational methods are also employed to improve the understanding of these structures. Ordinary differential equations (ODE) and Gillespie's algorithm for stochastic simulations are among the methods used for this end [10]. However, despite their ability to obtain valuable information, simulations are not capable of covering every possible situation, and might incur local minima of the model state space, therefore possible overlooking some events, such as ion depletion, where all ions of a cell side have been transferred to the other side.

3   Related Work

3.1   Experimental and Simulational Techniques

Previous researchers have investigated PTX and its interactions with the Na^+/K^+-ATPase [3]. They found that PTX drastically modifies the nature of the pump after binding to it, which changes the behavior of the pump to the one of an ion channel. They suggest that PTX could be an useful tool in experiments to discover the control mechanisms for opening and closing the gates of ion pumps. Rodrigues and co-workers [22] have also discussed this through mathematical simulations using non-linear ODEs and considering only states and reactions related to sodium and potassium exchange.

Interactions of PTX with the complete model for the Na^+/K^+-ATPase are analyzed in [23]. The series of works by Rodrigues and co-workers can be viewed as simulational approaches of the experimental results of [3].

The specific sodium-potassium pump present in cardiac cells is examined in [18] using different models of ODEs. Initially a thirteen state model is presented, however a reduction for the model containing only four states is obtained. It is demonstrated the central role of the sodium-potassium pump in maintaining the cellular concentration levels of calcium ions, essential for the cardiac muscle contraction. Also, a model is presented for the pump coupled with states and reactions related to cesium, a substance used to perform experiments, which interfere in the behavior of the pump in the same way as drugs and toxins.

3.2   Model Checking

The tools used in the formal verification of biological systems that are more closely related to this work are PRISM [16], BioLab [8], Ymer [26], Bio-PEPA [6] and SPiN [12].

PRISM supports different types of models, properties and simulators [16]. It has been largely used in several fields, i.e. communication and media protocols, security and power management systems. We have used PRISM in this work for several reasons, which include: exact PMC in order to obtain accurate results; Continuous-time Markov Chain (CTMC) models, suited for our field of study; rich modeling language that allowed us to build our model; and finally property specification using Continuous Stochastic Logic (CSL), which is able to express qualitative and quantitative properties.

Clarke and co-workers [8] have introduced a new algorithm called BioLab. Instead of building explicitly all states of a model, the tool generates the minimum number of necessary simulations, given error bounds parameterized for acceptance of false positives and false negatives of the properties to be verified. This algorithm is based on the works of [26], author of the approximate model checker Ymer. We did not use BioLab or Ymer because our initial analysis demanded exact results. Only after these preliminary results we could have used an approximate analysis.

In [27] the authors compare numerical and statistical methods for PMC, since exact model checking is not always possible due to timewise and computational resources restrictions. Therefore, approximate model checking is an alternative when it is acceptable to lose exact results that demand prohibitive execution time in order to obtain approximate results that are obtained in a timely manner. Ymer uses this technique.

The authors illustrate in [15] the application of PMC to model and analyze different complex biological systems for example the signaling pathway of Fibroblast Growth Factor (FGF), a family of growth factors involved in healing and embryonic development. The analysis of other signaling pathways such as MAPK and Delta/Notch can be seen in [14].

The use of PMC is demonstrated also in [13], where the authors examine and obtain a better understanding of mitogen-activated kinase cascades (MAPK cascades) dynamics, biological systems that respond to several extracellular stimuli, i.e. osmotic stress and heat shock, and regulate many cellular activities, such as mitosis and genetic expression.

4   The Na^+/K^+-ATPase Model

Our Na^+/K^+-ATPase model is written in the PRISM language (used by the PRISM model checker) and consists of modules for each of the molecules (Sodium or Na and Potassium or K) and one main module for the pump. This first part of the model does not include palytoxin, which is later included in Section 5. A fragment of the model is shown in Figure 4, and its complete version can be found in the supplementary material [1]. The complete model has 409 lines and 11 reactions.

Na+/K+-ATPase PRISM Model

```
module na
  naIn  : [0..(NI+NO)] init NI;        // Number of Na inside cell
  naOut : [0..(NI+NO)] init NO;        // Number of Na outside cell

  // reaction 2: 3naIn + E1 <-> NA3E1
  [r2]  naIn>=3          -> pow(naIn,3) : (naIn'=naIn-3);
  [rr2] naIn<(NI+NO-3) -> 1            : (naIn'=naIn+3);
endmodule

module pump
  E1    : [0..1] init 1;               // e1 conformational state
  NA3E1 : [0..1] init 0;               // e1 bound to three sodium ions

  // reaction 2: 3naIn + E1 <-> NA3E1
  [r2]  E1=1 & NA3E1=0 -> 1 : (E1'=0) & (NA3E1'=1);
  [rr2] E1=0 & NA3E1=1 -> 1 : (E1'=1) & (NA3E1'=0);
endmodule

// base rates
const double r2rate  = 2.00*pow(10,2)/(0.001*V*AV);
const double rr2rate = 8.00*pow(10,2);

// module representing the base rates of reactions
module base_rates
  [r2] true -> r2rate  : true;
  [rr2] true ->rr2rate : true;
endmodule
```

Fig. 2. Na+/K+-ATPase PRISM Model

Each molecule module contains a variable to store the current number of molecules (i.e. naIn for $[Na^+]^i$) and transitions that represent chemical reactions, which are responsible for changing the number of molecules. The concentration of sodium, potassium and palytoxin is discretized as described below in Section 4.1. A list of reactions can be found in [22] and in the supplementary material [1]. Reactions which involve more than one element of each type have to take into account the law of mass action as described below in Section 4.1.

The main module controls the pump, controlling its current state. The states are a boolean vector, where only one position can and must be true. The main module also has transitions which change the pump state.

The Albers-Post model [19] is a kinetic model that represents the Na+/K+-ATPase cycle (Figure 3 - left side). Its translation to the PRISM language is straightforward. According to it, the pump can be in different states, which change depending on different reactions involving sodium or potassium. The pump can be open or closed to the extra and intracellular sides. Two or three sodium ions can bind to the pump when it is open to its intracellular side. Two potassium ions can bind to the pump when it is open to its intracellular side. The reactions are bidirectional and their rates were obtained in [22].

In our model, the pump can be in five states: open to its inner side (E1, in our PRISM model); open to its outer side (E2); open to its inner side, with three sodium ions bound to it (NA3E1); closed to both sides with two sodium ions bound it (NA2E2); closed to both sides with two potassium ions bound it (K2E2).

KINETIC MODEL

**SODIUM AND POTASSIUM
INTERACTIONS
WITH PTX-PUMP**

**8 STATES
11 REACTIONS**

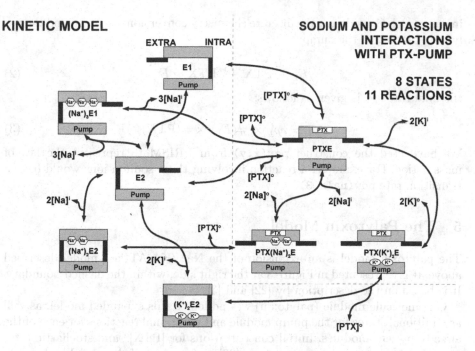

Fig. 3. The classical Albers-Post model [19], where $[Na^+]^i$ and $[Na^+]^o$ are the intra and extracellular sodium (Na) concentrations, $[K^+]^i$ and $[K^+]^o$ are the intra and extra cellular potassium (K) concentrations, and $[PTX]^o$ is the palytoxin (PTX) concentration. Adapted from [21].

4.1 Discrete Chemistry

The main components of our model are molecules (sodium and potassium) and the Na^+/K^+-ATPase, which can interact with each other through several elementary reactions. There is one additional molecule (PTX) in the palytoxin extension for this model, discussed below.

The concentration of each of these components is a discrete variable, instead of a continuous function. Therefore, we have converted the amount of initial concentration of molecules from molarity (M) to number of molecules. The stochastic rates for forward and backward transitions are from [21]. The substrates concentrations ($[Na]^i = 0.00500$, $[K]^i = 0.00495$, $[Na]^o = 0.00006$ and $[K]^o = 0.00495$) are from [5]. The *cell volume* is from [11].

In order to convert the initial amount of molecules given in molarity ([X]) into quantities of molecules (#X), we have used the following biological definition [2]:

$$\#X = [X] \times V \times N_A \tag{1}$$

where V is the cell volume and N_A is the Avogadro constant.

The law of mass action states that a reaction rate is proportional to the concentration of its reagents. Therefore, we take into account the reagent concentrations

in our model. Considering the discrete chemistry conversion discussed and the palytoxin binding to the pump:

$$E_1 + \text{PTX} \xrightarrow{rp_1'} \text{PTX} \sim E \tag{2}$$

the final rate rp_1 is given as follows:

$$rp_1 = rp_1' \times \#(E_1) \times \#(\text{PTX}) \tag{3}$$

We have used the construct `pow(x,y)` from PRISM to represent the law of
mass action. For example, a reaction involving three sodium ions would have a
transition rate `pow(naIn,3)`.

5   The Palytoxin Model

The palytoxin model is an extension of the Na^+/K^+-ATPase model described
above. It is represented in Figure 3 at the right side, within the dashed boundary.
It is based on the description by [22] and [3].

One molecule module (palytoxin) was added to this expanded model, as well
as additional states for the pump module and additional reactions for each of the
already present modules. Initial concentrations for $[\text{PTX}]^o$ and stochastic rates
for transitions between states are from [22]. A fragment of the model is shown in
Figure 5 and its complete version can be seen in the supplementary material [1].

The states correspond to the pump bound to PTX, when the pump is open
to both sides behaving like an ion channel. There are three additional states for
the pump: bound to a PTX molecule (`PTXE`, in our model); bound to a PTX
molecule, with two sodium ions bound to their binding sites (`PTXNA2E`); and
bound to a PTX molecule, with two potassium ions bound to their binding sites
(`PTXK2E`).

6   Results

6.1   Parameters and Model Complexity

Our model can be explored in six different dimensions: extracellular PTX concentration ($[\text{PTX}]^o$), intra and extracellular sodium concentrations ($[\text{Na}^+]^i$ and
$[\text{Na}^+]^o$, respectively), intra and extracellular potassium concentrations ($[\text{K}^+]^i$ and
$[\text{K}^+]^o$, respectively) and pump volume. Each dimension can be modified (increased or decreased) to affect one aspect of the model, which impacts directly
to model complexity regarding the number of states, transitions, topology, model
build time and property verify time.

Table 1 shows the changes in these values in function of different scenarios.
In the Control scenario, $[\text{Na}^+]^i = 22$ mM, $[\text{Na}^+]^o = 140$ mM, $[\text{K}^+]^i = 127$ mM,
$[\text{K}^+]^o = 10$ mM, $[\text{PTX}]^o = 0.001\,\mu\text{m}$ and the pump volume is 10^{-22} L. In the
High Sodium scenario, sodium concentrations are increased 10 times, therefore
$[\text{Na}^+]^i = 220$ mM, $[\text{Na}^+]^o = 1400$ mM, while the other parameters remain

```
Palytoxin PRISM Model

module ptx
  ptxOut : [0..(PTXO+1)] init PTXO;   // Number of PTX outside the cell

  // reaction p1: PTXo + E1 <-> PTXE
  [rp1]  ptxOut>=1         -> ptxOut : (ptxOut'=ptxOut-1);
  [rrp1] ptxOut<(PTXO-1) -> 1        : (ptxOut'=ptxOut+1);
endmodule

module pump
  PTXE : [0..1] init 0;               // non selective pump bound to ptx

  // reaction p1: PTXo + E1 <-> PTXE
  [rp1]  ptx!=0 & E1=1 & PTXE=0 -> 1 : (E1'=0) & (PTXE'=1);
  [rrp1] ptx!=0 & E1=0 & PTXE=1 -> 1 : (E1'=1) & (PTXE'=0);
endmodule

// base rates
const double r1rate = 1.00*pow(10,2);
const double rr1rate = 0.01;

// module representing the base rates of reactions
module base_rates
  [rp1]  true -> rp1rate : true;
  [rrp1] true -> rrp1rate : true;
endmodule
```

Fig. 4. Palytoxin PRISM Model

unchanged. Finally, in the High Potassium scenario, potassium concentrations are increased 10 times, which changes only potassium to $[K^+]^i = 1270$ mM, $[K^+]^o = 100$ mM.

The columns T_{Build}, T_{State} and T_{Rate} refer to the time to build the model, and to check a state and a transition reward properties. The experiments have been performed in a Intel(R) Xeon(R) CPU X3323, 2.50GHz which has 17 GB of RAM memory.

Table 1. Model complexity, build and check time for different scenarios

Scenario	States	Transitions	T_{Build}	T_{State}	T_{Rate}
Control	208	652	0.094 s	45.123 s	19.307 s
High Sodium	1880	6020	7.101 s	344.578 s	266.436 s
High Potassium	1274	7140	0.081 s	358.842 s	346.707 s

The standard animal cell volume is 10^{-12} L [11], which is prohibitive to represent in PMC since it would cause the classical problem of state space explosion. Our analysis is restricted to only one cell pump. As a consequence, it would also not be realistic to model the whole cell volume since it is shared between several pumps and other cellular structures. Our abstraction reduces the cell volume focusing our analysis in one or few pumps and their surroundings. We achieve this by maintaining the proportions between all interacting components. Therefore, our dimension for cellular volume is called pump volume and is usually 10^{-22} L. Even though those values are many orders of magnitude smaller than the real values, they still represent proper pump behavior, and can be interpreted as using a magnifying glass to investigate a portion of the cell membrane.

On the other hand, for some dimensions we have used more values than intuition suggests, ranging from three orders of magnitude below and above their literature reference values, shown in Section 4.1. This is particularly interesting because we can model different situations for pump behavior, including abnormal concentrations levels for $[Na^+]^i$ due to some disease or syndrome, and different degrees of exposure to $[PTX]^o$, from mild to fatal exposure.

Due to space limitations we have chosen to present the most important properties that we have formulated: state and transition rewards (Sections 6.2 and 6.3). There are also species depletion (reachability) properties (Section 6.4). These and other properties can be seen in the supplementary material [1].

6.2 High [Na⁺] Enhances PTX Action

States and rates of the model can be quantified through rewards, a part of PRISM language. One reward for each state and rate is created. Rewards are incremented each time its conditions are true. After calculating each reward we are able to determine state and rate probability. Figure 5 shows the rewards for state PTXE, the pump open to both sides and bound to a PTX molecule. Rewards for rates are nearly identical.

Now that the model has rewards for each state and rate, we are able to calculate the expected accumulated reward associated with each state and rate over time, with properties such as the one shown in Figure 5. The **R** operator allows us to quantify the reward for some given event, for example the number of times the model was in state PTXE. The operator **C** allows to quantify accumulated rewards for a given time T, therefore we are able to observe rewards over time.

Considering a single pump, a pump volume of 10^{-22} L, a Control scenario (described in the previous subsection), at instant T=100, the expected rewards associated with the state PTXE is 36.2195. In other words, in 100 seconds, the PTX inhibits the pump 36,11% of the time. In a High [Na⁺] scenario, the expected reward associated with PTXE changes to respectively 45.3599, 42.42% of the time. Therefore, as we increased [Na⁺], the likelihood of the pump to be bound exclusively to PTX increased 17,46%. This result can be seen in

State Rewards	Accumulated State Reward Property

`rewards "ptxe"`
`  (PTXE=1) : 1;`
`endrewards`
	R{"ptxe"}=? [**C**<=T]
	
	What is the expected accumulated reward for the state ptxe until time T?

Fig. 5. State Rewards and Accumulated State Reward Property

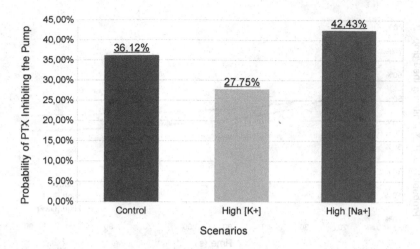

Fig. 6. Probability of PTX Inhibiting the Pump for Different Scenarios in 100 seconds: Control (normal ion concentration); High [K$^+$] scenario (10 times more potassium than normal) which reduces PTX effect by 23,17%; and High [Na$^+$] scenario (10 times more sodium than normal) which enhances PTX effect by 17,46%

Figure 6, which represents the probability of PTX inhibiting the pump for our three different scenarios, and also its time series version in Figure 7.

This result suggests that sodium enhances PTX action, and as consequence people with electrolyte disturbances would be more vulnerable to this toxin. Sodium disturbances appears in different forms (i.e. hypernatremia) and have different causes, such as diabetes insipidus, Conn's syndrome and Cushing's disease [25]. Sodium concentration could be reduced in order to reduce PTX action. However, this is a solution to be taken with caution since sodium is necessary for survival and its absence would shut down the pump. This is particularly interesting since PTX is found in marine species, which inhabit an environment with a high sodium concentration.

6.3 High [K$^+$] Inhibits PTX Action

As the potassium concentration increases, an event opposite to the one discussed the previous section is observed. In a High [K$^+$] scenario, the expected reward associated with PTXE changes to respectively 29.2241, 27.74% of the time. Therefore, as we increased [K$^+$], the likelihood of the pump to be bound exclusively to PTX decreased 23.17%. This result can be seen in Figures 6 and 7.

This result suggests that potassium inhibits PTX action. Therefore individuals with diets low in potassium, or with a pathology which decreases the potassium concentration in their metabolism could be more vulnerable to PTX. Potassium concentration could be increased to fight PTX action. In a similar way to sodium, there is another fine line here since a maximum amount of potassium is tolerated

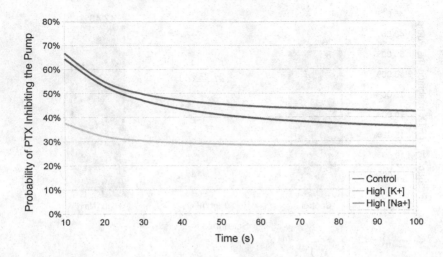

Fig. 7. Probability of PTX Inhibiting the Pump Time Series for Different Scenarios: Control (regular ions concentrations); High [K$^+$] scenario (10 times more potassium than regular concentration) which reduces PTX effect; and High [Na$^+$] scenario (10 times more sodium than regular concentrations) which enhances PTX effect

for one individual. There are a number of causes associated with a high potassium concentration (hyperkaulemia), such as renal insufficiency, Addison's disease, Gordon's syndrome and Rhabdomyolysis. Both results have been obtained from a parametric study of the state and transitions rewards of our model.

6.4   Species Depletion

We have also investigated properties related to species (ion or molecule) depletion events, i.e. there is no species in one side of the cell. For example, the event "naOutDepletion" where there is no external sodium, or the event "ptxAllBounded" where all palytoxin molecules are bound to the pump. These events can be created in PRISM using *labels* (Figure 8).

Species depletion properties state that these events eventually (**F** operator) will always happen (**P>=1** operator). For example, in every scenario the event "ptxAllBounded" eventually always happens. That is not the case for the event "naOutDepletion", which in every scenario it is not guaranteed that it will happen.

The event "kInDepletion" is sensitive to the parameter [K$^+$]– in the Control scenario, its property is true, while in the High [K$^+$]scenario, the property becomes false, because it is more difficult to deplete internal potassium since there is 10 times more potassium. One could check how long it takes for those events to happen. For that we have to use a time reward, and reward properties, such as the one shown in Figure 8. The event "ptxAllBounded" is expected to happen in 1.7513E-5 seconds.

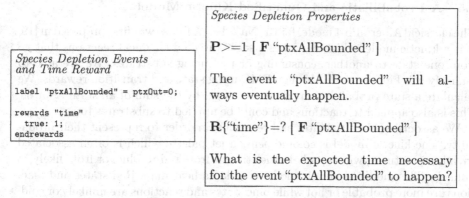

Species Depletion Events and Time Reward

```
label "ptxAllBounded" = ptxOut=0;

rewards "time"
  true: 1;
endrewards
```

Species Depletion Properties

$\mathbf{P}{>}={1}$ [**F** "ptxAllBounded"]

The event "ptxAllBounded" will always eventually happen.

$\mathbf{R}\{\text{"time"}\}{=}?$ [**F** "ptxAllBounded"]

What is the expected time necessary for the event "ptxAllBounded" to happen?

Fig. 8. Depletion Events and Properties, and Time Reward

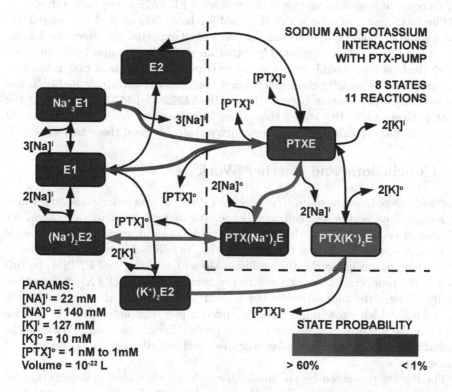

PARAMS:
[NA]^i = 22 mM
[NA]^o = 140 mM
[K]^i = 127 mM
[K]^o = 10 mM
[PTX]^o = 1 nM to 1mM
Volume = 10^{-22} L

SODIUM AND POTASSIUM
INTERACTIONS
WITH PTX-PUMP

8 STATES
11 REACTIONS

STATE PROBABILITY
> 60%   < 1%

Fig. 9. Heat Map: kinetic model for the Na$^+$/K$^+$-ATPase with state and rate probabilities represented as colors. Each state and rate is colored based on its probability. Red states/rates are likely while blue states/rates are improbable. This could be a valuable tool for biologists as it shows model dynamics and it could be used to suggest overlooked experiments.

6.5   A Probabilistic and Quantified Kinetic Model

The classical Albers-Post model for the Na^+/K^+-ATPase was first proposed in [19]. It is a kinetic model which describes a set of directed chemical reactions that go from one state to another, consuming or producing substrates. We are able to quantify this kinetic model through PMC using state and transition rewards. We calculate a state probability dividing its reward by the sum of all state rewards. This is also applied to reactions and could be applied to substrates too.

We associate colors to states and reactions, in order to represent their probability. The kinetic model is colored using a jet palette which is often associated with temperatures, where probabilities transit from red to blue, or from likely to unlikely. This modified kinetic model is called a heat map. Red states and reactions are more probable or hot while blue states and reactions are unlikely or cold. An example of the heat map can be seen in Figure 9, where the states PTXK2E and PTXE are more probable, and reactions involving PTXNA2E occur more often.

The heat map could be a valuable tool for biologists as it shows model dynamics and it could be used to suggest overlooked experiments. Since the kinetic model is an abstraction suggested by experimental data, it could be incomplete, which the heat map would assist towards its completion. The heat map raises several questions, especially about likely reactions involved with improbable states. For example, the reaction between the states NA2E2 and PTXNA2E is one of the most actives, while the states themselves are the most inactives. This could suggest that there might be an intermediary state between these two states.

7   Conclusions and Further Work

The sodium-potassium pump (Na^+/K^+-ATPase) is a cellular structure which exchanges ions across the cell membrane. Its regular behavior is critical for all animal cells, otherwise the individual could present some diseases or syndromes. A stochastic model representing the Na^+/K^+-ATPase has been built for a single pump using the Probabilistic Model Checking tool PRISM. In this model, the pump has been exposed to the toxin palytoxin (PTX), which drastically changes the pump regular behavior. PMC has allowed us to investigate the model, which show unpredictable and complex characteristics. Properties about biological events were expressed in probabilistic logics, e.g. "What is the probability of being in PTX related states?", which allowed the observation of rare events.

The results presented by the model have shown that high concentrations of sodium could enhance PTX effects. For example, when the sodium concentration is increased by 10 times its normal values, the probability of PTX inhibiting the pump increases 17,46%. This suggests that electrolyte disturbances could make an individual more susceptible to the toxin. Since PTX is found in an environment with a high concentration of sodium, this could represent some kind of evolutionary pressure.

An opposite behavior is observed regarding high concentrations of potassium. When potassium concentration is increased by 10 times its normal values, PTX effects are reduced by 23,17%. Both results suggest that electrolyte levels could be changed to reduce PTX effects on the pump by decreasing sodium and increasing potassium. Since electrolyte levels in the blood can be manipulated up to a certain degree, the study of their role and capability to change our Na^+/K^+-ATPase model behavior is even more important. PMC can improve our understanding of cell transport systems and its behavior, and can lead to the discovery and development of new drugs.

We have shown in this work that PMC can be used to obtain valuable information about cell transport systems in a simple and complete way. This type of analysis can provide a better understanding of how transmembrane ionic transport systems behave, helping in the discovery and development of drugs. Future work include performing electric current and ion concentration measurements; confront the results with experimental validation; explore other dimensions such as the number of pumps; and integrate to our model other toxins (e.g. ouabain) or drugs (e.g. digitalis).

References

1. http://www.dcc.ufmg.br/~fbraz/sbmf2012/
2. Aidley, D.J., Stanfield, P.R.: Ion channels: molecules in action. Cambridge University Press (1996)
3. Artigas, P., Gadsby, D.C.: Large diameter of palytoxin-induced na/k pump channels and modulation of palytoxin interaction by na/k pump ligands. J. Gen. Physiol. (2004)
4. Braz, F.A.F., Cruz, J.S., Faria-Campos, A.C., Campos, S.V.A.: A Probabilistic Model Checking Approach to Investigate the Palytoxin Effects on the Na+/k+-ATPase. In: de Souto, M.C.P., Kann, M.G. (eds.) BSB 2012. LNCS, vol. 7409, pp. 84–96. Springer, Heidelberg (2012)
5. Chapman, J.B., Johnson, E.A., Kootsey, J.M.: Electrical and biochemical properties of an enzyme model of the sodium pump. Membrane Biology (1983)
6. Ciocchetta, F., Hillston, J.: Bio-pepa: A framework for the modelling and analysis of biological systems. Theoretical Computer Science (2009)
7. Clarke, E.M., Emerson, E.A.: Design and synthesis of synchronization skeletons using branching-time temporal logic. In: Kozen, D. (ed.) Logic of Programs 1981. LNCS, vol. 131, pp. 52–71. Springer, Heidelberg (1982)
8. Clarke, E.M., Faeder, J.R., Langmead, C.J., Harris, L.A., Jha, S.K., Legay, A.: Statistical Model Checking in *BioLab*: Applications to the Automated Analysis of T-Cell Receptor Signaling Pathway. In: Heiner, M., Uhrmacher, A.M. (eds.) CMSB 2008. LNCS (LNBI), vol. 5307, pp. 231–250. Springer, Heidelberg (2008)
9. Crepalde, M., Faria-Campos, A., Campos, S.: Modeling and analysis of cell membrane systems with probabilistic model checking. BMC Genomics 12(suppl. 4), S14 (2011), http://www.biomedcentral.com/1471-2164/12/S4/S14
10. Gillespie, D.T.: Exact stochastic simulation of coupled chemical reactions. The Journal of Physical Chemistry 81(25), 2340–2361 (1977)
11. Hernández, J.A., Chifflet, S.: Eletrogenic properties of the sodium pump in a dynamic model of membrane transport. Membrane Biology 176, 41–52 (2000)
12. Holzmann, G.J.: The SPIN Model Checker: Primer and Reference Manual, 1st edn. Addison-Wesley Professional (September 2003)

13. Kwiatkowska, M., Heath, J.: Biological pathways as communicating computer systems. Journal of Cell Science 122(16), 2793–2800 (2009)
14. Kwiatkowska, M., Norman, G., Parker, D.: Quantitative Verification Techniques for Biological Processes. In: Algorithmic Bioprocesses. Springer (2009)
15. Kwiatkowska, M., Norman, G., Parker, D.: Probabilistic Model Checking for Systems Biology. In: Symbolic Systems Biology, pp. 31–59. Jones and Bartlett (2010)
16. Kwiatkowska, M., Norman, G., Parker, D.: PRISM 4.0: Verification of Probabilistic Real-Time Systems. In: Gopalakrishnan, G., Qadeer, S. (eds.) CAV 2011. LNCS, vol. 6806, pp. 585–591. Springer, Heidelberg (2011)
17. Nelson, D.L., Cox, M.M.: Lehninger Principles of Biochemistry, 3rd edn. (2000)
18. Oka, C., Cha, C.Y., Noma, A.: Characterization of the cardiac na+/k+ pump by development of a comprehensive and mechanistic model. Journal of Theoretical Biology 265(1), 68–77 (2010),
    http://www.sciencedirect.com/science/article/pii/S0022519310002274
19. Post, R., Refyvary, C., Kume, S.: Activation by adenosine triphosphate in the phosphorylation kinetics of sodium and potassium ion transport adenosine triphosphatase. J. Biol. Chem.
20. Queille, J.P., Sifakis, J.: A temporal logic to deal with fairness in transition systems. In: 23rd Annual Symposium on Foundations of Science, SFCS 2008, pp. 217–225 (1982)
21. Rodrigues, A.M., Almeida, A.C.G., Infantosi, A.F., Teixeira, H.Z., Duarte, M.A.: Model and simulation of na+/k+ pump phosphorylation in the presence of palytoxin. Computational Biology and Chemistry 32(1), 5–16 (2008)
22. Rodrigues, A.M., Almeida, A.C.G., Infantosi, A.F.C.: Effect of palytoxin on the sodium-potassium pump: model and simulation. Physical Biology 5(3), 036005 (2008), http://stacks.iop.org/1478-3975/5/i=3/a=036005
23. Rodrigues, A.M., Infantosi, A.F.C., Almeida, A.C.G.: Palytoxin and the sodium/potassium pump-phosphorylation and potassium interaction. Physical Biology (2009)
24. Sadava, D., Heller, H., Orians, G., Purves, W., Hillis, D.: Life: The Science of Biology. Sinauer Associates (2006)
25. Yamada, K., Inagaki, N.: ATP-sensitive K+ channels in the brain: Sensors of hypoxic conditions. Physiology 17(3), 127–130 (2002)
26. Younes, H.L.S.: Ymer: A Statistical Model Checker. In: Etessami, K., Rajamani, S.K. (eds.) CAV 2005. LNCS, vol. 3576, pp. 429–433. Springer, Heidelberg (2005)
27. Younes, H., Kwiatkowska, M., Norman, G., Parker, D.: Numerical vs. statistical probabilistic model checking. International Journal on Software Tools for Technology Transfer (STTT) 8(3), 216–228 (2006)

BETA: A B Based Testing Approach*

Ernesto C.B. de Matos and Anamaria Martins Moreira

Federal University of Rio Grande do Norte (UFRN), Natal, RN, Brazil
ernesto@forall.ufrn.br, anamaria@dimap.ufrn.br

Abstract. While formal methods provide ways to specify and verify software systems with mathematical accuracy, testing techniques can provide mechanisms to identify defects that were inserted in the system during its implementation. With that in mind, this paper presents an approach to generate test specifications based on a formal notation: the B-Method. Our approach is supported by a tool and uses restrictions described on a B specification, such as invariants, preconditions and conditional statements, to create unit tests for an operation. The approach uses equivalence classes and boundary value analysis techniques to partition the operation input space and relies on combinatorial criteria to select partitions to test. The approach and the tool were evaluated through a small case study using specifications for the FreeRTOS micro kernel.

Keywords: Testing, Formal Methods, Unit Testing, B-Method.

1 Introduction

The process of software verification and validation (V&V) is known to consume much of the time of the development process. Almost 50% of the time and costs of the development of a system is consumed by V&V activities [18]. It is difficult to ensure that a system is safe, robust and error-free. With that in mind, there are many methods and techniques that try to improve quality assurance in software development, such as software testing and formal methods. The cost of these methods and techniques is however an important issue, motivating developers and researchers to look for ways to improve quality assurance without increasing V&V costs.

Formal methods and testing are V&V techniques which complement each other. Formal verification is a static technique which can guarantee the validity of certain specific properties, while testing, a dynamic technique, is the one V&V technique that no one thinks of discarding in software development, although its goal is mostly to show the presence of defects in the software. Nowadays, there is an effort of both formal methods and testing communities to integrate both disciplines. Even though formal methods allow a system to be verified with mathematical accuracy, they are not enough to ensure that a system is

---

* This work is partly supported by CAPES and CNPq grants 306033/2009-7, 560014/2010-4 and 573964/2008-4 (National Institute of Science and Technology for Software Engineering—INES, www.ines.org.br).

R. Gheyi and D. Naumann (Eds.): SBMF 2012, LNCS 7498, pp. 51–66, 2012.

error-free. Thereby, software testing can complement formal methods, providing mechanisms to identify failures, exploiting possible defects that were inserted into the software code during its implementation or maintenance. Besides, as formal specifications usually describe requirements in a rigorous and unambiguous way, they can be used as basis to create good test cases. If not better than the ones created based on informal specifications of the system, at least, cheaper to produce when formal specifications are reused from former activities, as more automation is possible.

The generation of tests from formal specifications can be particularly useful in scenarios where formal methods are not followed strictly. Sometimes, due to time and budget restrictions, formal methods are only used in more abstract levels of specification and the implementation of the system is done in an informal way. In this scenario, tests generated from formal specifications would help verifying the cohesion between specification and implementation, checking whether the implementation is in accordance with the specification.

Different research groups have then been researching this integration in different ways, targeting different kinds of tests, using different formal input models, and with different levels of automation ([3,20,10,23,11,17,6,15,7,4,8]). This paper presents the approach BETA (B Based Testing Approach) to derive unit tests from formal specifications, contributing to this line of research. The approach is partially supported by a tool and uses B Method [1] state machines to generate test specifications for an operation under test. There is no restriction on the form and structure of the input B machine. The BETA approach uses input space partitioning techniques [5] to define positive and some negative test cases. Whilst positive test cases use valid input test data to test an operation, negative test cases use invalid input test data (data that goes against the restrictions imposed by the specification) to test it. Negative test cases are important to evaluate the level of safety of the system, since malicious users usually exploit this kind of errors. The negative test cases specified by the BETA approach aim to contribute to the analysis of the software behavior when the operation is used outside its input domain (i.e., when its preconditions are not respected).

The remainder of the paper is organized as follows: Section 2 gives a brief introduction about the B-Method; In Section 3 we discuss about related work; in Section 4 we present our approach to generate specifications of unit tests based on B specifications; In Section 5 we present the tool we developed to automate our approach; In Section 6 we discuss the results obtained on a case study; we conclude in Section 7 with discussions and future work.

2   The B-Method

The B Method is a formal method that uses concepts of first order logic, set theory and integer arithmetic to specify abstract state machines that represent a software behavior. These specifications can be verified using proof obligations that ensure the specification's consistence. The method also provides a refinement mechanism in which machines may pass through a series of refinements until it reaches an algorithmic level that can be automatically converted into code.

A B machine may have a set of variables that represent the software state and a set of operations that can modify it. Restrictions on possible values that variables can assume are stated by the machine's invariant. The method also has a precondition mechanism for operations of a machine. To ensure that an operation behaves as expected, it is necessary to ensure its precondition is respected. Figure 1 presents an example of B machine from [22] that is responsible for managing substitutions on a soccer team.

```
01 MACHINE Player                       14 OPERATIONS
02 SETS ANSWER = {in, out}; PLAYER      15 substitute(pp, rr) =
03 PROPERTIES                           16 PRE pp : PLAYER & pp : team &
04    card(PLAYER) > 11                 17    rr : PLAYER & rr /: team
05 VARIABLES team                       18 THEN team := (team \/ {rr}) - {pp}
06 INVARIANT                            19 END;
07    team <: PLAYER &                  20 aa <-- query(pp) =
08    card(team) = 11                   21 PRE pp : PLAYER & aa : ANSWER
09 INITIALISATION                       22 THEN IF pp : team THEN aa := in
10    ANY tt                            23     ELSE aa := out
11    WHERE tt <: PLAYER & card(tt) = 11 24     END
12    THEN team := tt                   25 END
13    END                              26 END
```

Fig. 1. Player machine specification[22]

The team squad is represented by a set *PLAYER* while the main team is stored on the state variable *team*. There are two restrictions on the machine's invariant which establish that, first, the main team must be a subset of the whole squad (line 7), and second, the main team must have exactly eleven players (line 8). The machine has two operations: *substitute* (lines 15-19) and *query* (lines 20-25). The *substitute* operation is responsible for making substitutions on the team. It receives as parameters a player *pp* who will be replaced in the team and a player *rr* who will take *pp*'s place. As preconditions, the operation establishes that *pp* must belong to the main team (line 16), *rr* must belong to the squad (also line 16) but should not be in the main team (line 17). The *query* operation can verify if a particular player *pp* is currently on the team. It has a return variable *aa* that will receive the value *in* if *pp* is indeed on the team or the value *out* in case it is not on the team.

3   Related Work

During our research we also considered work that aims to generate tests from formal specifications written in Z [24], Alloy [12], JML [13], VDM [19] and OCL [26]. We chose these notations due to similarities they share with the B notation, such as: the concept of abstract state machines, the transition between states using operations and the specification of functional requirements based on pre and post conditions and invariants.

We evaluated papers which focus on different levels of testing. Most of the available work based on these languages concerns the generation of test cases for the *module* level [5]: the level of testing that is right above unit testing. While unit tests are concerned with testing individual operations (such as functions and methods), module testing is concerned with testing the interaction between operations from a same collection, such as a class, a package or a file.

This is also the case for the reasearch that uses B models for test generation ([21], [20] and [10]), with very few focusing on unit testing [3]. For module testing, the most meaningful and recent work is the one proposed by Butler et al. in [20], in which they present an approach for test case generation based on model based formal notations (such as B). The proposed approach distinguishes itself from the others for its solution for scenarios with non-deterministic behavior and for its tool support.

Work concerning unit tests is available ([3], [4], [23], [11] and [6]) to specify or generate tests from other formal notations. However, it not always uses very clear testing criteria. This is probably due to the fact that traditional test literature concerning testing from specifications usually presents different variations of the same concepts, depending on the source. Only recently an important consolidation work has been carried out in [5] to present different levels of testing and different coverage criteria in an uniform framework. In our work we tried to improve this aspect, then, making clear how each software testing concept is used throughout the approach, using input space partitioning criteria and data combination criteria that is formally described in [5].

Besides, another problem found in related work – not only for B specifications but also for other formal notations – is the lack of tool support for the proposed approaches. Tool support is essential to industry adoption as we concluded after an initial case study for our approach [16]. In terms of tool support the most developed work is the *jmlunit* tool [7] which generate tests based on JML annotations. However, it only generates templates for test methods and requires the user to provide test data. Concerning B models, we have the tools introduced in [3], where the authors present the BZ-TT toolset which generates tests using a boundary values technique from B and Z specifications, and in [20], where the authors present an extension of the ProB animator to generate module tests. In both cases, the tools were not available for evaluation. In our research we developed a tool that automates most of the approach, generating test case specifications for a given B operation. We also support specifications structured in multiple components. Most of the available tools require the specification to be done in a single file, which is not pratical in real projects.

4   Test Generation Approach

The BETA test generation has as goal to define (1) situations to be tested (test cases) for each unit in a module, and (2) input data that create these situations. It defines its test cases based on *input space partitioning*, using formal information extracted from B models of the unit under test (or operation under test, using B terminology). This information, in the form of logical formulas, is first used to define the partitions, according to some partitioning strategy, and then used to define combinations of the blocks that compose each of these partitions, according to some combination pattern. Each formula resulting from this procedure specifies the input data requirements for a different test case for the unit under test. The selection of abstract data values that satisfy each test case formula is then carried out via constraint solving procedures. Expected abstract results for the selected input data can be obtained by referring to the original B model (manually or by using a B model animator). Concrete input values and expected results can be derived from the abstract ones by applying the inverse of the mapping from abstract data to their implementation (the inverse of the retrieval relation, when available). The result of the approach is the specification of a set of unit tests for the operation under test that can be easily coded in the implementation programming language to obtain concrete test case implementations.

In the following we more precisely describe the proposed test generation approach. An overview of the approach is presented in Figure 2. The white boxes represent artifacts that are used or produced during the approach while the gray ones represent its steps. The approach is automated by the BETA tool from steps 1 to 7 (more information in Section 5), until the generation of the test case specifications. Steps 8 and 9 must be performed manually to obtain the concrete test cases.

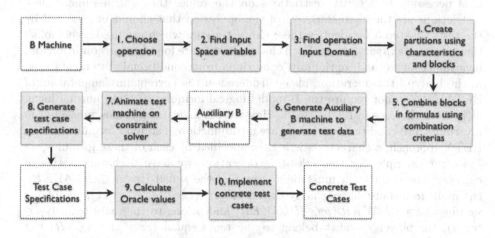

Fig. 2. Test generation approach overview

To illustrate the approach we will generate tests for the *substitute* operation of the *Player* machine we presented in Section 2. The first step is self-explanatory. For a given B machine, we must apply the approach on each operation we intend to generate tests for. Currently, we only consider abstract B machines as input for the whole generation process. Refinements or implementations could also be considered to gather extra information on the internals of an operation, but should not be the main reference for input space partitioning as they may omit preconditions, for instance. We assume that the given machine was specified and verified in a separate tool and does not contain specification errors.

4.1 Defining the *Input Space* and *Input Domain*

Once the operation to be tested is chosen, we have to identify the variables that compose the operation's *input space* and, as such, may influence its behavior. The input space of a B operation is composed of its formal parameters and of the machine state variables listed on its *VARIABLES* clause. However, the greater the number of variables in the input space, the greater the risk of combinatorial explosion on the number of test cases. On the other hand, in real problems it is common to have only a subset of the state variables influencing the behavior of an operation. For optimization purposes, then, we only consider a subset of the state variables: the ones mentioned in the operation's precondition and the ones which are related to them via invariant clauses, so that the value of one may represent further restrictions on the valid values of the other (a small fixpoint calculation is carried out to identify this set). Additionally, the body of the operation specification (e.g., conditionals) may also be analyzed to identify other variables in this input space. In our example, the input space of the *substitute* operation is composed of the parameters *pp* and *rr*, and of the state variable *team*.

After the definition of the input space variables for the operation under test it is necessary to identify restrictions on the values they can assume. These restrictions are the *characteristics* of the operation that should be assessed by the tests. In step 3 we identify these characteristics which are used to establish the operation's *input domain*. Such characteristics are found on precondition and invariant clauses (and, optionally, conditions from conditional statements used in the body of the operation, also considered in the current implementation of BETA). We do not require the B model logical formulas to be in normal form, as is often the case in related work. However, B logical conditions presented in invariants, pre-conditions and such, are a conjunction of simpler formulas. In the BETA approach, a characteristic is then specified by each of these formulas.

In our example, for the *substitute* operation, we have 6 characteristics to consider: the main *team* must be a subset of the squad ($team \subset PLAYER$), the main *team* must have exactly eleven players ($card(team) = 11$), the player *pp* must be a $PLAYER$ ($pp \in PLAYER$) and belong to the main team ($pp \in team$), the player *rr* must belong to the team squad ($rr \in PLAYER$) but should not belong to the main *team* ($rr \notin team$). The conjunction of these clauses results in the following formula that represents the valid input domain for the operation *substitute*:

$$team \subset PLAYER \ \& \ card(team) = 11 \ \& \ pp \in PLAYER \ \& \ pp \in team \ \&$$
$$rr \in PLAYER \ \& \ rr \notin team$$

In this example each characteristic corresponds to an atom, but we could as well have more complex, including quantified, formulas.

4.2   Creating Partitions and Defining Test Case Formulas

In step 4 we create partitions using the domain model constructed on the previous steps. Each characteristic gives rise to a partition composed of up to 4 blocks of test data, depending on the formula that defines it and the chosen partition strategy. The approach currently supports two partition strategies: *equivalence classes* and *boundary value analysis*.

In most of the cases, we generate two blocks for each characteristic: one block for positive tests, which satisfy the given formula (the block is defined by all values which satisfy the formula describing the characteristic), and another block for negative tests, which contain values that disrespect the restriction described by the formula (the block is defined by all values which satisfy the negation of the formula describing the characteristic). There are two exceptions to this rule:

- cases in which the formula states that some variable in the input space accepts values from a range of values, also called *interval* (e.g., $xx : 10..25$). In these cases, if we are using equivalence classes to partition, the partition is composed of three blocks: one block for values inside the interval, one block for values preceding the interval and one block for values following the interval. In cases where the boundary value analysis technique is chosen, the proposal is to cover it with four values, corresponding to the two valid limits of the range and its two invalid limits (immediately below and above the range). This can correspond to four blocks: one block containing the values below the limit, one block containing the values above the limit, and two blocks for the valid range, where each one contains one of the valid limits. An example of a pair of blocks satisfying this criterium is to have one singleton with the inferior limit of the range and the other block containing the rest of the range.
- cases in which the negation of the formula corresponds to situations for which we are not interested in generating test cases. In this case, the characteristics correspond to a trivial, one block, partition. Our approach considers 2 situations to be "not-interesting" for test generation: (1) to give value of a given type to a parameter or variable of a different type (usually corresponds to a compilation error); and (2) to have an invalid value (a value that does not satisfy the invariant) for a state variable at the operation input, meaning that the system was already in an invalid state before the execution of the operation under test. Although this is important for security analysis, when we may be interested in security breaches provoked by attackers, and will be considered in future work, it is not so for the basic testing schema that we propose here. This means that the input domain model may ignore the negation of typing and invariant characteristics, generating trivial partitions for them.

In our *substitute* operation example, the partitions are then the ones presented on Table 1.

Table 1. Characteristics and blocks for the substitute operation

Characteristic	Block 1	Block 2
$team \subset PLAYER$	$team \subset PLAYER$	-
$card(team) = 11$	$card(team) = 11$	-
$pp \in PLAYER$	$pp \in PLAYER$	-
$pp \in team$	$pp \in team$	$pp \notin team$
$rr \in PLAYER$	$rr \in PLAYER$	-
$rr \notin team$	$rr \notin team$	$rr \in team$

After the definition of the blocks, we have to choose which of these blocks we will use on our test cases. The first thought might be to test all possible combinations of blocks. Unfortunately, due to high number of blocks created, to test all possible combinations of blocks is usually impractical. Therefore, we need ways to choose more meaningful combinations of blocks; for this, we use test data combination criteria.

Our approach currently supports three combination criteria:

- *All-combinations*: all combinations of blocks from all characteristics must be tested. As we said, this criteria is usually impractical to perform, but we still give the test engineer the option to use it if needed;
- *Each-choice*: one value from each block for each characteristic must be present in at least one test case. This criteria is based on the classical concept of equivalence class partitioning, which requires that every block must be used in a test case of our test set;
- *Pairwise*: one value of each block for each characteristic must be combined to one value of all other blocks for each other characteristic. The algorithm we used for this criteria was the *In-Parameter-Order Pairwise*, presented in [25].

As a result of the combination of blocks using one of these criteria, we will have a set of formulas to test sub-domains of the operation. Each formula is a conjunction of the formulas describing a set of blocks, representing a (possibly empty) portion of the input domain, and corresponds to a test case to be executed. In our example, we obtain the following combinations for the Each-choice criterium:

1. $pp \in PLAYER$ & $card(team) = 11$ & $pp \in team$ & $rr \notin team$ &
   $rr \in PLAYER$ & $team \subset PLAYER$
2. $pp \in PLAYER$ & $card(team) = 11$ & $pp \notin team$ & $rr \in team$ &
   $rr \in PLAYER$ & $team \subset PLAYER$

And the following for the Pairwise or All-combinations criteria, which, in this case, give rise to the same set of test cases:

1. $pp \in PLAYER$ & $pp \notin team$ & $team \subset PLAYER$ & $rr \notin team$ &
   $rr \in PLAYER$ & $card(team) = 11$

2. $pp \in PLAYER$ & $pp \notin team$ & $team \subset PLAYER$ & $rr \in team$ & $rr \in PLAYER$ & $card(team) = 11$

3. $pp \in PLAYER$ & $pp \in team$ & $team \subset PLAYER$ & $rr \in team$ & $rr \in PLAYER$ & $card(team) = 11$

4. $pp \in PLAYER$ & $pp \in team$ & $team \subset PLAYER$ & $rr \notin team$ & $rr \in PLAYER$ & $card(team) = 11$

In order to obtain test input data for our test cases, we need to find values for each variable (and parameter) in the operation's input space that satisfy the test case input specification formula. If no such values exist, the specified test case is unfeasible. If different combinations of values satisfy the formula, any of them is selectable. The classical tool to verify this is a constraint solver. Because we are already dealing with B specifications, our implementation uses the *ProB* animator as constraint solver, and to do it, we have to use a small trick: in step 6 we create an auxiliary B machine that is animated to generate test data for the specified test cases.

This auxiliary machine contains one operation for each test case. The input space variables (state variables and parameters of the operation under test) are declared to be parameters of the test case operation and the test case input data description formula (each combination obtained in the previous step) is defined to be its precondition. The animator then uses constraint solving to identify values that satisfy the precondition. These values are then guaranteed to exercise the conjunction of blocks which should be tested in that specific test case. In Figure 3 we present an example of auxiliary machine to generate test data.

4.3   Creating Test Case Specifications

In step 7 we animate the auxiliary test machine presented in Figure 3 to obtain input data for our test cases. For the *substitute* operation, using the Each-choice combination criteria, the auxiliary machine may generate the following input data, where $PLAYER_i, i : 1..12$ are the values created by ProB to populate the abstract set $PLAYER$ for animation purposes:

1. *In:* pp=PLAYER1, rr=PLAYER12, team={PLAYER1, PLAYER2, ..., PLAYER11};
2. *In:* pp=PLAYER12, rr=PLAYER1, team={PLAYER1, PLAYER2, ..., PLAYER11};

In step 8 we use this data to create test case specifications. An example of test case specification generated by the tool is presented in Figure 4. Before each test case the document presents the test formula that originated it (lines 3-10). With this information, the user knows to which situation the test case corresponds. This may be useful for debugging, when the test case reveals an error, selecting test cases for execution, combining the generated test cases with others, completing them, etc. The test case then specifies the desired input state

```
01 MACHINE TestsForOp_substitute_From_Player

02 SETS ANSWER = {in, out}; PLAYER
03 PROPERTIES card(PLAYER) > 11

04 OPERATIONS
05 /* Equivalence Class test data for substitute */
06 substitute_test1(rr, team, pp) =
07 PRE card(team) = 11 & pp : PLAYER & pp : team &
08     rr /: team & rr : PLAYER & team <: PLAYER
09 THEN skip
10 END;
...
```

Fig. 3. Auxiliary test machine for substitute

(line 12). The state variables which are not on the operation's identified input space can assume any valid values in each test case and do not need to have their values specified. For instance, any value that they assume after initialization of the component is acceptable. And because of the fixpoint calculation done during the identification of the input space, we can be sure that the values of the variables of the input space are not influenced by the ones outside it. From the specified input state, the operation under test should be executed with test value parameters (line 13). The oracle values (lines 14-17) must be calculated manually by the test engineer or using the approach suggested in the next section.

4.4 Calculating Oracle Values and Implementing Concrete Test Cases

To complete our test cases we need to calculate the oracle values, in step 9, for each test operation. The oracle generated in this step aims to verify if, for the given input data, the results obtained after the execution of the operation under test are in accordance with its specification.

From this step on, the approach is not yet integrated on the BETA tool, but the calculation of positive test case oracles can easily be obtained from a specification animator such as ProB, at least when the operation specification is deterministic. Given some input data for an operation under test, the animator calculates the expected results through the calculus of post-conditions. The non-deterministic case requires some extra work to provide the description of the set of acceptable return values, but this is not a major problem. In the future, the BETA tool can be improved to generate oracle values for positive test cases automatically.

Negative tests, on the other hand, violate the operation's preconditions and this means that the behavior of the operation is not specified for them, at least, not in the formal model (this is the standard use of the pre-post condition, contract-based, specification paradigm). The criteria used by the oracle to

```
01 TEST REPORT
02 MACHINE: Player

03 /** Test Formula
04 card(team) = 11 &
05 pp : PLAYER
06 pp : team &
07 rr /: team &
08 rr : PLAYER &
09 team <: PLAYER
10 */
11 substituteTest1() {
12 set_team({PLAYER1,PLAYER2,PLAYER3,PLAYER4,PLAYER5,PLAYER6,
              PLAYER7,PLAYER8,PLAYER9,PLAYER10,PLAYER11});
13 substitute(PLAYER12, PLAYER1);
14 // Oracle Value must be calculated
15 expectedValueForTeam = nil;
16 actualValueForTeam = getTeam();
17 assertEquals(expectedValueForTeam, actualValueForTeam);
18 }
19 ...
```

Fig. 4. Example of test specification for the substitute operation

evaluate the results must be manually defined by the test engineer, according to some criteria (e.g. safety criteria) not included in the model.

Using an Animator to Calculate (Deterministic) Expected Values for Positive Test Cases. To use an animator to calculate the oracle values we need to animate the operation under test with the input data corresponding to each test case. For the presented test case specification in Figure 4 for the *substitute* operation, the steps are the following:

1. Set the *team* variable to its input state value. To do this we call the operation *set_team* passing as a parameter the required value for the *team* variable: *set_team({PLAYER1, ..., PLAYER10, PLAYER11});*
2. Animate the operation under test using the parameter test data we obtained previously: *substitute(rr=PLAYER12, pp=PLAYER1);*
3. Verify the new state of the machine (and/or operation outputs). In our test case the expected test result is the value for the *team* variable to be changed to *team = {PLAYER2, ..., PLAYER11, PLAYER12}*

The ProB tool can also be used (and we recommend it) to perform this process, though other animation tools could be used as well. Once the oracle values are filled on the test specification, the test engineer can implement the concrete test cases. Figure 5 presents an example of concrete test that was implemented based on the test case specification presented in Figure 4 and on an implementation using a java implementation of sets, and the abstract set $PLAYER$ was implemented by integer numbers, with the mapping from $PLAYER_i$ to i.

```
01 public class PlayerTest {
02   @Test
03   public void substituteTest1() {
04     Player player = new Player();

05     Integer[] team = {1,2,3,4,5,6,7,8,9,10,11};
06     player.setTeam(new HashSet<Integer>(Arrays.asList(team)));
07     player.substitute(12, 1);

08     Integer[] expectedTeam = {2,3,4,5,6,7,8,9,10,11,12};
09     Set<Integer> expectedResult =
               new HashSet<Integer>(Arrays.asList(expectedTeam));
10     Set<Integer> actualResult = player.getTeam();

11     assertEquals(expectedResult, actualResult);
12   }
13 }
```

Fig. 5. Example of concrete test implementation

5   The BETA Tool

To automate part of the approach, we developed the BETA tool. This tool automates the presented approach from steps 1 to 8, generating unit test specifications for the operation under test, such as the one presented in Figure 4. BETA is free and open-source. More information on the tool and links for download are available on: http://www.forall.ufrn.br/beta.

In Figure 6 we have an overview of the BETA architecture. The tool receives as input an abstract B machine (a) and passes it thought a parser (b) which checks if the specification is syntactically correct. If it is in fact correct, the parser outputs the specification's syntactic tree (c). As parser we used the *BParser* which is the same one used on the *ProB* tool [14].

The generated syntactic tree is then used by the partitioner module (d) to extract the information needed to implement the approach such as: machine operations, states variables, operation parameters, invariant and precondition clauses, and conditional statements. This information is then used by the partitioner module to generate blocks (e) of data based on characteristics from the input domain of the operation under test. The generated blocks are then combined into test formulas by the combinator module (f) using the chosen test data combination criteria (All-combinations, Each-choice or Pairwise).

To select input data for each test case, the resulting combination of test formulas (g) is passed through a constraint solver. BETA uses the *ProB* tool command line interface for this. To prepare the formulas for *ProB* they are passed to the machine builder module (h) which creates an auxiliary B machine that contains one test operation for each test formula generated (i). As result, we have an auxiliary test machine such as the one presented in Figure 3. The *ProB* model checker animator (j) then generates test data for the selected blocks. The data

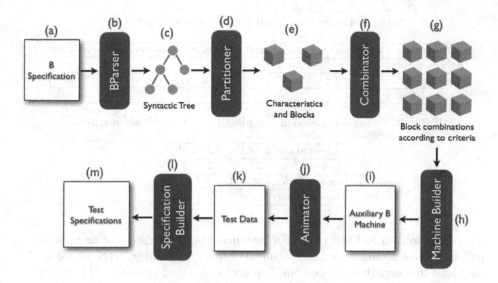

Fig. 6. The BETA architecture

generated by ProB is formatted in a file which is read by the specification builder module (l) to generate unit test specifications (m) for the operation under test.

6   Case Study

We evaluated the approach and the tool through a small case study using B specifications for *FreeRTOS* [9]. *FreeRTOS*[1] is a micro kernel for real time systems that provides a layer of abstraction between the application being developed and the hardware, making it easier for applications to access hardware features.

In our case study we generated test case specifications for the *Queue* module of *FreeRTOS*, which is responsible for managing message queues in the system. In this paper we will present the results for three of its operations: *q_queueCreate*, *q_queueDelete* and *q_sendItem*. These operations are respectively responsible for creating a new message queue on the system, deleting a message queue from the system and sending an item to a given queue. Table 2 presents some information obtained by the tool on these operations.

All the test cases were generated using equivalence classes partitioning. In Table 3 we present an overview of the unit tests generated in a run of BETA for these three operations. The table shows the number of test cases generated according to the chosen data combination criteria (AC = *All Combinations*, EC = *Each-choice* e PW = *Pairwise*) .

Not all of the specified test cases are feasible, however. Different reasons may cause a test case to be unfeasible, but usually, unfeasibility is due to a interdependence among different formulas specifying different blocks which should

---

[1] http://www.freertos.org

Table 2. Information about the operations from Queue

Operation	Variables	Characteristics	Blocks	Non-trivial Partitions
q_queueCreate	2	2	3	1
q_queueDelete	10	27	32	5
q_sendItem	12	28	34	6

Table 3. Test cases generated according to each combination criteria

Operation	AC	EC	PW
q_queueCreate	$2 = 2^1$	2	2
q_queueDelete	$32 = 2^5$	2	7
q_sendItem	$64 = 2^6$	2	8

indeed not lead to real test cases. For instance, the precondition of an operation which requires a parameter xx to be member of a set yy and yy to be non-empty, may lead to a negative test combination containing $xx : yy$ & $yy = \{\}$, which is clearly unsatisfiable. Then, there are two possibilities: either no other combination would lead to a satisfiable formula, such as in this case, and 100% coverage is not achievable, or extra tests can be added to cover specific situations (test requisites) which were not covered by automatic generation.

One other reason for not obtaining test input values in some cases is not intrinsic of the problem, but related to the ProB behavior. Considering the $q\_queueDelete$ operation, a problem we could find in some of the test formulas generated to $q\_queueDelete$ was the negation of a clause stating that the queue to be deleted should be an active queue ($pxQueue \in queues$), when the original specification did not contain the typing clause for $pxQueue$ ($pxQueue \in QUEUE$). The constraint solver can use $pxQueue \in queues$ to infer the type of $pxQueue$ but from the negated clause the constraint solver cannot infer the type of $pxQueue$ and, as consequence, is not able to animate these particular test formulas. One simple solution to increase the number of automatically defined input data in this case is to enforce explicit typing ($pxQueue \in QUEUE$), as it is already done in some B tools. Note that, as we are not considering negation of typing clauses, this extra information corresponds to a trivial partition and has no influence on the generated combinations.

Finally, the combination of multiple negative test blocks more often results in unfeasible scenarios. A different combination approach could be to only use one negative block per test formula, as it is recommended in classic equivalence partitioning methods. Besides the reduction of unfeasible scenarios, this could also make it easier to evaluate the results of the negative tests.

7   Discussions and Future Work

In this paper we presented an approach to generate unit test specifications from B machine specifications. The approach uses restrictions specified on these machines in the form of invariants, preconditions and conditional statements to

create partitions for an operation input space and then combine these partitions using test data combination criteria to generate test cases. The approach
is supported by a tool that is capable of generating part of the test specifications
automatically. We also evaluated the approach through a small case study using
B specifications for the *FreeRTOS* micro kernel.

There is still much room for improvement of the approach and the tool. There
are many open topics in the theme of generating tests from formal specifications
such as the generation of test oracles, the relation between abstract a concrete
test data, problems concerning testing operations with non-deterministic behavior among others.

As further work we plan to automate the process of oracle generation so the
whole test generation process can be completely automatic. Besides, we plan
to extend the approach to generate test cases for other levels of testing, such
as integration and system testing. We intend to develop a strategy to generate
test cases for the system level using Event-B [2] specifications. These tests could
complement the unit tests already generated with tests that are concerned with
a higher level of abstraction.

Acknowledgements. The authors would like to thank the anonymous reviewers whose comments helped to improve the quality of this paper.

References

1. Abrial, J.R.: The B Book: Assigning Programs to Meanings. Cambridge University
   Press (1996)
2. Abrial, J.R., Butler, M., Hallerstede, S., Hoang, T.S., Mehta, F., Voisin, L.: Rodin:
   an open toolset for modelling and reasoning in Event-B. STTT 12(6), 447–466
   (2010)
3. Ambert, F., Bouquet, F., Chemin, S., Guenaud, S., Legeard, B., Peureux, F.,
   Vacelet, N., Utting, M.: BZ-TT: A tool-set for test generation from Z and B using constraint logic programming. In: Proc. of Formal Approaches to Testing of
   Software, FATES, pp. 105–120 (2002)
4. Amla, N., Ammann, P.: Using Z Specifications in Category Partition Testing. In:
   Ehrig, H., Yu, Y. (eds.) Abstract Data Types 1992 and COMPASS 1992. LNCS,
   vol. 785, pp. 3–10. Springer, Heidelberg (1994)
5. Ammann, P., Offutt, J.: Introduction to Software Testing. Cambridge University
   Press (2008)
6. Burton, S.: Automated testing from Z specifications. Technical report, University
   of York (2000)
7. Cheon, Y., Leavens, G.T.: A Simple and Practical Approach to Unit Testing: The
   JML and JUnit Way. In: Deng, T. (ed.) ECOOP 2002. LNCS, vol. 2374, pp. 231–
   1901. Springer, Heidelberg (2002)
8. Dick, J., Faivre, A.: Automating the Generation and Sequencing of Test Cases from
   Model-based Specifications. In: Larsen, P.G., Wing, J.M. (eds.) FME 1993. LNCS,
   vol. 670, pp. 268–284. Springer, Heidelberg (1993)
9. Galvão, S.S.L.: Especificação do micronúcleo FreeRTOS utilizando Método B. Master Thesis, DIMAp/UFRN (2010)

10. Gupta, A., Bhatia, R.: Testing functional requirements using B model specifications. SIGSOFT Softw. Eng. Notes 35(2), 1–7 (2010)
11. Huaikou, M., Ling, L.: A test class framework for generating test cases from Z specifications. In: IEEE International Conference on Engineering of Complex Computer Systems (2000)
12. Jackson, D.: Alloy: a lightweight object modelling notation. ACM Trans. Softw. Eng. Methodol. 11, 256–290 (2002)
13. Leavens, G.T., Baker, A.L., Ruby, C.: JML: a java modeling language. In: Proceedings of Formal Underpinnings of Java Workshop, OOPSLA 1998 (1998)
14. Leuschel, M., Butler, M.: ProB: A Model Checker for B. In: Araki, K., Gnesi, S., Mandrioli, D. (eds.) FME 2003. LNCS, vol. 2805, pp. 855–874. Springer, Heidelberg (2003)
15. Marinov, D., Khurshid, S.: TestEra: A novel framework for automated testing of Java programs. In: International Conference on Automated Software Engineering, p. 22 (2001)
16. Matos, E.C.B., Moreira, A.M., Souza, F., Coelho, R.d.S.: Generating test cases from B specifications: An industrial case study. In: Petrenko, A., Simao, A., Maldonado, J.C. (eds.) Proceedings of 22nd IFIP International Conference on Testing Software and Systems: Short Papers, November 8-10, pp. 55–60, Natal, Brazil. CRIM (Centre de Recherche Informatique de Montréal) (2010) ISBN-13: 978-2-89522-136-4
17. Mendes, E., Silveira, D.S., Lencastre, M.: Testimonium: Um método para geração de casos de teste a partir de regras de negócio expressas em OCL. In: IV Brazilian Workshop on Systematic and Automated Software Testing, SAST (2010)
18. Myers, G.J.: The Art of Software Testing, 3rd edn. Wiley (2011)
19. Plat, N., Larsen, P.G.: An overview of the ISO/VDM-SL standard. SIGPLAN Not. 27, 76–82 (1992)
20. Satpathy, M., Butler, M., Leuschel, M., Ramesh, S.: Automatic Testing from Formal Specifications. In: Gurevich, Y., Meyer, B. (eds.) TAP 2007. LNCS, vol. 4454, pp. 95–113. Springer, Heidelberg (2007)
21. Satpathy, M., Leuschel, M., Butler, M.: Protest: An automatic test environment for B specifications. Electronic Notes in Theoretical Computer Science (2005)
22. Schneider, S.: B Method, An Introduction. Palgrave (2001)
23. Singh, H., Conrad, M., Sadeghipour, S., Singh, H., Conrad, M., Sadeghipour, S.: Test case design based on Z and the classification-tree method. In: First IEEE International Conference on Formal Engineering Methods, pp. 81–90 (1997)
24. Spivey, J.M.: The Z Notation: A Reference Manual, 2nd edn. Prentice-Hall (1992)
25. Tai, K., Lei, Y.: A test generation strategy for pairwise testing. IEEE Transactions on Software Engineering 28(1), 109–111 (2002)
26. Warmer, J., Kleppe, A.: The Object Constraint Language: Precise Modeling with UML. Addison-Wesley (1999)

A Process Algebra Based Strategy for Generating Test Vectors from SCR Specifications

Gustavo Carvalho, Diogo Falcão, Alexandre Mota, and Augusto Sampaio

Centro de Informática - Universidade Federal de Pernambuco
50740-560 Recife-PE, Brazil
{ghpc,dfdf,acm,acas}@cin.ufpe.br

Abstract. SCR is a formal requirements language and method designed to detect and correct errors during the requirements phase. In this paper we start with an SCR specification, translate it into a CSP model (particularly the CSP# variant) and then apply LTL model checking on the CSP# specification to generate test vectors as counter-examples. Before the actual test vector generation, our strategy supports the verification of properties like completeness and determinism of the model; this is one of the advantages of using a process algebra for an intermediate model representation. Our strategy has been assessed by considering typical system requirements of the Aviation Industry. We compared the test vectors generated by our strategy with test vectors written manually by specialists. With respect to the examples used, our strategy has proven to be feasible and was able to generate the same test vectors.

Keywords: CSP, Process Algebra, SCR, LTL, Generation, Test Vector.

1 Introduction

During the last fifty years, the industry has seen a significant increase of embedded HW-SW components in critical systems. A report from NASA [15] highlights that, from 1960 to 2000, the amount of functionalities provided to military aircrafts by embedded software has grown from 8% to 80%. This scenario is not a privilege of the Aviation Industry. The Automobile Industry, for instance, has become even more dependent on embedded components.

Clearly, this trend increases software size and complexity, and impacts specifically critical systems, as well as its safety and reliability. Currently, many researches are focusing on how to achieve the safety and reliability levels required for these systems. Some approaches to treat the problem are based on formal verification [4, 10], whereas others rely on Model-Based Testing (MBT) techniques [14, 5]. To avoid inconsistent and incomplete requirements, regardless of the adopted approach, most works use a (semi-)formal language as input, for example: UML2 (Unified Modeling Language) [14], ITML (IMA Test Modeling Language) [5], Lustre [1] and SCR (Software Cost Reduction) [7].

R. Gheyi and D. Naumann (Eds.): SBMF 2012, LNCS 7498, pp. 67–82, 2012.

Particularly, SCR was designed to detect and correct errors during the requirements phase. SCR-based tools, like T-VEC[1] and SCR Toolset[2], can formally evaluate properties of the system and consequently produce test vectors when the properties are valid. Internally, these tools rely upon constraint solvers.

In this paper, we propose a strategy for translating SCR specifications into the CSP process algebra (particularly the CSP# variant[11]). Besides generating test vectors, our strategy supports the verification of properties like completeness and determinism of the model, and we can check whether a particular test vector makes sense with respect to the specification without the need of previously generating all test vectors.

The contributions of this work are: (1) a translation from SCR specifications into CSP#, (2) a test vector generation strategy based on Linear Temporal Logic (LTL) model checking for CSP#, (3) a mechanism for verifying properties like completeness and determinism of the model, and (4) empirical results on a real case study provided by our industrial partner Embraer, a Brazilian aerospace company that produces commercial, military and executive aircraft.

The next section briefly presents background concepts. Section 3 details the proposed translation strategy. Section 4 describes how test vectors can be automatically generated from CSP# specifications as well as how other kinds of analyses can be performed. Section 5 presents evaluation results of our strategy applied to a real case study provided by Embraer. Section 6 addresses related work, and finalises the paper with our conclusions and future work.

2 Background Concepts

In what follows we briefly explain basic concepts of CSP# and SCR.

2.1 CSP#

Communicating Sequential Processes (CSP) is a formal language designed to describe behavioural aspects of systems. The fundamental element of a CSP specification is a process. For practical purposes, CSP has some machine readable versions (dialects). The two main dialects of CSP are CSP_M, processed by the FDR tool[3], and CSP#, used by the PAT tool[4]. These formalisms present some differences. For instance, CSP# provides communication via message passing as well as shared memory, whereas CSP_M provides only message passing. The tools provide different functionalities as well. FDR is based on process refinement whereas PAT adds to this the ability to perform LTL on-the-fly model checking. We chose CSP# and PAT as the main technology to support our proposal. We have actually developed a similar strategy for CSP_M/FDR, but it has not scaled, as further discussed in the concluding section.

---

[1] www.t-vec.com
[2] www.nrl.navy.mil/chacs/5546/scr_toolset/index.php
[3] www.fsel.com/fdr2_download.html
[4] www.comp.nus.edu.sg/~pat/

The behaviour of a process is described by the set of events it can communicate to other processes. An event is considered as a transition that changes the process behaviour or state. An event is also defined as an atomic operation. To define a process as a sequence of events, we use the prefix process $(ev \rightarrow P)$, where ev is an event and P a process. We can use the prefix process to create an infinite (recursive) process such as $P() = a \rightarrow b \rightarrow P()$. In CSP# events are naturally atomic, but if we want to make the behaviour of a process (a sequence of events) atomic, we shall use the $atomic\{P()\}$ operator. Two primitive processes are the one that represents the successful termination $(Skip)$ and the one that stands for an abnormal termination $(Stop)$, also interpreted as a deadlock.

In CSP#, we are also able to define constants, using the $\#define$ operator, as in $\#define\ Off\ 0$. To declare global variables we use the following syntax $(var\ v = initial\_value;)$. As a consequence, v becomes a shared memory used in communications. When we need to change the value of a global variable, we shall use a special type of event called data operation $(event\{v = new\_value; v2 = new\_value2; ...\})$. All assignments described inside a data operation are performed sequentially and atomically. CSP# also offers a special event name tau when we do not need a meaningful name for a particular event. This is usually used in conjunction with data operations, for instance, $P() = a \rightarrow tau\{x = 2; \} \rightarrow b \rightarrow Skip;$.

To define alternating behaviours, we use (external, internal, or conditional) choice operators. An external choice $([*])$ represents a deterministic choice between two processes, whereas the internal one $(<>)$ involves a non-deterministic choice. The conditional (if) choice operator is similar to the ones of standard programming languages. A particularity of CSP# is that the evaluation of a conditional choice is performed by an internal (not visible) event. Thus, there is another conditional choice operator, named ifa, where the evaluation of the condition does not create an event. Besides these operators, there is the guard operator $[condition]P$, which is a shortcut to $ifa(condition)\{P\}else\{Stop\};$.

Two other relevant operators are the sequential and parallel ones. For example, the following sequential composition $P() = P1(); P2();$ states that the behaviour of P is equivalent to the behaviour of $P1()$ followed by the behaviour of $P2$, exactly when P1() terminates successfully. Concerning the parallel composition, CSP# allows a composition with or without synchronisation between the processes being composed. In this work we use only the parallel composition without synchronisation, the interleaving operator $(P1|||P2)$.

From a CSP# specification, the PAT tool can check desirable properties, such as: (1) deadlock-freedom, (2) deterministic behaviour, (3) divergence-freedom, (4) successful termination, and (5) if a process satisfies some LTL formulae.

2.2 SCR

SCR is a requirements method created by the U.S. Navy for documenting the requirements of the U.S. Navy A-7 Aircraft [8]. It was designed to detect and correct errors during the requirements phase. Currently, SCR is being applied in several different control system industries. According to [7], SCR has been applied by organisations like Grumman, Bell Laboratories and Lockheed. The largest applicaton of SCR we currently know is the specification of the C-130J Flight Program requirements. This produced a source code with more than 250,000 LOC. Nowadays, there are some commercial tools that are able to process SCR specifications, such as, for instance: T-VEC [3] and the SCR Toolset [7].

In SCR, system requirements are defined in terms of monitored and controlled variables. Besides that, SCR also allows the use of mode classes, to model system states, and terms, internal variables declared for reuse purposes. A set of assumptions can be made to impose constraints on the variables. It is also possible to define assertions describing properties, such as security and safety.

The behaviour of the system is described using functions that specify how changes of the monitored variables, and even controlled ones, affect each controlled variable. In more details, the functions describe conditions (predicates) that (when satisfied) change a specific variable in a particular way. SCR allows two types of predicates: condition predicate (inside $if...fi$ scope) and event predicate (inside $ev...ve$ scope). The former is defined considering a single system state, whereas the latter takes into account the changes that happen between two states. An SCR event predicate has the form: $\dagger(c)\ WHEN\ d$, where $\dagger$ stands for $@T,\ @F,\ @C$. Considering that a dashed $(')$ variable stands for the variable value in the new state, and the undashed variable its value in the previous state, the precise meaning of these event predicates are: $@T(c)\ WHEN\ d = \neg c \wedge c' \wedge d$, $@F(c)\ WHEN\ d = c \wedge \neg c' \wedge d$, and $@C(c)\ WHEN\ d = c \neq c' \wedge d$. If $WHEN d$ is omitted, the meaning is defined not considering the value of d.

For a concrete example, consider Figure 1.1. It is an excerpt from a control System for Safety Injection in a nuclear power plant. The complete specification can be seen in [9]. Figure 1.1 shows how the mode class $mcPressure$ evolves according to changes of $mWaterPres$, a monitored variable. For example, line 3 states that if $mcPressure$ is $TooLow$ and $mWaterPres$ becomes higher than or equal to Low, then $mcPressure$ will be $Permitted$ in the next state.

Figure 1.1. SCR Specification Example

```
 1 var  mcPressure :=
 2    case  mcPressure
 3       []  TooLow  ev  []  @T(mWaterPres >= Low)  -> Permitted  ve
 4       []  Permitted
 5       ev
 6          []  @T(mWaterPres >= Permit)  -> High
 7          []  @T(mWaterPres < Low)  -> TooLow
 8       ve
 9       []  High  ev  []  @T(mWaterPres < Permit)  -> Permitted  ve
10 esac
```

From the SCR proposal, some extensions were introduced. For instance, *WHERE* and *WHILE*, besides *WHEN*: *WHERE*, means that d is true only in the next state and *WHILE* means that d is true in the previous and next states. Another important extension is the $DUR(p)$ operator. It represents the time duration since p became true. In SCR, the system time is represented by an implicit integer variable (*time*), nondecreasing and non-negative. For more details on SCR see, for instance, [7, 9].

3   Translating SCR Specifications into CSP# Processes

The SCR specification is translated into CSP# processes by the progressive application of 8 steps. In the first step, SCR types and constants are translated to #*define* clauses. The second step is responsible for creating CSP# variables for each SCR variable. After that, CSP# processes are created to model the input scenarios (values the monitored values may assume). The fourth step defines a CSP# process that models the time passing behaviour. The fifth step defines other CSP# processes, now for modeling the output scenarios (values the controlled variables, terms and mode classes may assume). The sixth step defines a loop where input values iteratively evolve modifying the system outputs.

The last two steps are optional and may be executed for optimization purposes: reduce the CSP# model state space by means of data abstraction and eliminate eventual CSP# variables that are not used. All the steps are detailed in the following subsections and exemplified also considering the Safety Injection System (SIS) specification presented in [9]. Currently, the translation is systematic and is implemented in a prototype tool, but it is informal; a proven correct translation is our current focus of investigation.

3.1   Step 1 - Mapping Types and Constants

The SCR enumerations and constants become #*define* clauses in CSP#. The SCR boolean types become CSP# int types, where 0 means false, and 1 means true. The SCR float types must be cast to CSP# int types. As PAT does not support floating numbers, we first abstract inexact numbers by multiplying all of them by the same slowest factor 10^n that is enough for eliminating the decimal precision. For instance, 3.2 becomes 32 and 0.5 becomes 5. In this case, n is 1. All related operations are abstracted as well. Figure 1.2 shows an example.

Figure 1.2. Definition in CSP# of SCR Constants

```
1 \\ ─────────────────────────── SCR ──────────────────
2 type_mcPressure: enum in {TooLow, Permitted, High};
3 Low=900:integer; Permit=1000 : integer;
4 \\ ─────────────────────────── CSP# ──────────────────
5 #define TooLow 0; #define Permitted 1; #define High 2;
6 #define Low 900; #define Permit 1000;
```

3.2   Step 2 - Mapping SCR Variables

For each monitored or controlled variable, term, and mode class we create two CSP# variables: one to hold the current state and another to keep the previous (suffix _*old*) state. The initial values of these variables are obtained directly from the initial values specified in the SCR specification.

These current and previous state variables are necessary to support the translation of @T, @F and @C events. For instance, @$T(input1)$ becomes the predicate $input1 == true$ && $input1\_old == false$. Therefore, the number of CSP# variables produced by this step doubles the number of SCR variables. Figure 1.3 shows an example.

Figure 1.3. Definition in CSP# of SCR Variables

```
1 \\ ────────────────────── SCR ──────────────────────────
2 mcPressure: type_mcPressure, initially TooLow;
3 \\ ────────────────────── CSP# ─────────────────────────
4 var mcPressure = TooLow; var mcPressure_old = TooLow;
```

3.3   Step 3 - Modeling Input Possibilities

Let mV_i be an SCR monitored variable, such that mV_i can assume the values $v\_1, ..., v\_n$. We create a process following the template presented in Figure 1.4.

Figure 1.4. Template - Definition in CSP# of Input Possibilities

```
1 V_i() = tau{ mV_old = mV; } ->
2       ( ( mV_v_1{ mV = v_1; } -> Skip) [*]
3       ... ( mV_v_n{ mV = v_n; } -> Skip));
4 MONITORED_VARIABLES() = V_1() ; ... ; V_n();
```

V_i (lines 1–3) models, using external choices, the possible values mV_i can assume. Before updating the mV_i value, the current value is stored in the $\_old$ variable (line 1). We create a process named *MONITORED_VARIABLES* to represent the assignment possibilities of all monitored variables. As each SCR monitored variable is independent of each other, with respect to the same time step, any updating order would produce the same result. We could use the interleaving operator to represent all updating orders, but, for optimization purposes, we compose the processes sequentially considering some order, which is valid as any of them would be as well. Figure 1.5 shows a concrete example.

Figure 1.5. Example - Definition in CSP# of Input Possibilities

```
1 \\ ────────────────────── SCR ──────────────────────────
2 yWPres: integer in [0, 2000]; mWaterPres: yWPres, initially 0;
3 mBlock, mReset: ySwitch, initially Off;
4 \\ ────────────────────── CSP# ─────────────────────────
5 WATERPRES() = tau{ mWaterPres_old = mWaterPres; } ->
6     ((mWaterPres_0{ mWaterPres = 0; } -> Skip) [*]
7     ... (mWaterPres_2000{ mWaterPres = 2000; } -> Skip));
8 BLOCK() = ... ; RESET() = ... ;
9 MONITORED_VARIABLES() = WATERPRES() ; BLOCK() ; RESET();
```

3.4   Step 4 - Representing Time Passing

A *CLOCK* process is created to represent the time passing. This is accomplished by means of a cyclic *tick* event that updates the current time of the system. To avoid an infinite CSP# process, a clock upper bound is defined. It represents the number of cycles the CSP# model for the SCR specification will evolve. Therefore, when the clock upper bound is reached, the system deadlocks. Figure 1.6 shows the code for an upper bound equal to 5.

Figure 1.6. Definition in CSP# of Time Passing

```
1  #define CLOCK_UPPER_BOUND 5;  var clock = 0;
2  CLOCK() = ifa ( clock < CLOCK_UPPER_BOUND ) { tick{clock++} -> Skip }
3                  else { time_limit -> Stop };
```

3.5   Step 5 - Mapping SCR Functions

Let cV_i be an SCR controlled variable, term or mode class, such that cV_i can assume the values $v\_1, ..., v\_n$ when the SCR predicates $p\_1, ..., p\_n$ are satisfied, respectively. Then we create a process following the template presented in Figure 1.7, where $cV\_i\_COND\_1, ..., cV\_i\_COND\_n$ are conditional expressions semantically equivalent to $p\_1, ..., p\_n$.

Figure 1.7. Template - Definition in CSP# of SCR Functions

```
1  #define cV_i_COND_1 p_1;  ...  #define cV_i_COND_n p_n;
2  V_i() = V_i_old{ cV_i_old = cV_i; } -> (
3              ([ cV_i_COND_1 ] V_i_condition_satisfied ->
4                 cV_i_COND_1_v_1{ cV_i_old = cV_i; cV_i = v_1;} Skip)
5          [*] ...
6              ([ cV_i_COND_n ] V_i_condition_satisfied ->
7                 cV_i_COND_n_v_n{ cV_i_old = cV_i; cV_i = v_n;} Skip)
8          [*]
9              ([ !cV_i_COND_1 && ... && !cV_i_COND_n ]
10                V_i_empty_condition -> Skip ));
11 OUT() = atomic{V_1()} ||| ... ||| atomic{V_n()};
```

V_i (lines 2–7) models, using external choice, the possible values cV_i can assume. However, before updating the cV_i value, the current value is stored in the _old variable (line 2). To update the value of cV_i to v_i, the conditional expression $cV\_i\_COND\_j$ (equivalent to the SCR predicate p_j of cV_i) must be true. This is ensured in this template by guards.

Lines 9–10 models a special case when all defined SCR predicates are false. In this situation, according to the SCR semantics, the value of the variable remains unchanged. These lines (9–10) may be removed in the CSP# when analysing completeness of the specification, as we are going to see in Section 4.

After that, we create a process named *OUT* to represent the update of all controlled variables, terms and mode classes. In SCR, the evaluation of a function is atomic. Therefore, in *OUT*, each process V_i is atomically performed

($atomic\{V\_i\}$ clause). Differently from monitored variables, controlled variables, terms and modes may be dependent of each other. In other words, the update order is relevant. To model all ordering possibilities, we compose the processes V_i using the interleaving operator. Figure 1.8 shows a concrete example.

An important aspect of this step is the definition of conditional expressions (c_i) semantically equivalent to SCR predicates (p_i). For @T, @F, @C events as well as conditions (without DUR operator) the translation is quite straightforward. We just need to follow the definition of events and conditions as depicted in Section 2.2. However, the DUR operator requires special attention.

Considering $DUR(p\_i)$, currently we restrict p_i to be of the form ($var \dagger value$), where $\dagger$ stands for $<, \leq, >, \geq, =, \neq$. For each p_i we create a variable to store the time stamp ($clock$ value) when p_i becomes true. To do this, we need to complement the processes defined by Step 3 with respect to this new information. For example, consider the following SCR predicate @$T(DUR(mWaterPres = 1) = 2)$. It represents the exact moment when $mWaterPres$ is equal to 1 for 2 time units.

We create a new variable ($mWaterPres\_eq1\_moment$) and complement the CSP# process of $mWaterPres$ as depicted in Figure 1.9. When $mWaterPres$ becomes equal to 1, we store the current clock value in $mWaterPres\_eq1\_moment$. In any other situation, we reset this variable to -1. However, we still need to consider the first iteration: if $mWaterPres$ becomes equal to 1, the current $clock$ will not be saved because the old value of $mWaterPres$ is also equal to 1 (recall that the initial values of the CSP# variables are obtained from the initial values specified in the SCR specification). Therefore, we also need to define a process to deal with the first cycle situation (in this case, $WATERPRES\_FIRSTCYCLE$). Based on these considerations, the SCR predicate previously mentioned, can be expressed in CSP# as $mWaterPres\_eq1\_moment\ != -1\ \&\&\ (clock - mWaterPres\_eq1\_moment) == 2$. Figure 1.9 shows the CSP# for this example.

Figure 1.8. Example - Definition in CSP# of SCR Functions

```
1  \\ ———————————————— SCR ————————————————
2  var mcPressure := ... (see Figure 1.1)
3  var tOverridden := ... var cSafety_Injection := ...
4  \\ ———————————————— CSP# ————————————————
5  #define mcPressure_COND_1
6  (mcPressure == TooLow && mWaterPres >= Low && mWaterPres_old < Low);
7  ...
8  #define mcPressure_COND_4
9  (mcPressure==High && mWaterPres < Permit && mWaterPres_old >= Permit);
10 PRESSURE() = tau{ mcPressure_old = mcPressure; } -> (
11    ([mcPressure_COND1] pressure_condition_satisfied ->
12      mcPressure_COND_1_Permitted{ mcPressure = Permitted; } -> Skip)
13    [*] ... [*]
14    ([mcPressure_COND4] pressure_condition_satisfied ->
15      mcPressure_COND_4_Permitted{ mcPressure = Permitted; } -> Skip)
16    [*]
17    ([!mcPressure_COND1 && ... && !mcPressure_COND4]
18      pressure_empty_condition -> Skip ));
19 OUT() = atomic{PRESSURE()} ||| ... ||| atomic{SAFETY_INJECTION()};
```

Figure 1.9. Adaptation in the CSP# Code to Support the SCR *DUR* Operator

```
1  WATERPRES() = tau{ mWaterPres_old = mWaterPres; } ->
2      (... [*] (mWaterPres_1{ mWaterPres = 1; } ->
3              ifa ( mWaterPres_old != 1 ) {
4                  tau{ mWaterPres_eq1_moment = clock; } -> Skip
5              } ; Skip)
6      [*] ... [*] (mWaterPres_2000{ mWaterPres = 2000;
7                      mWaterPres_eq1_moment = -1; } -> Skip ));
8  WATERPRES_FIRSTCYCLE() = ...
9      } else ifa ( mWaterPres == 1 ) {
10         tau{ mWaterPres_eq1_moment = clock; } -> Skip } ...
11     } else ifa ( mWaterPres == 2000 ) {
12         tau{ mWaterPres_eq1_moment = -1; } -> Skip };
13 MONITORED_VARIABLES_FIRSTCYCLE() = WATERPRES_FIRSTCYCLE() ; ...;
```

3.6   Step 6 - Representing the SCR Loop Behaviour

The formal semantics of SCR is given by a state machine $\Sigma = (S, S_0, E_m, T)$, where S is the set of states, $S_0 \subseteq S$ is the set of initial states, E_m is the set of monitored events and $T : E_m \times S \to S$ is the transition relation. In each transition, defined by T, only one monitored variable may have its value changed from one state to the next (*One Input Assumption*). Thus, when one monitored variable value changes the system evolves to a new state where the variables (controlled, terms and mode classes) that depend on this monitored variable are updated. After that, new changes may occur again.

In this step, we create a process to capture the semantics briefly described in the previous paragraph. It is important to note that we allow multiple changes of input values, what is not allowed by the SCR semantics. However, multiple changes of input values are equivalent to a sequence of SCR transitions, where intermediate values of controlled (and other) variables are not considered relevant. Consider the following example: a system has two monitored variables ($M1$ and $M2$) whose values shall change simultaneously (same value of T) from 0 to 1. When this happens, the system output changes from 0 to 2. In SCR, this behaviour is captured by three state transitions (Figure 1 - left side). In CSP# we will capture this as a single transition where intermediate states are discarded (Figure 1 - right side).

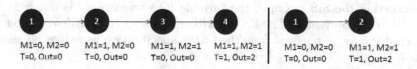

Fig. 1. P and Q LTS

Another difference in our case is that we do not allow indefinite changes. As previously said, to avoid an infinite process, we shall set a clock upper bound such that, when this is reached, the entire system deadlocks. In SCR this is not necessary as the system is symbolic modeled and analysed by constraint solvers.

Figure 1.10 shows the code that is generated in this step. In the first cycle, the system behaves as *MONITORED_VARIABLES_FIRSTCYCLE* due to the treatment related to the *DUR* operator, as explained in the previous section. After that, the time evolves and the system enters in a recursion.

Figure 1.10. Definition in CSP# of System Process to Model SCR Loop Behaviour

```
1 var first_cycle = true;
2 SYSTEM() =   ifa( !first_cycle) { MONITORED_VARIABLES()
3              } else { MONITORED_VARIABLES_FIRSTCYCLE() }
4              ; OUT() ; tau{first_cycle = false;} -> CLOCK() ; SYSTEM();
```

3.7   Step 7 - Data Abstraction

Data abstraction techniques, for instance the one discussed in [6], may be applied to reduce the CSP# specification state space. Particularly, we reduce the number of external choices produced in Step 3 to consider only meaningful values.

For example, if we carefully analyse the SIS specification [9] we notice that the *mWaterPres* value range can be split into three classes of equivalence: $mWaterPres < 900$, $900 <= mWaterPres < 2000$ and $mWaterPres = 2000$. Thus, we can simplify the definition of *WATERPRES* (see Figure 1.5) to the one presented in Figure 1.11

Figure 1.11. CSP# Optimization due to Data Abstraction

```
1 WATERPRES() = tau{ mWaterPres_old = mWaterPres; } ->
2     ((mWaterPres_899{ mWaterPres = 899; } -> Skip) [*]
3     (mWaterPres_900{ mWaterPres = 900; } -> Skip) [*]
4     (mWaterPres_1000{ mWaterPres = 1000; } -> Skip));
```

3.8   Step 8 - Elimination of Unnecessary Variables

Some of the CSP# _old variables declared in Step 2 might eventually not be used. This happens if the corresponding variable is never used inside an event predicate ($@T$, $@F$, $@C$). Thus, in this situation, we do not need to store the old value of this variable.

Considering the SIS example, the variable *tOverridden_old* is not used because there is no event ($@T$, $@F$, $@C$) with respect to *tOverriden*. Therefore, this variable may be removed from the CSP# specification as well as all assignments *tOverriden_old = tOverridden;*.

4   Generating Test Vectors from CSP# Specifications

After creating the *SYSTEM* process we can verify whether it satisfies some desired properties and generate test vectors automatically, supported by a strategy we propose based on LTL model checking. In the following subsections we focus on how this verification and generation can be performed.

4.1   Specification Properties

Specification Completeness. With respect to a clock upper bound with value n ($n > 0$), a CSP# specification is complete if and only if for all possible input values, at least one guard of each process created by Step 5 evaluates to true.

This property ensures that the specification dictates how the controlled variables, terms and mode classes shall evolve for each possible value of monitored variables. If this property is false, there is at least one input scenario (valuation of monitored variables) where the specification does not specify how the output shall be updated. Thus, this means that the desired reactive behaviour of the system for this input is undefined.

Theorem 1. Let dlf be a function that verifies if a system S (created in Step 6 of our translation strategy - with a clock upper bound equal to n, and $n > 0$) is deadlock free, ce_dlf be a function that returns a counter-example of deadlock freedom using Breadth First Search, a system S is complete if and only if S is not deadlock free and the last event of the counter-example is $time\_limit$. Formally: $\neg dlf(S) \wedge tail(ce\_dlf(S, BFS)) = time\_limit \leftrightarrow cmplt(S)$

Proof Sketch. Initially, it is necessary to note that there are only two possibilities of reaching a deadlock in S: (1) when the clock upper bound is reached, and the event $time\_limit$ occurs before the $Stop$ process, and (2) if all the guards of at least one process created by Step 5 (for modeling the SCR functions) evaluate to false (considering the guard semantics, this is equivalent to $Stop$). It is important to notice that the only deadlock introduced by the steps is the one after the $time\_limit$ event.

Thus, let the clock upper bound be n ($n > 0$). For $clock$ equal to 0 (first cycle), if the system is incomplete, then there is at least one input scenario (valuation for the monitored variables) that will not satisfy any guard of a process V_i (one of the processes created in the Step 5 for modeling the SCR functions). In this situation, the process V_i deadlocks due to the guard semantics. If V_i deadlocks, then S deadlocks as well. However, in this case, the last performed event will not be $time\_limit$ because $clock$ has not reached n. If the system is complete, then some output will be produced and the time will evolve to 1. If the system is incomplete, it will deadlock and the trace will not contain $time\_limit$ either. If S evolves until $time\_limit$ is performed, what only happens when $clock$ is equal to the clock upper bound n, then a deadlock has not happened before. If so, for all input scenarios previously evaluated, we always had at least one guard being satisfied. Thus, the system is complete.   □

Corollary 1. If S is complete for a clock upper bound equal to n, $m \leq n$ and $m > 0$ then S is complete with respect to m.

Corollary 2. If the guard [!cV_i_COND_1 && ... && !cV_i_COND_n] is considered then S is always complete.

Corollary 1 is a consequence of the inductive proof previously presented. Concerning Corollary 2, this happens because always one guard will be satisfied.

Briefly speaking: $cV\_i\_COND\_1 \parallel ... \parallel cV\_i\_COND\_n \parallel (!cV\_i\_COND\_1 \&\& ... \&\& !cV\_i\_COND\_n)$ is always true.

If we are modeling a system whose requirements must define the output for all combinations of input values, we should remove this guard. In this case, due to Corollary 2, the system is not necessarily complete. However, if we consider the value of controlled and terms variables, as well as mode classes, shall remain unchanged when a combination of input values (not covered by the system requirements) are provided, we should maintain the guard. In this last case, due to Corollary 2, the system will always be complete.

Specification Determinism. With respect to a clock upper bound equal to n ($n > 0$), a CSP# specification is deterministic if and only if for all possible input values, no more than one guard of each process created by Step 5 evaluates to true.

This property ensures that, for all input scenarios, no more than one output possibility is expected. To verify this property we use the determinism assertion of PAT. If we have a nondeterministic CSP# model, there is at least one input scenario that will satisfy at least two guards of a process V_i (one of the processes created in the Step 5). In this situation, the LTS produced to the CSP# model will have at least two events with the same name ($V\_i\_condition\_satisfied$) leading to different states. Considering the CSP semantics, this characterizes a non-deterministic behaviour.

An interesting property, a consequence of the Theorem 1 and the specification determinism definition, is that if a SYSTEM is complete and deterministic, then for all input scenarios exactly one guard of the processes created by Step 5 evaluates to true.

4.2 Generating Test Vectors

In this work, a test vector (TV) is defined as a non-empty sequence of mappings, as follows: $< in\_1 = iv\_1\_1, ..., in\_n = iv\_1\_n \rightarrow out\_1 = ov\_1\_1, ..., out\_m = ov\_1\_m, ..., in\_1 = iv\_k\_1, ..., in\_n = iv\_k\_n \rightarrow out\_1 = ov\_k\_1, ..., out\_m = ov\_k\_m >$, where in and out are prefixes for input and output variables, iv_i_j stands for the ith value of input variable in_j, and ov_i_j stands for the ith value of output variable out_j.

Each mapping of TV associates a tuple of the values of monitored variables to a corresponding tuple of the values of controlled variables. If the scenario we want to test implies in time passing, the TV will have more than one element, and we assume a *tick* has occurred (the time has evolved in one unit) between them. We do not consider the values of mode classes and terms in the test vector because we assume them as internal, and non-observable, elements of the system. For example, considering Figure 1, we could have the following test vector: <M1=0, M2=0, Out=0>.

Consider a controlled variable $cVar$, in the context of a CSP# process with n guards. If we want to generate test vectors for $cVar$ we shall find out all value combinations for the inputs that will make each ith guard evaluate to true. We can generate these value combinations using Linear Temporal Logic (LTL) formulae. The idea is to check whether SYSTEM *never* satisfies the ith condition;

if this is false (the ith condition can be satisfied by some value combination for the inputs), then PAT will return a counter-example (say ce_1).

```
#assert SYSTEM |= !(<> output1_i-th_condition); // false
#define ce_1 (input_1=v_1_1 && ... && input_n=v_n_1 && cVar=v_1 );
```

The input values can be inferred by the name of the events performed in ce_1. If we want to find another counter example, we should repeat the previous check, but stating that $SYSTEM$ will never satisfy the ith condition in a situation different from the one described by ce_1.

```
#assert SYSTEM |= !(<> (output1_i-th_condition && !ce_1) ); // false
#define ce_2 (input_1=v_1_2 && ... && input_n=v_n_2 && cVar=v_1 );
```

This idea can be repeated incrementally. When SYSTEM satisfies the predicate, then we will have generated all scenarios that satisfy the ith condition of $cVar$ with respect to the value defined to the clock upper bound.

Example. To illustrate the approach to automatic generation of test vectors, consider the Safety Injection System previously discussed. Test vectors for this system can be generated in the following manner:

```
=> First assertion for the first condition of cSafety_Injection
#assert SYSTEM |= !(<> cSafety_Injection_COND1_Off );

=> Counter example produced by PAT using BFS
<init -> tau -> pressure_empty_condition -> overriden_empty_condition ->
safety_injection_condition_satisfied -> cSafety_Injection_COND2_On -> tau -> tick -> tau ->
mWaterPres_899 -> tau -> mBlock_On -> tau -> mReset_Off -> overriden_condition_satisfied ->
tOverridden_COND1_true -> safety_injection_condition_satisfied -> cSafety_Injection_COND1_Off>

=> Test vector defined by the previous counter example
TV_1 = < (mWaterPres=0, mBlock=Off, mReset=Off -> cSafety_Injection=On),
     (mWaterPres=899, mBlock=On, mReset=Off -> cSfety_Injection=Off) >

=> State after the execution of TV1
#define cond1_state1 ( mWaterPres==899 && mBlock==On && mReset==Off &&
                       mcPressure==TooLow && tOverridden==1 && cSafety_Injection==Off );

=> Second assertion for the first condition of cSafety_Injection
#assert SYSTEM |= !(<> ( cSafety_Injection_COND1_Off && !cond1_state1 ) );

... and so on!
```

Based on each automatically generated test vector (TV_i), the behaviour of System Under Test (SUT) may be verified. The collection of the generated test vectors forms the test suite to be exercised against the SUT.

5   Empirical Analyses

In this section, we evaluate our strategy for generating test vectors focusing on two aspects: (1) the time required to generate test vectors, and (2) comparing the number of automatically generated test vectors with those created manually by domain specialists. As examples of specifications, we considered two typical aeronautical functions provided by our industrial partner (Embraer).

The first function (Priority Command) decides whether the pilot or the copilot will have priority in controlling the airplane side stick. The decision is based on: (i) if some side stick is not on the neutral position, (ii) if some side stick priority button has been pressed, and (iii) who pressed the priority button first. The second function (Fade In/Out) is responsible for linearly incrementing and decrementing a system output based on variations of two inputs.

Table 1 summarizes the empirical results. The first function was described by 8 system requirements. We created an SCR specification of 34 lines of code from these requirements. Running a prototype tool that implements the steps described in Section 3, we obtained a CSP# specification with 81 lines of code composed by 11 global variables. Domain specialists created 17 test vectors manually. Using the strategy described in Section 4, we were able to automatically generate 20 test vectors, containing the 17 test vectors produced by the specialists. Our generation strategy took only 6 seconds for generating them. The second line of Table 1 corresponds to a similar analysis performed on the second aeronautical function.

Table 1. Results for the Application of our Test Vector Generation Strategy

Spec	#Req	SCR LOC	CSP# LOC	CSP# Var.	#Man.	#Aut.	%	Time
Priority Cmd.	8	34	81	11	17	>17	100%	6s
Fade In/Out	5	33	60	9	12	12	100%	4s

We also evaluated our strategy for verifying properties of the specification. As a practical result, we identified that the original description of the aeronautical functions presented situations of nondeterminism and incompleteness. When we applied the verifications (deadlock-freedom and determinism assertion) we were able to identify these two problems: the Priority function did not specify who should gain priority when both priority buttons are pressed simultaneously (this led to a deadlock in the CSP# output function as we did not consider the clause produced by Step 5), and the Fade In/Out function had a scenario where two different outputs could be produced for the same inputs (this led to a nondeterminism as two guards of the CSP# output function were evaluated to true).

Despite the promising results, these empirical analyses have some threats to validity. The most relevant ones are: (1) threat to External Validity - we have just analysed two examples of one specific Domain, and (2) threat to Conclusion Validity - we do not have a proof of soundness for our translation from SCR to CSP#.

Concerning the first threat, we plan to perform more case studies for other examples of different domains. Regarding the second threat, we are currently working on the formalisation of the translation. However, the empirical analyses give some evidence that the generated CSP# specifications are meaningful and capture the semantics of the system requirements and of the SCR specification, as, from them, our generation strategy was able to produce only relevant test vectors: most of them coincided with those that have been written by the domain specialists, and the additional ones were also considered relevant by them (although they test conditions already verified by other vectors).

6   Conclusions

This paper presented a strategy based on the process algebra CSP (particularly the CSP# variation) for generating test vectors from high-level specifications written in SCR. This strategy relies on the application of 8 translation steps. Based on the CSP# model, using LTL-based model checking, test vectors are automatically generated. Moreover, the CSP# model is also suitable to perform some analysis with respect to specification completeness and determinism.

The proposed strategy was evaluated in the context of two typical functions of the aeronautical domain. The results are promising as the strategy was able to generate the same vectors that were manually written by domain specialists. Besides that, the strategy also identified specification problems concerning completeness and determinism.

The generation of test vectors is a well known problem and has been studied for many years. For instance, the work reported in [2] uses symbolic execution and model checking to produce test vectors for C programs; and the work [13] uses genetic algorithms for generating test vectors. Despite the use of different techniques, these works are different from the strategy proposed here because they assume as input a concrete specification (an implementation in some programming language), and time aspects are not considered.

SCR has been used for years to generate test vectors [3, 7–9] from high-level specifications with time aspects. These works apply constraint solvers to generate test vectors. They also allow verifying specification properties like the ones described in Section 4.

Our work can be regarded as an alternative technique, which uses process algebra instead of solvers, for generating test vectors. The advantage we foresee relies on particular properties of process algebras. For instance, using process refinement we may be able to compare if an SCR specification is a refinement of another SCR specification. Thus, we can combine model checking and testing in a uniform framework. We can also explore compositional testing and analysis by benefitting from the rich repertoire of CSP operators. However, probably this strategy will be slower than the usage of constraint solver.

Initially, we tried to use FDR. However, the CSP_M way of modeling shared memory led to larger state machines. Thus, it took an unfeasible time to perform deadlock and determinism assertions. When we used PAT we obtained smaller state machines, and the time required for analysing system properties and generating test vectors was considerably small.

There are some studies that already used process algebras to generate tests, such as, for example [12]. However, these works generate test procedures and not test vectors in the style presented here. Also, the generation strategy in [12] is based on refinement checking, whereas we have based our approach on LTL model checking, which seems to be more potentially scalable for the kind of analysis involved in test generation. Therefore, to our knowledge, our strategy is innovative concerning the usage of a process algebra for generating test vectors from high-level descriptions (in SCR) of systems.

We foresee many interesting future works: formalise the steps of our translation strategy from SCR to CSP#, which is our current focus of investigation; investigate the strategy concerning properties of composition, coverage and soundness of the generated test cases; and apply the strategy to other problems and domains, exploring more elaborate abstraction techniques.

Acknowledgments. This work was partially supported by the National Institute of Science and Technology for Software Engineering (INES[5]), funded by CNPq and FACEPE, grants 573964/2008-4 and APQ-1037-1.03/08, by CNPq grant 476821/2011-8 and by the Brazilian Space Agency (UNIESPACO 2009).

References

1. Bergerand, J.L.: Lustre, un Langage Déclaratif pour le Temps Réel. Ph.D. thesis, INPG (1986)
2. Beyer, D., Chlipala, A.J., Majumdar, R.: Generating tests from counterexamples. In: Proceedings of the 26th ICSE, pp. 326–335. IEEE Computer Society, Washington, DC (2004)
3. Blackburn, M., Busser, R., Fontaine, J.: Automatic Generation of Test Vectors for SCR-style Specifications. In: Proceedings of the 12th Annual Conference on Computer Assurance (1997)
4. Camus, J.L., Dion, B.: Efficient Development of Airborne Software with Scade Suite. Tech. rep., Esterel Technologies (2003)
5. Efkemann, C., Peleska, J.: Model-Based Testing for the Second Generation of Integrated Modular Avionics. In: Proceedings of ICSTW, pp. 55–62 (2011)
6. Farias, A., Mota, A.M., Sampaio, A.: Efficient CSP_Z Data Abstraction. In: Boiten, E.A., Derrick, J., Smith, G.P. (eds.) IFM 2004. LNCS, vol. 2999, pp. 108–127. Springer, Heidelberg (2004)
7. Heitmeyer, C., Bharadwaj, R.: Applying the SCR Requirements Method to the Light Control Case Study. Journal of Universal Computer Science 6 (2000)
8. Heninger, K., Parnas, D., Shore, J., Kallander, J.: Software Requirements for the A-7E Aircraft - TR 3876. Tech. rep., U.S. Naval Research Laboratory (1978)
9. Leonard, E.I., Heitmeyer, C.L.: Program Synthesis from Formal Requirements Specifications Using APTS. Higher Order Symbol. Comput. 16, 63–92 (2003)
10. Mota, A., Jesus, J., Gomes, A., Ferri, F., Watanabe, E.: Evolving a Safe System Design Iteratively. In: Schoitsch, E. (ed.) SAFECOMP 2010. LNCS, vol. 6351, pp. 361–374. Springer, Heidelberg (2010)
11. National University of Singapore: PAT: User Manual, version 3.3.0. (2011)
12. Nogueira, S., Sampaio, A., Mota, A.M.: Guided Test Generation from CSP Models. In: Fitzgerald, J.S., Haxthausen, A.E., Yenigun, H. (eds.) ICTAC 2008. LNCS, vol. 5160, pp. 258–273. Springer, Heidelberg (2008)
13. Papadakis, M., Malevris, N., Kallia, M.: Towards automating the generation of mutation tests. In: Proceedings of the 5th Workshop on Automation of Software Test, AST 2010, pp. 111–118. ACM, New York (2010)
14. Peleska, J., Honisch, A., Lapschies, F., Löding, H., Schmid, H., Smuda, P., Vorobev, E., Zahlten, C.: A Real-World Benchmark Model for Testing Concurrent Real-Time Systems in the Automotive Domain. In: Wolff, B., Zaïdi, F. (eds.) ICTSS 2011. LNCS, vol. 7019, pp. 146–161. Springer, Heidelberg (2011)
15. West, A.: NASA Study on Flight Software Complexity. Tech. rep., NASA (2009)

---

[5] http://www.ines.org.br/

Specification Patterns for Properties over Reachable States of Graph Grammars*

Simone André da Costa Cavalheiro[1], Luciana Foss[1], and Leila Ribeiro[2]

[1] Universidade Federal de Pelotas, Centro de Desenvolvimento Tecnológico
Rua Gomes Carneiro, 1, 96010-610, Pelotas - RS, Brazil
{simone.costa,lfoss}@inf.ufpel.edu.br
[2] Universidade Federal do Rio Grande do Sul, Instituto de Informática,
Av. Bento Gonçalves, 9500, 91501-970, Porto Alegre - RS, Brazil
leila@inf.ufrgs.br

Abstract. Essential characteristics of the behavior of a system may be described by properties. These descriptions must be precise and unambiguous to enable verification through (semi-)automated tools. There are many appropriate mathematical languages for writing system requirements, but they are often difficult to be applied by user without a good mathematical background. Patterns for property specifications capture recurring solutions for common problems, simplifying this task. This paper presents specification patterns for properties over reachable states of graph grammars, that is, properties of complex graph structures. This proposal may be used to aid the verification of systems where states are represented as graphs.

1 Introduction

During the past two decades, various case studies and industrial applications [1, 2] have been confirming the significance of the use of formal methods to improve the quality of both hardware and software designs. The description of a system by a formal specification language has shown to provide a solid foundation to guide later development activities and obtain, through verification, a high confidence that the system satisfies its requirements. Well-formed specifications, validated with respect to critical properties, have supplied a basis for generating correct and efficient source code.

Nevertheless, the employment of such methods is far from trivial: it typically requires some mathematical expertise. Despite a significant number of successful stories, the software engineering community has not been convinced to widely use formal approaches on a large scale [3]. The most cited reasons for not using formal methods in practice are the extension of cycle development, the need for extensive personnel training, the difficulties in finding suitable abstractions and the mathematical knowledge required. Several improvements are needed to turn the use of these methods and their support tools into a common practice in software development process.

One of the main advantages of the use of formal descriptions of systems is the possibility to use analysis methods to guarantee that the system fulfills its requirements.

* The authors gratefully acknowledge financial support received from CNPq and FAPERGS, specially under Grants, ARD 11/0764-9, PRONEM 11/2016-2 and PRONEX 10/0043-0.

R. Gheyi and D. Naumann (Eds.): SBMF 2012, LNCS 7498, pp. 83–98, 2012.

Independently of the verification technique chosen to be applied, a description of both the system and its desired properties in some formal specification language is needed. The level of maturity and experience required to write these specifications is one of the first obstacles to the adoption of such techniques. This paper provides a contribution towards making the specification of properties easier.

Graph grammars [4, 5] are appealing as specification formalism because they are formal and based on simple, but powerful, concepts to describe behavior. At the same time they also have a nice graphical layout that helps even non-theoreticians to understand a specification. The basic idea of this formalism is to model the states of a system as graphs and describe the possible state changes as (graph) rules The operational behavior of the system is expressed via applications of these rules to graphs depicting the current states of the system. Graph grammars have been used in a variety of applications [6]. In previous work [7, 8] we proposed a relational approach to graph grammars, providing an encoding of graphs and rules into relations. This enabled the use of first-order logic formulas to express properties of reachable states of a graph grammar. Verification of infinite-state systems specified as graph grammars is possible using our approach using theorem proving techniques [9]. However, during the development of the case studies, we noticed that, although the specification of the behavior of the system could be rather intuitively described with graph grammars, the specification of properties was not trivial. Properties over (reachable) states are properties over graphs, typically composed of different kinds of edges and vertices. Logical formulas describing graph properties are not always straightforward to express and understand.

The goal of this paper is to propose patterns for the presentation, codification and reuse of property specifications. The patterns are based on functions that describe typical characteristics or elements of graphs (like the set of all edges of some type, the cardinality of vertices, etc.). These functions make the approach more flexible, enabling its use in other formalisms that use graphs as states. The pattern provides the first steps in the direction of helping and simplifying the task of stating precise requirements to be verified. Besides, it should prevent ambiguities and inaccuracies during the validation stage. Differently from most existing approaches [10–12] we focus on properties about reachable states for (infinite-)state verification, where states are described by graphs. Most of existing patterns for property specification describe properties about traces for finite-state verification tools. These two approaches are complementary.

The next section brings the presentation of the graph grammar specification language together with an example. Section 3 defines a standard library of functions to be used in the specifications. Section 4 describes our taxonomy and explain the patterns. Section 5 concludes and present future works.

2   Graph Grammars

Graph grammars generalize Chomsky grammars from strings to graphs: they specify a system in terms of states, described by graphs, and state changes, described by rules having graphs at the left- and right-hand sides.

2.1 Attributed Graph Grammars

Basically, a graph is composed by a set of vertices and edges connecting them. We consider directed edges, therefore the source and target vertices of each edge must be defined. Both edges and vertices can be enriched with additional information, like labels and attributes. Graphs in which vertices (and edges) can be associated to attributes of some data type are often called attributed graphs. Attributed graphs generally consist of two parts: a graph-part and a data-part. We use algebraic specifications to define data types, and algebras to describe the values that can be used as attributes. We assume that the reader is familiar with algebraic specifications. Basic concepts will be informally introduced in the next paragraph.

A *signature* $SIG = (S, OP)$ consists of a set S of sorts and a set OP of constants and operations symbols. Given a set of variables X (of sorts in S), the *set of terms* over SIG is denoted by $T_{OP}(X)$ (this is defined inductively by stating that all variables and constants are terms, and then all possible applications of operation symbols in OP to existing terms are also terms). An *equation* is a pair of terms $(t1, t2)$, and is usually denoted by $t1 = t2$. A *specification* is a pair $SPEC = (SIG, Eqns)$ consisting of a signature and a set of equations over this signature. An *algebra* for specification $SPEC$, or $SPEC$-algebra, consists of one set for each sort symbol of SIG, called *carrier set*, and one function for each operation symbol of SIG such that all equations in $Eqns$ are satisfied (satisfaction of one equation is checked by substituting all variables in the equation by values of corresponding carrier sets and verifying whether the equality holds, for all possible substitutions). Given two $SPEC$-algebras, a homomorphism between them is a set of functions mapping corresponding carrier sets that are compatible with all functions of the algebras. The set obtained by the disjoint union of all carrier sets of algebra A is denoted by $\mathcal{U}(A)$.

The following definition describes graphs whose vertices may be attributed by values from some data type. Relations between attributed graphs are defined by morphisms, that assure that there is a structural compatibility between the graphs, as well as an attribution compatibility.

Definition 1 (Attributed graph and attributed graph morphism). *A graph G is a tuple $(vertG, edgeG, sourceG, targetG)$, where $vertG$ is a set of (regular) vertices, $edgeG$ is a set of edges, and $sourceG, targetG: edgeG \rightarrow vertG$ are total functions, defining source and target of each edges, respectively.*

*Given a specification $SPEC$, an **attributed graph** is a tuple $AG = (G, A, AttrG, valG, elemG)$, where G is a graph, A is a $SPEC$-algebra, $Attr_G$ is a set, and $valG: AttrG \rightarrow \mathcal{U}(A)$, $elemG: AttrG \rightarrow vertG$ are total functions. Vertices belonging to $AttrG$ are called **attribute vertices**.*

Given two graphs $G = (vertG, edgeG, sourceG, targetG)$ and $H = (vertH, edgeH, sourceH, targetH)$, a (partial) graph morphism $f: G \nrightarrow H$ is a tuple $(f\_V: vertG \nrightarrow vertH, f\_E: edgeG \nrightarrow edgeH)$ such that f commutes with source and target functions, i.e.

$$\forall e \in dom(f\_E) \cdot f\_V(sourceG(e)) = sourceH(f\_E(e)) \text{ and}$$
$$\forall e \in dom(f\_E) \cdot f\_V(targetG(e)) = targetH(f\_E(e))$$

*A **(partial) attributed graph morphism** g between attributed graphs AG and AH is a triple $g = (g_{Graph}, g_{Alg}, g_{Attr})$ consisting of a graph morphism $g_{Graph} = (g\_V, g\_E)$, an algebra homomorphism g_{Alg} and a partial function g_{Attr} between the corresponding components that are compatible with the attribution, i.e.*

$$\forall a \in dom(g_{Attr}) \cdot g_{Alg}(valG(a)) = valH(g_{Attr}(a)) \text{ and}$$
$$g\_V(elemG(a)) = elemH(g_{Attr}(a))$$

An attributed graph morphism g is called total or injective if all components are total or injective, respectively.

The role of the type graph is to define the types of vertices and edges of instance graphs. It is thus adequate that the part of the type graph describing data elements consists of names of types. Therefore, we require that the algebra of the type graph is a final one, that is, an algebra in which all carrier sets are singletons. In practice, we will use the name of the corresponding sort as the only element in a carrier set interpreting it. With respect to the attributes, there may be many different kinds of attribute vertices for the same vertex, and this is described by the existence of many of such vertices connected to the same vertex of the type graph. For example, Fig. 1(a) shows a type graph T. T is composed of: two regular vertices (represented by boxes) Ant and Usr; two attribute vertices (represented by circles) max and cn; and three edges: Acn, Ucn and Cal. Moreover, in T we can see one type of attribute: natural number. Functions $valG$ and $elem$ are depicted as arrows, connecting an attribute vertex to an attribute type or to a regular vertex, resp. For a better visualization, we will use the notation shown in Fig. 1(b) to represent this type graph. We use different images to represent each regular vertex, as well as, different arrow shapes to represent each edge. Attributes are represented by dotted arrows connecting regular vertices to attribute type. The (conditional) algebraic specification used in this graph is shown in Fig. 2. It defines the types natural numbers and booleans and some operations that will be used in the graph grammar specification. Graph $G0$ (Fig. 1(c)) is typed over T (the type morphism is given implicitly by using the same graphical notation to mapped items). The morphism on the algebra component is not shown: the algebra of T will have as carrier sets $T_{Nat} = \{Nat\}$ and $T_{Bool} = \{Bool\}$, and the algebra for $G0$ will have $G_{Nat} = \{0, 1, 2, 3, 4, 5, \ldots\}$ and $G_{Bool} = \{true, false\}$. The mapping between algebras of G and T associates all natural numbers to the element Nat and $true$ and $false$ to $Bool$.

Definition 2 (Attributed type graph, typed attributed graphs). *Given a specification SPEC, an **attributed type graph** is an attributed graph $AT = (T, A, AttrT, valT, elemT)$ in which all carrier sets of A are singletons.*

*A **typed attributed graph** is a tuple $AG^{AT} = (AG, tAG, AT)$, where AG is an attributed graph, called instance graph, AT is an attributed type graph and $tAG : AG \to AT$ is a total attributed graph morphism called attributed typing morphism.*

*A **typed attributed graph morphism** between graphs AG^{AT} and AH^{AT} with attributed type graph AT is an attributed graph morphism g between AG and AH such that $tAG \geq tAH \circ g$ (that is, g may only map between elements of the same type).*

Since in the following we will be dealing only with typed attributed graphs, we will omit the word "typed".

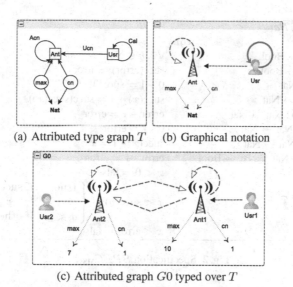

(a) Attributed type graph T (b) Graphical notation

(c) Attributed graph $G0$ typed over T

Fig. 1. Type and initial graphs for the mobile system

A rule consists of a left-hand side, describing items that must be present in a state to enable the rule application and a right-hand side, expressing items that will be present after the rule application. We will restrict possible attributes in left- and right-hand sides to be variables, and the possible relations between these variables will be expressed by equations associated to each rule. When applying a rule, all its equations will be required to be satisfied by the chosen assignment of values to variables. Moreover, we require that rules do not collapse vertices or edges and do not delete vertices. Since here our aim is to find a finite representation of attributed graph grammars, we use just terms as attributes, that is, we use the term algebra over the signature of the specification as attribute algebra (in the definition below, we equivalently use the term algebra over a specification without equations). In such an algebra, each carrier set consists of all terms that can be constructed using the operations defined for the corresponding sort, functions just represent the syntactical construction of terms (for example for a term t and algebra operation op^A corresponding to an operator op in the signature, we would have $op^A(t) = op(t)$). Consequently, all terms are considered to represent different values in a term algebra, since they are syntactically different. The satisfaction of the equations will be dealt with in the match construction, in a rule application.

Definition 3 (Attributed rule). *Given a specification $SPEC = (SIG, Eqns)$. An **attributed rule with NACs** over $SPEC$ with type AT is a triple $attRule = (\alpha, X, ruleEqns)$, where*

- *X is a set of variables over the sorts of $SPEC$;*
- *$\alpha : AL^{AT} \rightarrowtail AR^{AT}$ is an injective attributed graph morphism over the specification $(SIG, \varnothing)$, with $AL = (L, T_{OP}(X), AttrL, valL, elemL)$ and $AR = (R, T_{OP}(X), AttrR, valR, elemR)$, in which $\alpha\_V : vertL \rightarrowtail vertR$ is a total*

MSys : sorts *Bool, Nat*

    opns   **eqns**

               true : $\rightarrow$ Bool $\forall x, y \in$ Nat:

               false: $\rightarrow$ Bool $\mathrm{succ}(\mathrm{error}) = \mathrm{error}$

               0 : $\rightarrow$ Nat $0 + 1 = \mathrm{succ}(0)$

               error : $\rightarrow$ Nat $\mathrm{succ}(x) + 1 = \mathrm{succ}(\mathrm{succ}(x))$

               succ(_) : Nat $\rightarrow$ Nat $\mathrm{error} + 1 = \mathrm{error}$

               _ + 1 : Nat $\rightarrow$ Nat $0 - 1 = \mathrm{error}$

               _ - 1 : Nat $\rightarrow$ Nat $\mathrm{succ}(x) - 1 = x$

               _ < _ : Nat $\times$ Nat $\rightarrow$ Bool $\mathrm{error} - 1 = \mathrm{error}$

                                            $x < 0 = \mathrm{false}$

$$x < \mathrm{succ}(y) = \begin{cases} \mathrm{true} & \text{if } \mathrm{succ}(x) = \mathrm{succ}(y) \\ & \wedge\, x \neq \mathrm{error} \\ x < y & \text{if otherwise.} \end{cases}$$

                                            $x < \mathrm{error} = \mathrm{false}$

Fig. 2. Specification $SPEC_{\text{MSys}}$

function on the set of vertices and the algebra component is the identity on the term algebra $T_{OP}(X)$;

– $ruleEqns$ *is a set of equations using terms of* $T_{OP}(X)$;

In last definition we do not require that variables that appear only in the right-hand side of the rule are involved in equations. The effect of this situation in a rule application is that a value for the corresponding attribute will be generated non-deterministically.

Rule $r5$ in Fig. 3 is an example of attributed rule. Variables x and y are used as attribute values in its left-hand side. There is one equation that restricts the application of this rule. It states that the rule can only be applied if the max attribute of node Ant1 is less than the cn attribute of the same node. By abuse of notation, we write $x < y$ instead of $x < y$ =true. To apply this rule, besides finding a match for the graphical part of the rule, we have to find an assignment of values to variables x and y that satisfies the equation of the rule. The application of this rule will change both graph- and data-parts. The effect of the application on the graph-part will be that a node Usr1 will be created, as well as, an edge connecting Usr1 to Ant1; and the effect of the application on attributes will be that the value of the cn of Ant1 will be increased of one unit.

An attributed graph grammar with respect to some specification of data types $SPEC$ is composed of an *attributed type graph*, an *initial graph* and a *set of rules*.

Definition 4 (Attributed Graph Grammar). *Given a specification $SPEC$ and a $SPEC$-algebra A, a **(typed) attributed graph grammar** is a tuple $AGG = (AT, AG0, R)$, such that AT (the type of the grammar) is an attributed type graph over $SPEC$, AG0 (the initial graph of the grammar) is an attributed graph typed over AT using algebra A, and R is a set of rules over $SPEC$ with type AT .*

The behavior of a graph grammar system is given by successive applications of the rules of the grammar to the initial graph. Applications are done by finding matches of the left-hand sides of rules in the graph that represents the actual state of the system.

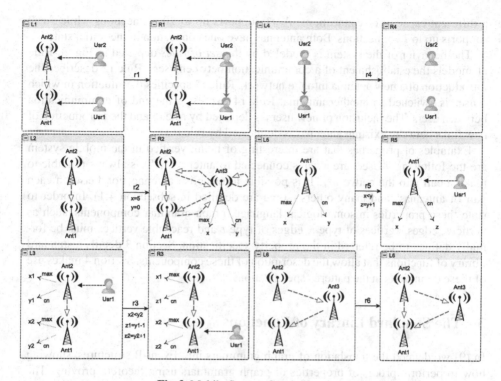

Fig. 3. Mobile System Graph Grammar

Matches of attributed rules must take into account not only the graphical part, but must assure that all equations of the rule are satisfied by the chosen assignment of values to the variables. Since the purpose of this paper is to define properties of (attributed) graphs, we will not present the formal definitions of rule application and semantics of graph grammars. The reader may find these definitions, for example, in [8].

2.2 Specification of a Mobile System Using Graph Grammars

We describe the use of graph grammars specifying a very simple mobile system. The system consists of a network of interconnected antennas and mobile users. Each user, connected to a single antenna, may start/finish a communication with another user. The user may be switched to another antenna. New antennas and users can be added to the system at any time. Each antenna has a maximal capacity of simultaneous connections, which blocks new connection.

Fig. 1(b) shows the type graph T of the system. It describes two types of nodes Ant (Antenna) and Usr (User), three types of edges Acn (connection between antennas), Ucn (connection between users and antennas) and Cal (communication between users). Nodes of type Ant have two attributes max (maximum connection) and cn (number of connections). The *initial graph*, illustrated in Fig. 1(c), represents the initial state of the system. G0 specifies a system with two antennas and two users. Each antenna has a different capacity of connections: Ant1 supports up to 10 connections while Ant2 supports up to 7 connections. Both antennas have one connection in the initial state.

The behavior of the system is modeled by the *set of rules* depicted in Fig. 3. Rule r1 models the establishment of a communication between users. Rule r2 describes the introduction of a new antenna into the network. Rule r3 specifies the situation in which a user is switched to another antenna. Rule r4 expresses the end of communication between users. The inclusion of new users is depicted by rule r5 and the introduction of new links between existing antennas is delineated by rule r6.

Examples of properties that are interesting of being verified in the mobile system are the following: "Users are always connected to antennas", "It is always possible to make a call into the network", "It is possible to establish a connection between each pair of antennas" and many others (some are detailed in subsection 4.1). In order to state these properties in some logical language, graph grammar components, such as vertices, edges, vertices of type t, edges of type t and reachable vertices must be formally defined to be referred in the property specification. Section 3 details a standard library of functions that allow the description of these components. Section 4 makes use of these definitions in the patterns specifications.

3   The Standard Library of Functions

In [9] we defined the translation of graph grammars into Event-B structures, showing how to perform proofs of properties of graph grammars using theorem proving. The strategy used to develop proofs is the following. First, we specify the system as a graph grammar (according to definitions of previous section). Then, the property to be verified is stated as an invariant (using first-order logic enriched with set theory), indicating that it must be true for all reachable states of the system. Finally, proofs are developed by induction: in base case, the property is verified for the initial graph and, at the inductive step, the property is verified for the graph resulting from the application of each rule of the grammar to a reachable graph G, considering that the property is valid for G. On the one hand, the use of this approach requires user interaction during the development of the proofs, but on the other hand, it allows the verification of systems with huge or infinite state spaces. During the development of case studies, we noticed the need for some help to express properties of graphs. We concluded that it would be very helpful to have a set of pre-defined functions over (typed)graphs to build the formulas representing graph properties. This is what is presented in this section. Besides helping to express properties, the library makes the approach more flexible to be used by other formalisms that also use the notion of graph as state: all it is needed is to describe (or implement) the functions of the library in the other formalism and one would be able to use the property patterns to aid the analysis of systems specified in this other formalism.

Tables 1 and 2 present the library functions $\mathcal{L}$. The library is not complete and should grow over as new functions are recognized as relevant to express graph properties. Considering that the properties describe the structure of reachable states (graphs), at the first moment we define functions that describe common characteristics or typical elements of graphs. Depending on the description, functions may return a set (as (1) to (15) and (20) to (21)), a natural number (as (16) to (19)) or a boolean (as (22) to (24)). Many functions and sets used in definitions come from the definitions of the previous section. For instance, function (2) *tvert* returns the vertices of type t of a typed graph G. It is defined restricting the elements of typing morphism tG_V for those with image in t. Any property that states about vertices of a specific type must use such function in its description. If another formalism should be used instead of graph grammars, one should describe how to obtain the corresponding sets and functions in the chosen formalism.

Additionally, we use $Graph(VertG, EgdeG)$ to represent all graphs containing vertices and edges from $VertG$ and $EdgeG$, resp.; analogously for $Graph(VertT, EgdeT)$; $TypedGraph(VertG \cup VertT, EdgeG \cup EdgeT)$ denotes the set of all typed graphs whose type graph contains only vertices and edges from $VertT$ and $EdgeT$, resp., and instance graph contains only vertices and edges from $VertG$ and $EdgeG$, resp; $TypedAGraph(VertG \cup VertT, EdgeG \cup EdgeT, A, AttrG \cup AttrT)$ denotes the set of all attributed typed graphs whose attributed type graph contains vertices and edges from $VertT$ and $EdgeT$, resp., and attribute vertices from $AttrT$, instance attributed graph contains vertices and edges from $VertG$ and $EdgeG$, resp., and attribute vertices from $AttrG$, and A denotes the union of the algebras of G and T. We assume that $VertG \cap VertT = \varnothing$, $EdgeG \cap EdgeT = \varnothing$ and $AttrG \cap AttrT = \varnothing$.

This collection should help the developer not only to state the properties specification but also in the construction of proofs. The idea is to build later a theory including such functions together with a series of theorems that may be used to simplify proofs of properties which involves functions of the standard library. Space limitations prohibit the proof of well-definedness of each function of the library.

4 Property Patterns

Patterns are developed to capture recurrent solutions to design and coding problems. According to Dwyer et al. [10], through a pattern system, the specifier can identify similar requirements, select patterns that fit to those requirements and instantiate solutions that incorporate the patterns. A state property specification pattern is a generalized description of a frequently occurring requirement on the admissible states of a system. It describes the essential arrangement of some aspect of the states of the system and provides expression of this arrangement.

Now we define a collection of patterns for state property specifications. Instead of specifying state properties just as forbidden or desired graphs as frequently done, we adopt first-order logic formulas to describe them. As emphasized in [13], formulas over graph structure are more expressive than pattern graphs. We attempt to give a collection of independent patterns from which a set of interesting specifications about the states of systems can be constructed. We do not intend to provide the smallest set of patterns that can generate all useful specifications. We indeed try to specify patterns which commonly appear as state property specifications and expect that this collection be expanded, as new property specifications do not match with the existing patterns.

The patterns should assist developers into the process of mapping descriptions of the states of the system into the formalism, allowing the specification of state properties without much expertise. To help the user in finding the appropriate pattern for each situation, we organized the patterns using the taxonomy in Table 3.

Table 1. Standard Library

Ref.	Description	Function Definition
(1)	Edges of specific type	$tedg : TypedGraph(VertG \cup VertT, EdgeG \cup EdgeT) \times EdgeT \to 2^{EdgeG}$ $tedg(G,t) = dom(tG\_E \rhd \{t\})$ ($\rhd$ is the range restriction operator)
(2)	Vertices of specific type	$tvert : TypedGraph(VertG \cup VertT, EdgeG \cup EdgeT) \times VertT \to 2^{VertG}$ $tvert(G,t) = dom(tG\_V \rhd \{t\})$
(3)	Pairs of loop edges of specific types with source and target in the same vertex	$ploop : TypedGraph(VertG \cup VertT, EdgeG \cup EdgeT) \times EdgeT \times$ $\times EdgeT \to 2^{EdgeG \times EdgeG}$ $ploop(G, t_1, t_2) = \{(e,f) \mid e \neq f \wedge e \in edgeG \wedge f \in edgeG \wedge$ $\wedge tG\_E(e) = t_1 \wedge tG\_E(f) = t_2 \wedge$ $\wedge \exists x[sourceG(e) = x \wedge targetG(e) = x \wedge$ $\wedge sourceG(f) = x \wedge targetG(f) = x]\}$
(4)	Edges with specific source	$edgs : TypedGraph(VertG \cup VertT, EdgeG \cup EdgeT) \times VertT \to 2^{EdgeG}$ $edgs(G,t)\quad = \{x \mid x \in edgeG \wedge$ $\wedge \exists y[sourceG(x) = y \wedge tG\_V(y) = t\}$
(5)	Edges with specific target	$edgt : TypedGraph(VertG \cup VertT, EdgeG \cup EdgeT) \times VertT \to 2^{EdgeG}$ $edgt(G,t)\quad = \{x \mid x \in edgeG \wedge$ $\wedge \exists y[targetG(x) = y \wedge tG\_V(y) = t\}$
(6)	Edges with specific source and target	$edgl : TypedGraph(VertG \cup VertT, EdgeG \cup EdgeT) \times VertT \times$ $\times VertT \to 2^{EdgeG}$ $edgl(G, t_1, t_2)\quad = \{x \mid x \in edgeG \wedge$ $\wedge \exists y, z[sourceG(x) = y \wedge targetG(x) = z \wedge$ $\wedge tG\_V(y) = t1 \wedge tG\_V(z) = t2\}\}$
(7)	Loop edges	$loop : Graph(VertG, EdgeG) \to 2^{EdgeG}$ $loop(G)\quad = \{x \mid x \in edgeG \wedge$ $\wedge \exists y[sourceG(x) = y \wedge targetG(x) = y]\}$
(8)	Source vertices	$verto : Graph(VertG, EdgeG) \to 2^{VertG}$ $verto(G)\quad = \{x \mid x \in vertG \wedge \exists y[y \in edgeG \wedge sourceG(y) = x] \wedge$ $\wedge \nexists y[y \in edgeG \wedge targetG(y) = x]\}$
(9)	Sink vertices	$verti : Graph(VertG, EdgeG) \to 2^{VertG}$ $verti(G)\quad = \{x \mid x \in vertG \wedge \exists y[y \in edgeG \wedge targetG(y) = x] \wedge$ $\wedge \nexists y[y \in edgeG \wedge sourceG(y) = x]\}$
(10)	Isolated vertices	$ivert : Graph(VertG, EdgeG) \to 2^{VertG}$ $ivert(G)\quad = \{x \mid x \in vertG \wedge \nexists y[y \in edgeG \wedge$ $\wedge (sourceG(y) = x \vee targetG(y) = x)]\}$
(11)	Vertices that are source of specific edges	$verts : TypedGraph(VertG \cup VertT, EdgeG \cup EdgeT) \times EdgeT \to 2^{VertG}$ $verts(G,t)\quad = \{x \mid x \in vertG \wedge$ $\wedge \exists y[y \in edge(G) \wedge sourceG(y) = x \wedge tG\_E(y) = t]\}$
(12)	Vertices that are target of specific edges	$vertt : TypedGraph(VertG \cup VertT, EdgeG \cup EdgeT) \times EdgeT \to 2^{VertG}$ $vertt(G,t)\quad = \{x \mid x \in vertG \wedge$ $\wedge \exists y[y \in edge(G) \wedge targetG(y) = x \wedge tG\_E(y) = t]\}$
(13)	Vertices that are reachable from a specific vertex	$rvert : Graph(VertG, EdgeG) \times VertG \to 2^{VertG}$ $rvert(G,v)\quad = \{x \mid [x = v \wedge v \in vertG] \vee \exists y, z [y \in rvert(G,v) \wedge$ $\wedge z \in edgeG \wedge sourceG(z) = y \wedge targetG(z) = x]\}$
(14)	Value of specific attributes	$tattr : TypedAGraph(VertG \cup VertT, EdgeG \cup EdgeT, A, AttrG \cup AttrT) \times$ $\times AttrT \to 2^{\mathcal{U}(A)}$ $tattr(G,t)\quad = \{x \mid x \in \mathcal{U}(a) \wedge \exists a [a \in attrG \wedge$ $\wedge tG\_attrV(a) = t \wedge valG(a) = x]\}$
(15)	Pairs of vertices and values of specific attributes	$tattrv : TypedAGraph(VertG \cup VertT, EdgeG \cup EdgeT, A, AttrG \cup AttrT) \times$ $\times AttrT \to 2^{VertG \times \mathcal{U}(A)}$ $tattrv(G,t)\quad = \{(v,x) \mid v \in vertG \wedge \exists a [a \in attrG \wedge elemG(a) = v \wedge$ $\wedge tG\_attrV(a) = t \wedge valG(a) = x]\}$

Table 2. Standard Library (Cont.)

Ref. Description	Function Definition
(16) Cardinality of vertices	$cardV : Graph(VertG, EdgeG) \rightarrow \mathbb{N}$ $cardV(G) = \sharp vertG$ ($\sharp$ is the cardinality operator)
(17) Cardinality of edges	$cardE : Graph(VertG, EdgeG) \rightarrow \mathbb{N}$ $cardE(G) = \sharp edgeG$
(18) Cardinality of specific vertices	$tcardV : TypedGraph(VertG \cup VertT, EdgeG \cup EdgeT) \times VertT \rightarrow \mathbb{N}$ $tcardV(G, t) = \sharp(tG\_V \triangleright \{t\})$
(19) Cardinality of specific edges	$tcardE : TypedGraph(VertG \cup VertT, EdgeG \cup EdgeT) \times EdgeT \rightarrow \mathbb{N}$ $tcardE(G, t) = \sharp(tG\_E \triangleright \{t\})$
(20) Transitive closure of specific edges	$tranc : TypedGraph(VertG \cup VertT, EdgeG \cup EdgeT) \times EdgeT \rightarrow$ $\rightarrow 2^{VertG \times VertG}$ $tranc(G, t) = \{(x, y) \mid \exists e[e \in edgeG \wedge tG\_E(e) = t \wedge sourceG(e) = x \wedge$ $\wedge targetG(e) = y] \vee [(x, z) \in tranc(G, t) \wedge (z, y) \in tranc(G, t)]\}$
(21) Root vertices	$root : Graph(VertG, EdgeG) \rightarrow 2^{VertG}$ $root(G) = \{x \mid x \in vertG \wedge \nexists y[y \in edgeG \wedge targetG(y) = x] \wedge$ $\wedge \exists y[y \in edgeG \wedge sourceG(y) = x]\}$
(22) Ring topology	$ring : TypedGraph(VertG \cup VertT, EdgeG \cup EdgeT) \times EdgeT \rightarrow$ $\rightarrow \{True, False\}$ $ring(G, t) = \forall x\,[x \in vertG \rightarrow (x, x) \in tranc(G, t)] \wedge$ $\wedge \forall e, f, x[e \in edgeG \wedge sourceG(e) = x \wedge tG\_E(e) = t \wedge$ $\wedge f \in edgeG \wedge sourceG(f) = x \wedge tG\_E(f) = t \rightarrow e = f] \wedge$ $\wedge \forall x, z\,[x \in vertG \wedge z \in vertG \rightarrow (x, z) \in tranc(G, t)]$
(23) Tree topology	$tree : Graph(VertG, EdgeG) \rightarrow \{True, False\}$ $tree(G) = \exists!x\,[x \in root(G)] \wedge$ $\wedge \forall x\,[x \notin root(G) \rightarrow \exists!y[y \in edgeG \wedge targetG(y) = x]] \wedge$ $\wedge \nexists x, y\,[x \in edgeG \wedge sourceG(x) = y \wedge targetG(x) = y] \wedge$ $\wedge \forall x, y, z, w\,[x \in edgeG \wedge sourceG(x) = y \wedge targetG(x) = z \wedge$ $\wedge w \in edgeG \wedge sourceG(w) = y \wedge targetG(w) = z \rightarrow x = w] \wedge$ $\wedge \forall x, y\,[x \in vertG \wedge y \in root(G) \rightarrow x \in rvert(G, y)]$
(24) Star topology	$star : Graph(VertG, EdgeG) \rightarrow \{True, False\}$ $star(G) = \exists x\,[x \in vertG \wedge \forall y\,[(y \in vertG \wedge y \neq x) \rightarrow$ $\rightarrow (\exists w\,[w \in edgeG \wedge sourceG(w) = x \wedge targetG(w) = y] \wedge$ $\wedge \nexists z\,[z \in vertG \wedge z \neq x \wedge z \neq y \wedge y \in rvert(G, z)])]]$

We define three levels of hierarchy. The first level differentiates properties that express *functional* aspects of the system from properties that specify *structural* characteristics of the states. The functional pattern is divided in the second level according to the kind of information that it describes: the pattern *resources* deal with relations between vertices, edges (that do not describe attributes) and their types; the pattern *data* handle attribute edges. The structural pattern considers the arrangement between vertices and edges: in its second level, the *topology* pattern depicts the physical configuration of the states, determining how the vertices are connected, while the *adjacency* pattern treats the neighboring between vertices, edges and their types. The third level distinguishes, for each specificity, if the properties occur, do not occur or occur for all items of definite characteristics. This level still discriminates properties that deal with cardinality and dependence of specific items. In the following, we briefly describe the formulas of the third level of the taxonomy. Important to notice that each property is always specifying a characteristic that must hold for all reachable states.

Absence: state formulas specifying the non-occurrence of particular characteristics.

Table 3. A Pattern Taxonomy

1. Functional	2. Structural
1.1 Resources	2.1 Topology
1.1.1 Absence	2.1.1 Absence
1.1.2 Existence	2.1.2 Existence
1.1.3 Universality	2.2 Adjacency
1.1.4 Cardinality	2.2.1 Absence
1.1.5 Dependence	2.2.2 Existence
1.2 Data	2.2.3 Universality
1.2.1 Absence	2.2.4 Cardinality
1.2.2 Existence	2.2.5 Dependence
1.2.3 Universality	
1.2.4 Cardinality	
1.2.5 Dependence	

Existence: state formulas specifying the occurrence of particular characteristics.

Universality: state formulas specifying characteristics of all vertices or edges (possibly of some specific type).

Cardinality: state formulas specifying characteristics about the number of vertices or edges (possibly of some specific type).

Dependence: conditional state formulas.

Table 4 depicts the patterns. For Resources, Data and Adjacency, P_A describes the absence pattern, P_E the existential pattern, P_U the universality pattern, P_C the cardinality pattern and P_D the dependence pattern. The set S and the binary relation S' that can appear in atoms definitions $A(y)$ and $A(y_1, y_2)$ is what differentiate the patterns. Table 5 specifies them according to the pattern. Roughly speaking, the functions of the standard library allowed in each pattern are what effectively characterize the requirement. Table 4 also defines the Topology pattern. P_{AT} specifies the absence of topology pattern and P_{ET} the existence of topology pattern.

4.1 Properties Specification for the Mobile System

Considering the mobile system described in subsection 2.2, the pattern system and the standard library previously presented can assist, for example, in the statement of the properties detailed in Table 6. The specification of properties can be done according to the following steps:

SP1 Textual and informal description of the property;

SP2 Identification of the state-graph elements that guarantee the requirement described in step **SP1** and rewrite of the property according to the graph structure;

SP3 Identification of the pattern and the necessary functions in the standard library;

SP4 Formal specification (instantiation) of the property.

These steps will be illustrated by specifying two properties of the mobile system described in Section 2.2.

Table 4. Property Patterns

Property Patterns for Resources, Data and Adjacency

$P_A : \nexists x_1, \ldots, x_n[P(x_1, \ldots, x_n)]$
$\quad\;\; \nexists x_1, \ldots, x_n[P(x_1, \ldots, x_n) \wedge U(x_1, \ldots, x_n)]$

$P_E : \exists x_1, \ldots, x_n[P(x_1, \ldots, x_n)]$
$\quad\;\; \exists x_1, \ldots, x_n[P(x_1, \ldots, x_n) \wedge U(x_1, \ldots, x_n)]$

$P_U : \forall x_1, \ldots, x_n[P(x_1, \ldots, x_n) \to Q(x_1, \ldots, x_n)]$

$P_C : (E \mid card(\{x \mid P(x)\}))\, \alpha\, (E \mid card(\{x \mid P'(x)\})),$ such that
$\quad\;\; \alpha \in \{<, \leq, >, \geq, =, \neq\},$ and
$\quad\;\; E$ is a numeric expression possibly with some free non-negative integer variables or a
$\quad\;\;$ value returned by functions (16) to (19) in $\mathcal{L}$.

$P_D : A(x_1, \ldots, x_n) \to B(x_1, \ldots x_n)$

considering

$P(x_1, \ldots, x_n) := A \mid A \wedge P(x_1, \ldots, x_n) \mid A \vee P(x_1, \ldots, x_n) \mid \neg P(x_1, \ldots, x_n)$
$\quad\quad\quad\quad A := A(y) \mid A(y_1, y_2) \mid R(y_1, y_2)$
$\quad\quad\quad\quad\quad A(y) := y \in S \mid y \notin S$ such that $y \in \{x_1, \ldots, x_n\}$ and S is a set (see Table 5)
$\quad\quad\quad\quad A(y_1, y_2) := y_1 \mapsto y_2 \in S' \mid y_1 \mapsto y_2 \notin S',$ such that $y_1, y_2 \in \{x_1, \ldots, x_n\} \cup C,$
$\quad\quad\quad\quad\quad\quad\quad\quad\quad$ where C is a set of constants and S' is a relation (see Table 5)
$\quad\quad\quad\quad R(y_1, y_2) := E_1\, \alpha\, E_2,$ such that
$\quad\quad\quad\quad\quad\quad\quad\quad\quad \alpha \in \{<, \leq, >, \geq, =, \neq\}$
$\quad\quad\quad\quad\quad\quad\quad\quad\quad E_1, E_2$ are boolean or numeric expressions possibly with some
$\quad\quad\quad\quad\quad\quad\quad\quad\quad$ variables or values returned by functions (14) to (19) in $\mathcal{L}$ or
$\quad\quad\quad\quad\quad\quad\quad\quad\quad$ the result of $card(\{x \mid P(x)\})$

$Q(x_1, \ldots, x_n) := P(x_1, \ldots, x_n) \mid \exists y_1, \ldots y_k.P(y_1 \ldots y_k) \mid \nexists y_1, \ldots y_k.P(y_1 \ldots y_k) \mid$
$\quad\quad\quad\quad\quad\quad \mid U(x_1, \ldots, x_n)$

$U(x_1, \ldots, x_n) := \forall y_1, \ldots, y_n[P(y_1, \ldots, y_n) \to P'(y_1, \ldots, y_n)]$

$A(x_1, \ldots, x_n) := P_A \mid P_E \mid P_U \mid P_C$

$B(x_1, \ldots, x_n) := P_A \mid P_E \mid P_U \mid P_C$

Property Patterns for Topology

$P_{AT} : f(x) \equiv false$ $\quad\quad\quad\quad\quad\quad\quad\quad\quad\quad$ $P_{ET} : f(x) \equiv true$

such that f is one of the functions (22) to (24) in $\mathcal{L}$

Table 5. Specification of S and S' according to the pattern

	S may be...	S' may be...
Resources	$vertG, edgeG$ or the sets returned by functions (1), (2), (4) to (9), (11), (12) or (16) to (19) in $\mathcal{L}$	$tG\_V, tG\_E, sourceG, targetG$ or the set of ordered pairs returned by function (3) in $\mathcal{L}$
Data	$vertG, attrG$ or the set returned by functions (1), (2), (14) in $\mathcal{L}$	$tG\_attr, tG\_Alg, valG, elemG$ or the set of ordered pairs returned by function (15) in $\mathcal{L}$
Adjacency	$vertG, edgeG$ or the sets returned by functions (1), (2), (10) to (13) or (21) in $\mathcal{L}$	$tG\_V, tG\_E, sourceG, targetG$ or the set of ordered pairs returned by function (20) in $\mathcal{L}$

Step SP1. Textual and informal description of the property. This step is accomplished by describing textually the requirements. For instance we want to specify the following requirements: (P1) "Users are always connected to antennas"; and (P2) "There is no antenna with more connections than its capacity".

Step SP2. Identification of the state-graph elements that guarantee the requirement described in step SP1 and rewrite of the property according to the graph structure. In this step we have to identify the elements of graph structure that will guarantee the requirements. In case of property (P1), a user will be connected to an antenna when the vertex of type Usr, which models the user, is source of an edge of type Ucn, which models the connection of a user with an antenna. That is, (P1) must be rewritten as "All vertices of type Usr are source of edges of type Ucn." For (P2), the value of attribute vertices cn and max associated to a vertex of type Ant are what determine, respectively, the number of connections and the capacity of the antenna. Then, it can be rewritten as: "For all vertices of type Ant , the cn attribute is not great than the max attribute".

Step SP3. Identification of the pattern and the necessary functions in the standard library. In case of property (P1), we want to establish a requirement that must be true for all vertices of type Ucn. Functions to be used of $\mathcal{L}$ are functions (2) $tvert$ (which returns vertices of specific type) and (11) $verts$ (which returns vertices that are source of specific edges). Then, the pattern is the universality of resources (1.1.3). In case of property (P2), we want to establish a requirement that must be true for all vertices of type Ant. Functions to be used of $\mathcal{L}$ are functions (2) $tvert$ (which returns vertices of specific type) and (15) $tattrv$ (which returns pairs of vertices and values of specific attributes). Then, in such case, we are in the pattern universality of data (1.2.3).

Step SP4. Formal specification (instantiation) of the property. Both properties fit on the pattern P_U. For (P1) the antecedent $P(x)$ must select vertices of type Usr and the consequent $Q(x)$ must guarantee that they are source of edges of type Ucn. Thus, the instantiated formula must be $\forall x \, [x \in tvert(G, \mathsf{Usr}) \rightarrow x \in verts(G, \mathsf{Ucn})]$. For (P2) the antecedent $P(x)$ must select vertices of type Ant and the consequent $Q(x)$ must guarantee that there is no cn attribute that is great than the max attribute. So, the instantiated formula is $\forall x \, [x \in tvert(G, \mathsf{Ant}) \rightarrow \neg \exists y, z \, [(x,y) \in tattrv(G, \mathsf{max}) \land (x,z) \in tattrv(G, \mathsf{cn}) \land z > y]]$.

Table 6. Properties Specification for the Mobile System

Description	Property	Formula	Pattern
It is always possible to make a call into the network.	There is an edge of type Acn.	$\exists x\ [x \in tedg(G, \mathsf{Acn})]$	1.1.2
Users are always connected to antennas.	All vertices of type Usr are source of edges of type Ucn.	$\forall x\ [x \in tvert(G, \mathsf{Usr}) \to x \in verts(G, \mathsf{Ucn})]$	1.1.3
There are at least two antennas into the network.	The number of vertices of type Ant is great or equal to 2.	$card(\{x \mid x \in tvert(G, \mathsf{Ant})\}) \geq 2$	1.1.4
There is no antenna with more connections than its capacity.	For all vertex of type Ant, the cn attribute is not great than max attribute.	$\forall x\ [x \in tvert(G, \mathsf{Ant}) \to \neg\exists y, z\ [(x, y) \in tattrv(G, \mathsf{max}) \wedge (x, z) \in tattrv(G, \mathsf{cn}) \wedge z > y]]$	1.2.3
There are no disconnected users.	There are no isolated vertices of type Usr.	$\nexists x[x \in ivert(G) \wedge x \in tvert(G, \mathsf{Usr})]$	2.2.1
It is possible to establish a connection between each pair of antennas.	For all pairs of Ant vertices, one is reachable from another.	$\forall x, y[x \in tvert(G, \mathsf{Ant}) \wedge y \in tvert(G, \mathsf{Ant}) \to y \in rvert(G, x)]$	2.2.3

5   Conclusions and Future Work

In this paper we presented the first step towards specification patterns for properties over states in the context of graph grammars. This proposal contains 17 pattern classes in which functional and structural requirements of reachable states can be formulated. We believe that this pattern system provides enough help for the specification of properties over reachable states of graph grammars. Based on the statement of these properties, techniques used to prove over infinite domains such as structural induction can be applied to ensure that a system meets its requirements. Additionally, this work provided a standard library of functions that are commonly needed to state properties over graphs. These functions were used to construct the patterns, and provide flexibility to the proposed approach: other formalisms may use the approach to state properties, what is needed is to identity in these formalisms the graph components used in this library.

Most of the existing pattern systems [14, 10–12] are oriented to classify and express properties over computations of systems. These are typically described using some temporal logics. The focus of our approach has been to describe properties of reachable states of systems, where the description of the state is modeled by a graph. Our intent was to provide the first steps in order to simplify the stating of properties about the structure of states. For this reason, together with the definition of the standard library of functions, the pattern has the purpose of offering several possible direct instantiations of properties over states or simply of guiding the developer of about functions that may be used in the specifications. Although it is possible (to some extent) to encode properties over states in computations and the other way around, we believe that such encodings give rise to non-intuitive and often very complex logical formulas, making the proof process more difficult. We believe that our pattern system complements the existing approaches and provides the first steps in the direction of a pattern for infinite-state verification through graph grammars.

Several directions for future work are possible. We have used event-B and its theorem provers in the Rodin platform [15] to specify the graph grammar systems[9]. Adopting theorem proving, the process of proof is usually semi-automated. Recently, a new tool was integrated in the Rodin platform that allows the creation and use of theories to define data types. Thus, the standard library could be implemented as a *Graph Theory*, together with a set of theorems that could aid the process of proving properties of graph grammars. Moreover, it is possible to define the property patterns together with strategies for proving them, Also, the description of requirements with higher-order logics is a natural extension of the patterns. We should, finally, complement and evaluate our pattern system surveying an appropriate number of case studies.

References

1. Butterfield, A., et al.: Selected papers from the 9th international workshop on formal methods for industrial critical systems. Formal Methods in System Design 30(3) (2007)
2. Craigen, D., Gerhart, S., Ralston, T.: Industrial applications of formal methods to model, design and analyze computer systems. Noyes Publications, Park Ridge (1995)
3. Bowen, J.P., Hinchey, M.G.: Ten commandments of formal methods..ten years later. Computer 39(1), 40–48 (2006)
4. Ng, E.W., Ehrig, H., Rozenberg, G. (eds.): Graph Grammars 1978. LNCS, vol. 73. Springer, Heidelberg (1979)
5. Rozenberg, G. (ed.): Handbook of graph grammars and computing by graph transformation: vol. I. Foundations. World Scientific Publishing Co., River Edge (1997)
6. Ehrig, H., et al. (eds.): Handbook of graph grammars and computing by graph transformation: vol. II: Applicationss. World Scientific Publishing Co., River Edge (1999)
7. da Costa, S.A., Ribeiro, L.: Formal verification of graph grammars using mathematical induction. Electronic Notes Theoretical Computer Science 240, 43–60 (2009)
8. da Costa, S.A., Ribeiro, L.: Verification of graph grammars using a logical approach. Sci. Comput. Program. 77(4), 480–504 (2012)
9. Ribeiro, L., Dotti, F.L., da Costa, S.A., Dillenburg, F.C.: Towards theorem proving graph grammars using event-b. ECEASST 30 (2010)
10. Dwyer, M.B., Avrunin, G.S., Corbett, J.C.: Patterns in property specifications for finite-state verification. In: Proc. of ICSE 1999, pp. 411–420. ACM, New York (1999)
11. Chechik, M., Paun, D.O.: Events in Property Patterns. In: Dams, D.R., Gerth, R., Leue, S., Massink, M. (eds.) SPIN 1999. LNCS, vol. 1680, pp. 154–167. Springer, Heidelberg (1999)
12. Salamah, S., et al.: Verification of automatically generated pattern-based ltl specifications. In: Proc. of HASE 2007, pp. 341–348. IEEE Comp. Soc., Washington (2007)
13. Strecker, M.: Modeling and verifying graph transformations in proof assistants. ENTCS 203(1), 135–148 (2008); Proc of TERMGRAPH 2007
14. Dwyer, M.B., Avrunin, G.S., Corbett, J.C.: Property specification patterns for finite-state verification. In: Proc. of FMSP 1998, pp. 7–15. ACM, New York (1998)
15. DEPLOY: Event-b and the rodin platform (2008), http://www.event-b.org/ (last accessed May 2012); Rodin Development is supported by European Union ICT Projects DEPLOY (2008 to 2012) and RODIN (2004 to 2007)

Compositionality and Refinement in Model-Driven Engineering

Jim Davies, Jeremy Gibbons, David Milward, and James Welch

Department of Computer Science, University of Oxford, Oxford OX1 3QD, UK
{jim.davies,jeremy.gibbons,david.milward,james.welch}@cs.ox.ac.uk

Abstract. Model-driven engineering involves the automatic generation of software artifacts from models of structure and functionality. The use of models as 'source code' has implications for the notions of composition and refinement employed in the modelling language. This paper explores those implications in the context of object-oriented design: establishing a necessary and sufficient condition for a collection of classes to be treated as a component, identifying an appropriate notion of refinement for the generation process, and investigating the applicability of data and process refinement to object models.

Keywords: formal methods, model driven, object orientation, compositionality, refinement, inheritance.

1 Introduction

Compositionality is a fundamental notion in software engineering, and an important property of design methods and modelling languages. A language is compositional for a notion of meaning M when the meaning of a compound expression is determined by the meanings of its components. That is, for every means of composition $\oplus$ in the language, there is a function $f_\oplus$ such that

$$M [\![A \oplus B]\!] = f_\oplus (M [\![A]\!], M [\![B]\!])$$

This is an essential tool for tackling complexity: a system may be designed, implemented, and analysed as a collection of smaller components.

Refinement describes the intended relationship between specification and implementation, or between a given component and a suitable replacement; the intention being that the meaning of the implementation should be consistent with that of the specification. In this context, meaning is often described in terms of the range of possible behaviours or effects, and B is a refinement of A, written $A \sqsubseteq B$, if and only if every behaviour of B is also a behaviour of A: that is

$$A \sqsubseteq B \Leftrightarrow M [\![A]\!] \supseteq M [\![B]\!]$$

Refinement is another essential tool for tackling complexity, allowing the comparison of descriptions at different levels of abstraction, and checking that one component may be safely replaced with another.

R. Gheyi and D. Naumann (Eds.): SBMF 2012, LNCS 7498, pp. 99–114, 2012.

Model-driven engineering is the automatic generation of software artifacts from models of structure and functionality. Where the artifacts in question are at a lower level of abstraction than the models then this may be seen as a process of automatic refinement. The additional information needed is introduced by transformations that provide context or describe implementation strategies within a particular domain. This affords a significant factorisation of effort: the same transformations can be used in the development of many different systems, or many different versions of the same system.

A model-driven approach allows the developer to work at a higher level of abstraction, with concepts and structures that are closer to the users, or the processes, that the software is intended to support. The *model-driven architecture* (MDA) proposed for object-oriented development [1] has been characterised as "using modeling languages as programming languages" [2]. For such an approach to work, the concepts and structures of the modeling language must admit a precise, formal interpretation within the chosen domain, even if this is expressed only in terms of the transformation and the generated code.

A considerable amount of research has been published concerning the formal interpretation of the most widely-used object-oriented modelling language, the Unified Modeling Language (UML). However, code generation from UML models is typically limited to the production of data structures and default, primitive methods for structures such as JavaBeans [3], and the implementation of more complex, user-defined methods remains a manual task—error-prone, and time-consuming. The principal reason for this is the lack of any suitably-abstract means of describing intended behaviour: in most cases, it is easier to express and understand design intentions directly in terms of executable code.

In a sequential context, behaviour can be described in the transformational or state-based style characteristic of formal techniques such as Z [4], and the Refinement Calculus [5], and adopted in more recent developments such as the Object Constraint Language (OCL) [6]. Here, operations are specified in terms of the relationship between the state of the system before and after the operation has been performed, together with the values of any inputs and outputs. The specification is usually given as a pair of constraints: a precondition and a postcondition. The Z notation differs, notably, in regarding the precondition as a derived property, calculated as the domain of the resulting relation.

Where formal techniques are used in the design of novel programs or algorithms, the specifications may describe precisely what is to be achieved, but are unlikely to support the automatic generation of a suitable implementation. Within a specific domain, however, it is entirely possible to establish a useful set of heuristics, transformations, or strategies for translating abstract specifications into program implementations: this is formally-based, model-driven engineering in practice. For the domain of *information systems*, in particular, most postconditions are readily translated into combinations of guarded assignments: for example, the constraint that $a \in S$ could be translated to the action `S.insert(a)`.

In earlier work [7,8], we presented a formal language for the model-driven development of information systems; we have applied this language, and the corresponding model transformation techniques, to the production of several, large systems, including a secure, online patient monitoring system. In the course of this work, it became clear that the original characterisation of the generation process in terms of data refinement, presented in [8], was problematic. It became clear also that a suitable notion of composition was required for models, in order that a large system might be designed and maintained in several parts.

In this paper, we identify a suitable notion of composition for object models in this context. We revisit our characterisation of the generation process, concluding that data refinement is an unrealistic expectation, and arriving at an improved characterisation in terms of trace refinement or partial correctness. We consider the question of when one object model might usefully refine another in this context, and the related question of when a class might usefully be defined as a subclass of another. These points are illustrated using a small example model, and placed in the context of related work.

2 Object Models and Abstract Data Types

In object-oriented programming, a class may be seen as "an implementation of an abstract data type" [9]. In object-oriented modelling, the situation is not so straightforward: the interpretation of a particular class may depend upon information presented elsewhere in the model; consideration of the class declaration itself may not be enough. For example, consider the two classes, described using the notation of UML and OCL, shown in Figure 1. The operation increment on A should increase the value of attribute m by 1; however, its applicability may be constrained by the value of n in any corresponding instance of class B.

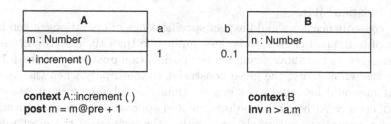

Fig. 1. A constraint between associated classes

A mapping of A and B to separate abstract data types may not admit an adequate interpretation of operation increment. Instead, the operation increment should be considered as an operation on a component whose state encompasses both A and B objects, and this component should be mapped to a single abstract data type, whose state is an indexed collection of A and B objects.

We may use the schema notation of Z [4] to describe the corresponding data type. In this description, the given set I denotes the set of object references, and $[0 . . 1]$ a postfix, generic abbreviation for sets of cardinality at most one—in combination with the unique selection operator μ, a simple way of representing optionality. The state of the data type is described by the schema $System\_State$, in combination with the local schemas A_State and B_State, and the single data type operation by the schema $A\_Increment$.

$$
\begin{array}{|l}
\hline \_A\_State \rule{5em}{0pt} \\
\hline
m : \mathbb{N} \\
b : I[0 . . 1] \\
\hline
\end{array}
\qquad
\begin{array}{|l}
\hline \_B\_State \rule{5em}{0pt} \\
\hline
n : \mathbb{N} \\
a : I \\
\hline
\end{array}
$$

$$
\begin{array}{|l}
\hline \_System\_State \rule{4em}{0pt} \\
\hline
as : I \twoheadrightarrow A\_State \\
bs : I \twoheadrightarrow B\_State \\
\hline
\forall\, b : \operatorname{ran} bs \bullet (as\, b.a).m < b.n \\
\hline
\end{array}
\qquad
\begin{array}{|l}
\hline \_A\_Increment \rule{3em}{0pt} \\
\hline
\Delta System\_State \\
this : I \\
\hline
this \in \operatorname{dom} as \\
(as'\, this).m = (as\, this).m + 1 \\
\hline
\end{array}
$$

In this description, the constraint upon the applicability of the operation is captured implicitly within the global state schema. We could make it explicit by adding the conjunct $(as\, this).b \neq \emptyset \Rightarrow (as\, this).m < (bs\,(\mu\,((as\, this).b))).n$ to the operation schema. The complexity of this conjunct, even in such a simple example, is representative of the difficulty posed by constraints that extend across associations.

Nevertheless, we should expect to find this kind of constraint in object models. For example, the *opposite* property for "mutually-constrained attributes" is part of the core UML language definition; the principal reference texts for OCL, including that for OCL in MDA [6], include many examples of constraints upon attributes of associated classes; and the class-responsibility-collaboration approach developed by Beck and Cunningham [10] insists that "objects do not exist in isolation" [11].

As a consequence, we should expect specifications of operations, given in the context of individual classes, to be less applicable than their precondition part would suggest. In the above example, the specification **post** m = m@pre + 1 does not tell the whole story; the given constraint cannot apply when the resulting value of m would be equal to or greater than the value of n in an associated object of class B. Although the object-oriented approach affords the convenience of defining operations within classes—within the context of the most relevant data, or the most obvious reference point—a complete understanding of the operation may require a consideration of other parts of the model.

It should be clear that the ADT corresponding to the model containing both A and B cannot be derived from the ADTs corresponding to A and B: for our implicit mapping M from models to data types, there is no function $f_\oplus$ such that

$$M(A \oplus B) = f_\oplus(M(A), M(B))$$

where $\oplus$ denotes the combination of class declarations within a model.

Observation 1. *Classes are not necessarily components in the context of model-driven development. In particular, they may not be an appropriate unit of composition for behavioural information.*

3   Model-Driven Development

Where the model is to be used as *source code*, as the basis for the automatic generation of a working system, the specification provided for each operation is *final*: the constraint information provided in the model is all that the compiler has to work with. In particular, then the compiler will need to determine what is to happen if the operation is called in circumstances where the constraint is not applicable: that is, for combinations of state and input values that lie outside the calculated precondition.

If the generated system holds data of any value, then it would not seem sensible to allow an arbitrary update to the state: in the absence of any default action, the effect of calling an operation outside its precondition should leave the state of the system unchanged. Further, if we wish to adopt a compositional approach, in the sense that a composite operation should be inapplicable whenever one or more of its components is inapplicable, then it is not enough for the operation to leave the state unchanged; instead, its inapplicability must be recorded or communicated.

Within the precondition, the specification is applicable, and the intended effect of the operation is known. However, it may be that the compiler does not know how to achieve this effect: that is, part of the constraint information may lie outside the domain of the model transformation rules that are used to generate the implementation. For example, the constraint

$$x = y - 1 \land y = 2x - 3$$

describes a condition achievable by the assignment $x, y := 4, 5$, but it is quite possible that the model transformations used in the compiler do not address the solution of such a system of simultaneous equations.

Where this is the case, then the intended effect of the operation is known, but is not achievable; in the generated implementation, the operation should not be allowed to proceed—unless, of course, the desired condition already holds, in which case the effect can be achieved simply by doing nothing. Again, the inapplicability of the specification should be reflected by the exceptional, or blocking, behaviour of the implementation.

In practice, we are more likely to encounter a constraint that readily admits two or more different implementations, any of which could be easily generated, but for which the intention behind the specification is unclear. That is, although an implementation could be generated that would satisfy the constraint, it seems more likely that the user would prefer to extend or qualify the specification, rather than accept—or be surprised by the behaviour of—the generated implementation.

Consider, for example, the situation illustrated by the class diagram of Figure 2, in which the operation cleanUp has the effect of ensuring that the two associations d1 and d2 are disjoint. If an object d is present in both associations when the operation cleanUp() is called, the intention in the model is unclear: should we remove d from d1 or from d2?

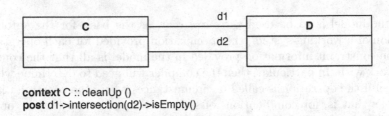

context C :: cleanUp ()
post d1->intersection(d2)->isEmpty()

Fig. 2. A postcondition admitting multiple implementations

While it could be the case that either alternative is equally acceptable, it is more likely that the designer has failed to make their intentions clear. Deleting one of these links may have consequences for other data: it may even be that, to achieve a new state in which the model constraints are satisified, deletions need to be propagated across the whole system. Is this what the designer intends? For information systems, where the data may be of considerable value, it may be better to generate an implementation that blocks when intentions are unclear, instead of making unexpected or unintended modifications.

The nature of refinement associated with code generation for model-driven engineering should now be clear: it is neither failures refinement, where the concurrent availability of interactions is preserved; nor is it data refinement, where sequential availability is preserved. We argue instead that it should be *trace refinement*: if the implementation is able to perform an operation, then its postcondition is achieved; however, it may be that the implementation blocks in some, or even all, circumstances where the precondition applies.

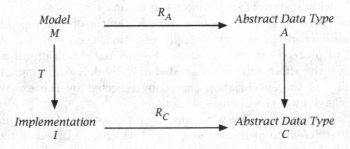

Fig. 3. Abstract data type semantics of model and implementation

To see this, consider the commuting diagram of Figure 3, in which T denotes the code-generating transformation, and A and C denote the representation of the model and the implementation, respectively, as abstract data types. As the model is intended as source code for system generation, it is reasonable to assume that the data model contained within it will be reflected in the implementation, to the extent that data types A and C have equivalent state components and initialisations. It is reasonable to assume also that the model and implementation present the same interface in terms of operation names, inputs, and outputs.

We will write R_A to denote the mapping from a model operation to the corresponding operation on an abstract data type, and R_C to denote a similar mapping for implementation-level operations, then the correctness constraint upon our model transformation is simply that

$$R_C [\![\, T\,(op)\,]\!] \subseteq R_A [\![\, op\,]\!]$$

for every operation op: the transformation should respect the precondition and postcondition, along with any related model constraints. There is no requirement that $\mathrm{dom}\, R_A [\![\, op\,]\!]$ should be contained within $\mathrm{dom}\, R_C [\![\, T\,(op)\,]\!]$, and hence no guarantee that C is a data refinement of A [4,5].

However, if we consider the processes PA and PC, defined using the notation of Communicating Sequential Processes (CSP) as follows:

$$PA(s) =$$
$$\Box\, op : Op \bullet$$
$$s \in \mathrm{dom}\, R_A [\![\, op\,]\!]\ \&\ \underline{op} \to \sqcap s' : R_A [\![\, op\,]\!](\{s\}) \bullet PA(s')$$

$$PC(s) =$$
$$\Box\, op : Op \bullet$$
$$s \in \mathrm{dom}\, R_C [\![\, T(op)\,]\!]\ \&\ \underline{op} \to \sqcap s' : R_C [\![\, T(op)\,]\!](\{s\}) \bullet PC(s')$$

where the event $\underline{op}$ represents a successful, completed execution of the operation op, chosen from the set of all operations Op defined in the model, and $\&$ denotes the guard operator: in the expression $g\ \&\ P$, the actions of process P are available only if g is true. For any code-generating model transformation T satisfying the correctness constraint above, it should be clear that

$$PA(init) \sqsubseteq_T PC(init)$$

where $init$ represents the initial state of the system, and $\sqsubseteq_T$ denotes trace refinement.

Observation 2. *The correctness of a code-generating model transformation may be characterised as trace refinement between specification and implementation: guaranteeing safety, but not liveness.*

4   Model Refinement

In model-driven development, improvements are made to an implementation by updating the model used to generate it. Some updates can be characterised as formal refinements, in the sense that data type corresponding to the new model is a refinement of the data type corresponding to the old. In this case, it would be useful to know whether the old and new implementations are related in the same way: if they are, then any testing, integration, or further development based upon the generated code, rather than the model, need not be repeated. (Of course, we would prefer an approach to development in which any such activity is based solely upon the model, but this is not always possible.)

In a sequential context, the notion of model refinement that we will consider is based upon data refinement of the corresponding abstract data types. A model M_2 will refine another model M_1 precisely when the effect of any sequence of operations upon the corresponding data type A_2, in terms of the possible changes in state and outputs generated, is contained within the effect of the same sequence upon the corresponding data type A_1. The fact that such a refinement relationship exists is shown most often by exhibiting a forward simulation.

If schema s_1 denotes the set of all states—the state space—of data type A_1, s_2 denotes the state space of A_2, and i_1 and i_2 are subsets representing the initial configurations of each data type, then f is a forwards simulation precisely when $i_2 \subseteq i_1 \mathbin{\mathrm{\char59}} f$ and

$$\mathrm{dom}\, R_A \llbracket\, Op_1 \,\rrbracket \lhd (f \mathbin{\mathrm{\char59}} R_A \llbracket\, Op_2 \,\rrbracket) \subseteq R_A \llbracket\, Op_1 \,\rrbracket \mathbin{\mathrm{\char59}} f$$
$$\mathrm{ran}(\mathrm{dom}\, R_A \llbracket\, Op_1 \,\rrbracket \lhd f) \subseteq \mathrm{dom}\, R_A \llbracket\, Op_2 \,\rrbracket$$

for every corresponding pair of operations Op_1 and Op_2, where R_A denotes the relational semantics of the operation at the model level, $\lhd$ denotes domain restriction, and $\mathbin{\mathrm{\char59}}$ denotes forward relational composition. This is the characterisation of [4], with the omission of the identity relation for input and output.

In the case where the two models have precisely the same classes, attributes, associations, and initialisation, this reduces to a constraint upon the updates made to the specification of each operation:

$$\mathrm{dom}\, R_A \llbracket\, Op_1 \,\rrbracket \lhd R_A \llbracket\, Op_2 \,\rrbracket \subseteq R_A \llbracket\, Op_1 \,\rrbracket$$
$$\mathrm{dom}\, R_A \llbracket\, Op_1 \,\rrbracket \subseteq \mathrm{dom}\, R_A \llbracket\, Op_2 \,\rrbracket$$

where Op_2 represents the updated version of Op_1. Thus we may produce a refinement of the model by weakening the precondition of an operation—that is, extending the domain of the corresponding relation—while strengthening the postcondition. To guarantee that the generated implementation is refined in the same way, we need to know also that

$$\mathrm{dom}\, R_C \llbracket\, T(Op_1) \,\rrbracket \lhd R_C \llbracket\, T(Op_2) \,\rrbracket \subseteq R_C \llbracket\, T(Op_1) \,\rrbracket$$
$$\mathrm{dom}\, R_C \llbracket\, T(Op_1) \,\rrbracket \subseteq \mathrm{dom}\, R_C \llbracket\, T(Op_2) \,\rrbracket$$

where R_C denotes the semantics of the operation at the implementation level.

The argument of the previous section tells us that any suitable code-generating model transformation T will guarantee that

$$R_C \llbracket\, T(Op) \,\rrbracket \subseteq R_A \llbracket\, Op \,\rrbracket$$

for any operation Op, but this is not enough. The following monotonicity property of T would suffice:

$$R_A [\![Op]\!] \subseteq R_A [\![Op']\!] \Rightarrow R_C [\![T(Op)]\!] \subseteq R_C [\![T(Op')]\!]$$

for any pair of operations Op and Op'. However, this property is unlikely to hold in practice: it requires that the refinement proposed by the designer is one that is performed automatically in the course of code generation. While this would produce a model in which more of the corresponding implementation is made explicit, it seems unlikely that we would wish to propose such a refinement in the context of model-driven engineering.

To see why, consider the definitions of Op_1 and Op_2 presented as operation schemas upon a state $State \; \widehat{=} \; [x : \mathbb{N}]$, with their implementations $T(Op_1)$ and $T(Op_2)$ written in an extended language of guarded commands. In a data type with state $State$, and attribute x accessible, replacing Op_1 with Op_2 would produce a data refinement.

Op_1
$\Delta State$
$x = 0 \wedge x' \in \{0, 1\}$

Op_2
$\Delta State$
$x = 0 \wedge x' = 1$

$$T(Op_1) \; \widehat{=} \; x = 0 \rightarrow \mathsf{skip} \qquad T(Op_2) \; \widehat{=} \; x = 0 \rightarrow x := 1$$

Here, T represents a plausible implementation strategy. If Op_1 is called when $x = 0$, then the subsequent value of x should be 0 or 1: the implementation $T(Op_1)$ might quite sensibly leave the value of a variable unchanged when the current value would satisfy the postcondition. In the new specification, Op_2, this nondeterminism in Op_1 has been resolved, and $T(Op_2)$ must change the value of x when x is initially zero. The data type corresponding to the second implementation is not a refinement of the one corresponding to the first.

Observation 3. *A model refinement in which postconditions are strengthened may lead to the generation of a system that is different to, and not a refinement of, the current implementation.*

There is however a circumstance in which refinement at the model level can be guaranteed to produce refinement in the implementation: when the domain or precondition of an operation is extended, but the applicable postconditions are left unchanged. Such a circumstance is quite likely to arise in the course of iterative development. Having specified an operation, a designer may find that the specification is less applicable than they had expected: that there are cases that have not been considered. If they then extend the specification to cover these cases, then they might reasonably expect that the behaviour of the implementation would remain the same for those cases already covered: that is, those within the domain of the existing specification.

For this to be the case, the following property must hold of transformation T: for any set of states S,

$$S \lhd R_A [\![Op]\!] = S \lhd R_A [\![Op']\!] \Rightarrow S \lhd R_C [\![T(Op)]\!] = S \lhd R_C [\![T(Op')]\!]$$

That is, if Op and Op' have the same relational semantics for that region of the state space, then so do their respective implementations. For any pair of operations for which the specifications agree within the domain of the first:

$$\operatorname{dom} R_A [\![Op_1]\!] \lhd R_A [\![Op_2]\!] = R_A [\![Op_1]\!]$$
$$[\text{specifications agree where } Op_1 \text{ defined}]$$

$$\Rightarrow \operatorname{dom} R_A [\![Op_1]\!] \lhd R_A [\![Op_2]\!] = \operatorname{dom} R_A [\![Op_1]\!] \lhd R_A [\![Op_1]\!]$$
$$[\text{domain restriction}]$$

$$\Rightarrow \operatorname{dom} R_A [\![Op_1]\!] \lhd R_C [\![T(Op_2)]\!] = \operatorname{dom} R_A [\![Op_1]\!] \lhd R_C [\![T(Op_1)]\!]$$
$$[\text{property above}]$$

$$\Rightarrow \operatorname{dom} R_A [\![Op_1]\!] \lhd R_C [\![T(Op_2)]\!] \subseteq R_C [\![T(Op_1)]\!]$$
$$[\text{domain restriction}]$$

$$\Rightarrow \operatorname{dom} R_C [\![T(Op_1)]\!] \lhd R_C [\![T(Op_2)]\!] \subseteq R_C [\![T(Op_1)]\!]$$
$$[\text{partial correctness of } T, \text{ domain restriction}]$$

The second condition for refinement, that the domain of the operation is preserved, follows from the same condition. The correctness of transformation T guarantees that $\operatorname{dom} R_C [\![T(Op_1)]\!] \subseteq \operatorname{dom} R_A [\![Op_1]\!]$ and hence

$$\operatorname{dom} R_A [\![Op_1]\!] \lhd R_C [\![T(Op_2)]\!] = \operatorname{dom} R_A [\![Op_1]\!] \lhd R_C [\![T(Op_1)]\!]$$
$$[\text{third line of argument above}]$$

$$\Rightarrow \operatorname{dom} R_A [\![Op_1]\!] \lhd R_C [\![T(Op_2)]\!] = R_C [\![T(Op_1)]\!]$$
$$[\text{partial correctness of } T, \text{ domain restriction}]$$

$$\Rightarrow \operatorname{dom}(\operatorname{dom} R_A [\![Op_1]\!] \lhd R_C [\![T(Op_2)]\!]) = \operatorname{dom} R_C [\![T(Op_1)]\!]$$
$$[\text{property of domain operator dom}]$$

$$\Rightarrow \operatorname{dom} R_A [\![Op_1]\!] \cap \operatorname{dom}(R_C [\![T(Op_2)]\!]) = \operatorname{dom} R_C [\![T(Op_1)]\!]$$
$$[\text{domain restriction}]$$

$$\Rightarrow \operatorname{dom} R_C [\![T(Op_1)]\!] \subseteq \operatorname{dom} R_C [\![T(Op_2)]\!]$$

Observation 4. *A model refinement in which preconditions are weakened, but already-applicable postconditions are left unchanged, will produce a corresponding refinement of the implementation.*

The condition that T should produce the same implementation from Op_1 and Op_2, when restricted to the domain of Op_1, can be translated into a constraint upon the interaction of T and the grammar of our modelling language. As we suggested above, the constraints

$$x = 4 \wedge y = 5 \qquad \text{and} \qquad x = y - 1 \wedge y = 2x - 3$$

may produce the same relational semantics, but it may be that only the first of them is successfully translated into an implementation. To guarantee a refinement at the implementation level, we need to know that the constraints of Op_1 and Op_2 will be treated in the same way by transformation T.

In practice, the easiest way to ensure this is to have an operator "or" within the modelling language that corresponds to disjoint union in the relational semantics, and extend the precondition of the specification so that

$$Op_2 \mathrel{\widehat{=}} Op_1 \text{ or } Op_e$$

where Op_e describes the intended behaviour of the operation in circumstances left uncovered by Op_1, so that $\operatorname{dom} R_A [\![Op_1]\!] \cap \operatorname{dom} R_A [\![Op_e]\!] = \emptyset$.

The suitability of a data refinement will depend upon our interpretation of preconditions at the implementation level. In Section 3, we argued that—where data is important—we should interpret preconditions as guards. Weakening a precondition may make an operation available in some circumstance where it is currently blocked, perhaps with good reason. For example, if the precondition for an edit() operation includes the constraint that the current value of user matches the value of owner, then weakening this condition might not constitute an improvement in the design.

The difficulty here is that we are not distinguishing between a constraint that has been included deliberately—and is intended as a restriction upon availability— and one that appears as a consequence of "underspecification". A simple solution is to include a description of the intended availability of an operation, or of a sequence of operations, as part of the model. If we treat this as part of the precondition for the purposes of code generation, then we can guarantee that it will be respected in the implementation. However, as a separate, distinguished part of the specification, it can be excluded from consideration in any subsequent, manual refinements.

The same approach allows us to address the issue of *liveness* in the implementation. Since the correctness of the code generation process is characterised as trace refinement, we have no guarantee that the implementation will do anything at all. If we have an indication A of the intended availability of an operation, or sequence of operations, then we may compare this with the precondition P of the generated implementation: if $A \neq P$, then the operation is less available than A would suggest. As the comparison involves determining the semantic equivalence of two different predicates, we would not in general be able to rely upon fully-automatic verification. However, restrictions upon the form of the specifications, coupled with the expected regularity of preconditions for implementations, should mean that automation is a perfectly feasible proposition.

Observation 5. *In the model-driven engineering of information systems, we can establish "safety properties", or partial correctness, automatically. Liveness or availability properties may require manual intervention, through semi-supervised testing or proof.*

5   Generalisation and Inheritance

In object-oriented design, a distinction is often drawn between *generalisation* and *inheritance*. For example, the UML reference manual [12] states that:

> Generalisation is a taxonomic relationship among elements. It describes what an element is. Inheritance is a mechanism for combining shared incremental descriptions to form a full description of an element. They are not the same thing, although they are closely related.

In this view, *generalisation* is a modelling concept and *inheritance* a programming concept. This begs a question: in the context of model-driven engineering, where we are using a modelling language as a programming language, which of these concepts is applicable?

If we define one class B as a specialisation of another class A—being the inverse of generalisation—then we expect everything that we know about A to remain true of B. Any class invariant should be strengthened, and so too should any operation specifications. This means that an operation specification declared in the context of A may be less applicable when considered in the context of B. As an example, consider the classes shown in Figure 4, where the operation setWidth(w:Number) should have the effect of setting the width of the current figure to w.

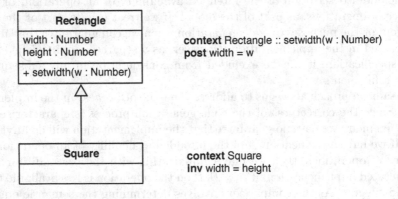

Fig. 4. Square and Rectangle

We would argue that the most appropriate strategy for code generation, in the face of such a specification, is to produce an assignment to the attribute width and—in the context of Rectangle—to leave the value of all other attributes unchanged. Any other approach might come as something of a surprise to the user, and thus reduce the utility of the notation as a programming language. However, when we consider setWidth in the context of Square, we find that it has the implicit precondition w = height.

It should be immediately apparent that we cannot simply use an instance of Square whenever we might have used an instance of Rectangle: a setWidth operation in which the width is set to anything other than the current height would fail for an instance of Square, when it would have succeeded for an instance of Rectangle. Whether this amounts to a violation of the substitivity condition of Liskov and Wing [13]—

Let $P(x)$ be a property provable about objects x of type T. Then $P(y)$ should be true for objects y of type S where S is a subtype of T.

—depends upon the notion of properties involved. Certainly, if setWidth is performed on an instance of Square, then we know at least as much about the states of the object before and after the operation as we would if it had been performed on an instance of Rectangle. However, if we were to consider the availability of the operation as a property of interest, then the condition would indeed be violated.

As was the case with code-generating model transformations, the fact that preconditions are strengthened rather than weakened means that specialisation may not characterised simply as data refinement. Instead, a more appropriate characterisation may be that of trace refinement, under the assumption that no new operations are introduced—or, at least, that no new operations are introduced that may update the state in such a way as to affect the availability or effect of one or more of the existing operations.

Observation 6. *In the context of model-driven development, specialisation need not correspond to subtyping in the programming sense; for transformational specifications, trace refinement may be a more appropriate notion.*

Of course, in the design of an object-oriented program, the relationship of Figure 4 may well have been reversed. The class Rectangle might have been introduced as an extension of Square, with the addition of a distinct *height* property. Consider the two fragments of Java code shown below

```
class Square{                    class Rectangle extends Square{
  float width;                     float height;
  float getArea(){ ... }           float getArea(){ ... }
}                                }
```

Here, Rectangle will inherit the attributes of class Square, and will redefine the method getArea()—to use both width and height. This form of inheritance represents code re-use, and it is certainly possible to exhibit specifications in which Rectangle is a refinement of Square, in terms of corresponding abstract data types. For example, we might imagine a specification for Square.getArea() that stated

```
post (self.oclIsKindOf(Rectangle) and result = width * height)
  or
  (self.oclIsKindOf(Square) and result = width * width)
```

If `Rectangle.getArea()` were assigned the same specification, or merely the first disjunct above, then we could exhibit a forward simulation between the two corresponding data types.

Such specifications might be produced in the course of a post-hoc activity in which existing Java code is annotated with specifications that take account of any inheritance hierarchy. However, in a model-driven context, our purpose in supplying specifications is to enable the generation of an implementation: a suitable specification for `Square.getArea()` would be **post** result = width * width, and one for `Rectangle.getArea()` would be **post** result = width * height. These specifications would not produce a forward simulation, or a data refinement, in the corresponding abstract data types.

Furthermore, in model-driven development the emphasis is upon specification re-use, rather than the specification of code re-use. In this example, the potential for re-use is in the other direction: Square should be seen as a specialisation of Rectangle, inheriting the constraints as additional conjuncts alongside any new specification provided. This will also support the expected refinement relationship—trace refinement—between classes in an inheritance hierarchy.

Observation 7. *In model-driven development, re-use is afforded by specialisation rather than inheritance.*

6   Discussion

In this paper, we have argued that classes are not a suitable basis for behavioural composition in the context of model-driven engineering. For the purposes of code generation, a component is a closed collection of associated classes: *closed* in the sense that every constraint refers only to attributes declared in classes within the collection. This applies whether the component is implemented as a separate system, communicating by means of a messaging protocol, or whether it is used to generate part of the applications programming interface for a larger system.

We have argued also that the notion of correctness associated with code generation, and with specification re-use, should be that of trace refinement. This reflects our understanding that the model transformations used to generate the code may not be able to resolve all of the nondeterminism within the specifications supplied: either because the specification 'problem' cannot be solved, or because it is unclear which of the possible solutions corresponds to the intentions of the designer. Our strategy for the verification of liveness properties is to provide a separate constraint specifying the intended availability of a given operation, or a given sequence of operations. This can be compared with the generated guard or availability constraint in the implementation: if it is stronger, then we may wish to modify the model and repeat the generation process.

Finally, we have argued that refinements to the model need not correspond to refinements of the implementation. We identified a necessary and sufficient condition for this to be the case, but argued that this would be an unrealistic objective in practice. We then identified a necessary condition that would be eminently achievable in the iterative development of operation specifications.

If the existing description is correct, but fails to address all of the relevant combinations of state and input values, then we may extend the specification with an appropriate alternation operator, and repeat the generation process, without the need to repeat any testing or development based on the previous, generated implementation.

The question of whether classes can be treated as components has been addressed before, although not in this context. Most relevant is the work of Szyperski [14], who characterises a *component* as a unit of independent deployment and of composition, with no externally observable state, and an *object* as a unit of instantiation that may have an externally observable state. If we interpret 'observability' as the ability to refer to an attribute in an externally-declared constraint, then his argument that components are collections of classes, rather than individual classes, is in line with that presented in this paper. In the area of formal techniques, Barnett and Naumann [15] come to the same conclusion about association constraints in 'real-life situations', and provide a mechanism for working with collections of 'cooperating classes'.

The formal technique *Object-Z* [16] allows the definition of object references, and constraints can mention attributes of other classes. Such *object coupling* induces additional conditions upon the constraint information in a model in order to achieve individual class refinement [5]: in object-oriented design, as we have argued, these conditions may not be fulfilled. Some authors [17,18] rule out such constraints, insisting that read access to attributes is through accessor methods only, or aligning preconditions of component methods by introducing derived input attributes. A similar approach is taken in *OhCircus* [19]. The result is a semantics that aligns closely with that of CSP: each class is a separate process, with no externally observable state.

CSP-OZ [20] and TCOZ [21], building upon earlier work on action systems [22], allow the definition of a separate guard, as well as a precondition, for each operation. In these methods, the guard and the precondition together define the operation. Our approach is different in that the user-supplied precondition is treated as an upper bound on availability: if it does not hold, then the operation should be blocked. In the code generation process, our preconditions are treated as (partial) guards. There is value in providing a second, separate piece of information, analogous to a guard, that corresponds to a *lower bound* upon the intended availability: a liveness constraint. This could be used as the basis for the generation of a suite of tests, or as a property to be checked using a theorem prover.

Our objective is to add useful, formal support for model-driven, object-oriented development. In doing so, we have identified a need for two different notions of composition: one in which classes are combined to produce a complete description of a sequential component, and one in which sequential components are combined to produce a complete working system. In this paper, we have focussed our attention on the first of these, where the notion of composition is purely static: the behaviours of the sequential component cannot be derived from the behaviours of the individual classes; instead they emerge as the result of the combination of classes and associations.

114   J. Davies et al.

References

1. Kleppe, A., Warmer, J., Bast, W.: MDA Explained, The Model Driven Architecture: Practice and Promise. Addison-Wesley (2003)
2. Frankel, D.: Model Driven Architecture: applying MDA to enterprise computing. OMG Series. Wiley (2003)
3. Matena, V., Stearns, B., Demichiel, L.: Applying Enterprise JavaBeans: Component-Based Development for J2EE. Pearson (2003)
4. Woodcock, J., Davies, J.: Using Z. Prentice Hall (1996), http://www.usingz.com
5. Derrick, J., Boiten, E.: Refinement in Z and Object-Z: foundations and advanced applications. Springer (2001)
6. Warmer, J., Kleppe, A.: The Object Constraint Language: Getting Your Models Ready for MDA. Addison-Wesley (2003)
7. Faitelson, D., Welch, J., Davies, J.: From predicates to programs. In: Proceedings of SBMF 2005, vol. 184 (2007)
8. Davies, J., Faitelson, D., Welch, J.: Domain-specific semantics and data refinement of object models. ENTCS 195 (2008)
9. Meyer, B.: Object-Oriented Software Construction. Prentice Hall (2000)
10. Beck, K., Cunningham, W.: A laboratory for teaching object oriented thinking. SIGPLAN Not. 24(10) (September 1989)
11. Wirfs-Brock, R.: Responsibility-driven design. The Smalltalk Report (1991)
12. Rumbaugh, J., Jacobson, I., Booch, G.: The Unified Modeling Language Reference Manual. Addison-Wesley Professional (2004)
13. Liskov, B., Wing, J.: A behavioral notion of subtyping. ACM Transactions on Programming Languages and Systems 16(6) (1994)
14. Szyperski, C.: Component Software: Beyond Object-Oriented Programming, 2nd edn. Addison-Wesley (2002)
15. Barnett, M., Naumann, D.A.: Friends Need a Bit More: Maintaining Invariants Over Shared State. In: Kozen, D. (ed.) MPC 2004. LNCS, vol. 3125, pp. 54–84. Springer, Heidelberg (2004)
16. Smith, G.: The Object-Z Specification Language. Kluwer (2000)
17. McComb, T., Smith, G.: Compositional Class Refinement in Object-Z. In: Misra, J., Nipkow, T., Sekerinski, E. (eds.) FM 2006. LNCS, vol. 4085, pp. 205–220. Springer, Heidelberg (2006)
18. Smith, G.: A fully abstract semantics of classes for Object-Z. Formal Aspects of Computing 7 (1995)
19. Cavalcanti, A., Sampaio, A., Woodcock, J.: Unifying classes and processes. Software and Systems Modeling 4 (2005)
20. Fischer, C.: How to Combine Z with a Process Algebra. In: Bowen, J.P., Fett, A., Hinchey, M.G. (eds.) ZUM 1998. LNCS, vol. 1493, pp. 5–25. Springer, Heidelberg (1998)
21. Mahony, B., Dong, J.S.: Blending Object-Z and Timed CSP: An introduction to TCOZ. In: Proceedings of ICSE 1998. IEEE Press (1998)
22. Back, R.J.R., von Wright, J.: Trace refinement of action systems. In: Structured Programming. Springer (1994)

Identifying Hardware Failures Systematically

André Didier and Alexandre Mota

Universidade Federal de Pernambuco - Centro de Informática
Av. Jornalista Anibal Fernandes, s/n - Cidade Universitária - Zip 50.740-560
{alrd,acm}@cin.ufpe.br
http://www.cin.ufpe.br

Abstract. Critical control systems can only be used after approval of certification authorities due to safety reasons, among other aspects. Undetected failures in such systems can be catastrophic, including the loss of human lives or huge amounts of money. The safety assessment process aims to minimize such problems. But actually it still is largely dependent on human support (engineer's experience). To decrease this human dependency, we propose a systematic hardware-based failure identification strategy. Following common practices in industry, which use Simulink diagrams to design (critical) control systems, the starting point of our proposed strategy is Simulink diagrams. The systematic identification is performed by the model checker FDR [11]. Therefore, we translate Simulink diagrams into CSP_M specifications [30]. With our strategy, engineers only need to label certain Simulink elements as hardware and choose specific failure names for the generic ones our strategy provides. We illustrate our work on a simple but real case study supplied by our industrial partner EMBRAER.

Keywords: fault injection, failure logic, safety assessment, Simulink, CSP_M.

1   Introduction

The development process of (critical) control systems is based essentially on the rigorous execution of guides and regulations [2,8,9,31]. Moreover, specialized agencies (like FAA, EASA and ANAC in the aviation field) use these guides and regulations to certify such systems.

Control systems are traditionally based on Simulink diagrams [23,26]. These diagrams are models of real systems, aiming at cost reduction by avoiding tests and simulations on real incorrectly designed systems.

Safety is another concern of great importance for these systems and it is the responsibility of the safety assessment process. ARP-4761 [31] defines several techniques to perform safety assessment. One of them is FMEA (Failure Mode and Effects Analysis). It has two categories: functional and piece-part FMEA. IF-FMEA [28] (Interface Focused FMEA) extends the piece-part FMEA to perform compositional analysis. This allows failures modes, annotated on known components, to be used to derive failures on higher layers. These versions of

R. Gheyi and D. Naumann (Eds.): SBMF 2012, LNCS 7498, pp. 115–130, 2012.

FMEA are used to obtain information to perform other analyses—for example, FTA (Fault Tree Analysis) [31]. The table depicted in Figure 1 shows an example of an IF-FMEA table with annotated failure logic[1] in the style of HiP-HOPS [28] (Hierarchically Performed Hazard Origin and Propagation Studies).

Component	Deviation	Port	Annotation	
PowerSource	LowPower	Out1	PowerSourceFailure	
Monitor	LowPower	Out1	(SwitchFailure AND (LowPower-In1 OR LowPower-In2)) OR (LowPower-In1 AND LowPower-In2)	(A)
Reference	OmissionSignal	Out1	ReferenceDeviceFailure OR LowPower-In1	
	CorruptedSignal	Out1	ReferenceDeviceDegradation	

Fig. 1. Annotations table of the *ACS* provided by EMBRAER

The work [24] reports a way of integrating functional verification with safety assessment. Failure logic makes such a connection. But in that work failure logic is provided manually by engineers, as well as in the example shown in Figure 1.

In this work we propose a systematic hardware-based failure identification strategy. We focus on hardware failures because we assume that software does not fail. This is the view of our industrial partner and we agree with it in the sense that the functional behaviour is completely analysed by functional verification [32]. To follow industry common practices, we assume Simulink diagrams as a starting point. But our strategy is stated in terms of the formal language CSP_M [30] (this variant is the machine-readable version of CSP) that allows an automatic analysis by the model checker FDR. Thus, our strategy requires the translation from Simulink to CSP_M [15].

As this work is a result of a partnership with EMBRAER, most terms and artifacts are related to the aviation field. Nevertheless, our strategy applies, in principle, to any critical control system.

Our main contributions in this paper are:

1. Extract failure logic from nominal behaviour of simple components expressed as a Simulink model;
2. Connect functional analysis and safety assessment [24];
3. Improve an existing translation from Simulink to CSP_M [15] to allow fault injection;
4. Apply the strategy to a real case study provided by our industrial partner.

As we will show in this paper our failure logic is at least the same as that stated by highly experienced safety engineers. It can be strengthened based on previous knowledge or testing. We leave this decision to the safety specialist.

This paper is organized as follows: in Section 2 we show the concepts and tools used as basis for our strategy, Section 3 presents our strategy, and Section 4 the case study. In Section 5 we report the related work and present our conclusions and future work in Section 6.

---

[1] Failure logic means failure conditions, expressed as a boolean expression, where each operand expresses the occurrence of a fault on the component, as annotated in the column *Annotation*, in Figure 1.

2   Background

In what follows we present CSP$_M$ in Section 2.1 and Simulink in Section 2.2.

2.1   The CSP$_M$ Language

The CSP$_M$ language combines the concurrent and functional paradigms in a single language. Expressing a complex behaviour requires few lines, unlike other languages even those that support concurrency. In this section we briefly present its notation and operators tailored to this work, as well as the traces refinement theory which is the basis of our strategy.

The supported data types are: integers (32 bits), booleans, sets, sequences, tuples and enumerations. Although CSP$_M$ does not support floating-point numbers, we use data abstraction techniques [6,7,10] to deal with them in terms of integers.

Concerning data structures we have sequences and sets. Sequences use the symbols < and >, and sets the symbols { and }. The language supports set declarations as set comprehension, for example, { (x,y) | x<-X, y<-Y } represents the cartesian product of X and Y. This is similar for sequences.

It is also possible to declare functions, including anonymous ones (*lambda*). For example: \x,...,z @ expr(x,...,z) is a function with parameters (x,...,z), and result given by expr.

The language identifiers are characters with no spaces, with the following naming convention: (i) all in upper case for processes (MONITOR, ACTUATOR), (ii) first letter in upper case for types and type constructors (SwitchValues, RelationalOperatorValues) and all in lower case for functions and channels (input, output_monitor).

It has keywords for declaring types and channels. For types, there are two: nametype (to state an abbreviation) and datatype (for enumerations). For channels and events, CSP$_M$ uses the keyword channel.

A process behaviour is basically described through its *traces*. Traces are defined in [30] as the set of all event sequences that a process can perform. By definition, every process can communicate nothing (thus, the empty trace). The set of possible traces are defined by the use of the process operators. In Table 1 we summarize the meaning of the operators that we use in our work. Other operators are explained deeply in [30]. Just for illustration, the traces of the process P = a -> STOP is the set $\{\langle\rangle, \langle a\rangle\}$, because the process STOP (deadlock) cannot perform any trace.

Model-checking is an exhaustive technique to verify system properties. Traditionally, it uses temporal logic, where $M \models f$ means that the temporal formula f is valid in the model M. For CSP [30], there is an alternative for temporal logic that is based on a refinement theory of processes. CSP uses a technique named *refinement checking*, where $M \models f$ becomes $P_f \sqsubseteq M^2$ such that both P_f and M are CSP processes and P_f is the most non-deterministic process that is known to satisfy f. Refinement checking is supported by the FDR tool [11].

---

[2] In this work we only use traces refinement, defined following.

Table 1. Some CSP$_M$ operators

CSP$_M$ operator	Meaning
P ||| Q	Interleaving. P and Q communicate without any synchronization.
P [] Q	External choice. The environment chooses behaving like P or Q.
P [[b <- a]]	All events b of P are replaced by a.
P [| X |] Q	Sharing in X. The processes synchronize in the events of the set X.
P [X || Y] Q	Alphabetized parallel. The processes synchronize in the intersection of X and Y.
if b then P else Q	If b is true, P is enabled, otherwise, Q.
b & P	Guard. The same as if b then P else STOP.

The traces refinement is the simplest refinement relation. The refinement $P \sqsubseteq_T Q$, written in CSP$_M$ using the statement P [T= Q, is defined as $traces(Q) \subseteq traces(P)$ [30]. This refinement relation is used as the basis of our strategy.

To be exhaustive, model-checking requires the state space to be finite. Data abstraction [7,18] is the most powerful technique to do that. Data abstraction consists of mapping concrete elements (normally infinite) into abstract elements (potentially finite) and proposing new corresponding operations to handle these abstract elements, so that analyses on the abstract model correspond to analyses on the concrete model [5]. When it is possible, data independence [18] can be used, as presented in [6,10], to make data abstraction completely automatic.

2.2   System Modelling and Simulation with Simulink

Control system modelling using Simulink block diagrams is recommended in [26]. We follow this recommendation in this work.

Simulink [23] is a complementary tool of Matlab [22]. In fact, it works as a graphical interface to Matlab. A Simulink model has blocks and connections between these blocks, named signals. Each block has inputs and outputs and an internal behaviour expressed by its mathematical formula, which defines a function of the inputs for each output. There are many predefined blocks in the tool; it is also possible to create new blocks or use subsystems that encapsulate other blocks. A simulation adds extra parameters to a block diagram, like elapsed time and time between states. The elapsed time of a simulation is an abstraction for the quantity of possible simulation states and the time between states is related to the lowest common denominator of the sample time. Some components define different sample times, depending on their mode of operation. Usually, the value for this property is set to *auto*, allowing Simulink to choose a proper value automatically.

Nowadays, control systems are usually composed of an electromechanical part and a processor. Figure 2 shows the components of a feedback system [3] which was provided by EMBRAER. In this system, the feedback behaviour is given by the *Controller* (1), *Actuator* (2) and *Sensor* (3). A command is received by the *Controller*, which sends a signal to the *Actuator* to start its movement. The *Sensor* detects the actual position of the *Actuator* and sends it back to the *Controller*, which adjusts the given command to achieve the desired position. This loop (feedback) continues until the desired position given by the original command is reached.

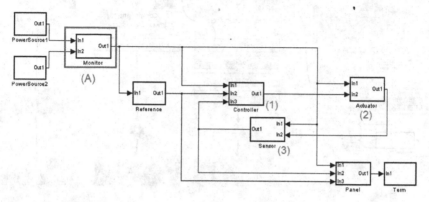

Fig. 2. Block diagram of the *ACS* provided by EMBRAER

Figure 3 shows the internal elements of the monitor component (Figure 2 (A)), which is used as case study in Section 4 to illustrate our strategy. The outputs of the hardware elements are annotated with *HW*, which are the two power sources and an internal component of the monitor (switch command).

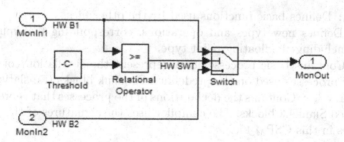

Fig. 3. Internal diagram of the monitor component (Figure 2 (A))

3   Systematic Strategy to Find Failures

In our proposed strategy (Figure 4), the engineer creates a system model in Simulink (A) and annotates the signals that represent hardware component communications (2); this is illustrated in Figure 3. The tool reported in [15] (with the changes we explain in the following subsections) is used to generate a CSP_M specification (B), from such an annotated Simulink diagram. In this work, that

CSP_M specification also includes our strategy files (C) which have a refinement relation verification (CSP_M assert clause). We load this specification in FDR and perform the refinement checks. This gives several counterexamples (D) that represent the failures of the system. From these traces, we extract the failure logic (4) automatically, with a tool that we also created.

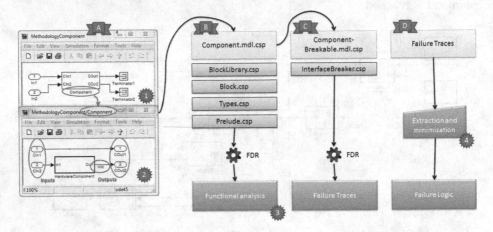

Fig. 4. Overview of the strategy for finding failures in nominal models

3.1 Proposed Changes on the Translation From **Simulink** to CSP_M

The translation strategy from Simulink to CSP_M [15] contains a compiler based on four auxiliary files:

Prelude$_{.csp}$: Defines basic functions used by the other files.

Types$_{.csp}$: Defines new types and operations, corresponding to Simulink elements, including the floating point type.

Block$_{.csp}$: Contains basic processes that represent the simulation control and the base processes used on the predefined Simulink blocks translation.

BlockLibrary$_{.csp}$: Contains the declarations of the processes that represent the predefined Simulink blocks. The compiler uses the signatures of the declared processes in this CSP_M file.

As a result of the translation, each Simulink component is converted into a CSP_M process and the signals are translated into channels. For example, for a block $SIMPLE$ with one input port ($In1$), one output port ($Out1$) and a signal connecting them, the translation yields:

```
TIn1 = { ... }
LO2_SIMPLE =
  let  In1 = B_Inport(1, TIn1)(sig.NO2_SIMPLE.1)(Sampler__CONTINUOUS)
       Out1 = B_Outport(1, TIn1)(sig.NO2_SIMPLE.1)(Sampler__CONTINUOUS)
       CS = {  (In1, {| tick, in.1.xD, sig.NO2_SIMPLE.1.xD | xD<-TIn1 |}),
               (Out1, {| tick, sig.NO2_SIMPLE.1.xD, out.1.xD | xD<-TIn1 |}) }
  within B_Subsystem(CS)
```

The processes In1 and Out1 are put in parallel with the synchronization on the channel (sig.NO2.SIMPLE.1) using the set CS as a parameter of the process B_Subsystem, in a way that the data flow on the channels corresponds to the data flow on the signals. The process B_Subsystem is defined as:

```
B_Subsystem(CS) = || (p,cs): CS @ [ cs ] p \ signals(Union(ran(CS)))
```

where signals is a function to match each sig event to hide the internal communications of the component. Note that the parameter CS is a set of pairs, where each pair (p, cs) is formed by a process (p) and its communicating events as a set (cs). The synchronization sets contain the channels that correspond to the signals that connect the Simulink blocks.

We proposed changes to the compiler to capture the information of which components are annotated as hardware, adding the SW/HW information on the channels, as well as enabling the fault injection on the signals. We also needed to change the files of the translation strategy (Types.$_{csp}$ and Block.$_{csp}$). Finally, the Breaker Process shown in Section 3.2 uses those structures to compare the nominal (without injected faults) and fallible (with injected faults) behaviours through a traces refinement to generate where these behaviours differ, what determines a failure.

One of the proposed changes is the Simulink signal representation in CSP_M. Originally, a signal, which is the connection between blocks, is translated into a CSP_M channel. We propose to represent a signal as two channels and a process: a channel for the connected output port (cout), another channel for the input port of the next component (sig) and a process to connect the values between these channels (Signal or HwSignal). This change is fairly simple and easily automated. It enables fault injection on signals. We present below the process that represents a signal:

```
Signal(o, i, Tin) = tick -> o?v:Tin -> i!v -> Signal(o, i, Tin)
```

This process has three parameters: o corresponds to the output of a component, i the input of another component and Tin the set of values channel o can communicate. These parameters are usually instantiated with channels cout of a component, a sig of a connected component and the type for cout. The behaviour of Signal is simply communicating a tick event, followed by an output communication restricted by Tin (o?v:Tin) and an input (i!v) in an infinite recursion. The tick event is used in the translation strategy [15] to represent time passing on a Simulink simulation. To enable fault injection, we change the behaviour of this process for the hardware signals. Therefore, the process that represents a hardware signal is written as:

```
HwSignal(o, i, Tin) = tick -> o?vo:Tin -> i?vi:Tin -> HwSignal(o, i, Tin)
```

The only difference on the behaviour is the independence of values communicated on the output and input channels. It allows the value received on the following component (input channel) to be different of the value observed on the output channel. Although it is a small change, it is significant for the fault injection to work properly. The Breaker Process controls these values to obtain the nominal behaviour ($vi = vo$) and the fallible behaviour ($vi \neq vo$).

Changes in Block.$_{csp}$. The Breaker Process requires the communication channels of the components to be controlled. To achieve that, we created a different structure for a subsystem: rather than defining a subsystem as a process, we define it as a set of communications (CS). We use this set to initialize a process during the analysis. The original version [15] uses this set to define the final behaviour of the process with a replicated alphabetized parallel operator and hides the internal signals to externalize only the input and output channels of a component. In our strategy, the visibility control is defined by the Breaker Process, which externalizes the internal hardware channels, the inputs and outputs and the faults documentation, when they are present, which are used to extract the failure logic, shown on Section 3.2. The behaviour with the replicated alphabetized parallel operator is kept to correspond to the behaviour in the original strategy.

Thus, the processes of the components under analysis are defined as the internal processes and their signals. If an internal element is also a subsystem, then its internal signals are also externalized to be controlled by the Breaker Process.

Only the behaviour of the component under analysis is changed. It is necessary to keep both behaviours in this layer: the original, as a process, for the other components, and as set, for the components under analysis.

Changes in Types.$_{csp}$. In this layer, the basic types are defined, like integers, booleans, floating-point numbers and vectors. The relational operators (like *greater than*, *less than* and *equals*) and mathematical operations (like *sum*, *division* etc.) are defined for these types.

To detect failures related to signal omission, we perform a lifting by adding a new data type "omission" (OMISSION), which can be communicated in any channel. We changed the comparison functions and the mathematical operators to support this new data type.

Generated CSP$_M$ Specification. To prepare the generated CSP$_M$ specification to run with the Breaker Process, we need to do the following:

1. Add the signal omission on the types of the input channels;
2. Replace `Signal` processes by `HwSignal` processes for components annotated as hardware;
3. Change the behaviour of the component under analysis from process to a set. The internal elements which are subsystems also need to be converted from process to a set.

By applying our adjustments to the translation from Simulink to CSP$_M$, the *SIMPLE* process becomes:

```
TIn1 = { OMISSION, ... }
LO2_SIMPLE =
   let  In1 = B_Inport(1, TIn1)(cout.SW.NO2_SIMPLE.1)(Sampler__CONTINUOUS)
        Sig_NO2_SIMPLE = Signal(cout.SW.NO2_SIMPLE.1,
                              sig.SW.NO2_SIMPLE.1, TIn1)
        Out1 = B_Outport(1, TIn1)(sig.SW.NO2_SIMPLE.1)(Sampler__CONTINUOUS)
        CS = { (In1, {| tick, in.1.xD, sig.SW.NO2_SIMPLE.1.xD | xD<-TIn1 |}),
               (Sig_NO2_SIMPLE,  {| tick, cout.SW.NO2_SIMPLE.1.xD,
                              sig.SW.NO2_SIMPLE.1.xD | xD<-TIn1 |}),
               (Out1, {| tick, sig.SW.NO2_SIMPLE.1.xD | out.1.xD | xD<-TIn1 |}) }
   within CS
```

If the connecting signal (sig.SW.NO2_SIMPLE.1) was annotated as hardware in the Simulink model, then we should use HwSignal instead of Signal to declare the process Sig_NO2_SIMPLE.

3.2 Breaker Process

The Breaker Process aims at: (i) controlling the fault injection on the components and (ii) documenting the counterexample traces with enough information to assemble the failure logic. The infrastructure of this process is composed of:

1. A generic process named ComponentBehaviour, parametrized by (i) the set of pairs of processes and theirs communications[3], (ii) the function that handles the hardware channels' behaviour and (iii) the function that documents the failures:

```
ComponentBehaviour(CS, fFailure, fDoc) =
   let
      Component = B_Diagram(CS)
      (...)
      SignalsSync = Union({ ComponentInputs, ComponentOutputs, HwOutputs, HwInputs })
      HiddenSignals = Union({ HwInputs, HwOutputs, SwSignals, FEvaluations, {tick} })
      (...)
      SignalsBehaviour = ... -- it uses fFailure and fDoc
   within (Component [|SignalsSync|] SignalsBehaviour) \ HiddenSignals
```

where B_Diagram(CS) = || (p,cs): CS @ [cs] p (replicated alphabetized parallel).

2. Two instances of ComponentBehaviour, one representing nominal behaviour (Nominal) and another for fallible behaviour (Breakable):

```
Nominal(CS) =
   ComponentBehaviour(CS,
      \ v, vs @ {v},              -- fFailure
      \ vi, vs @ vs)              -- fDoc

Breakable(CS) =
   ComponentBehaviour(CS,
      \ v, vs @ diff(vs, {v}), -- fFailure
      \ vi, vs @ {vi})            -- fDoc
```

---

[3] It is the set CS, which is used on the alphabetized parallel operator to put all internal elements in parallel.

where the function `fFailure` of the nominal behaviour enables only the communication of the event `v`, returning the set `{v}` and, in the failure behaviour, all, except `v` (`diff(vs, {v})`). The function `fDoc`, enables the documentation of any fault in the nominal behaviour, returning the set `vs` and, for the fallible behaviour, enables only the fault event, through the set `{vi}`.

3. Documentation channels, named `failure.Hardware` with extra parameters to identify faulty channels.

The main idea behind the Breaker Process is to add documentation channels of the faults and to control the communication of the signal values. The nominal behaviour allows the documentation of any faults, but limits the behaviour of the hardware channels to the nominal behaviour. On the other hand, the fallible behaviour allows the communication of any value except the nominal value on the hardware channels and its corresponding fault is documented on the special channel (`failure`). The original translation from Simulink to CSP_M [15] exposes the inputs and outputs of the component under analysis through the channels `in` and `out`. Our strategy compares these channels in the nominal and fallible behaviour in a way that, if, for the same values on the input channels, the output channels have different values of the the nominal behaviour, the generated trace is a failure trace. FDR generates the counterexamples by processing the following assertion:

```
assert Nominal(CS_COMPONENT) [T= Breakable(CS_COMPONENT)
```

where `CS_COMPONENT` is the set of pairs of type (`p`, `cs`), such that `p` is a process of an internal element of the component and `cs` is the communications set of the internal element, as shown in Section 3.1. Always a component has at least one hardware element, FDR will generate counterexamples, where each one is a failure condition in terms of individual hardware component faults. For the `LO2_SIMPLE` process, this command is written as:

```
assert Nominal(LO2_SIMPLE) [T= Breakable(LO2_SIMPLE)
```

To be able to obtain any amount of counterexamples we use FDR in batch mode[4]. For instance,

```
fdr2 batch -max <K> -trace <file.csp>
```

instructs FDR to find at most K counterexamples. As the number of counterexamples can be large in some situations, we created a tool that extracts the combinations of fault occurrences automatically.

To create the failure logic, we see each trace as a conjunction where events become propositions. After converting each trace into a conjunction, we combine them into a big disjunction. If needed we can simplify this disjunction using tool support [33]. This will be illustrated in more detail in the next section.

---

[4] The FDR GUI is preconfigured to report at most 100 counterexamples.

4   Case Study

EMBRAER provided us with the Simulink model of an Actuator Control System (depicted in Figure 2). The failure logic of this system (that is, for each of its constituent components) was also provided by EMBRAER (Figure 1). In what follows we illustrate our strategy using only the Monitor component (A) to save space.

The monitor component is a system commonly used for fault tolerance [27,17]. Initially, the monitor connects the main input (power source on input port 1) with its output. It observes the value of this input port and compares it to a threshold. If the value is below the threshold, the monitor disconnects the output from the main input and connects to the secondary input. We present the Simulink model for this monitor in Figure 3.

We translated the monitor to CSP_M according to the changes presented in Section 3. We present part of the generated code in what follows (we omit some parts to save space[5]):

```
B_LO2_S_Monitor(threshold) =
let
  MonIn1 = B_Inport(1, Tbattery1)(cout.HW.NO4_MonIn1.1)(...)
  Sig_NO4_MonIn1_1 = HwSignal(cout.HW.NO4_MonIn1.1, sig.HW.NO4_MonIn1.1, Tbattery1)
  (...)
  RelOperator = B_GTE(<Tbattery1,Tthreshold>)(...)
    [[ in.1.x1 <- sig.HW.NO4_MonIn1.1.x1, in.2.x2 <- sig.SW.NO4_Threshold.1.x2,
       out.1.xB <- cout.HW.NO4_RelOperator.1.xB
       | x1<-Tbattery1, x2<-Tthreshold, xB<-Tboolean ]]
  (...)
CS = {
  (MonIn1, {| tick, in.1.xI, cout.HW.NO4_MonIn1.1.xI | xI<-Tbattery1 |}),
  (Sig_NO4_MonIn1_1, {| tick, cout.HW.NO4_MonIn1.1.xI, sig.HW.NO4_MonIn1.1.xI
                      | xI<-Tbattery1 |}),
  (...)
  (RelOperator,
     {| tick, sig.HW.NO4_MonIn1.1.x1, sig.SW.NO4_Threshold.1.x2,
        cout.HW.NO4_RelOperator.1.xB | x1<-Tbattery1, x2<-Tthreshold, xB<-Tboolean |}),
  (...) }
within CS
```

We then execute the following assertion:

```
assert Nominal(LO2_S_Monitor(I.3)) [T= Breakable(LO2_S_Monitor(I.3))
```

in FDR, obtaining the following traces:

```
--TRACE 1:
in.1.I.5
failure.Hardware.NO4_RelOperator.1.EXP.B.true
failure.Hardware.NO4_RelOperator.1.ACT.B.false
in.2.I.5
failure.Hardware.NO4_MonIn2.1.EXP.I.5
failure.Hardware.NO4_MonIn2.1.ACT.OMISSION
out.1.OMISSION

-- TRACE 2:
in.1.I.5
```

```
failure.Hardware.NO4_MonIn1.1.EXP.I.5
failure.Hardware.NO4_MonIn1.1.ACT.OMISSION
in.2.I.5
failure.Hardware.NO4_MonIn2.1.EXP.I.5
failure.Hardware.NO4_MonIn2.1.ACT.OMISSION
out.1.OMISSION

-- TRACE 3:
in.1.I.5
failure.Hardware.NO4_MonIn1.1.EXP.I.5
```

---

[5] The complete specification can be downloaded from
   http://www.cin.ufpe.br/~alrd/2012SBMF/2012SBMF.zip. Unzip and open the file
   "Monitor-InterfaceBreaker.mdl.csp" in FDR.

```
failure.Hardware.N04_MonIn1.1.ACT.OMISSION      failure.Hardware.N04_MonIn1.1.EXP.I.5
in.2.I.5                                        failure.Hardware.N04_MonIn1.1.ACT.OMISSION
failure.Hardware.N04_RelOperator.1.EXP.B.false  failure.Hardware.N04_RelOperator.1.EXP.B.false
failure.Hardware.N04_RelOperator.1.ACT.B.true   failure.Hardware.N04_RelOperator.1.ACT.B.true
out.1.OMISSION                                  in.2.I.5
                                                failure.Hardware.N04_MonIn2.1.EXP.I.5
-- TRACE 4:                                      failure.Hardware.N04_MonIn2.1.ACT.OMISSION
in.1.I.5                                        out.1.OMISSION
```

To briefly understand which fault information each trace carries with it, consider the first trace (**TRACE 1**). This trace presents two faults: the expected value (labelled **EXP**) on the relational operator control input (**N04_RelOperator**) is **true**, but the actual observed value is **false** (labelled **ACT**). On the second input port (**N04_MonIn2**), the value 5 is expected, but the signal omission (**OMISSION**) was observed. Thus, the failure condition this trace captures is: **N04_RelOperator** AND **N04_MonIn2**.

By applying our strategy to all traces found and taking their disjunction, we obtain the following failure logic:

```
(RelOperator.1 AND MonIn2.1) OR (MonIn1.1 AND MonIn2.1) OR
(MonIn1.1 AND RelOperator.1) OR (MonIn1.1 AND RelOperator.1 AND MonIn2.1)
```

which can be simplified to:

```
(RelOperator.1 AND (MonIn1.1 OR MonIn2.1)) OR (MonIn1.1 AND MonIn2.1)
```

This is exactly (except for naming conventions) the failure logic provided by EMBRAER (Figure 1 (A)), written manually by safety engineers.

We also applied our strategy to the actuator component (Figure 2), where FDR found 8.820 counterexamples. After this exercise, due to the large number of traces, we realised the need to develop a tool to extract the failure logic automatically. We implemented such a tool. As result, we extracted a failure logic weaker (that is, our logic considers more cases) than the one provided by the EMBRAER engineers. We leave the decision on eventually discarding certain parts of this logic to the safety specialists. It is worth noting that our failure logic is at least the same as that stated by highly experienced safety engineers.

Another noteworthy aspect of our strategy is that because it is component-wise and the component's behaviour is in general relatively simple, our strategy does not suffer from the state explosion problem. If the component's behaviour is in fact more complex, we can use our strategy to lower level components and then use HiP-HOPS to derive the failure logic of the higher level component.

5   Related Work

The work reported in [20] presents a similar strategy, but it uses tables to create fault trees. Rather than using tables, we capture the nominal behaviour from the Simulink block diagrams [23,15,28] and use an existing technique to perform safety assessment [12].

The search for failures in systems by fault injection is a technique that has been used both directly in hardware [32,25] (with patents [14,21]) or in models [16,1,34,19]. In real components it is expensive, because, generally, it requires the damage of these components to observe their fallible behaviour.

The work reported in [34] presents a strategy for fault injection in a Simulink model similar to ours. They provide values for all input signals (*stimuli* file). Furthermore, it is possible to select failure modes for each input port using the tool they created. In our work, it is not necessary to provide possible input values, nor the failure modes: we instruct FDR to search for these fault values. Another similarity with our work is the comparison of the failure behaviour against the nominal behaviour, which in [34] is called "the golden run".

The work reported in [19] presents a strategy to generate fault trees automatically from annotated nominal behaviour. The final goal of our work is also the generation of fault trees, as reported in [12]. The difference to this work is that we do not need to annotate nominal behaviour because it is extracted directly from the Simulink model.

6 Conclusion

In our work we presented a systematic strategy to obtain failure logic from a nominal model. This failure logic is essential for system safety assessment [28,15,12]. We use Simulink as starting point because it is a standard tool in the control systems industry. Furthermore, our work connects the strategy presented in [24] with the works reported in [15] (functional analysis) and in [12,28] (safety assessment) through the failure conditions found by our strategy.

Our strategy is based on exhaustive search (model checking) to find failures. To handle large finite sets or infinite sets specifications, we consider data abstraction [10,6]. Due to the exhaustive aspect, we can find failures that are even unlikely to occur in a statistical sense (its probability of occurrence can be negligible in practice). Therefore, our strategy is particularly suitable for new systems, where there is no historical records to be used by safety engineers. Our strategy finds all possible (untimed) failures and we leave to engineers the decision on whether such and such failure must be considered or not.

Another contribution of our work is that we have improved the translation strategy reported in [15]. We identified some missing Simulink blocks, which had not their behaviour declared in the layer BlockLibrary.$_{csp}$. We implemented functions for floating-point number calculations (which is not directly supported by FDR) in terms of integers that were not completely implemented in [15].

A limitation of our work is that we cannot detect time related failures, like too early or too late failures [4,13]. In principle, we could follow two approaches to solve this: the first is to extract the discrete time passing information, already present in [15], to represent them in the counterexample traces. The second is to represent the time in a continuous domain and use timed-CSP [29]. The drawback with this second way is that we need to use a theorem prover instead of a model checker and thus we will not have counterexamples to create the failure logic. This is a topic for future research.

Another future work we intend to do is to implement our strategy completely. Currently our implementation is limited to extract the failure logic from the counterexamples found. The connection with [15] and [12] is through the failure logic in the form of boolean expressions. We intend to make this connection through a tool.

Instead of changing the translation strategy reported in [15], maybe it would be easier to apply refactoring rules on the Simulink diagrams. Such a transformation would add new blocks for each signal. By applying [15] as originally proposed, without changing it, maybe the resulting CSP_M specification is equivalent to the one presented here with less effort. We need to investigate this issue as well.

We plan to apply our strategy in the COMPASS[6] project which is related to SoS (Systems of Systems). We may adapt our strategy to SysML (Systems Modelling Language), which uses diagrams and is semi-formal, and CML (COMPASS Modelling Language), the underlying formal language specific to SoS, based on CSP_M and VDM (Vienna Development Method).

Acknowledgements. We would like to thank **Felipe Ferri** and **Edson Wanatabe** from EMBRAER for providing us with the case study. We also thank **Adriano Gomes**, **Joabe Jesus Jr.** and the anonymous referees of **SBMF 2012** for comments in drafts of this work. This work was partially supported by the National Institute of Science and Technology for Software Engineering (INES[7]), funded by CNPq and FACEPE, grants 573964/2008-4 and APQ-1037-1.03/08, by CNPq grant 476821/2011-8 and by the Brazilian Space Agency (UNIESPAÇO 2009).

References

1. Akerlund, O., Bieber, P., Boede, E., Bozzano, M., Bretschneider, M., Castel, C., Cavallo, A., Cifaldi, M., Gauthier, J., Griffault, A., Lisagor, O., Luedtke, A., Metge, S., Papadopoulos, C., Peikenkamp, T., Sagaspe, L., Seguin, C., Trivedi, H., Valacca, L.: ISAAC, a framework for integrated safety analysis of functional, geometrical and human aspects. In: 3rd Embedded Real Time Software, Toulouse, France (January 2006)
2. ANAC: Aeronautical product certification. DOU N⁰ 230, Seção 1, p. 28, (December 01, 2011) (November 2011), http://www2.anac.gov.br/biblioteca/resolucao/2011/RBAC21EMD01.pdf
3. Astrom, K.J., Murray, R.M.: Feedback Systems: An Introduction for Scientists and Engineers. Princeton University Press, Princeton (2008)
4. Bondavalli, A., Simoncini, L.: Failure classification with respect to detection. In: Second IEEE Workshop on Future Trends of Distributed Computing Systems, pp. 47–53 (October 1990)
5. Cousot, P.: Abstract interpretation. ACM Comput. Surv. 28, 324–328 (1996)

---

[6] Comprehensive Modelling for Advanced Systems of Systems,
http://www.compass-research.eu
[7] http://www.ines.org.br

6. Damasceno, A., Farias, A., Mota, A.: A Mechanized Strategy for Safe Abstraction of CSP Specifications. In: Oliveira, M.V.M., Woodcock, J. (eds.) SBMF 2009. LNCS, vol. 5902, pp. 118–133. Springer, Heidelberg (2009)
7. Derrick, J., Wehrheim, H.: On using data abstractions for model checking refinements. Acta Informatica 44, 41–71 (2007)
8. FAA: RTCA, Inc., Document RTCA/DO-178B. U.S. Dept. of Transportation, Federal Aviation Administration, Washington, D.C. (1993)
9. FAA: Part 25 - airworthiness standards: Transport category airplanes. Tech. rep., Federal Aviation Administration (FAA), USA (2007)
10. Farias, A., Mota, A.C., Sampaio, A.: Compositional Abstraction of CSPZ Processes. J. Braz. Comp. Soc. 14(2), 23–44 (2008)
11. FSEL: FDR2 User Manual, version 2.91. Formal Systems (Europe) Ltd. (2010), http://fsel.com/fdr2_manual.html
12. Gomes, A., Mota, A., Sampaio, A., Ferri, F., Buzzi, J.: Systematic Model-Based Safety Assessment Via Probabilistic Model Checking. In: Margaria, T., Steffen, B. (eds.) ISoLA 2010, Part I. LNCS, vol. 6415, pp. 625–639. Springer, Heidelberg (2010)
13. Grunske, L., Winter, K., Yatapanage, N., Zafar, S., Lindsay, P.A.: Experience with fault injection experiments for FMEA. Software: Practice and Experience 41(11), 1233–1258 (2011)
14. Hamlin, J.W., Logan, B.C., Richards, W.A., Sanders, M.T., Wyckoff, R.C.: Automatic fault insertion system (AFIS). US Patent 4835459 (May 1989)
15. Jesus, J., Mota, A., Sampaio, A., Grijo, L.: Architectural Verification of Control Systems Using CSP. In: Qin, S., Qiu, Z. (eds.) ICFEM 2011. LNCS, vol. 6991, pp. 323–339. Springer, Heidelberg (2011)
16. Joshi, A., Heimdahl, M.P.E.: Model-Based Safety Analysis of Simulink Models Using SCADE Design Verifier. In: Winther, R., Gran, B.A., Dahll, G. (eds.) SAFECOMP 2005. LNCS, vol. 3688, pp. 122–135. Springer, Heidelberg (2005)
17. Koren, I., Krishna, C.M.: Fault Tolerant Systems. Morgan Kaufmann Publishers Inc., San Francisco (2007)
18. Lazić, R.: A Semantic Study of Data Independency with Applications to Model Checking. Master's thesis, Oxford University (1999)
19. Mader, R., Armengaud, E., Leitner, A., Kreiner, C., Bourrouilh, Q., Grießnig, G., Steger, C., Weiß, R.: Computer-Aided PHA, FTA and FMEA for Automotive Embedded Systems. In: Flammini, F., Bologna, S., Vittorini, V. (eds.) SAFECOMP 2011. LNCS, vol. 6894, pp. 113–127. Springer, Heidelberg (2011)
20. Majdara, A., Wakabayashi, T.: Component-based modeling of systems for automated fault tree generation. Reliability Engineering and System Safety 94(6), 1076–1086 (2009)
21. Mathewes Jr., J.K., Chancellor, C.A., Howes, H.F.: Transient and intermittent fault insertion. US Patent 4875209 (October 1989)
22. MathWorks: Matlab® (2010), http://www.mathworks.com/products/matlab
23. MathWorks: Simulink® (2010), http://www.mathworks.com/products/simulink
24. Mota, A., Jesus, J., Gomes, A., Ferri, F., Watanabe, E.: Evolving a Safe System Design Iteratively. In: Schoitsch, E. (ed.) SAFECOMP 2010. LNCS, vol. 6351, pp. 361–374. Springer, Heidelberg (2010)
25. Nadeau-Dostie, B., Hulvershorn, H., Adham, S.M.I.: A new hardware fault insertion scheme for system diagnostics verification. In: International Test Conference, pp. 994–1002 (October 1995)
26. Nise, N.S.: Control systems engineering. Benjamin-Cummings Publishing Co., Inc., Redwood City (1992)

27. O'Connor, P., Newton, D., Bromley, R.: Practical reliability engineering. Wiley (2002)
28. Papadopoulos, Y., McDermid, J., Sasse, R., Heiner, G.: Analysis and synthesis of the behaviour of complex programmable electronic systems in conditions of failure. Reliability Engineering & System Safety 71(3), 229–247 (2001)
29. Reed, G.M., Roscoe, A.W.: A timed model for communicating sequential processes. Theor. Comput. Sci. 58, 249–261 (1988)
30. Roscoe, A.W.: The Theory and Practice of Concurrency. Prentice Hall PTR, Upper Saddle River (1997)
31. SAE: SAE ARP4761 Guidelines and Methods for Conducting the Safety Assessment Process on Civil Airborne Systems and Equipment (1996)
32. Snooke, N., Price, C.: Model-driven automated software FMEA. In: Reliability and Maintainability Symposium, pp. 1–6 (January 2011)
33. Sontrak: Logic Friday, http://www.sontrak.com
34. Svenningsson, R., Vinter, J., Eriksson, H., Törngren, M.: MODIFI: A MODel-Implemented Fault Injection Tool. In: Schoitsch, E. (ed.) SAFECOMP 2010. LNCS, vol. 6351, pp. 210–222. Springer, Heidelberg (2010)

Investigating Time Properties
of Interrupt-Driven Programs

Yanhong Huang[1], Yongxin Zhao[1], Jianqi Shi[1],
Huibiao Zhu[1], and Shengchao Qin[2]

[1] Shanghai Key Laboratory of Trustworthy Computing
East China Normal University, Shanghai, P.R. China
{yhhuang,yxzhao,jqshi,hbzhu}@sei.ecnu.edu.cn
[2] School of Computing, Teesside University
S.Qin@tees.ac.uk

Abstract. In design of dependable software for real-time embedded systems, time analysis is an important but challenging problem due in part to the randomicity and nondeterminism of interrupt handling behaviors. Time properties are generally determined by the behavior of the main program and the interrupt handling programs. In this paper, we present a small but expressive language for interrupt-driven programs and propose a timed operational semantics for it which can be used to explore various time properties. A number of algebraic laws for the computation properties that underlie the language are established on top of the proposed operational semantics. We depict a number of important time properties and illustrate them using the operational semantics via a small case study.

Keywords: time, interrupt, operational semantics.

1 Introduction

With the rapid development of the computer industry, multitudinous operating systems spring up in the past forty years. An operating system (OS), as a particular software running on computers, not only manages the computer hardware, but also provides the common platform for efficient execution of various application software. It acts as a bridge between the computer hardware and application programs. A real-time OS is a multitasking OS that aims at executing real-time applications. This kind of OS involves both logical correctness and timeliness. Usually the interrupt mechanism is introduced as a technique to support multi-threads, device drivers and OS in real-time computing, which enables OS to handle time-sharing tasks and concurrency.

An interrupt-driven system indicates that the OS can schedule the tasks' execution and perform reasonable allocation of time and other resources in the form of hardware interrupt or software interrupt. The interrupts are usually implemented in terms of asynchronous signals and synchronous events. The generation of interrupt requests (signals/events) is usually random and nondeterministic,

R. Gheyi and D. Naumann (Eds.): SBMF 2012, LNCS 7498, pp. 131–146, 2012.

which make interrupt behaviors extremely difficult to reason about in the development of OS.

The analysis and verification of interrupt therefore becomes the focus of attention in both industry and academia. There have been proposals suggesting that interrupts can be regarded as threads and may be verified like threads using some similar verification methods [2–5]. Some researchers have attempted to apply different formal methods to the interrupt programs [6–8]. In an earlier work, we have developed a formal model of interrupt programs from a probabilistic perspective, designed the probabilistic operational semantics for interrupt program to capture the potential properties, and specified the time constraint of interrupt programs [1].

Most real-time operating systems require responsive interrupt handling to meet the real-time requirements. As this kind of OS has been widely used in our society, the correctness of timing behavior in this kind of OS becomes increasingly important. There has been work reported on analyzing the time properties of interrupt-driven programs. Jens Palsberg et al. have performed a series of studies on interrupt-driven Z86-based software. They have developed a tool to analyze interrupt latencies, stack sizes, deadline as well as verified fundamental safety and liveness properties [9–12]. John Regehra has proposed a set of design rules for interrupts in real-time and embedded software, where he believes it is necessary to consider the stack overflow, interrupt overload and real-time analysis problems [13].

There has also been work reported to improve the performance of the interrupt mechanism, in order to make real-time embedded operating systems to provide correct and timely services in the presence of constrained resources. Eleidermacher suggests that the most important characteristic that makes an operating system a real-time system is the ability to handle interrupts quickly. He proposes a few rules to minimize interrupt response time in worst case [14]. Jinkyu et al. [15] suggest a novel scheme to minimize the performance degradation in embedded operating systems with real-time support, where they present transparent and selective real-time interrupt services which transparently monitor the system and postpone interrupt handling that are not relevant to real-time tasks.

With the development of various formal methods and emergence of the corresponding tools, such as automata theory, B method, Z notation, CSP, VDM, etc., formal methods can be applied with the assistance of automated and human-assisted tools. This makes the analysis and verification of programs more and more viable. In this paper, we develop a formal model of interrupt-driven programs from a timing perspective, in order to analyze time properties during the development of such programs. We propose an interrupt-driven programming language and define a timed operational semantics for interrupt-driven programs written in this language and explore various time properties using the semantics. The main contributions of our work includes:

- **Interrupt-driven Programs.** We present a language of the interrupt-driven programs including some interrupt operators like enable/disable/set. In our model, the system can enable or disable interrupts to decide whether the system should enable/disable the interrupt mechanism which is to interact with the environment via interrupt handling. Moreover, the system can request any interrupt itself by setting a interrupt signal which help the system schedules multiple tasks.

- **Timed Operational Semantics.** Time is introduced into operational semantics to specify the meanings of the interrupt-driven programs. We provide two ways to handle the interrupt requests. One is an ordinary way that the received interrupt requests are always handled, and the other is a safe way that the system may ignore some interrupts so as to make sure that the program always meet the deadline. Meanwhile, the algebraic laws [16] that underlie the language are established in terms of the suggested operational semantics.

- **Time Properties.** We depict a number of important time properties which are essential to the real-time embedded operating systems in our framework: interrupt response time, interrupt activated time, interrupt overload and deadline. The analysis of four properties will help the analysis of the real-time embedded OS. Based on these, we give an example to present the feasibility and effectiveness of our approach.

The remainder of the paper is organized as follows: Section 2 introduces the interrupt handling mechanism which we discuss about in this paper and provides an approach to describing the program's operating environment. Section 3 defines the language which has two parts, i.e., the main program and the interrupt handlers. Section 4 is devoted to a timed operational semantics for our interrupt-driven language. Section 5 lists some interesting algebra laws for the computation properties of our programs. The time properties of interrupt programs are specified and a corresponding case study is presented in Section 6, followed by our concluding remarks in Section 7.

2   Overview of the Interrupt Mechanism

In this section, we depict the interrupt mechanism in our model, which has been used in some real-time embedded operating systems. The interrupt mechanism provides an efficient way for an operating system to interact with and react to its operating environment. Such a mechanism is illustrated in Figure 1. In our model, the interrupts are implemented in terms of signals which can be produced by either the software program or the hardware device; in other words, by either the system or the environment. Firstly, when an interrupt is received, the program that is currently running is suspended and its state is saved. Secondly, the code that has already been associated with the interrupt starts to run. Such code can be found in the interrupt vector. At last, the control returns to where the interrupt has occurred and all the preserved states should be returned as if the interrupt has never happened.

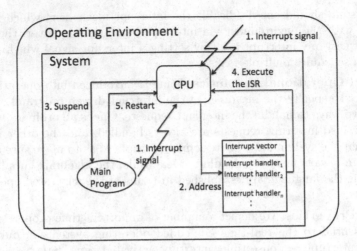

Fig. 1. The Mechanism of Interrupt

Based on the interrupt mechanism, we give an informal introduction about the system and the environment in our model in what follows.

2.1   System

In our model, the system is divided into two parts, i.e., the main program and the interrupt handlers. The main program provides basic services and can be expressed as a particular sequential program. The interrupt handlers interact with the environment to make sure the system can provide correct and timely services. Although they both are programs from a coding perspective, they still have their own characteristics due to different duties.

The main program's characteristics:

- A real-time embedded operating system usually supports multiple tasks, and it always has a scheduling strategy to manage the tasks and to locate the limited resources. In our model, we assume there is one processor and only one task is running at all time. So the system can be described as a sequential program ("the main program" called here).
- The main program can enable or disable the interrupt handling. An interrupt signal is used to denote an interrupt request. Only when the interrupt handling is enabled, the system can receive interrupt signals which are then handled by the corresponding interrupt handlers in the order in which they were received. On the other hand, if the interrupt handling is disabled, the system ignores all interrupt signals received during the disabled period. Moreover, when the interrupt handling option is switched from enabled to disabled, the accumulated interrupt requests are cleared.
- The main program prevents itself from continuously being interrupted by requiring itself to step forward once returning back from an interrupt handler.

The interrupt handlers' characteristics:

- An operating system usually tries to ensure that the time spent on interrupt-handling is kept to a minimum. It saves the state of the interrupted program when the context is switched to that of an interrupt handler. In our model, interrupt handlers may require a little handling time but they will not modify the data states of their interrupted programs. Moreover, for simplicity, we assume no priorities for interrupt handlers here; all interrupt requests are therefore dealt with in the order they were received. It is acceptable for the system to ignore some interrupt signals in order to meet its deadline.
- Both the system and environment can request interrupts by issuing interrupt signals. In our model, the system may issue any interrupt signal in any place wherever it needs. Meanwhile, the environment may also produce any interrupt signal unexpectedly at any time. As we mentioned above, only when the interrupt handling is enabled, interrupt requests can be received and handled as soon as possible (but not necessarily immediately). In our model, we assume that there would not be two or more interrupt signals happened at the same time (such a scenario rarely happens in fact).
- In our model, the system forbids interrupt nesting. But during the execution of an interrupt handler, the system can still receive and record interrupt requests.

2.2   Environment

The correctness of an real-time embedded operating system depends not only on its logical correctness but also its correct response to the operating environment. For better interaction with the environment, the system must respond the interrupts timely on one hand, and the main program of the system must meet its time deadline on the other hand. So analyzing such kind of systems must take into account the variable environment.

In our model, we assume there are only a finite number of different kinds of interrupt signals, and the environment may produce different sequences of interrupt requests made up of these signals. For a given sequence, we can analyze the behavior of the system in the corresponding environment and investigate its time properties. To have a better analysis of the behavior of the system in a specific environment, we assume that each signal in the sequence is labeled with its arrival time. Despite of the randomicity and nondeterminism of the interrupts, we would still expect that any user-given interrupt sequence can reflect the real scenarios to a large extent, so that our analysis can reveal more accurate performance of the system in such reasonable situations.

3   The Language

In this section, we present our language to specify interrupt-driven programs, which includes some ordinary program constructs as well as three new constructs related to interrupt handling, namely enable, disable and set. We also define a function to estimate the execution time of program which supports the time analysis of interrupt-driven programs.

3.1   Syntax

In our model, a system is composed of a main program and a set of interrupt handlers. We use the notation $Sys ::= [M, I]$ to describe a system, where M and I denotes the main program and the set of interrupt handlers respectively. The main program can be interrupted by interrupt signals corresponding to any of the interrupt handlers in the interrupt set I. As mentioned earlier, the interrupt nesting is forbidden in our model. That is, an interrupt handler cannot be interrupted by other handlers. The abstract syntax of the language is defined in the following.

$$M ::= \text{enable} \mid \text{disable} \mid \text{set}(is) \mid P \mid M; M \mid$$
$$M \lhd b \rhd M \mid [b * M]^n$$

$$(is \to P) \in I$$

When the system starts, the interrupts are usually enabled so that the system can interact with the environment timely. After that, the main program can enable or disable interrupts. The main program itself can also set an interrupt signal is via $\text{set}(is)$ to take the initiative to request an interrupt. The notion $(is \to P) \in I$ denotes an interrupt handler P identified by the interrupt signal is. Note that P, which appears in both the main program and interrupt handlers above, stands for an ordinary program and is defined in what follows.

$$P ::= \text{skip} \mid x := e \mid P; P \mid P \lhd b \rhd P \mid [b * P]^n \mid \text{atomic}(P)$$

skip is a program that does not change anything. $x := e$ assigns the value of e to the variable x. The programs $P; Q$ denotes the sequential composition of P and Q (similarly for $M_1; M_2$). The program $P \lhd b \rhd Q$ behaves like P if the boolean expression b is true, or Q otherwise (similarly for $M_1 \lhd b \rhd M_2$). The iteration $[b * P]^n$ iterates P whenever b is true. For simplicity, we assume the number of iterations is statically known and is given by the annotation n. The assignment $x := e$ and the evaluation of boolean expression b are atomic, that is, their computation cannot be interrupted. Informally $\text{atomic}(P)$ behaves like P except that any interrupts occurred would not dealt with during the execution. However, it is not equal to $(\text{disable}; P; \text{enable})$. The difference lies in that the system can still receive interrupt requests during the execution of $\text{atomic}(P)$ while $(\text{disable}; P; \text{enable})$ will make the system to ignore all interrupt requests including previously received ones.

3.2   Workload Function

In this subsection, we give a definition of *workload function* $f : M \times \sigma \to \mathbb{N}$ to estimate the execution time of program. The time that elapses during the program's execution is interrelated with the program's structure and data states. If the initial state of program is definite, then the finial state is definite. M is program while σ stands for the program's current data states. And $\mathbb{N}$ is natural number denoting time. The user can define the execution time of each program by f, here we assume that the interrupt operations enable, disable and set don't cost any time and all of them can be considered as instantaneous operation following the previous ones, where $f(\text{enable}, \sigma) = 0$, $f(\text{disable}, \sigma) = 0$ and $f(\text{set}(is), \sigma) = 0$. In particular, we define skip won't cost time $f(\text{skip}, \sigma) = 0$. Moreover, we assume the computation of expression e or b won't cost time as they are prepared to evaluate their values in the former operations.

Our group has developed a virtual machine called $xBVM$ which we introduced in [17]. This machine which based on $xBIL$ language can be used to execute the $xBIL$ code and calculate the program's execution time. With this example, we can assure that the workload function is feasible and practical. Absolutely, the user can use any feasible machine to help estimate the program's execution time, which makes better use of our approach for analyzing the time properties of programs.

Property 1. For a sequential program $P; Q$, its execution time is the sum of the time cost by P and Q. The program P starts with initial state σ and Q performs at the state passed from P which is a definite state $P(\sigma)$.

P-1 $f(P; Q, \sigma) = f(P, \sigma) + f(Q, P(\sigma))$

Property 2. This function distributes over conditional operator.

P-2 $f(P \triangleleft b \triangleright Q, \sigma) = f(P, \sigma) \triangleleft b(\sigma) \triangleright f(Q, \sigma)$

Property 3. The atomic(P) costs the same time as program P.

P-3 $f(\text{atomic}(P), \sigma) = f(P, \sigma)$

Property 4. The execution time of iteration program is interrelated with the boolean expression and loop times.

P-4 $f([b * P]^n, \sigma) = f(P; [b * P]^{n-1}, \sigma) \triangleleft b(\sigma) \triangleright f(\text{skip}, \sigma)$

4 Operational Semantics

In the section, we present an operational semantics for the interrupt-driven program. The operational semantics specifies how the effect of a computation is produced. It is given in terms of transitions between *configuration*. The configuration is defined as a tuple $\langle M, \sigma, t, i, q \rangle$ consisting of the following components:

- M describes the program to be executed. We can use *workload function* to estimate the execution time of this program.
- A state $\sigma \in \Sigma : Vars \to \mathbb{N}$ which is a mapping of the given finite set $Vars$ of variables to the set $\mathbb{N}$ of natural numbers. The data states of the main program and the interrupt handlers have no intersection.
- $t \in \mathbb{N}$ denotes the time spent by the running program.
- The identifer i indicates the running state of the system. It has three values, i.e., 0, 1, and 2. 0 stands for the interrupts are enabled and the main program can be interrupted at any time. 1 denotes that the interrupts are enabled, but the main program cannot be interrupted until progressing one step. And

it makes there won't be more than one interrupt handled in the same place. At last, 2 stands for the interrupts are disabled.
- We employ interrupt signals queue q to record the received signals.

We give a few of the operational rules for the interrupt-driven program as follows. In our framework, each program has a deadline (denoted by d) which is given in specification to help analyze the behavior and time properties of program. For all the transitions, we assume they satisfy a precondition that a good program M to be executed will always meet its deadline, so there exists such a invariance $f(M, \sigma) \leq d$ during the program normally running. Moreover, the system contains a set of interrupt handlers, and the arrow $\rightarrow_I$ means the transition happens within the interrupt set I.

Nontermination
We employ $\langle M, \sigma, t, i, q \rangle$ where $t > d$ to indicate the nontermination of the program. The notation $t > d$ means program M has already missed its deadline.

Assignment
$$\langle x := e, \sigma, t, 0, nil \rangle \rightarrow_I \langle \text{skip}, \sigma[e/x], t', 0, q \rangle$$
$$\langle x := e, \sigma, t, 1, q \rangle \rightarrow_I \langle \text{skip}, \sigma[e/x], t', 0, q' \rangle$$
$$\langle x := e, \sigma, t, 2, nil \rangle \rightarrow_I \langle \text{skip}, \sigma[e/x], t', 2, nil \rangle$$
$$\text{where } t' = t + f(x := e, \sigma)$$

The assignment $x := e$ is an atomic action which cannot be interrupted. We write $\sigma[e/x]$ for the state that agrees with σ except at x, which is mapped to $\sigma(e)$. The $\sigma(e)$ means the natural number value of e in σ.

There are three kinds of transitions for assignment. Firstly, system is in 0 state, the assignment can execute only when $q = nil$, otherwise the interrupt in q will be handled before the assignment running. During its execution, the environment may produce interrupt signal, where nil may change into q. Secondly, system is in 1 state which means the system returns from handling an interrupt just now, the assignment will always execute no matter whether there is any more interrupt request in q or not. And q may extend to q' as the environment may issue interrupt signal. The assignment is considered as one step, the system can turn its state from 1 to 0 after it executed. At last, when the system is in 2 state, there shouldn't be any interrupt. When the assignment finishes, the execution time t adds the time consumed by itself.

Sequential Composition
$$\frac{\langle M_1, \sigma, t, i, q \rangle \rightarrow_I \langle \text{skip}, \sigma', t', i', q' \rangle}{\langle M_1; M_2, \sigma, t, i, q \rangle \rightarrow_I \langle M_2, \sigma', t', i', q' \rangle}$$
$$\frac{\langle M_1, \sigma, t, i, q \rangle \rightarrow_I \langle M_1', \sigma', t', i', q' \rangle}{\langle M_1; M_2, \sigma, t, i, q \rangle \rightarrow_I \langle M_1'; M_2, \sigma', t', i', q' \rangle}$$

The sequential composition of two programs $M_1; M_2$ is executed by running M_1 first and running M_2 until M_1 terminates. If M_1 is unable to terminate, so is $M_1; M_2$.

Choice

$$\frac{b(\sigma) = \text{true}}{\langle M_1 \lhd b \rhd M_2, \sigma, t, i, q \rangle \rightarrow_I \langle M_1, \sigma, t, i, q \rangle}$$

$$\frac{b(\sigma) = \text{false}}{\langle M_1 \lhd b \rhd M_2, \sigma, t, i, q \rangle \rightarrow_I \langle M_2, \sigma, t, i, q \rangle}$$

The notation $b(\sigma)$ is defined for the boolean value of b in σ, and the evaluation of expression b cannot be interrupted. In our framework, we assume b's computation won't cost time as it is prepared to evaluate true or false in the former operations. The program behaves like M_1 if the boolean expression b is true, or M_2 if false.

Iteration

$$\frac{b(\sigma) = \text{true} \wedge n \geq 1}{\langle [b * M]^n, \sigma, t, i, q \rangle \rightarrow_I \langle M; [b * M]^{n-1}, \sigma, t, i, q \rangle}$$

$$\frac{b(\sigma) = \text{false} \vee n = 0}{\langle [b * M]^n, \sigma, t, i, q \rangle \rightarrow_I \langle \text{skip}, \sigma, t, i, q \rangle}$$

The iteration is similar with the choice program that the interrupt cannot happen during the evaluation of b. The real-time embedded system usually forbids infinite iteration, especially the interrupt handlers, so it is always limited to a number of cycles.

Atomic Action

$$\langle \text{atomic}(\text{skip}), \sigma, t, i, t \rangle \rightarrow_I \langle \text{skip}, \sigma, t, i, q \rangle$$

$$\frac{\langle P, \sigma, t, 0, nil \rangle \rightarrow_I \langle P', \sigma', t', 0, q \rangle}{\langle \text{atomic}(P), \sigma, t, 0, nil \rangle \rightarrow_I \langle \text{atomic}(P'), \sigma', t', 0, q \rangle}$$

$$\frac{\langle P, \sigma, t, 1, q \rangle \rightarrow_I \langle P', \sigma', t', 0, q' \rangle}{\langle \text{atomic}(P), \sigma, t, 1, q \rangle \rightarrow_I \langle \text{atomic}(P'), \sigma', t', 0, q' \rangle}$$

$$\frac{\langle P, \sigma, t, 2, nil \rangle \rightarrow_I \langle P', \sigma', t', 2, nil \rangle}{\langle \text{atomic}(P), \sigma, t, 2, nil \rangle \rightarrow_I \langle \text{atomic}(P'), \sigma', t', 2, nil \rangle}$$

$$\text{where } t' = t + (f(P, \sigma) - f(P', \sigma'))$$

The user can define atomic action to ensure a series of actions complete without interrupted. The behavior of $\text{atomic}(P)$ is the same as program P without interrupt. It has three kinds of transitions like the assignment.

Enable/Disable Interrupt

$$\langle \text{enable}, \sigma, t, i, q \rangle \rightarrow_I \langle \text{skip}, \sigma, t, 0, q \rangle$$

$$\langle \text{disable}, \sigma, t, i, q \rangle \rightarrow_I \langle \text{skip}, \sigma, t, 2, nil \rangle$$

The statement enable is an atomic action which can change the system' state into 0. So that the program can receive the interrupt request and handle the interrupt as soon as possible. The disable is also an atomic action and it makes the system's state turn into 2 and empties the interrupt signals queue q. Once the system is disabled, the received and the new interrupt requests are all be ignored. In our model, we mentioned both of the two operations are considered to take no time.

Request Interrupt

$\langle \text{set}(is), \sigma, t, 0, nil \rangle \to_I \langle \text{skip}, \sigma, t, 0, is \rangle$

$\langle \text{set}(is), \sigma, t, 1, q \rangle \to_I \langle \text{skip}, \sigma, t, 0, q^\frown is \rangle$

$\langle \text{set}(is), \sigma, t, 2, nil \rangle \to_I \langle \text{skip}, \sigma, t, 2, nil \rangle$

The main program can request any interrupt actively. The $\text{set}(is)$ denotes that the main program requests the is interrupt. $\text{set}(is)$ is an atomic action and it has the same transitions as assignment except that it won't cost time. Only when the interrupts enabled, the request signal will be accepted and put into the queue in occurred order.

Handle Interrupt

$$\frac{head(q) = is \land \langle I(is), \sigma_I, t, 2, nil \rangle \to_I \langle \text{skip}, \sigma'_I, t', 2, nil \rangle}{\langle M, \sigma, t, 0, q \rangle \to_I \langle M, \sigma, t', 1, q' \rangle}$$

$$\text{where } t' = t + f(I(is), \sigma_I)$$

As we mentioned before, there is no intersection of data states between the main program and interrupt handlers, where $\sigma \cap \sigma_I = \emptyset$. When the interrupts can be executed, they are always handled in *First In First Out* order. So the head signal is got out of queue and the corresponding interrupt handler executes. The interrupt handler cannot be interrupted, so its state is set to 2 and q is nil.

After the interrupt terminates, the time t of the main program should also records the time spent by the interrupt. And the system'state changes from 0 to 1 to denote the main program cannot be interrupted again in the same place. The environment may produce interrupt signal during the execution of interrupt handler, so $q' = is^\frown q$ or $q' = is^\frown q^\frown q''$. If the interrupt consumes so much time that make the main program miss the deadline, the deadline is negative.

Handle Interrupt Safely

In our model, we also provides a mechanism that can make the program always meet the deadline. Before the ready interrupt handler running, the system will evaluate whether there is enough time for the main program's execution. We use the arrow $\xrightarrow{s}_I$ to denote the transition is based on the safe mechanism.

$$\frac{head(q) = is \land f(I(is), \sigma_I) \leq T \land \langle I(is), \sigma_I, t, 2, nil \rangle \xrightarrow{s}_I \langle \text{skip}, \sigma'_I, t', 2, nil \rangle}{\langle M, \sigma, t, 0, q \rangle \xrightarrow{s}_I \langle M, \sigma, t', 1, q' \rangle}$$

$$\text{where } T = d - f(M, \sigma) \text{ and } t' = t + f(I(is), \sigma_I)$$

$$\frac{head(q) = is \land f(I(is), \sigma_I) > T}{\langle M, \sigma, t, 0, q \rangle \xrightarrow{s}_I \langle M, \sigma, t, 0, q' \rangle}$$

$$\text{where } T = d - f(M, \sigma)$$

The safe transition is the same as the normal transition when there is enough time for the interrupt to be executed, in other words, the inequality $f(I(is), \sigma_I) \leq (d - f(M, \sigma))$ establishes. If there isn't enough time and the system adopts safe transition, the system may reject the interrupt request to make the main program meet its deadline. The states of the system remain the same except removing the ignored interrupt signal out of q.

We present two equivalence relations in our framework like bisimulation [18, 19]. We assume two programs M_1 and M_2 with the same interrupt set I execute in the same environment, and they have same initial states except deadline. Formally, let $\to_I^1$ mean one step and $\to_I^*$ mean 0 or more steps under the operational semantics.

Definition 1. We say an equivalence relation $=_t$ over the interrupt-driven programs. $M_1 =_t M_2$ iff for any state σ,

if $\quad \langle M_1, \sigma, t_1, 2, nil \rangle \to_I^* \langle skip, \sigma_1', t_1', 2, nil \rangle$ and
$\qquad \langle M_2, \sigma, t_2, 2, nil \rangle \to_I^* \langle skip, \sigma_2', t_2', 2, nil \rangle$
then $\quad (\sigma_1' = \sigma_2') \wedge (t_1' - t_1 = t_2' - t_2)$

When discussing about $=_t$-equivalence, we assume the interrupt mechanism is disabled to analyze the main program's own behavior. When the two programs terminate, their data states are still same and they consume same execution time.

Definition 2. We define an equivalence relation $\mathcal{R}$ over configurations as a I-bisimulation if $\langle M_1, \sigma, t, i, q \rangle \mathcal{R} \langle M_2, \sigma, t, i, q \rangle$ implies,

if $\quad \langle M_1, \sigma, t, i, q \rangle \to_I^1 \langle M_1', \sigma_1', t_1', i_1', q_1' \rangle$
then $\quad \langle M_2, \sigma, t, i, q \rangle \to_I^* \langle M_2', \sigma_2', t_2', i_2', q_2' \rangle$ and
$\qquad \langle M_1', \sigma_1', t_1', i_1', q_1' \rangle \mathcal{R} \langle M_2', \sigma_2', t_2', i_2', q_2' \rangle$

if $\quad \langle M_2, \sigma, t, i, q \rangle \to_I^1 \langle M_2', \sigma_2', t_2', i_2', q_2' \rangle$
then $\quad \langle M_1, \sigma, t, i, q \rangle \to_I^* \langle M_1', \sigma_1', t_1', i_1', q_1' \rangle$ and
$\qquad \langle M_1', \sigma_1', t_1', i_1', q_1' \rangle \mathcal{R} \langle M_2', \sigma_2', t_2', i_2', q_2' \rangle$

Definition 3. (a) Two configurations C_1 and C_2 are I-bisimilar, written as $C_1 =_I C_2$, if there exists a I-bisimulation $\mathcal{R}$ such that $C_1 \mathcal{R} C_2$. (b) Two programs M_1 and M_2 are I-bisimilar, denoted as $M_1 =_I M_2$, if for any states σ, t, i and q, $\langle M_1, \sigma, t, i, q \rangle \mathcal{R} \langle M_2, \sigma, t, i, q \rangle$.

According to the definition of operational semantics and the two kinds of equivalences, we can educe if $=_I$-bisimilar establishes, then $=_t$-equivalence must establish. Define if $M_1 =_I M_2$ then $M_1 =_t M_2$.

Example. $(x := x) \neq_t skip$ since they may have different execution time. Moreover, $(disable\ x := 1\ enable) =_t (x := 1)$ but $(disable\ x := 1\ enable) \neq_I (x := 1)$. Although they cost same time, the latter can receive interrupt quest. So they may have different system state and interrupt queue.

5   Algebraic Laws

Program properties can be expressed as algebraic laws (equations or inequations), which can be verified by using the formalized semantics. We explore a set of important and useful algebraic laws which hold for the interrupt-driven program in this section. Proofs that the laws are sound with respect to the operational semantics are straightforward and have been omitted due to space limit.

Algebra is well-suited for direct use by engineers in symbolic calculation of parameters and the structure of an optimal design. Algebraic proof by term rewriting is the most promising way in which computers can assist in the process of reliable design [16]. From the point of view of language design it is desirable to impose as few constraints as possible on the programming constructs, and make the laws as widely applicable as possible. Here we will confine ourselves to those laws involving the introduced operators.

Atomic Statement

Atomic statement is idempotent.

A-1 $\mathsf{atomic}(P) =_I \mathsf{atomic}^2(P)$.

Atomic statement distributes over conditional choice.

A-2 $\mathsf{atomic}(P \lhd b \rhd Q) =_I \mathsf{atomic}(P) \lhd b \rhd \mathsf{atomic}(Q)$.

Interrupt Operation

The programs enable and disable are idempotent.

I-1 $\mathsf{enable}; P =_I \mathsf{enable}; \mathsf{enable}; P$

I-2 $\mathsf{disable}; P =_I \mathsf{disable}; \mathsf{disable}; P$

Program disable makes the following program set(is) no sense.

I-3 $\mathsf{disable}; \mathsf{set}(is) =_I \mathsf{disable}$

The atomic operator between disable and enable behaves no sense.

I-4 $\mathsf{disable}; \mathsf{atomic}(P); \mathsf{enable} =_I \mathsf{disable}; P; \mathsf{enable}$.

6   Time Properties and a Case Study

Real-time embedded operating systems support real-time applications; therefore, the designers of such systems should consider their real-time features. The correctness of this kind of operating systems involves both the logical correctness and timeliness. In this section, we will analyze some time properties about our interrupt-driven programs listed as below.

Interrupt Response Time. The system usually takes time to respond to an interrupt request. This is the time between the arrival of the interrupt signal and the start of the execution of the corresponding interrupt handler. In order for the system to have better interaction with the environment, the system should handle the interrupt request timely. So we think the analysis of interrupt-driven programs should take this property into account. The system requirement usually give worst-case upper bounds on interrupt response time. In our model, we use σ_w to denote the worst case response time of the analyzed program.

Interrupt-Activated Time. This time denotes the total period when the interrupts are enabled. The system allows the main program to enable or disable interrupts. The system requirement usually extends interrupt activated time to make sure that the system can interact with the environment promptly. So it is necessary to consider the interrupt activated time in a specified environment to evaluate the system's real-time behaviors.

Interrupt Overload. If there come too many interrupt requests, the system may not have enough time to handle all of them, or it may miss its deadline. Interrupt overload is a problem to consider in real-time analysis. The designer usually adopts a few strategies to help make interrupt overload less likely or impossible in real-time embedded operating systems. For example, they may keep the execution time of interrupt handlers short or bound the arrival rates of interrupt signals. Given its importance, we shall also analyze this property of the system in a given environment.

Deadline. A reliable real-time embedded operating system should be such a system that it meets its deadline in most cases but may miss its deadline very rarely (the probability for such cases is so low that it can be tolerated). There may be a deadline for every program, but we assume the interrupt handler always meet its deadline in our model. Here we just consider whether the main program meet the deadline or not in a variable environment.

The Case Study

To carry out the study, we can define a specific environment which contains a sequence of interrupt signals to happen as well as their happening time. For instance, the user can assume that there are three kinds of interrupts in the system, denoted as is_1, is_2, and is_3. For convenience, we assume each of the interrupt handlers costs the same time in different data states, and we assume that $f(I(is_1), \sigma_I) = \tau$, $f(I(is_2), \sigma_I) = 2\tau$ and $f(I(is_3), \sigma_I) = 4\tau$, where τ indicates the time unit. We also assume that the environment may produce a sequence such as $\langle is_1^{2\tau}, is_1^{3\tau}, is_2^{4\tau} \rangle$ or another sequence: $\langle is_1^{\tau}, is_2^{3\tau}, is_3^{5\tau} \rangle$, e.g., $is_1^{2\tau}$ means at the second time unit, the environment will produce the interrupt signal is_1. We can analyze the behavior and the time properties about the system in such given environments.

A main program P whose deadline is 10τ is defined as below, and meanwhile the interrupts are enabled at the very beginning. We define the execution time for the program begins in a unique initial data state σ by workload function f. Here we assume $\sigma = \sigma_w$ that the analyzed program is running in the worst case scenario. We use superscripts like (n) to label each operation for simplicity.

$$P =_{df} x := 1^{(1)}; y := 2^{(2)};$$
$$\text{atomic}(x := x + 1; y := y + 1)^{(3)};$$
$$z := x + y^{(4)}; \text{disable}^{(5)}; x := x - 2^{(6)};$$

$f(x := 1, \sigma) = \tau$

$f(y := 2, \sigma_1) = \tau$ where $\sigma_1 = x := 1(\sigma)$

$f(x := x + 1, \sigma_2) = \tau$ where $\sigma_2 = y := 2(\sigma_1)$

$f(y := y + 1, \sigma_3) = \tau$ where $\sigma_3 = x := x + 1(\sigma_2)$

$f(z := x + y, \sigma_4) = \tau$ where $\sigma_4 = y := y + 1(\sigma_3)$

$f(x := x - 2, \sigma_5) = \tau$ where $\sigma_5 = z := x + y; disable(\sigma_4)$

Case 1: The program P executes in such an interrupt sequence: $\langle is_1^{2\tau}, is_1^{3\tau}, is_2^{4\tau} \rangle$. The table below has four parts: P presents the last executed program, t denotes the execution time of program, i indicates the system's state, and q certainly denotes the interrupt signal queue. Take the row 2 for example, when $x := 1$ finishes running, it costs one time unit τ. The system state is 0 and the interrupt queue has no interrupt signal.

Table 1. Steps shown in the case 1

	P	t	i	q
1		0	0	nil
2	1	τ	0	nil
3	2	2τ	0	is_1
4	$I(is_1)$	3τ	1	is_1
5	3	5τ	0	$is_1 \frown is_2$
6	$I(is_1)$	6τ	1	is_2
7	4,5	7τ	2	nil
8	6	8τ	2	nil

We analyze four properties we mentioned above in case 1. The average of the interrupt response time is τ, where $(0 + 2\tau)/2 = \tau$ that the first two interrupt requests are handled. The interrupt activated time is the sum of time when the system in 0 and 1 states, and it is 6τ in case 1. During the whole execution of program P, there comes three interrupts but only two are handled before it finishes. At last, $t = 8\tau < d$ indicates P meet its deadline.

Case 2a: The program P executes in another interrupt sequence: $\langle is_1^{\tau}, is_2^{3\tau}, is_3^{5\tau} \rangle$.

Table 2. Steps shown in the case 2a

	P	t	i	q
1		0	0	nil
2	1	τ	0	is_1
3	$I(is_1)$	2τ	1	nil
4	2	3τ	0	is_2
5	$I(is_2)$	5τ	1	is_3
6	3	7τ	0	is_3
7	$I(is_3)$	11τ	1	nil

Case 2b: According to Case 2a, we get program P miss the deadline where $t = 11\tau > d$ at last. Here we analyze the behavior of the system by following the safe interrupt handler transition rules. In this case, the is_3 interrupt which costs so much time won't be handled so P would meet the deadline.

We compare the performance of program P in the same environment but following different transition rules, namely, an ordinary rule in case 2a, and a safe rule in case 2b. The interrupt response time is respectively $2/3\tau$ and 0.

Table 3. Steps shown in the case 2b

	P	d	i	q
1		0	0	nil
2	1	τ	0	is_1
3	$I(is_1)$	2τ	1	nil
4	2	3τ	0	is_2
5	$I(is_2)$	5τ	1	is_3
6	3	7τ	0	is_3
7	4,5	8τ	2	nil
8	6	9τ	2	nil

The interrupt activated time is respectively 11τ and 7τ. Three interrupts are all handled in case 2a, while only the first two interrupts are handled in case 2b. Due to the is_3 interrupt executes or not, P misses the deadline in case 2a, but meets the deadline in case 2b.

According to the examples above, it's convenient for the user to analyze the time properties of the interrupt-driven program through the language and the timed operational semantics in our framework.

7   Conclusion and Future Work

It remains a challenging problem to analyze time properties for programs in the presence of interrupts. In this paper we make a small step forward in tackling this problem. We provide a small interrupt-driven programming language and propose a timed operational semantics for it. To simplify the analysis, we consider only finite programs where the number of iterations are statically known. We make use of a workload function to estimate the execution time of programs. We also have some preliminary discussions on algebraic laws based on the proposed operational semantics. Several time properties for such programs are introduced and analyzed under several scenarios with the help of the operational semantics.

As for future work, we will extend the model to cover more advanced issues, such as interrupt priorities, interrupt nesting, enabling/disabling some interrupt services (but not all). We shall also try to provide a formal specification for the time properties and offer a more formal analysis as to how good a programming model would behave in terms of those time properties.

Acknowledgment. This work is supported by National Basic Research Program of China (No. 2011CB302904), China Core Electronic Components, High-end Universal Chips and Infrastructure Software series Significant Project (No. 2009ZX01038-001-07), National High Technology Research and Development Program of China (No. 2011AA010101 and No. 2012AA011205), National Natural Science Foundation of China (No. 61061130541 and No. 61021004), Shanghai Leading Academic Discipline Project (No. B412), and East China Normal University Overseas Research Foundation (No. 79622040).

References

1. Zhao, Y., Huang, Y., He, J., Liu, S.: Formal Model of Interrupt Program from a Probabilistic Perspective. In: ICECCS (2011)
2. Regehra, J., Coopridera, N.: Interrupt Verification via Thread Verification. ENTCS (2007)
3. Regehra, J.: Random testing of interrupt-driven software. ACM (2005)
4. Kleiman, S., Eykholt, J.: Interrupts as threads. In: ACM SIGOPS (1995)
5. Feng, X., Shao, Z., Guo, Y., Dong, Y.: Certifying Low-Level Programs with Hardware Interrupts and Preemptive Threads. J. Autom. Reasoning 42(2-4) (2009)
6. Hills, T.: Structured interrupts. In: ACM SIGOPS (1993)
7. Cobben, T., Engels, A.: Interrupt and Disrupt in MSC: Possibilities and Problems (1998)
8. Baeten, J.C.M., Bergstra, J.A., Klop, J.W.: Syntax and Defining equations for an interrupt mechanism in process algebra. In: FIIX (1986)
9. Brylow, D., Damgaard, N., Palsberg, J.: Static Checking of Interrupt-driven Software. In: ICSE (2001)
10. Palsberg, J., Ma, D.: A Typed Interrupt Calculus. In: Damm, W., Olderog, E.-R. (eds.) FTRTFT 2002. LNCS, vol. 2469, pp. 291–310. Springer, Heidelberg (2002)
11. Chatterjee, K., Ma, D., Majumdar, R., Zhao, T., Henzinger, T.A., Palsberg, J.: Stack Size Analysis for Interrupt-driven Programs. In: Cousot, R. (ed.) SAS 2003. LNCS, vol. 2694, pp. 109–126. Springer, Heidelberg (2003)
12. Brylow, D., Palsberg, J.: Deadline Analysis of Interrupt-Driven Software. IEEE Transactions on Software Engineering (2004)
13. Regehra, J.: Handbook of Real-Time and Embedded Systems. In: Safe and Structured Use of Interrupts in Real-Time and Embedded Software (2007)
14. Kleidermacher, D.: Minimizing Interrupt Response Time, Design Strategies and Methodologies 4(1) (2005)
15. Jeong, J., Seo, E., Kim, D.-S., Kim, J.-S., Lee, J., Jung, Y.-J., Kim, D.-H., Kim, K.: Transparent and Selective Real-Time Interrupt Services for Performance Improvement. In: Obermaisser, R., Nah, Y., Puschner, P., Rammig, F.J. (eds.) SEUS 2007. LNCS, vol. 4761, pp. 283–292. Springer, Heidelberg (2007)
16. Hoare, C.A.R., He, J.: Unifying Theories of Programming, Prentice Hall International Series in Computer Science (1998)
17. Shi, J., Zhu, L., Huang, Y., Guo, J., Zhu, H., Fang, H., Ye, X.: Binary Code Level Verfication for Interrupt Safety Properties of Real-Time Operating System. In: TASE (2012)
18. Milner, R.: Communication and Comcurrency. Prentice Hall International Series in Computer Science (1990)
19. Milner, R.: Communication and Mobile System: $\pi-$ caculus. Cambirdge University Press (1999)

Specifying and Verifying Declarative Fluent Temporal Logic Properties of Workflows

Germán Regis[1], Nicolás Ricci[1,2], Nazareno M. Aguirre[1,2], and Tom Maibaum[3]

[1] Departamento de Computación, FCEFQyN,
Universidad Nacional de Río Cuarto, Argentina
{gregis,nricci,naguirre}@dc.exa.unrc.edu.ar
[2] Consejo Nacional de Investigaciones Científicas y Técnicas (CONICET), Argentina
[3] Dept. of Computing & Software, McMaster University, Canada
tom@maibaum.org

Abstract. In this paper, we present a characterization of workflows as labeled transition systems, focusing on an encoding of workflow specifications based on workflow patterns. This encoding models tasks in a convenient way, enabling us to exploit fluent linear time temporal logic formulas for capturing typical constraints on workflows. Fluents enable us to flexibly characterize the activities associated with workflow tasks, and also to easily express a wide range of constraints on workflows. Moreover, our characterization of workflows as labeled transition systems, and the use of fluent linear time temporal logic as a language to express workflow properties, allows us to employ model checking for automatically guaranteeing that a property is satisfied by a workflow, or generating violating workflow executions when such property does not hold.

We use YAWL as a language for expressing workflows. Our characterization of workflows as labeled transition systems is implemented in a tool that translates YAWL models into FSP, and then employs the LTSA tool to automatically verify properties of workflows, expressed as fluent linear time temporal logic properties, on the resulting FSP models.

1 Introduction

The importance of efficiency in companies requires constant improvement to their organizational processes. This has led to the need for expressing such processes, typically referred to as *workflows*, and to the proposal of various workflow languages. Indeed, there exist many workflow languages, differing in their degree of formalization (e.g., informal, only with a formal syntax, with a formal syntax and semantics, etc.), their corresponding approaches for workflow description (e.g., declarative or procedural), their expressiveness (e.g., some support advanced conditional routing and some not), their support for automated analysis, etc. An aspect that we consider particularly important is formal semantics. This aspect is crucial for the analysis of models in the language, and is also strongly related to expressiveness, since more expressive languages are more difficult to fully formalize. Furthermore, expressiveness and automation in analysis are typically conflicting aspects, and the design of a good language involves the search of

R. Gheyi and D. Naumann (Eds.): SBMF 2012, LNCS 7498, pp. 147–162, 2012.

an adequate balance between these aspects. This applies not only to the language in which a workflow is expressed, but also to the language used for describing declarative properties of a workflow. The importance of declarative properties of workflows is acknowledged by several researchers (see for instance [10,19,14,21]). In particular, in [19] a declarative approach to business process modeling and execution is proposed, where declarative behavioral properties of workflow models are a central characteristic.

In this paper, we present a characterization of workflows as labeled transition systems, focusing on an encoding of workflow specifications based on workflow patterns. This encoding models tasks in a convenient way, enabling us to exploit *fluent linear time temporal logic* (FLTL) [7], to describe declarative behavioral properties of workflow models. As we show later on, fluents enable us to flexibly characterize the activities associated with workflow tasks, and also to easily express a wide range of constraints on workflows. Our characterization of workflows as labeled transition systems has as an additional motivation (besides enabling for the use of FLTL as a language to express properties of workflows) the possibility of using Model Checking [5] for automatically verifying that a workflow satisfies a given property. Thus, our encoding of workflows as labeled transition systems allows us to use FLTL to express properties of workflows, as well as to automatically verify these properties via model checking on the resulting transition systems, generating violating workflow executions when these properties do not hold. This mechanism for the analysis of declarative properties of workflows is very flexible, as opposed to existing tools for workflow analysis that focus on specific properties such as soundness or deadlock-freedom (e.g., the tool in [2]).

Our approach is in essence language independent, and could in principle be applied to any formal workflow language. In this paper, we choose to use YAWL (Yet Another Workflow Language) [2] models to express workflows. YAWL is a powerful workflow language based on the use of workflow patterns [1], that is supported by an open source toolset, and has a formal semantics based on Petri Nets. It is considered an expressive formalism, as various works dealing with its expressiveness in relation to other business process or workflow languages (e.g., Business Process Modeling Notation, Event-Driven Process Chains, etc) demonstrate [9]. Indeed, the use of YAWL allows us to ensure the applicability of our approach to other workflow languages, in many cases via the use of available automated tools mapping other formalisms into YAWL.

The paper proceeds as follows. In the next section, we discuss workflows, and present the use of the YAWL tool for their specification. We then argue about the importance of being capable of expressing properties of workflows, as well as guaranteeing their validity. In section 3 we provide the formal foundations of our work. In section 4, we propose an automated way of encoding YAWL specifications as Finite State Processes (FSP), characterizing tasks as *fluents*. We show how convenient fluents are for expressing behavioral properties, in the context of fluent temporal logic. In order to do that, we develop in detail a case study, taken from the YAWL toolset, whose complexity enables us to illustrate the advantages of the approach. Finally, we discuss related work in the area and draw some conclusions.

2   Business Processes, Workflows and Patterns

In the last decade, several languages and tools have been developed in order to provide an organized view of the structural behavior of systems. One of the main goals of these languages and tools is to provide a setting for describing and analyzing procedural descriptions (workflows) of the activities that take place on the system. As part of these efforts, the Workflow Pattern Initiative was created with the aim of identifying and providing a conceptual basis for business process specifications. This resulted in the specification of a wide range of workflow patterns (control flow, data, resource, etc.), and the development of a formally founded language (and accompanying toolset), known as YAWL [2].

2.1   Workflow Specification Using YAWL

Yet Another Workflow Language (YAWL) is a language for modeling workflows. YAWL has a formal foundation based on Petri Nets (PN) [8], and its models are specified using *workflow patterns* [1]. In this paper, we concentrate on control flow patterns; these are composed of tasks, conditions and a flow relation between tasks and conditions. The semantics of a given model is influenced by that of PNs, in the sense that a task is enabled when there are enough tokens in its input conditions, according to the pattern behavior. When a task is executed, it takes tokens out of the input conditions and puts tokens in its output conditions. As opposed to the case of PNs, in a YAWL specification one can connect two tasks directly. A distinguishing feature of YAWL is that it provides direct support for the so-called *cancel region* pattern. This pattern enables one to model situations in which a task can have a cancellation set associated with it. When a task is executed, all tasks in its cancellation set are aborted (i.e., disabled if these were not running, canceled if these were in the middle of a process).

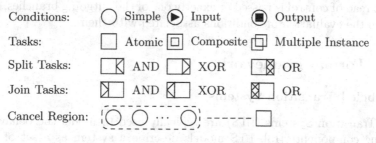

Fig. 1. YAWL Symbols

A workflow specification (control flow perspective) in YAWL is a set of hierarchically organized YAWL nets. Figure 1 shows the symbols corresponding to the elements of the language. A YAWL net is composed of:

- A single *input (start) condition* and a single *output (end) condition*.
- *Tasks*: the language provides three types of tasks, namely: *atomic*, *composite* and *multiple instance*.

- *Atomic* tasks are at the lowest description level of the system.
- *Composite* tasks are associated with corresponding YAWL nets, modeling their behavior. It is assumed that there exists a main YAWL net, which is not associated with any composite task.
- *Multiple instance* (MI) tasks have corresponding lower and upper bounds on the number of instances created when the task is "started up"; MI tasks also have a modifier indicating whether instance creation is *static* or *dynamic* (i.e., indicating whether all instances are created at once, or if these are dynamically created during the execution of the system).

A task T can be related to a *cancel region*, i.e., a set of conditions and tasks that will be aborted when A is completed.

- Specific control flow patterns for the net. The control flow constructs used for pattern definition are those depicted in Fig. 1. Their intended meaning is the following:

  - AND-join: a task associated with this construct starts when all of the incoming branches have been enabled, i.e., all the preceding tasks or associated conditions were completed.
  - OR-join: a task associated with this construct starts when at least one of the incoming branches has been enabled.
  - XOR-join: the associated task starts when exactly one of the incoming branches has been enabled.
  - AND-split: when the incoming branch of this construct is enabled, the thread of control is passed to all of the branches associated with it.
  - OR-split: when the incoming branch of the OR-split is enabled, the thread of control is passed to one or more of the branches following the OR-split, based on the evaluation of conditions associated with each of the outgoing branches.
  - XOR-split: when the incoming branch of the XOR-split is enabled, the thread of control is passed to exactly one of the outgoing branches, based on the evaluation of conditions associated with them.

3   The Formal Framework

3.1   Labeled Transition Systems

Labeled Transition Systems (LTS) are typically used to model the behavior of interacting components [13]. LTS models describe a system as a set of interacting components characterized by states and transitions between them. The transitions represent events in the system, and different components synchronize via shared events. The behavior of the whole system is the result of the parallel composition of its components, understood as the interleaving of the behaviors of the components. Formally, an LTS P is a quadruple $\langle Q, A, \delta, q_0 \rangle$, where: Q is a finite set of states, A is the *alphabet* of P, a subset of the universe Act of events; $\delta \subseteq Q \times A \cup \{\tau\} \times Q$ is a labeled transition relation and q_0 is the initial state.

The semantics of an LTS P is its set of *executions*, i.e., the set of sequences of events that P can perform, starting in its initial state and following P's transition relation. For systems with more than a few states, their representation as LTSs becomes impractical. In such situations, a representation of systems as processes in the process algebra FSP, is more convenient [13]. FSP expressions can be automatically mapped into finite LTS, and vice versa.

An FSP specification contains two sorts of process definitions: primitive processes and composite processes. Primitive processes are expressed using event prefix "->", choice "|" and recursion. Conditional choices can be expressed by means of "when" clauses or "if" expressions. Both event labels and local process names may be indexed, and primitive processes can be parameterized. As an example, consider the following specification of a simple bounded buffer, and its corresponding LTS.

```
BUFF(N=3) = STATE[0],
STATE[i:0..N] = (
  when (i<N) put[i] ->STATE[i+1]
| when (i>0) get[i] ->STATE[i-1]).
```

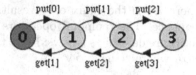

Fig. 2. FSP Buffer specification   **Fig. 3.** LTS of the previous buffer

In Fig. 2, the specification contains a primitive process, parameterized with a bound for the buffer (a default value for the parameter is provided). The possible behaviors of the buffer are specified by means of a primitive process which contains a choice for the two available actions, put and get. These actions are "multiplied" via indexing, and the resulting behavior is illustrated in the LTS in Fig. 3.

Processes can be composed in a sequential (";") or parallel ("||") way. The parallel composition combines the behavior of two processes by synchronizing the events common to their alphabets, and interleaving the remaining events. Continuing with our previous example, consider two processes PROD and CONS, representing a producer and a consumer, respectively, as specified below. These processes are composed in parallel with a buffer, instantiated with a Size (constant declaration); they are synchronized via the relabeling operator "/". Relabeling is a relation between actions; in our example, this is used to synchronize all put (resp. get) actions with the action produce (resp. consume).

```
PROD = (produce ->PROD).    CONS = (consume ->CONS).
|| BOUNDEDBUFFER = (PROD || BUFF(Size) || CONS)
/{ put[0..Size-1]/produce, get[1..Size]/consume }.
```

3.2   Linear Time Temporal Logic

In order to reason about the behaviors of an LTS, one needs a *logic* in which to express properties of these behaviors. Linear Time Temporal Logic (LTL) [15,16] is a language that is able to predicate about infinite sequences of states. Each formula expresses a property of the executions of an LTS. Given a set of atomic propositions $\mathcal{P}$, a well-formed formula is defined inductively using the standard boolean operators and the temporal operators $\mathbf{X}$ (next) and $\mathbf{U}$ (strong until), in the following way: *(i)* every $p \in \mathcal{P}$ is a formula, and *(ii)* if ϕ and ψ are formulas, then so are $\neg\phi$, $\phi \vee \psi$, $\phi \wedge \psi$, $\mathbf{X}\phi$, $\phi\mathbf{U}\psi$.

An infinite word $w = x_0x_1x_2\ldots$ over the power set of propositions $\mathcal{P}$ satisfies an LTL formula ϕ, written $w \models \phi$, if the following conditions hold:

- $w \models p \Leftrightarrow p \in x_0$
- $w \models \phi \vee \psi \Leftrightarrow (w \models \phi)$ or $(w \models \psi)$
- $w \models \neg\phi \Leftrightarrow$ not $w \models \phi$
- $w \models \phi \wedge \psi \Leftrightarrow (w \models \phi)$ and $(w \models \psi)$
- $w \models \mathbf{X}\phi \Leftrightarrow w_1 \models \phi$
- $w \models \phi\mathbf{U}\psi \Leftrightarrow \exists i \geq 0 : w_i \models \psi$ and $\forall 0 \leq j \leq i, w_j \models \phi$

where w_1 is the suffix of w resulting from removing the first element in the sequence. The temporal operators $\mathbf{F}$ (eventually), $\mathbf{G}$ (always) and $\mathbf{W}$ (weak until) are defined as follows: $\mathbf{F}\phi \equiv \text{true}\mathbf{U}\phi$, $\mathbf{G}\phi \equiv \neg\mathbf{F}\neg\phi$, and $\phi\mathbf{W}\psi \equiv ((\phi\mathbf{U}\psi) \vee \mathbf{G}\phi)$, where "true $\equiv \phi \vee \neg\phi$".

3.3   Fluent Linear Time Temporal Logic

Fluent Linear Time Temporal Logic (FLTL) is a variant of LTL, that is particularly well suited for describing properties of event-based discrete systems (e.g., LTSs) [13]. Basically, FLTL provides a convenient way of expressing state properties of a labeled transition system, associated with the occurrence of events in the system. More precisely, FLTL extends LTL by incorporating the possibility of describing certain abstract states, called *fluents*, characterized by events of the system. As defined in [17], Fluents are time-varying properties of the world, which hold at particular instants of time if they have been initiated by a triggering event (occurring at some earlier instant in time), and have not been terminated by any terminating event since its initiation. Similarly, a fluent is false at a particular time instant if none of its triggering events ever occurred, or if it has been previously terminated (by one of its associated terminating events) and not yet re-initiated. More formally, $Fl = \langle\{s_1,\ldots,s_n\}, \{e_1,\ldots,e_n\}\rangle$ *initially* B defines a fluent Fl, where B is a boolean value indicating if the fluent is true or not in the initial state, and $\{s_1,\ldots,s_n\}$ and $\{e_1,\ldots,e_n\}$ are disjoint sets of events; when any of the initiating events $\{s_1,\ldots,s_n\}$ occurs, the fluent starts to be true, and it becomes false again when any of the terminating events $\{e_1,\ldots,e_n\}$ occurs. If the term *initially* B is omitted then Fl is initially *false*.

LTSA, a tool for the analysis of FSP descriptions, has direct support for fluent-based specifications. Consider as an example the following characterization of the states `full` and `empty`, capturing the obvious associated properties of the bounded buffer:

```
fluent Full = < put[Size-1], get[1..Size]>
fluent Empty = < get[1], put[0..Size-1]> initially True
```

3.4   Model Checking

In the last two decades, the development of algorithmic methods for software and hardware verification has led to powerful analysis mechanisms. One of these is model checking [5]. Model checking provides an automated method for verifying finite state systems, by determining whether or not a property described by a (typically temporal) formula holds on the system's state graph. Various alternative model checking approaches have been proposed, which vary in the representation of the system's state transitions (e.g., explicit state or symbolic), in the logic used for describing properties (e.g., linear time temporal logic, or computation tree logic, etc.), and the language in which systems are actually described (e.g., directly as code in a programming language, or as a model in some more abstract modeling language, etc.). Moreover, tools are available for many of these alternative approaches. In our case, we will use Labelled Transition System Analyzer (LTSA), a verification tool for concurrent systems models. A system in LTSA is modeled as a set of interacting finite state machines. LTSA supports Finite State Process notation (FSP) for concise description of component behavior, and directly supports FLTL property verification. Following the previous examples, we can employ the model checker behind LTSA in order to verify that the buffer cannot simultaneously be empty and full; this is captured by the following FLTL formula: `assert CORRECT_BUFFER = [](!(Full && Empty))`.

4   From YAWL Workflows to Labeled Transition Systems

In this section, we present an encoding of YAWL nets into FSP processes. Basically, this encoding, which is fully automated, will allow us to interpret YAWL (procedural) workflows as FSP processes, and thus we will be able to express properties of workflows, using FLTL formulas over their corresponding encoding in FSP. As we mentioned previously, this encoding will enable us to employ the LTSA model checker for *verifying* behavioral properties of task activities of the business process (BP) specifications. The basic intuition behind the encoding of a YAWL net (control flow perspective) into FSP is the following. A system's behavior is characterized by the occurrence of its tasks. In an abstract way, we can capture a task as an entity having some activity in the system between its *start* and *end* events. So, a trace of these events describes a possible execution of the system. In this way, a system's behavior, i.e., all its possible runs, is captured by the set of all its execution traces. These traces are obviously constrained according to the control flow of the system.

According to our previous observation, it is straightforward to see that a task activity can be captured by means of a *fluent*, becoming *true* when its *start* event takes place, and turning back to *false* when its *end* event task occurs. In order to capture the behavior of the workflow's control flow, we will need to introduce appropriate event synchronizations and process compositions, relating the events related to the tasks that conform the workflow. Once we achieve a characterization of workflows as FSP processes, we can express properties of the workflows by expressing temporal formulas, employing task-related fluents as the basic ingredient.

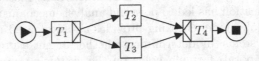

Fig. 4. Simple YAWL net with XOR-split and XOR-join control flow

In order to illustrate the intuition behind our encoding of YAWL into FSP, and our motivation in doing so, let us consider the simple YAWL net shown in Fig.4. According to the YAWL semantics, the set of all possible task occurrences for this net is: $\{T_1T_2T_4, T_1T_3T_4\}$. Each of these corresponds to a trace of events of the system; for instance, $[T_1.start\ T_1.end\ T_2.start\ T_2.end\ T_4.start\ T_4.end$] corresponds to the first of the above task occurrences. We will capture the activity of a task straightforwardly via a fluent. For instance, T_2's activity is captured by the fluent $\langle\{T_2.start\}, \{T_2.end\}\rangle$. Now, these fluents can be used in expressing properties of the system's execution, in a declarative way. A basic sample property of the above workflow would be to guarantee that tasks T_2 and T_3 are always run mutually exclusively. This is expressed by the FLTL formula $\mathbf{G}\neg(T_2 \wedge T_3)$.

To formally describe our translation from YAWL into FSP, we consider a formal semantics of YAWL nets [9], given in terms of Reset Petri Nets. Taking into account this semantics, we propose an encoding for tasks and conditions, with a particular treatment for *input* and *output* conditions. For conditions, and due to constraints of finite LTSs (the formalism underlying our approach), we limit their behavior to a *bounded* number of tokens in them. Even though we have this significant limitation, every YAWL model can be encoded as an FSP model. The mismatch between (unbounded) condition tokens and our intrinsically bounded setting will be reflected when analyzing properties of workflows, via false positives reporting deadlocks. However, the analysis is still *conservative*: if no violations to a property are detected, then it is guaranteed that no violations exist.

It is worth mentioning that FSP supports nondeterministic choice, and therefore branching constructs such as non-free choice and deferred choice can be faithfully captured. Also, since our property language is FLTL, there is no need to consider a branching semantics for our processes (nor a bisimulation semantics) for the purpose of property verification: all possible executions (i.e., all possible interleavings of parallel processes) are taken into account by the model checking tool, thus exhaustively covering all behaviours of the system.

In order to represent a net behavior, we specify how to compose tasks and conditions. In this composition we consider the control flow operators associated with the tasks of the net, and provide an encoding for them. Finally, we address especially sophisticated elements of YAWL nets, such as *cancel regions* and *composite tasks*. Multiple instance tasks are simply treated as abbreviations of nets composed of as many instances as the tasks indicate. The dynamic evolution of multiple instance tasks is characterized via sequential compositions and OR operations.

Definition 1. *A YAWL net is a tuple* $(nid, C, i, o, T, T_A, T_C, M, F, Split, Join,$ $Default, Rem, Nofi)$ *where:*

- *nid is the unique identification of the YAWL net.*
- *C is a set of conditions, $i \in C$ and $o \in C$ are the input (start) and output (end) conditions, respectively;*
- *T is a set of tasks; $T_A \subseteq T$ is the set of atomic tasks, and $T_C \subseteq T$ is the set of composite tasks. $M \subseteq T$ is the set of multiple instance tasks;*
- *$F \subseteq (C\backslash\{o\} \times T) \cup (T \times C\backslash\{i\}) \cup (T \times T)$ is the control flow relation; every node in the graph $(C \cup T, F)$ is on a directed path from i to o;*
- *$Split : T \nrightarrow \{AND, XOR, OR\}$ specifies the split behavior of each task;*
- *$Join : T \nrightarrow \{AND, XOR, OR\}$ specifies the join behavior of each task;*
- *$Default \subseteq F$ denotes the default arc for the OR-Split, ensuring that at least one outgoing arc is enabled;*
- *$Rem : T \nrightarrow \mathbb{P}^+(T \cup C\backslash\{i,o\})$ specifies the tokens to be removed and the tasks that should be canceled as a consequence of an instance of the task completing its execution;*
- *$Nofi : M \to \mathbb{N} \times \mathbb{N}^{inf} \times \mathbb{N}^{inf} \times \{dynamic, static\}$ specifies the configuration of multiple instance tasks: lower and upper bounds, the threshold for continuation, and its creation's behavior.*

Let N be a YAWL net. The process representing the *input*(i) and *output*(o) conditions, starting and ending N, is the following:

```
YNET = (i_cond ->o_cond -> YNET).
```

For each $t \in T_A$ (atomic task), we generate an FSP process characterizing its *start* and *end* events:

```
TASK = (start ->end -> TASK).
```

As mentioned before, the encoding of conditions are restricted to a bounded number of tokens. With this limitation, we represent the conditions in a way similar to a bounded buffer, but with two parameters indicating the possible input and output connections. The bound for tokens is the amount of input connections given by default.

```
CONDITION (IN=2,OUT=2) = STATE[0], STATE[i:0..IN] =
(when(i<IN) in[i:1..IN]->STATE[i+1]|when(i>0) out[j:1..OUT]->STATE[i-1]).
```

The input/output connections are encoded as the *in* and *out* actions, and we refer to them as *ports*. Let $tsk_1, tsk_2 \in T_A \wedge (tsk_1 \notin Dom(Split) \wedge tsk_2 \notin Dom(Join))$ be atomic tasks of N, without split and join decorations, respectively; let $c \in C\backslash\{i,o\}$ be a condition with n and m input and output ports, respectively. In order to compose tsk_1 and tsk_2, we have:

- Sequential composition of tsk_1 and tsk_2: achieved by synchronizing $tsk_1.end$ and $tsk_2.start$, by means of relabeling.

```
|| SYSTEM = tsk[1..2]:TASK /{tsk[2].start/tsk[1].end}
```

- Composition of tsk_1 with tsk_2 through c (condition in between two tasks): achieved by connecting the finalization of tsk_1 with some input port of c, and the start of tsk_2 with some output port of c.

```
|| SYSTEM = tsk[1..2]:TASK || c:CONDITION(n,m)
/{c.in[i]/tsk[1].end, tsk[2].start/c.out[j]}
```

where $1 \leq i \leq n$ and $1 \leq j \leq m$.

- Composition with decorations: Consider $T \in T_A \wedge (T \in Dom(Split) \vee T \in Dom(Join))$, i.e., T is an atomic task with some *and* or *join* decoration (AND, OR, XOR). Let us call these decorations *gates*. For each possible gate, we generate a process according to its behavior. These processes are parameterized by the corresponding input and output *ports* (e.g., the process corresponding to a *join* gate may have $2..n$ input ports and only one output). As shown in Fig. 5, if T has some join (j) or split (s) gate associated, the interconnection between T and the gates will be achieved by the synchronization of $J.out$ with $T.start$, and $T.end$ with $S.in$, respectively. Let us consider tsk_1, tsk_2 to be tasks of the system. In order to compose tsk_1 with tsk_2 through T, we synchronize $tsk1.end$ with some input port of J, and $tsk2.start$ with some output port of S.

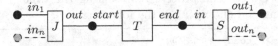

Fig. 5. Task gates configurations

In order to model the task occurrences in the system, for every task T_i we define a *fluent* of the form $T_i = \langle \{tsk_i.start\}, \{tsk_i.end\} \rangle$. This fluent predicates that T is active between the occurrences of its *start* and *end* events. As an example, the encoding for the YAWL net of Fig. 4 as an FSP process is the following:

```
|| SYSTEM=(YNET ||tsk[1..4]:TASK ||xors: XOR_SPLIT(2) ||xorj:XOR_JOIN(2))
/{ TSK[1].start/i_cond, TSK[4].end/o_cond,
xors.in/TSK[1].end, TSK[2].start/xors.end[1], TSK[3].start/xors.end[2],
xorj.in[1]/TSK[2].end, xorj.in[2]/TSK[3].end, TSK[4].start/xorj.out }.
fluent T[i:1..4] = <{tsk[i].start}, {tsk[i].end}>
```

4.1   Encoding of Gates

For each kind of gate we will generate a corresponding FSP process capturing its behavior. These processes are parameterized by input and output ports. Due to space limitations, we present the encodings only for some gates.

For *AND-split*, *XOR-split* and *OR-split*, the FSP processes are characterized by one input port and $N > 1$ output ones. The processes will be parameterized with N and their encodings depend on the corresponding behavior, e.g., for the AND-split we generate a process of the form:

```
AND_SPLIT_TRIGGER(N=1) = (in ->out[I] ->ANDSPLIT_TRIGGER).
|| AND_SPLIT(N=2) = ( forall [i:1..N] ANDSPLIT_TRIGGER(i)).
```

The AND_SPLIT process triggers as many *out* actions as specified by the parameter which shares the *in* action (`forall` is an abbreviation for parallel "||" composition). When the *in* action occurs, *all* the *out* are made available, i.e., the control (token) is passed to all connected output tasks or conditions.

Notice that, in the XOR and OR split gates, we use state variables in order to encode the corresponding guard conditions. Due to restrictions in the datatypes supported by LTSA, we only consider integer and boolean types. The choices for the out ports are constrained by formulas involving those variables, used as conditional *when* clauses in the obvious way.

The *XOR-join* encoding is simply a choice over its incoming events; once one of them arrives, the outgoing event must occur: `XOR_JOIN (N=2) = in[1..N] -> out -> XOR_JOIN)`.

OR-join: Due to its non local semantics, this kind of gate has different interpretations across different business process specification languages. In [9], there is a survey of the *OR-join* semantics in Business Process Modeling Notation (BPMN), in Event-driven Process Chains (EPCs) (see also [11]), etc., and the complications in the analysis of these gates in the presence of cancel regions, loops, or multiple instances. In YAWL, the evaluation of the gate in order to determine if an OR-join can be fired is made via *backward firing* and *coverability* analyses in reset nets. The encoding of the OR-join gates employed to perform our analysis of the models mimic the informal semantic of the OR-join (cf. [9], p. 104), that prioritizes all possible incoming events before firing the out port. In order to encode this gate, the following process is generated:

```
OR_JOIN(N=2) = OR_JOIN_DEF[0], OR_JOIN_DEF[b:0..1] =
                ( in[1..N] -> OR_JOIN_DEF[1] | when (b!=0) out ->OR_JOIN ).
```

where all incoming events are "listened to", and if at least one of them is activated, the outgoing event will be fired. The priority on accept incoming events before firing the output is encoded by means of the *priority* operator of FSP, giving *lower* (>>) priority to the *out* action.

4.2   Cancel Regions and the Encoding of Composite Tasks

Cancel Regions provide the ability of disabling a set of tasks in a process instance. If any of the tasks belonging to this region is already being executed (or is currently enabled), then they are immediately terminated. Cancelation captures the interference of an activity in the execution of others. In order to model this interference in YAWL, a *canceling task* can be associated with a cancel region,

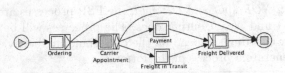

Fig. 6. YAWL net corresponding to the Order Fullfilment Process

indicating a set of tasks or conditions to be canceled. In order to encode cancel regions in FSP, first we consider an extended version for the encoding of tasks and conditions belonging to a *cancelable region*. For these tasks, instead of the original FSP process, we define a process representing a task that *starts* and, either the task *ends*, or the task can be *canceled*. In a similar way, we define the processes corresponding to the cancelable conditions. In this setting, the *start* action of a canceling task is synchronized with the *cancel* actions of the canceled tasks and conditions.

```
CANCELABLE_TASK = CTASK_INACTIVE,
CTASK_INACTIVE = ( start ->CTASK_ACTIVE | cancel ->CTASK_INACTIVE ),
CTASK_ACTIVE = ( end ->CTASK_INACTIVE | cancel ->CTASK_INACTIVE ).
```

For systems involving *composite tasks*, each of these tasks will have an associated YAWL net specifying its corresponding behavior. So, in order to encode the system, we generate a process CT_i for each net associated with a composite task, following the above procedure. Then, in the net encoding corresponding to the main system, we declare an instance of each CT_i, and we connect them synchronizing their i_cond and o_cond with the corresponding input and output task or condition. Finally, the activities corresponding to the composite tasks are defined by fluents whose logical values depend on the occurrence of their i_cond and o_cond actions in the expected way. Note that we can specify the activity of a task t_i belonging to a composite task CT_k on the main process, prefixing the task with the name of the composite task, i.e., $CT_k.t_i$.

5   Case Study

We take a case study accompanying the YAWL tool, that we consider to be a complex and complete model, involving all kinds of components of the YAWL language. The sources of the YAWL model can be downloaded[1]. The case study describes the process of order fulfillment followed in a fictitious company, which is divided into the following phases: ordering, logistics (which includes carrier appointment, freight in transit, freight delivered), and payment. The order fulfillment process model is shown in Fig. 6, where each of the above phases is captured by a composite task. Due to space limitations, we only explain in more detail one of the subtasks, the Carrier Appointment process. The YAWL model corresponding to the CA is show in Fig. 7. Basically, the model specifies that after confirmation of a Purchase Order on the previous phase, a *route guide* needs

---

[1] http://www.yawlfoundation.org

to be prepared and the *trailer usage* needs to be estimated. These operations are performed in parallel. If either task takes too long (calculated by the task *Carrier Timeout*), a timeout is triggered, which leads the termination of the overall process. If not, the task *Prepare Transportation Quote* takes place, by establishing the cost of shipment. After this task, a distinction is made among shipments that require a *full truck load (FTL)*, those that require *less than a truck load (LTTL)* and those that simply concern a *single package (SP)*. In order to simplify the view of the model, we depict FTL and LTTL as composite tasks. After the FTL and LTTL, there are subsequent opportunities to modify the appointments information until a *Shipment Notice* is produced; after that, the freight can be picked up. For SP the process is straightforward.

The encoding of YAWL specifications into FSP processes is fully automated, and a tool called YAWL2FSP was developed for this task. This tool is publicly available[2]. The FSP specification was automatically generated and the resulting LTS for the complete Order Fulfillment net (58 tasks, 30 gates, 36 conditions, 2 cancel regions) was generated in 0.298 seconds, using 28,96 Mbytes of memory, with the tool LTSA. The LTS contains 13164 states and 59722 transitions. The analysis for the system was performed in two phases. First, we verified properties over tasks based on the templates published in the Declare Tool [9], including precedence, non-coexistence, response, etc. Next, and taking advantage of the *fluent* characterizations and FLTL expressiveness, we verified properties of the system involving "sub-traces" of the execution, e.g. activities of a subtask, or properties where the desired behavior is characterized by the occurrence of a disjoint set of events. Due to space limitations, we only report here some of the most relevant properties, and show how these are captured in FLTL:

1. *If timeout occurs in CA, then no shipment notice can be produced.*

```
assert PROPERTY_1 = (CarrierTimeout ->!ProduceShipmentNotice)
```

Notice that this property uses two fluents, that capture the execution of corresponding atomic actions. The previous section describes the details on how these fluents are defined; for instance, for CarrierTimeout, the fluent is: `fluent CarrierTimeout = <C_A.task[5].start,C_A.task[5].end>`,   where C_A references the Carrier Appointment net, and `task[5]` represents the FSP process id corresponding to the CarrierTimeout task.

2. *Tasks belonging to different ways of transportation cannot occur simultaneously.* To capture this property we define three fluents, corresponding to the whole activity of the FTL, LTTL or SP ways of transportation. For example, `FullTruckLoad=<C_A.ftl.i_cond,C_A.ftl.o_cond>`, where `ftl` is the FSP id of the translated sub-net, and `i/o.cond` are the *initial* and *end* events, respectively. The property is specified as:

```
assert PROPERTY_2 = !( (FullTruckLoad && LessThanTruckLoad) ||
     (FullTruckLoad && SinglePackage)      ||
     (SinglePackage && LessThanTruckLoad) )
```

---

[2] http://sourceforge.net/projects/yawl2fsp/

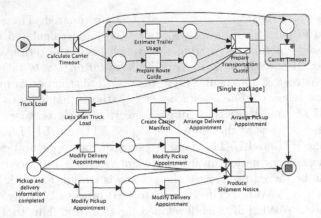

Fig. 7. YAWL net corresponding to Carrier Appointment Process

3. *If Shipment Notice was produced, necessarily a delivery and pickup appointment were arranged.* We define two fluents, characterizing the arranging appointment activities, i.e., pickup and delivery. These fluents will be activated by any of the corresponding activities of the three possible ways of transportation (FTL, LTTL or SP). Here we can appreciate the flexibility of fluents in order to describe abstract states in the model. As example consider the fluent corresponding to `Delivery Appointment Arranged`, which is enabled by the occurrence of an event corresponding to the main net and events of the FTL and LTTL sub-nets: <{C_A.task[7].end,C_A.ftl.task[2,3,7].end, C_A.ltl.task[2,5].end},C_A.o_cond> . The property is expressed as follows:

```
assert PROPERTY_3 = ( ShipmentNoticeProduced ->
    (DeliveryAppointmentArranged && PickupAppointmentArranged))
```

The time consumption associated with the verification of the above properties was: (1) 154ms, (2) 152ms and (3) 185ms, and the memory consumption (1) 11.8MB, (2) 11.9MB and (3) 16.6MB. The encoding and verification were performed using an Intel Core 2 Duo 2.2 Ghz processor, 2 GB 667 Mhz DDR2 SDRAM memory and a Unix based Operating System. Although we are unable to provide a fully-developed example due to space limitations, it is important to notice that in case some property does not hold, the model checker underlying LTSA would provide a trace reproducing the erroneous behavior of the system; this is extremely useful information, that is normally used in order to correct the model, or the corresponding workflow.

6   Related Work and Conclusions

The formal specification and verification of business processes has gained relevance in the last decade, not only in academic settings but also, and most importantly, in industry, where business process optimization is a crucial task. Various languages and methods for business process description have been proposed, most of which were initially informal, but for which different formal characterizations have been proposed. In [18] a general survey for BP specification can be found and in [4] a survey of formalizations for the Business Process Execution Language (BPEL) is analyzed. Other formal approaches include that presented in [20], where a semantics based on timed automata is proposed for the verification of Product Process Modeling Language (PPML) models. Since our work is essentially a formalization of workflows in terms of labeled transition systems, there exist some relevant related works; in particular, in [10] an automata-based method for formalizing workflow schemas is proposed, but the approach suffers from expressive power limitations, in relation to YAWL (beyond our bounded condition tokens limitation).

We have presented an encoding of YAWL (procedural) workflows into FSP processes. This encoding, which can be performed automatically and has been implemented in a tool, models tasks in a convenient way, enabling us to exploit fluent linear time temporal logic formulas for capturing typical constraints on workflows, and to use the model checker behind LTSA for verifying such constraints. The encoding adequately maps YAWL constructs to FSP elements, in order to make intensive use of *fluents*, in particular to capture workflow tasks, and their properties. Workflows, and in particular those based on a control-flow pattern, are inherently event-based, and thus using state-based formal languages such as LTL makes it more complicated to express declarative properties. FLTL, on the other hand, allows one to more naturally describe execution situations in workflows, via abstract activating/disabling events, as our encoding and examples in this paper illustrate.

We are currently conducting some experiments regarding a comparison of ease of use of LTL vs. FLTL for the specification of properties of workflows. In this respect, our work is twofold: we are working on a tool for automatically translating Declare constraint models to FLTL formulas, in order to verify those constraints over a procedural YAWL workflow, and we are developing a front-end (graphical tool) to assist the end user in the description of properties via FLTL and to represent violation executions when counterexamples are reported.

We have chosen to base our work on YAWL because it has a formal foundation, and it supports a wide range of workflow patterns, providing an expressive environment for BP specification. As we mentioned, the YAWL toolset provides the verification of some properties of workflows such as soundness and deadlock-freedom [3], but it does not provide a suitable flexible language for declaratively expressing other behavioral properties of its models. In this respect, the Declare tool might be applicable, but only to monitor executions of YAWL models, or analyzing the consistency of different declarative, linear temporal logic, constraints on a procedural YAWL workflow. In particular, Declare does not provide features for the verification of properties of executions. In this aspect, works closer to our approach are those presented in [12,6], where the SPIN model checker is used to automatically verify properties of YAWL models. However, in these works, standard LTL is employed as a property language, which is better suited for state-based settings but less appropriate for event-based frameworks, as is the case of workflow descriptions [7].

Acknowledgements. The authors would like to thank the anonymous referees for their helpful comments. This work was partially supported by the Argentinian

Agency for Scientific and Technological Promotion (ANPCyT), through grants PICT PAE 2007 No. 2772 and PICT 2010 No. 1690, and by the MEALS project (EU FP7 programme, grant agreement No. 295261).

References

1. van der Aalst, W.M.P., ter Hofstede, A.H.M., Kiepuszewski, B., Barros, A.P.: Workflow Patterns. Distributed and Parallel Databases 14, 5–51 (2003)
2. van der Aalst, W.M.P., ter Hofstede, A.H.M.: YAWL: yet another workflow language. Inf. Syst. 30, 245–275 (2005)
3. van der Aalst, W.M.P., et al.: Soundness of workflow nets: classification, decidability, and analysis. Formal Asp. Comput. 23(3), 333–363 (2011)
4. van Breugel, F., Koshkina, M.: Models and Verification of BPEL (2006), http://www.cse.yorku.ca/~franck/research/drafts/tutorial.pdf
5. Clarke, E., Grumberg, O., Peled, D.: Model Checking. MIT Press (2000)
6. Rabbi, F., Wang, H., MacCaull, W.: YAWL2DVE: An Automated Translator for Workflow Verification. In: SSIRI, pp. 53–59 (2010)
7. Giannakopoulou, D., Magee, J.: Fluent model checking for event-based systems. In: ESEC / SIGSOFT FSE, pp. 257–266 (2003)
8. Girault, C., Valk, R.: Petri Nets for Systems Engineering: A Guide to Modeling, Verification, and Applications. Springer (2002)
9. ter Hofstede, A.H.M., van der Aalst, W.M.P., Adams, M., Russell, N.: Modern Bussiness Process Automation. Springer (2010)
10. Karamanolis, C.T., Giannakopoulou, D., Magee, J., Wheater, S.M.: Model Checking of Workflow Schemas. In: EDOC, pp. 170–181 (2000)
11. Kindler, E.: On the semantics of EPCs: Resolving the vicious circle. Data Knowl. Eng. 56(1), 23–40 (2006)
12. Leyla, N., Mashiyat, A.S., Wang, H., MacCaull, W.: Towards workflow verification. In: CASCON, pp. 253–267 (2010)
13. Magee, J., Kramer, J.: Concurrency: State Models and Java Programs. John Wiley & Sons (1999)
14. Maggi, F.M., Montali, M., Westergaard, M., van der Aalst, W.M.P.: Monitoring Business Constraints with Linear Temporal Logic: An Approach Based on Colored Automata. In: Rinderle-Ma, S., Toumani, F., Wolf, K. (eds.) BPM 2011. LNCS, vol. 6896, pp. 132–147. Springer, Heidelberg (2011)
15. Manna, Z., Pnueli, A.: The Temporal Logic of Reactive and Concurrent Systems - Specification. Springer (1991)
16. Manna, Z., Pnueli, A.: Temporal Verification of Reactive Systems -Safety. Springer (1995)
17. Miller, R., Shanahan, M.: The Event Calculus in Classical Logic - Alternative Axiomatisations. Linkoping Electronic Articles in Computer and Information Science 4(16), 1–27 (1999)
18. Morimoto, S.: A Survey of Formal Verification for Business Process Modeling. In: ICCS 2008, pp. 514–522 (2008)
19. Pesic, M., Schonenberg, H., van der Aalst, W.M.P.: Declarative Workflow. In: Modern Business Process Automation, pp. 175–201 (2010)
20. Regis, G., Aguirre, N., Maibaum, T.: Specifying and Verifying Business Processes Using PPML. In: Breitman, K., Cavalcanti, A. (eds.) ICFEM 2009. LNCS, vol. 5885, pp. 737–756. Springer, Heidelberg (2009)
21. Wong, P.Y.H., Gibbons, J.: Property specifications for workflow modelling. Sci. Comput. Program 76(10), 942–967 (2011)

Composition of Model Transformations: A Categorical Framework

Christoph Schulz, Michael Löwe, and Harald König

FHDW Hannover University of Applied Sciences,
Freundallee 15, 30173 Hannover, Germany
{Christoph.Schulz,Michael.Loewe,Harald.Koenig}@fhdw.de

Abstract. Consistency management in evolving information systems is hard, for two reasons. On the one hand, large databases exist which have to be adjusted. On the other hand, many programs access those data. Data and programs all have to be synchronized in a consistent manner. It cannot be relied upon, however, that no running processes exist during such a migration. Consequently, a restructuring of an information system needs to take care of the migration of object-oriented systems comprising data, programs, and processes. This co-evolution together with the notion of model transformation and instance migration has been introduced in earlier papers. This paper builds upon this exploratory work and analyses under which circumstances composed model transformations are compatible with composed instance migrations. We develop the notion of shortcut paths and show that composition is possible if shortcut paths are reflected by the underlying model transformations.

Keywords: Composition, Model transformation, Instance migration, Data synchronization, Data-schema co-evolution.

1 Introduction

Software systems are subject to many kinds of changes. Obviously, this is because the environment in which software development is performed is very pliable. As Brooks once wrote, "The software entity is constantly subject to pressures for change. [...] Partly it is because software can be changed more easily—it is pure thought-stuff, infinitely malleable." [2, p. 184–185] Consequently, managers, team leaders and sometimes even developers expect changes in software requirements to be processed quickly.

But reality is different: Changing software is hard. There are two aspects which are independent of the modelling and programming language used to describe the software and which have a considerable impact on its changeability:

1) Is there any persistent data associated with the software to be changed?
2) Do processes (running instances) exist?

At least, the answer to the first question is "yes". For example, ERP software tends to have very large data bases associated, the contents of which possess

R. Gheyi and D. Naumann (Eds.): SBMF 2012, LNCS 7498, pp. 163–178, 2012.

important business value. No one will risk changing existing software with the consequence of losing valuable data. The second question is important in environments with a high demand for software running 24/7/365. Obviously needed in critical environments as nuclear power plants, this requirement has in the meantime also reached the business world over the last decade, as being able to do business without interruptions has become very important, especially for globally positioned companies. Consequently, running applications should not be disturbed or terminated by software updates whenever possible. Generally, we think that model evolution becomes agile only if consistency between models and dependent artifacts is spontaneously maintained.

Facing these challenges, we propose a formal method based on universal algebra and some basic facts from category theory that is capable of describing *complete* object-oriented systems. By this, we mean the combined software and data model (MOF[1] level "M1") together with data, programs, and processes, which build together the instances (MOF level "M0") and are typed in the model. Endogeneous model transformations[2] at medium or fine granularity, i.e. changes at the level of class structures or attribute assignments, are described by special relations between old and new model. The strength of this approach is the possibility to *automatically* induce a correct migration of *all* instances, i.e. data, programs, and processes, for a given model transformation. Here, "correct" firstly means that the resulting instances are correctly typed in the target model. Secondly, our formal method provably guarantees that the various migrated instances are adapted as much as necessary and as little as possible, due to sound constructions which are categorically founded. All these properties allow us to apply several model transformations to the current model and expect the migrated system to perform as the former system but to be typed in the new (improved) model. This is exactly what is desired when doing refactoring in software development.

But refactoring can almost never be done at one go. On the contrary, a good refactoring is characterized by applying a set of primitive and well-defined steps [8]. This is typically motivated by giving the developers the ability to test their software at several points during the refactoring process in order to ensure that the changes are sound. But even if the underlying refactoring framework can guarantee a correct result, it is reasonable to be able to model refactorings by a series of small atomic model transformations. Some advantages of this approach are e.g. that the single steps may be more understandable than the complete transformation, they may be documented separately, they can serve as a foundation for a refactoring tool offering arbitrary model transformations, and they aid in finding modelling errors more easily if the migration outcome is not what was desired. However, the ability of composing a big refactoring out of a set of elementary model transformations is also desired, for two reasons. First, it allows to build meaningful abstractions which can be reused to cut down the complexity of any problem. Second, applying the composed refactoring may perform better

---

[1] "Meta Object Facility", see http://www.omg.org/mof/ for details.
[2] A model transformation is called *endogenous* if both the source and target models possess the same meta model [18].

than applying its steps, due to potential synergy effects. So it is reasonable to analyze how to compose model transformations and what consequences emerge when migrating instances along such composed transformations.

The whole formal model has been developed in [21]. In [22, 23], we presented the modelling of data, programs, and processes. Correctness formulated in categorical terms has been invented in [14]. In this paper, we focus on the composition problem. After describing the basic data modelling features in the section 2, we recap in section 3 model transformations and induced instance migrations. In section 4, we present the requirements for sound composition of model transformations and show that not all model transformations meet these requirements. We finally develop a sufficient criterion for model transformations which enforces composability and relies on the reflection of so-called shortcut paths. In section 5 we give an overview over related work. Finally, in section 6 an outlook is given over future research related to our work. Due to space limitations, this paper neither discusses the migration of programs and processes nor does it include all proofs; they can be found in [13, 21].

2   Modelling Data

The model and the instance level of object-oriented systems are modelled by systems wrt. an extended specification.[3] An *extended specification* $Spec = (\Sigma, H)$ is an extended signature together with a set of positive Horn formulas H over a set of variables X. An *extended signature* $\Sigma = (S, OP, P)$ consists of a set of *sorts* S, a family of *operation symbols* $OP = (OP_{w,s})_{w \in S^*, s \in S}$, and a family of *predicates* $P = (P_w)_{w \in S^*}$ such that $=_s \in P_{s\,s}$ for each sort $s \in S$. A *system* A wrt. an extended signature $\Sigma = (S, OP, P)$, for short a Σ-*system*, consists of a family of *carrier sets* $(A_s)_{s \in S}$, a family of *operations* $(op^A: A_w \to A_s)_{w \in S^*, s \in S, op \in OP_{w,s}}$, and a family of *relations* $(p^A \subseteq A_w)_{w \in S^*, p \in P_w}$ such that $=_s^A \subseteq A_s \times A_s$ is the diagonal relation for each sort s.[4] A *system* A wrt. an extended specification $Spec = (\Sigma, H)$ is a Σ-system such that all axioms are valid in A. A Σ-*homomorphism* $h: A \to B$ between two Σ-systems A and B wrt. an extended signature $\Sigma = (S, OP, P)$ is a family of mappings $(h_s: A_s \to B_s)_{s \in S}$ such that the mappings are compatible with the operations and relations, i.e., $h_s \circ op^A = op^B \circ h_w$ for all operation symbols $op: w \to s$ and $h_w(p^A) \subseteq p^B$ for all predicates $p: w$ where $w = s_1 s_2 \ldots s_n \in S^*$.[5] Each Σ-homomorphism $h: A \to B$ between two $Spec$-systems A and B wrt. an extended specification $Spec = (\Sigma, H)$ is called a $Spec$-homomorphism.

We model object-oriented systems by externalizing the typing relation and consider only graphs for depicting models as well as data or processes [22, 23]. Typing an instance graph I in a model graph S is done by a homomorphism $I \xrightarrow{type} S$. Additional structure is provided by certain predicates:

---

[3] See [17] for the special case when signatures consist of one sort only.

[4] Given $w = s_1 s_2 \ldots s_n$, A_w is an abbreviation for the product set $A_{s_1} \times A_{s_2} \times \cdots \times A_{s_n}$.

[5] Given $w = s_1 s_2 \ldots s_n$, the term $h_w(x_1, x_2, \ldots, x_n)$ is a shorthand notation for the term tuple $(h_{s_1}(x_1), h_{s_2}(x_2), \ldots, h_{s_n}(x_n))$.

Definition 1 (Specification MP). *The specification MP is defined as below:*

$MP =$
sorts
$\quad N, E$ (nodes and edges)
opns
$\quad s, t: E \rightarrow N$ (source and target node of an edge)
prds
$\quad under, rel: N\ N$ (subnode of/related to)
axms

(MP.1)	$x \in N : under(x, x)$
(MP.2)	$x, y \in N : under(x, y) \wedge under(y, x) \Rightarrow x = y$
(MP.3)	$x, y, z \in N : under(x, y) \wedge under(y, z) \Rightarrow under(x, z)$
(MP.4)	$x, y \in N : rel(x, y) \Rightarrow rel(y, x)$
(MP.5)	$x, y, z \in N : rel(x, y) \wedge rel(y, z) \Rightarrow rel(x, z)$
(MP.6)	$x, y \in N : under(x, y) \Rightarrow rel(x, y)$

□

Nodes correspond to classes or object particles and edges correspond to associations or links, depending on the context. Note that in our model, objects are expressed as a conglomerate of so-called *particles* which resemble the typing hierarchy of the object's class. This allows us to type an object with possibly incoming and outgoing links into the model by the use of a simple homomorphism. The predicate *under* models the inheritance relation between classes and the subparticle relation between object parts. The predicate *rel* encompasses a symmetric and transitive closure of the *under* relation and builds components from the inheritance structure on classes and objects.[6] It is needed to be able to express the typing condition T.1 presented below.

In order to ensure that the modelling of object-oriented systems is sound, we extend the specification by the two *typing conditions* T.1 and T.2:

typing conditions

(T.1)	$x, y \in N : rel(x, y) \wedge type(x) = type(y) \Rightarrow x = y$
(T.2)	$x, y \in E : s(x) = s(y) \wedge type(x) = type(y) \Rightarrow x = y$

Condition T.1 prevents one object to contain more than one particle for the same type which is a typical requirement of object-oriented languages. Condition T.2 forces all associations to be many-to-at-most-one. This simplifies programmatic dereferencing at the instance level.[7]

---

[6] Note, however, that with positive Horn formulas, it is not possible to specify that *rel* is *exactly* the symmetric and transitive closure – the *rel* relation may be larger.

[7] Nevertheless, multi-valued associations can be used by employing a container such as a linked list using single-valued associations only.

We use the following notation: $\mathbf{Alg}(MP)$ denotes the category of MP-systems and MP-homomorphisms. Given a fixed model S, the slice category $\mathbf{Alg}(MP){\downarrow}S$ expresses the category of $\mathbf{Alg}(MP)$-arrows $I \xrightarrow{type} S$ and compatible morphisms between them, and the category $\mathbf{Sys}(S)$ denotes the full subcategory of $\mathbf{Alg}(MP){\downarrow}S$ whose objects (i.e. $type$-like arrows) satisfy the typing conditions.

See [14, 23] for the proof of the following proposition which expresses that for each system that does not satisfy the typing conditions, it is possible to find a minimal and uniquely determined set of changes such that the typing conditions are valid in the resulting system:

Proposition 2 (Free functor $\mathcal{F}^S$). *For each MP-system S, there is a functor $\mathcal{F}^S\colon \mathbf{Alg}(MP){\downarrow}S \to \mathbf{Sys}(S)$ which is left-adjoint to the inclusion functor $\mathcal{I}^S\colon \mathbf{Sys}(S) \to \mathbf{Alg}(MP){\downarrow}S$.* □

Summarizing our results so far, an object-oriented model is described by an MP-system S. An instance of this model consists of an MP-system I and a typing MP-homomorphism $type\colon I \to S$ such that $I \xrightarrow{type} S$ is an object of the category $\mathbf{Sys}(S)$. Every instance $I \xrightarrow{type} S$ in $\mathbf{Alg}(MP){\downarrow}S$ can freely be transformed into an object of the category $\mathbf{Sys}(S)$ by the free functor $\mathcal{F}^S$.

3   Modelling Transformations

In this section we introduce model transformations that can uniquely be extended to instance migrations.

Definition 3 (Transformation). *A transformation $t\colon S \rightsquigarrow S'$ in the category $\mathbf{Alg}(MP)$ is a span $S \xleftarrow{l^t} \overline{S} \xrightarrow{r^t} S'$.* □

A general transformation allows reduction and unfolding (or copying) as well as extension and folding (or identifying) through the use of non-surjective homomorphisms (reduction and extension) and non-injective homomorphisms (unfolding and folding) on the left and right side of the span, respectively. It expresses a relation between the old model S and the new model S'. In the following, we use the term *model transformation* if the span consists of model objects, and *(instance) migration* if the span consists of instance objects.

Given a typed instance $I \xrightarrow{type_I} S$ and a model transformation $S \xleftarrow{l^t} \overline{S} \xrightarrow{r^t} S'$, the migration is performed as follows (visualized in Fig. 1):

1) $\mathcal{P}^{l^t}$, the pullback functor along l^t, is applied to $I \xrightarrow{type_I} S$, resulting in the typed instance $\overline{I} \xrightarrow{type_{\overline{I}}} \overline{S}$.[8] This part of the transformation is responsible for unfolding instance elements if l^t is not injective, and for deleting elements if l^t is not surjective.

---

[8] This corresponds to the construction of the pullback of $type_I$ and l^t in $\mathbf{Alg}(MP)$ which is known to exist as $\mathbf{Alg}(MP)$ is complete, see [23].

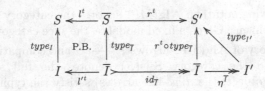

Fig. 1. Model transformation and instance migration

2) $\mathcal{F}^{r^t}$, the composition functor along r^t, is applied to $\overline{I} \xrightarrow{type_{\overline{T}}} \overline{S}$, resulting in the typed instance $\overline{I} \xrightarrow{r^t \circ type_{\overline{T}}} S'$. This part of the transformation is used to retype instance elements and to add new types without any instances.

3) $\overline{I} \xrightarrow{r^t \circ type_{\overline{T}}} S'$ may violate the typing conditions T.1 and T.2. To fix this, we apply $\mathcal{F}^{S'}: \mathbf{Alg}(MP){\downarrow}S' \to \mathbf{Sys}(S')$ from Proposition 2 to it, obtaining the typed instance $I' \xrightarrow{type_{I'}} S'$. This part of the transformation is responsible for identifying instance elements due to the application of the typing conditions.

Composing these functors yields the *migration functor* (compare [14]):

Definition 4 (Migration functor). *Let* $S \xleftarrow{l^t} \overline{S} \xrightarrow{r^t} S'$ *be a model transformation. The* migration functor $\mathcal{M}^t: \mathbf{Sys}(S) \to \mathbf{Sys}(S')$ *is then defined as* $\mathcal{M}^t ::= \mathcal{F}^{S'} \circ \mathcal{F}^{r^t} \circ \mathcal{P}^{l^t}$. □

We now give two examples of simple model transformations. We have customers (class "C") and third-party insurance products (class "TPI") which are connected by the association "prod" (product). The first transformation t_1 introduces insurances (class "I") as an abstraction of third-party insurances (see Fig. 2a). The second transformation t_2 moves the association end of "prod" to the new superclass "I", thereby allowing customers to be linked to more general insurance products (see Fig. 2b). Both model transformations represent actions that are typical for the development of object-oriented software.

Now we show how to migrate the instance in Fig. 3a, typed in the model on the left side of t_2.[9] In the first step, the instance is pulled back along l^{t_2}, yielding the instance in Fig. 3b. In the second step, this instance is only retyped, yielding the instance in Fig. 3c. Note that the object *2* of class *TPI* now possesses two particles of the type *I*. This instance violates the typing condition T.1. So applying the free functor $\mathcal{F}^{S'}$ identifies these two particles, resulting in the final instance shown in Fig. 3d.

A catalogue of supported model transformations is presented in [21].

---

[9] The model transformation t_2 has been chosen as it makes the migration more interesting.

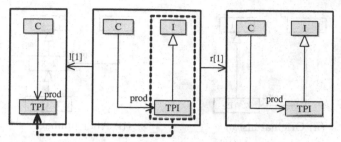

(a) First transformation t_1: Creating superclass

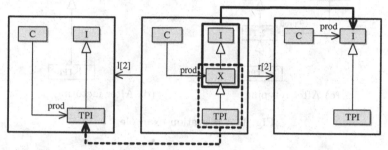

(b) Second transformation t_2: Moving association end to superclass

Fig. 2. Two simple model transformations

4   Composition of Model Transformations

Given two model transformations $t_1 ::= S \xleftarrow{l^{t_1}} \overline{S} \xrightarrow{r^{t_1}} S'$ and $t_2 ::= S' \xleftarrow{l^{t_2}} \overline{\overline{S}} \xrightarrow{r^{t_2}} S''$, a composed model transformation $t_2 \circ t_1$ has to fulfil two requirements:

1) *(syntactical)* $t_2 \circ t_1$ has to be a span $S \xleftarrow{l} X \xrightarrow{r} S''$ for some object X.
2) *(semantical)* Migrating a typed instance along the composed model transformation has to result in the same typed instance as the two-step migration along the two separate model transformations:

$$\mathcal{M}^{t_2 \circ t_1} = \mathcal{M}^{t_2} \circ \mathcal{M}^{t_1} \qquad \text{(migration compatibility condition)}$$

The syntactical requirement is easily fulfilled: As transformations are spans, they can be composed by taking the pullback of the "inner" span homomorphisms:

Definition 5 (Composition of model transformations). *Let two model transformations* $t_1 ::= S \xleftarrow{l^{t_1}} \overline{S} \xrightarrow{r^{t_1}} S'$ *and* $t_2 ::= S' \xleftarrow{l^{t_2}} \overline{\overline{S}} \xrightarrow{r^{t_2}} S''$ *be given. Then the composition* $t_2 \circ t_1$ *is defined to be the span* $S \xleftarrow{l^{t_1} \circ \overline{l}^{t_2}} P^S \xrightarrow{r^{t_2} \circ \overline{r}^{t_1}} S''$, *where* $\overline{S} \xleftarrow{\overline{l}^{t_2}} P^S \xrightarrow{\overline{r}^{t_1}} \overline{\overline{S}}$ *is pullback of* $\overline{S} \xrightarrow{r^{t_1}} S' \xleftarrow{l^{t_2}} \overline{\overline{S}}$ *(see Fig. 4).*

□

The semantical requirement, however, is more involved. The following counterexamples demonstrate that the migration compatibility condition is not always

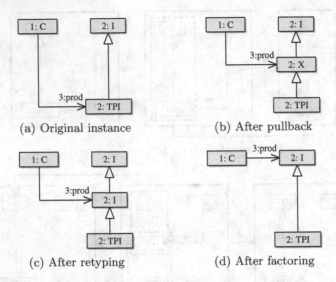

(a) Original instance   (b) After pullback

(c) After retyping   (d) After factoring

Fig. 3. A migration example

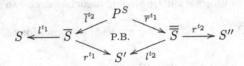

Fig. 4. Composition of transformations

true for arbitrary model transformations. In the first example (see Fig. 5), the second model transformation $M_1 \xleftarrow{l^{t2}} M_{12} \xrightarrow{r^{t2}} M_2$ deletes an association which results from merging two separate associations by the first model transformation $M_0 \xleftarrow{l^{t1}} M_{01} \xrightarrow{r^{t1}} M_1$ (5a). If the migration is done step-by-step (5b), the first model transformation causes instances of the merged associations to identify their targets if they start at the same particle due to typing condition T.2. When migrating along the composed model transformation (5c), the deletion is done earlier as the right side of the first model transformation and the left side of the second model transformation are interchanged. The effect of this is that no particles are identified on the right side of the composed transformation, as there are no associations to be merged at all at this point.

In the second example (see Fig. 6), the first transformation $M_0 \xleftarrow{l^{t1}} M_{01} \xrightarrow{r^{t1}} M_1$ merges the two related classes B and C (i.e. $(B, C) \in rel^{M_0}$, indicated by the squiggly line between B and C).[10] The second transformation $M_1 \xleftarrow{l^{t2}} M_{12} \xrightarrow{r^{t2}}$

---

[10] Note that B is neither a superclass nor a subclass of C.

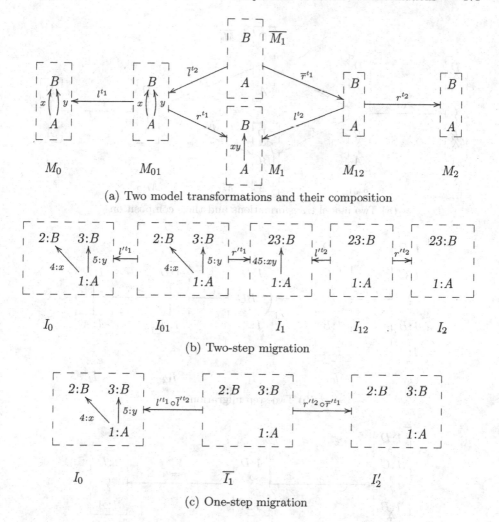

(a) Two model transformations and their composition

(b) Two-step migration

(c) One-step migration

Fig. 5. Composition incompatible with migration (1)

M_2 deletes the merged class (6a).[11] If I_0 is migrated step-by-step (6b), the missing inheritance link from $1{:}A$ to $1{:}D$ is added to I_1 by the free functor $\mathcal{F}$ due to axiom MP.3. If I_0 is migrated at once (6c), B and C are deleted before being merged as l'^{t_2} is effectively interchanged with r'^{t_1}. Hence, there is nothing to merge and so no inheritance link is added between the particles $1{:}A$ and $1{:}D$.

Because of these two effects, we need a compatibility condition for model transformations. First, observe that the counterexamples are based on the fact that the pullback functor $\mathcal{P}^{l^{t_2}}$ interacts badly with the free functor $\mathcal{F}^{M_1}$. The next

---

[11] Note that due to the axioms MP.4, MP.5, and MP.6, the property holds that if two classes are directly or indirectly connected via the *under* and/or *rel* predicates, they are also directly connected via *rel*.

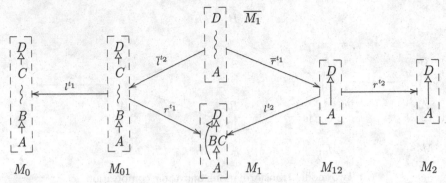

(a) Two model transformations and their composition

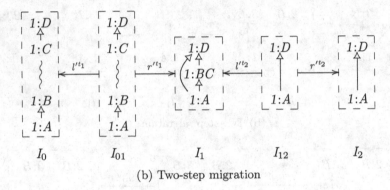

(b) Two-step migration

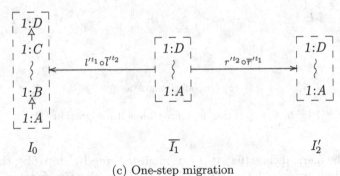

(c) One-step migration

Fig. 6. Composition incompatible with migration (2)

proposition develops this idea and states that if a certain *commutativity* property between these functors is given, composition is compatible with migration.

Proposition 6 (Composition of migrations [13, Theorem 26]). *Let two model transformations* $t_1 ::= S \xleftarrow{l^{t_1}} \overline{S} \xrightarrow{r^{t_1}} S'$ *and* $t_2 ::= S' \xleftarrow{l^{t_2}} \overline{\overline{S}} \xrightarrow{r^{t_2}} S''$ *be given. If the pullback functor on the left-hand side of the second migration and*

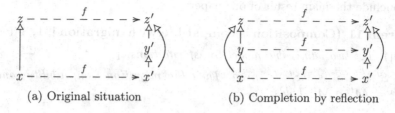

(a) Original situation   (b) Completion by reflection

Fig. 7. Example of a homomorphism reflecting shortcut paths

the free functor can be swapped, i.e. if $\mathcal{P}^{l_{t_2}} \circ \mathcal{F}^{S'} = \mathcal{F}^{\overline{S}} \circ \mathcal{P}^{l_{t_2}}$, then the migration compatibility condition $\mathcal{M}^{t_2 \circ t_1} = \mathcal{M}^{t_2} \circ \mathcal{M}^{t_1}$ holds.   □

It remains to find a criterion for ensuring the condition above. In the first counterexample, the problem arises from identifying associations. So we require that model transformations are not allowed to identify associations on the right side. We call such model transformations "proper":

Definition 7 (Proper transformation). *A transformation $S \xleftarrow{l^t} \overline{S} \xrightarrow{r^t} S'$ in* $\mathbf{Alg}(MP)$ *is proper if r^t is injective on associations, i.e., if $r_E^t(x) = r_E^t(y) \Rightarrow x = y$ holds for all x, $y \in \overline{S}_E$.*

The problem that arises in the second counterexample can be solved by requiring that the left-hand side of a model transformation reflect inheritance "shortcuts". Consider again Fig. 6: In M_1, the inheritance path $A \dashrightarrow D$ is a shortcut for the (longer) inheritance path $A \dashrightarrow BC \dashrightarrow D$. In M_{12}, however, the dotted inheritance relation is not a shortcut path. This leads to the anomaly where the free functor does not adapt instances due to missing elements. So we define

Definition 8 (Homomorphisms reflecting shortcut paths). *Let $f: A \to B$ be a MP-homomorphism. Then f is said to* reflect shortcut paths *if for every triple $(x, y', z) \in A_N \times B_N \times A_N$ with $(x, z) \in under^A$, $(f_N(x), y') \in under^B$, and $(y', f_N(z)) \in under^B$ there is some $y \in A_N$ with $f_N(y) = y'$, $(x, y) \in under^A$, and $(y, z) \in under^A$ (see Fig. 7).*

                                                                        □

Definition 9 (Admissible model transformations). *Let t be a model transformation $S \xleftarrow{l^t} \overline{S} \xrightarrow{r^t} S'$. Then t is said to be* admissible *if it is proper and if l^t reflects shortcut paths.*   □

It is easy to show that admissible model transformations are closed under composition. It remains to show that composing admissible model transformations is compatible with migration:

Proposition 10 (Pullback and free functor commute [21, Proposition 11.49]). *Let two* admissible *model transformations $t_1 ::= S \xleftarrow{l^{t_1}} \overline{S} \xrightarrow{r^{t_1}} S'$ and $t_2 ::= S' \xleftarrow{l^{t_2}} \overline{\overline{S}} \xrightarrow{r^{t_2}} S''$ be given. Then $\mathcal{P}^{l_{t_2}} \circ \mathcal{F}^{S'} = \mathcal{F}^{\overline{\overline{S}}} \circ \mathcal{P}^{l_{t_2}}$ holds.*   □

We conclude the main result of our paper:

Theorem 11 (Composition is compatible with migration [21, Theorem 11.50]). *Let two admissible model transformations* $t_1 ::= S \xleftarrow{l^{t_1}} \overline{S} \xrightarrow{r^{t_1}} S'$ *and* $t_2 ::= S' \xleftarrow{l^{t_2}} \overline{\overline{S}} \xrightarrow{r^{t_2}} S''$ *be given. Then the migration compatibility condition* $\mathcal{M}^{t_2 \circ t_1} = \mathcal{M}^{t_2} \circ \mathcal{M}^{t_1}$ *holds.*

Proof. This follows directly from Proposition 10 and Proposition 6.

Consider again the first counterexample Fig. 5. If t_1 is replaced by the proper identity model transformation t'_1, migrating I_0 along t'_1 results in I_1 being identical to I_0. Applying t_2 to it deletes both links $4{:}x$ and $5{:}y$, resulting in a system equal to I'_2. Now consider the second counterexample in Fig. 6. If t_2 is replaced by the model transformation t'_2 which equals t_2 except that the dotted inheritance relation in M_{12} is removed, t'_2 reflects shortcut paths on the left side as there are no inheritance paths in M_{12} at all anymore. Migrating I_1 along t_2 leads to systems I_{12} and I_2 without an inheritance link between $1{:}A$ to $1{:}D$. Hence, with the dotted path removed, migrating I_0 along t_1 and then I_1 along t_2 yields the same system as the migraton of I_0 along $t_2 \circ t_1$, according to Theorem 11.

It remains to discuss whether restricting oneself to admissible model transformations is a serious limitation. Regarding the reflection of shortcut paths, recall that shortcuts in models generally result from the transitive closure of the inheritance graph. So transforming a shortcut path into a non-shortcut path on the left side of a model transformation means that some indirect superclass becomes a direct superclass due to the removal of an intermediate class (e.g. D becomes a direct superclass of A on the left side of t_2). In our opinion, this is not a "natural" model transformation, as the data and operations associated with the removed intermediate class simply disappear which may lead to problems wrt. the semantics of the model. One would rather merge the intermediate class with one of its super- or subclasses in order to retain the associated data and operations. So restricting oneself to model transformations reflecting shortcut paths on the left side only rules out transformations that are problematic from a semantics point of view. Identifying associations on the right side is slightly more useful but generally unsafe as it may lead to object merging (see the first counterexample). Additionally, [21] shows that identifying associations causes problems when migrating programs ([22] describes how to model programs and processes with our model). So sticking to proper model transformations is sensible.

Now we continue the example of section 3. Let the model on the left side of t_1 be called the *source* model and the model on the right side of t_2 be called the *target* model. Then both t_1 and t_2 are syntactically composable as the left side of t_2 is equal to the right side of t_1. Moreover, they are both admissible: Both of them do not identify associations on the right side, and they reflect shortcut paths on the left side simply because there are no shortcut paths on the left side of both t_1 and t_2. By composing the spans according to Def. 5, we obtain the composed model transformation t_{1+2} as shown in Fig. 8. Fig. 9 presents the underlying pullback construction in more detail.

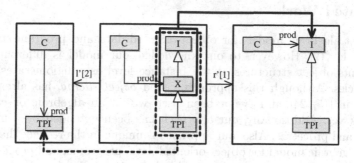

Fig. 8. Composed transformation t_{1+2}

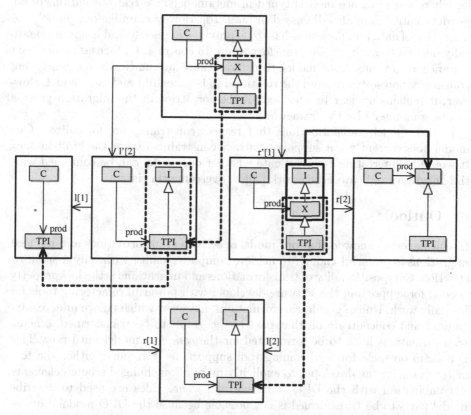

Fig. 9. Construction of the composed model transformation t_{1+2}

If, for example, we assume an instance identical to the source model (one customer linked to one third-party insurance product), it is easy to see that migrating this instance along t_1 and t_2 yields the same result as migrating the same instance along t_{1+2} (in both cases, an instance identical to the target model is produced).

5 Related Work

There exist algebraic models for object-oriented data and program structures, e.g. [6, 7, 11, 12]. However, to our knowledge, our model is different in that it represents object structures at the instance level as conglomerates of separate particles. Although this approach, called *object slicing*, has already been described in [15, 24], it has not been used within an algebraic or categorial framework yet. Additionally, our approach has been extended by a model for programs and processes. Also, our approach is unique in the respect that it combines an algebraic model for object-oriented data, programs, and processes with a model for schema transformations and induced instance migrations.

The transformation of typed instances using pullbacks is described e.g. in [5] where instances are models typed in metamodels. Co-transformations of dependent entities are also discussed in [3, 9, 10]. However, unlike our model, the migration of data and programs has to be provided explicitly and is not automatically derived from the model transformation. In contrast, [1] focuses on deriving instance migrations from model transformations automatically by generating transformation software from the relationship between old and new model. However, it remains unclear to what extent the correction of the migration process can be guaranteed by the framework.

In [19], model transformations that respect constraints are formalized. Our model does currently not support arbitrary constraints except the built-in ones. It would be interesting to investigate whether our model can be combined with the Diagram Predicate Framework [20] to overcome this issue.

6 Outlook

In this paper we showed that our model of schema transformations and induced migrations is powerful enough to achieve compositionality with only a small restriction. Compositionality of transformations and migrations is the key property needed for supporting the software developer with powerful refactoring tools for his daily work. Unlike graph transformations, however, which ignore unnecessary context and concentrate on that part of the graph to be transformed, schema transformations have to be formulated for the *complete* model until now. This is a main obstacle for forthcoming tool support, as it requires either the tool or (even worse) the developer to explicitly mark all unchanged schema elements. A combination with the DPO framework [6] where rules are used to describe model parts to be transformed is not possible because the DPO model requires the rule morphisms to be injective, whereas our model is dependent on the possibility to specify non-injective spans. Here more powerful graph transformation frameworks as sesqui pushout [4] or span rewriting [16] have to be examined and combined with the transformation model as presented in this paper.

The results of this paper are also valid when migrating programs and processes as described in [22]. In particular, disallowing the identification of associations on the right side is important if one wants to achieve that methods remain consistent during a migration. Details can be found in [21, Chapter 11.3].

For the time being, multiplicities and other complex conditions (e.g. OCL constraints) are not supported by our model and subject to future research.

References

[1] Aboulsamh, M., Crichton, E., Davies, J., Welch, J.: Model-Driven Data Migration. In: Trujillo, J., Dobbie, G., Kangassalo, H., Hartmann, S., Kirchberg, M., Rossi, M., Reinhartz-Berger, I., Zimányi, E., Frasincar, F. (eds.) ER 2010. LNCS, vol. 6413, pp. 285–294. Springer, Heidelberg (2010)

[2] Brooks, F.P.: The Mythical Man-Month: Essays on Software Engineering, Anniversary edn. Addison-Wesley (1995)

[3] Clève, A., Henrard, J., Hainaut, J.L.: Co-transformations in information system reengineering. Electronic Notes in Theoretical Computer Science 137(3), 5–15 (2005)

[4] Corradini, A., Heindel, T., Hermann, F., König, B.: Sesqui-Pushout Rewriting. In: Corradini, A., Ehrig, H., Montanari, U., Ribeiro, L., Rozenberg, G. (eds.) ICGT 2006. LNCS, vol. 4178, pp. 30–45. Springer, Heidelberg (2006)

[5] Diskin, Z., Dingel, J.: A metamodel independent framework for model transformation: Towards generic model management patterns in reverse engineering. In: Proceedings of the 3rd International Workshop on Metamodels, Schemas, Grammars and Ontologies for Reverse Engineering (ateM 2006) Johannes-Gutenberg-Universität Mainz (2006)

[6] Ehrig, H., Ehrig, K., Prange, U., Taentzer, G.: Fundamentals of Algebraic Graph Transformation. Springer (2006)

[7] Ehrig, H., Ehrig, K., Prange, U., Taentzer, G.: Formal integration of inheritance with typed attributed graph transformation for efficient VL definition and model manipulation. In: Proceedings of the 2005 IEEE Symposium on Visual Languages and Human-Centric Computing (VLHCC 2005), pp. 71–78. IEEE Computer Society, Washington, DC (2005)

[8] Fowler, M.: Refactoring: Improving the Design of Existing Code. Addison-Wesley (1999)

[9] Hainaut, J.L.: The Transformational Approach to Database Engineering. In: Lämmel, R., Saraiva, J., Visser, J. (eds.) GTTSE 2005. LNCS, vol. 4143, pp. 95–143. Springer, Heidelberg (2006)

[10] Henrard, J., Hick, J.M., Thiran, P., Hainaut, J.L.: Strategies for data reengineering. In: Proceedings of the 9th Working Conference on Reverse Engineering (WCRE 2002), pp. 211–220. IEEE Computer Society, Washington, DC (2002)

[11] Kastenberg, H., Kleppe, A.G., Rensink, A.: Defining Object-Oriented Execution Semantics Using Graph Transformations. In: Gorrieri, R., Wehrheim, H. (eds.) FMOODS 2006. LNCS, vol. 4037, pp. 186–201. Springer, Heidelberg (2006)

[12] Kastenberg, H., Kleppe, A.G., Rensink, A.: Engineering object-oriented semantics using graph transformations. Tech. Rep. TR-CTIT-06-12, University of Twente, Department of Computer Science (2006)

[13] König, H., Löwe, M., Schulz, C.: Functor semantics for refactoring-induced data migration. Tech. Rep. 02007/01, Fachhochschule für die Wirtschaft Hannover (2007)

[14] König, H., Löwe, M., Schulz, C.: Model Transformation and Induced Instance Migration: A Universal Framework. In: Simao, A., Morgan, C. (eds.) SBMF 2011. LNCS, vol. 7021, pp. 1–15. Springer, Heidelberg (2011)

178   C. Schulz, M. Löwe, and H. König

[15] Kuno, H.A., Ra, Y.G., Rundensteiner, E.A.: The object-slicing technique: A flexible object representation and its evaluation. Tech. Rep. CSE-TR-241-95, University of Michigan, Department of Elec. Engineering and Computer Science (1995)
[16] Löwe, M.: Graph Rewriting in Span-Categories. In: Ehrig, H., Rensink, A., Rozenberg, G., Schürr, A. (eds.) ICGT 2010. LNCS, vol. 6372, pp. 218–233. Springer, Heidelberg (2010)
[17] Mal'cev, A.I.: Algebraic systems. Springer (1973)
[18] Mens, T., Gorp, P.V.: A taxonomy of model transformation. Electronic Notes in Theoretical Computer Science 152, 125–142 (2006)
[19] Rutle, A., Rossini, A., Lamo, Y., Wolter, U.: A formal approach to the specification and transformation of constraints in MDE. Journal of Logic and Algebraic Programming 81(4), 422–457 (2012)
[20] Rutle, A., Wolter, U., Lamo, Y.: A diagrammatic approach to model transformations. In: Proceedings of the 2008 Euro American Conference on Telematics and Information Systems (EATIS 2008), pp. 1–8. ACM (2008)
[21] Schulz, C.: Transformation Objektorientierter Systeme basierend auf algebraischen Graphtransformationen. Ph.D. thesis, Technische Universität Berlin, Berlin, Deutschland (2010)
[22] Schulz, C., Löwe, M., König, H.: Categorical framework for the transformation of object-oriented systems: Operations and methods. Electronic Communications of the EASST 26, 1–21 (2010)
[23] Schulz, C., Löwe, M., König, H.: A categorical framework for the transformation of object-oriented systems: Models and data. Journal of Symbolic Computation 46(3), 316–337 (2011)
[24] Young-Gook, R., Rundensteiner, E.A.: A transparent schema-evolution system based on object-oriented view technology. IEEE Transactions on Knowledge and Data Engineering 9(4), 600–624 (1997)

Verification Rules for Exception Handling in Eiffel

Emil Sekerinski and Tian Zhang

McMaster University, Hamilton, ON, Canada
{emil,zhangt26}@mcmaster.ca

Abstract. The Eiffel exception mechanism supports two methodological aspects. First, a method specification by a pre- and postcondition also determines when the method exits exceptionally, namely when the stated postcondition cannot be satisfied. Secondly, the rescue and retry statements combine catching an exception with a loop structure, thus requiring a dedicated form of correctness reasoning. We present verification rules for total correctness that take these two aspects into account. The rules handle normal loops and retry loop structures in an analogous manner. They also allow the Eiffel's mechanism to be slightly generalized. The verification rules are derived from a definition of statements by higher-order predicate transformers and have been checked with a theorem prover.

1 Introduction

Programming languages offer exception handling for responding to detected failures, for dealing with rare or undesired circumstances, and for allowing for imperfections in the design (like an incomplete implementation). Compared to treating these situations by an explicit case analysis—with testing for permissibility of an operation *a priori* or testing for success of an operation *a posteriori*—exception handling allows the original, idealized design to remain largely unchanged and *separates the concern* of exceptional situations.

The exception mechanism of Eiffel is particularly methodological in that it is combined with the specification of methods by pre- and postconditions that are evaluated at run-time [16]. When a precondition does not hold, it is the caller's fault and an exception is signalled in the caller. When a postcondition does not hold, it is the callee's fault and an exception is signalled in the callee. If the callee cannot establish the desired postcondition by alternative means, the callee propagates the exception to the caller. Thus, a single postcondition determines whether a method exits normally or exits exceptionally, i.e. *fails*. This is in contrast to the view that exceptions provide an alternative exit from methods (like "item not found"), and as such have to be mentioned in method interfaces, together with the condition when they are raised and the postcondition in that case [12,14,15]. The second methodological aspect in Eiffel is that an exception handler may *retry* a method, in which case execution continues at the beginning of a method. The exception handler has to ensure that the precondition of the

R. Gheyi and D. Naumann (Eds.): SBMF 2012, LNCS 7498, pp. 179–193, 2012.

method holds, independently of where the exception in the body occurred, as in following fragment:

```
meth
  require
    pre
  do
    body
  ensure
    post
  rescue
    handler
    retry
  end
```

Here, *handler* is invoked if *post* does not hold at the end of *body*. The retry statement will restart the method, hence *handler* has to establish *pre*. Unlike in the *termination model* (as in Java) and the *resumption model* (as in Mesa), the *retrying model* of exception handling leads to a loop structure [5,24]. In this paper we are concerned with the correctness theory of exception handling in the retrying model of Eiffel.

The main contribution of this paper is a mechanically formalized verification theory for total correctness based on weakest precondition predicate transformers. Predicate transformers, as introduced by Dijkstra, define the input-output behaviour of statements and at the same time allow the extraction of verification conditions. The treatment of exception handling with predicate transformers goes back to Cristian [7]: statements have one entry and multiple exits (one of those being the normal one) and are defined by a set of predicate transformers, one for each exit. As King and Morgan point out, this disallows nondeterminism [11], which is useful for the specification and development of sequential programs and necessary for defining concurrent programs. The solution is to use a single *weakest exceptional precondition* predicate transformer with one postcondition for each exit instead. Leino and Snepscheut derive weakest exceptional preconditions of statements from a trace semantics [13]. Here we start immediately with weakest exceptional preconditions. Jacobs gives a mechanical formalization of try-catch-finally statements [10]. However, that formalization includes all the other "abrupt termination" modes of Java, which we do not need for Eiffel, and uses state transformers rather than predicate transformers, which again precludes nondeterminism.

Verification rules for *partial correctness* of Eiffel statements have been proposed by Nordio et al. [17]. The present work extends these rules by considering *total correctness*, which necessitates loop variants for normal loops and *retry variants* for methods with a retry statement. Loop variants were originally considered in Eiffel, but not retry variants [16]. Nordio et al. justify the rules with respect to an operational semantics; here we derive the rules from a (denotational) predicate transformer semantics. Another difference is the linguistic form for retrying. Eiffel originally has a *retry statement* which can appear only in the exception handler.

Nordio et al. propose instead to have a *retry variable*, a boolean variable which determines if at the end of an exception handler the body is attempted again. Tschannen et al. use this form of retrying for translating Eiffel into the Boogie intermediate verification language [21]. Here we consider retry statements, as they are of interest on their own and as the current versions of EiffelStudio (version 7) and SmartEiffel (version 2.3) only support retry statements. As a consequence, all statements have three exits, the normal, exceptional, and retry exit.

All theorems (formulae (1) to (23)) have been checked with the Isabelle/HOL theorem prover; for this reason, we allow ourselves to omit proofs [1]. The formalization is a *shallow embedding* in which each statement is directly defined as a term in the logic. This style goes back to Gordon [8] and has been explored for program verification and refinement, e.g. [4,23,18]. As noted by Harrison [9], this is a more natural formalization compared to a *deep embedding*, in which the syntax of statements and their meaning are inductively defined. A shallow embedding has also the advantage that all data types and operators of the underlying logic are immediately available in the programming language for specification and reasoning. The advantage of a deep embedding, to allow proofs over the structure of statements, is not needed here. The second contribution of this paper is to work out a shallow embedding of Eiffel statements with three exits. By comparison, the formalization of Jacobs uses a deep embedding [10]. Programming languages have partially defined expressions (pointer dereferencing, array indexing, arithmetic operations) and conditional boolean operators (**and then** and **or else**), which cannot be expressed directly in HOL, a logic of *total functions*. In order to avoid a dedicated logic with partial functions, the approach is to introduce partial functions within HOL only for program expression and to continue using total functions for reasoning about statements.

An elegant way to define loops is in terms of *strong iteration* S^ω, which stands for S being repeated zero or more times, i.e., **skip**, S, S ; S, ..., but possibly infinitely often. (Weak iteration S^* repeats S only finitely often.) Such a definition allows the algebraic properties of loops to be derived, which are useful for transformations like splitting/merging loops and atomicity refinement, e.g. as in [3,6,22]. The third contribution of this paper is to explore an algebraic style of defining retry loops. Here we have statements with three exits, i.e. with three kinds of "sequential composition", one for each exit. Thus three kinds of strong iteration are defined, one for each exit.

This work originated in an effort to identify and formalize design patterns for exception handling; one of those patterns is a simpler form of retrying [19]. The formalization here covers specifically the Eiffel mechanism of retrying. The authors' work on a new notion of *partial correctness* was inspired by the methodological aspects of exception handling in Eiffel [20].

Outline. As a prelude, the meaning of program expressions with undefinedness and conditional operators is given in Section 1. The definition of Eiffel statements is split in two parts. First a core language is defined by weakest preconditions

---

[1] The Isabelle/HOL formalization is available at
http://www.cas.mcmaster.ca/~zhangt26/SBMF/

in Section 2. The remaining statements of Eiffel are defined in terms of the core statements in Section 3. Correctness assertions are derived from the weakest preconditions for all statements in Section 4. This allows the conditions for method correctness to be derived in Section 5. The example of computing the square root by binary search is used to illustrate the application of the rules in Section 6. We conclude with a summary and discussion.

Notation. Following higher order logic, every term has a type and *predicates* are boolean terms. We write $=$ for the equality of terms and $\equiv$ for the equality of predicates. Arithmetic operators bind stronger than $=$, which itself binds stronger than boolean operators, which themselves bind stronger than $\equiv$.

2   Program Expressions

Before embarking on defining statements, we need to determine on how to treat possible *undefinedness* in expressions. We distinguish *terms* in the underlying logic, here higher order logic, from *program expressions*, here those of Eiffel. A boolean term, even one like $x/y > 0$ and $a[i] < k$ is always true or false. However, the program expressions $x/y > 0$ and $a[i] < k$ may not always yield a result. For program expression E its *definedness* ΔE and *value* 'E' are in part determined by the underlying machine; the result of ΔE and 'E' are terms. Formally, a program expression of type T is a total function whose range is either some element of T or *None*.

We consider a subset of Eiffel operators on booleans and integers: assuming that c is a constant, x a variable, and $\approx$ is $=, <$ or another relational operator, $\circ$ is $+, -,$ or $*$, and $|$ is $//$ or $\backslash\backslash$ (integer division and modulo), we have

$$
\begin{aligned}
&\Delta c &&\mathrel{\widehat{=}} \textit{True} &&\text{`}c\text{'} &&\mathrel{\widehat{=}} c \\
&\Delta x &&\mathrel{\widehat{=}} \textit{True} &&\text{`}x\text{'} &&\mathrel{\widehat{=}} x \\
&\Delta(E \textbf{ and } F) &&\mathrel{\widehat{=}} \Delta E \wedge \Delta F &&\text{`}E \textbf{ and } F\text{'} &&\mathrel{\widehat{=}} \text{`}E\text{'} \wedge \text{`}F\text{'} \\
&\Delta(E \textbf{ or } F) &&\mathrel{\widehat{=}} \Delta E \wedge \Delta F &&\text{`}E \textbf{ or } F\text{'} &&\mathrel{\widehat{=}} \text{`}E\text{'} \vee \text{`}F\text{'} \\
&\Delta(E \textbf{ and then } F) &&\mathrel{\widehat{=}} \Delta E \wedge (\text{`}E\text{'} \Rightarrow \Delta F) &&\text{`}E \textbf{ and then } F\text{'} &&\mathrel{\widehat{=}} \text{`}E\text{'} \wedge \text{`}F\text{'} \\
&\Delta(E \textbf{ or else } F) &&\mathrel{\widehat{=}} \Delta E \wedge (\neg \text{`}E\text{'} \Rightarrow \Delta F) &&\text{`}E \textbf{ or else } F\text{'} &&\mathrel{\widehat{=}} \text{`}E\text{'} \vee \text{`}F\text{'} \\
&\Delta(E \approx F) &&\mathrel{\widehat{=}} \Delta E \wedge \Delta F &&\text{`}E \approx F\text{'} &&\mathrel{\widehat{=}} \text{`}E\text{'} \approx \text{`}F\text{'} \\
&\Delta(E \mid F) &&\mathrel{\widehat{=}} \Delta E \wedge \Delta F \wedge \text{`}F\text{'} \neq 0 &&\text{`}E \mid F\text{'} &&\mathrel{\widehat{=}} \text{`}E\text{'} \mid \text{`}F\text{'} \\
&\Delta(E \circ F) &&\mathrel{\widehat{=}} \Delta E \wedge \Delta F \wedge &&\text{`}E \circ F\text{'} &&\mathrel{\widehat{=}} \text{`}E\text{'} \circ \text{`}F\text{'} \\
&&&\quad \textit{min\_int} \le \text{`}E \circ F\text{'} \\
&&&\quad \le \textit{max\_int}
\end{aligned}
$$

where *min_int* and *max_int* are the smallest and largest machine-representable integers, operators **and** and **or** evaluate both operands, and operators **and then** and **or else** evaluate conditionally. For example, assuming that $\textit{min\_int} \le 0 \le l \le u \le \textit{max\_int}$, we can show for program expression $(l + u) // 2$ that

$$\Delta((l + u) \;//\; 2) \equiv l + u \leq max\_int \qquad\qquad (1)$$
$$\text{`}(l + u) \;//\; 2\text{'} \quad = (l + u) \;//\; 2 \qquad\qquad (2)$$

and:

$$\Delta(l + (u - l) \;//\; 2) \equiv True \qquad\qquad (3)$$
$$\text{`}l + (u - l) \;//\; 2\text{'} \quad = l + (u - l) \;//\; 2 = (l + u) \;//\; 2 \qquad\qquad (4)$$

That is, program expressions $(l + u) \;//\; 2$ and $l + (u - l) \;//\; 2$ have the same value, namely the term $(l + u) \;//\; 2$, but the later is always defined under above assumption, whereas the former is not. We give the proof of (4):

$$
\begin{aligned}
& \text{`}(l + (u - l) \;//\; 2)\text{'} = (l + u) \;//\; 2 \\
\equiv\ & l + (u - l) \;//\; 2 = (l + u) \;//\; 2 && \text{definition of } val \\
\equiv\ & l * 2 + (u - l) \;//\; 2 * 2 = (l + u) \;//\; 2 * 2 && \text{congruence, distribution} \\
\equiv\ & l * 2 + (u - l) = l + u && \text{as } x \;//\; y * y = x \text{ if } y \neq 0 \\
\equiv\ & l + u = l + u && \text{arithmetic}
\end{aligned}
$$

The distinction between terms in the logic and program expressions keeps the logic simple, e.g. all familiar laws of the boolean algebra like the law of the excluded middle still hold, while allowing to capture all restrictions of an underlying machine.

3   Core Statements

We consider a core language of statements with three exits, namely *normal*, *exceptional*, and *retry* exit. The statement **abort** is completely uncontrollable and the statement **stop** blocks execution. The statements **skip**, **raise**, **retry** do not modify any variables, but jump to each of the three exits directly instead. **skip** terminates normally, **raise** terminates exceptionally, and **retry** terminates retrying.

Let a, b, c be predicates. In a language with single exit, the statement **assume** a or $[a]$ terminates if a is true and blocks if a is false. With three exits, the statement $[a, b, c]$ terminates normally if a is true, terminates exceptionally if b is true, terminates retrying if c is true, and blocks if all are false. If several conditions are true, the choice among the corresponding exits is nondeterministic. The *assignment* $x := e$, where x is a variable and e is a term, always terminates normally. The *nondeterministic choice* $S \sqcap T$ executes either S if S does not block and executes T if T does not block. If both do not block, the choice is nondeterministic. The *normal (sequential) composition* $S \,;\, T$ starts with statement S and continues with statement T on normal termination of S, the *exceptional (sequential) composition* $S;_E T$ continues with T on exceptional termination of S, and the *retrying (sequential) composition* $S;_R T$ continues with T on retrying termination of S.

This is formalized by a generalization of Dijkstra's weakest precondition predicate transformers. For predicates q, r, s,

$$wp\,{}^\backprime S^\prime\,(q, r, s)$$

is the weakest precondition such that S terminates, on normal termination q holds finally, on exceptional termination r holds finally, and on retrying termination s holds finally [2]:

$$wp\,{}^\backprime\mathbf{abort}^\prime\,(q, r, s) \mathrel{\widehat{=}} \mathit{False}$$
$$wp\,{}^\backprime\mathbf{stop}^\prime\,(q, r, s) \mathrel{\widehat{=}} \mathit{True}$$
$$wp\,{}^\backprime\mathbf{skip}^\prime\,(q, r, s) \mathrel{\widehat{=}} q$$
$$wp\,{}^\backprime\mathbf{raise}^\prime\,(q, r, s) \mathrel{\widehat{=}} r$$
$$wp\,{}^\backprime\mathbf{retry}^\prime\,(q, r, s) \mathrel{\widehat{=}} s$$
$$wp\,{}^\backprime[a, b, c]^\prime\,(q, r, s) \mathrel{\widehat{=}} (a \Rightarrow q) \wedge (b \Rightarrow r) \wedge (c \Rightarrow s)$$
$$wp\,{}^\backprime x := e^\prime\,(q, r, s) \mathrel{\widehat{=}} q[x \backslash e]$$
$$wp\,{}^\backprime S \sqcap T^\prime\,(q, r, s) \mathrel{\widehat{=}} wp\,{}^\backprime S^\prime\,(q, r, s) \wedge wp\,{}^\backprime T^\prime\,(q, r, s)$$
$$wp\,{}^\backprime S\,;\,T^\prime\,(q, r, s) \mathrel{\widehat{=}} wp\,{}^\backprime S^\prime\,(wp\,{}^\backprime T^\prime\,(q, r, s), r, s)$$
$$wp\,{}^\backprime S;_{\mathsf{E}}\,T^\prime\,(q, r, s) \mathrel{\widehat{=}} wp\,{}^\backprime S^\prime\,(q, wp\,{}^\backprime T^\prime\,(q, r, s), s)$$
$$wp\,{}^\backprime S;_{\mathsf{R}}\,T^\prime\,(q, r, s) \mathrel{\widehat{=}} wp\,{}^\backprime S^\prime\,(q, r, wp\,{}^\backprime T^\prime\,(q, r, s))$$

As a direct consequence, we have that $\mathbf{stop} = [\mathit{False}, \mathit{False}, \mathit{False}]$, $\mathbf{skip} = [\mathit{True}, \mathit{False}, \mathit{False}]$, $\mathbf{raise} = [\mathit{False}, \mathit{True}, \mathit{False}]$, and $\mathbf{retry} = [\mathit{False}, \mathit{False}, \mathit{True}]$. For local variable declarations, let X_0 be the initial value of variables of type X and let q, r, s be predicates that do not mention variable x:

$$wp\,{}^\backprime\mathbf{local}\,x : X\ S^\prime\,(q, r, s) \mathrel{\widehat{=}} (wp\,{}^\backprime S^\prime\,(q, r, s))[x \backslash X_0]$$

One more construct is needed for defining loops. In a language with single-exit statements, the *iteration* S^ω repeats S an arbitrary number of times, i.e. intuitively is $\mathbf{skip} \sqcap S \sqcap (S\,;\,S) \sqcap (S\,;\,S\,;\,S)\ldots$, until S blocks. While-loops can be defined in terms of iteration by $\mathbf{while}\,g\,\mathbf{do}\,S\,\mathbf{end} = ([g]\,;\,S)^\omega\,;\,[\neg g]$. Here, statements have three exits, so three variants of iteration exist: S^ω repeats S on normal termination; if S terminates exceptionally or retrying, S^ω terminates immediately. The iteration $S^{\omega_{\mathsf{E}}}$ repeats S on exceptional termination; if S terminates normally or retrying, $S^{\omega_{\mathsf{E}}}$ terminates immediately. Finally, the iteration $S^{\omega_{\mathsf{R}}}$ repeats S on retrying termination; if S terminates normally or exceptionally, $S^{\omega_{\mathsf{R}}}$ terminates immediately.

Iterations are defined in terms of fixed points. We skip the definition here and instead give the main rule for reasoning about iterations [3]. The formulation

---

[2] In the formalization with Isabelle/HOL, a statement is *identified* with its predicate transformer, thus we would write $S(q, r, s)$ instead of $wp\,{}^\backprime S^\prime\,(q, r, s)$. We use the latter notation here for familiarity.

[3] The Isabelle/HOL formalization contains the details.

follows the treatment of statements with single exits by Back and von Wright [2]. Let $W \neq \emptyset$ be a well-founded set, i.e. a set in which there are no infinitely decreasing chains, and let p_w for $w \in W$ be an indexed collection of predicates called *ranked predicates* of the form $p_w \equiv p \wedge v = w$. Here p is the *invariant* and v the *variant*. We define $p_{<w} \equiv (\exists\, w' \in W \cdot w' < w \wedge p_{w'})$ to be true if a predicate with lower rank than p_w is true:

$$(\forall w \in W \cdot q_w \Rightarrow wp\,`S\text{'}\,(q_{<w}, r, s)) \Rightarrow (q \Rightarrow wp\,`S^{\omega}\text{'}\,(q, r, s)) \qquad (5)$$

$$(\forall w \in W \cdot r_w \Rightarrow wp\,`S\text{'}\,(q, r_{<w}, s)) \Rightarrow (r \Rightarrow wp\,`S^{\omega E}\text{'}\,(q, r, s)) \qquad (6)$$

$$(\forall w \in W \cdot s_w \Rightarrow wp\,`S\text{'}\,(q, r, s_{<w})) \Rightarrow (s \Rightarrow wp\,`S^{\omega R}\text{'}\,(q, r, s)) \qquad (7)$$

The first of these rules states that if under q_w statement S terminates normally while decreasing the rank of q_w, then under q statement S terminates eventually with q; if S terminates exceptionally with r or retrying with s, then S^{ω} terminates likewise. Similarly, the last of these rules states that if under s_w statement S terminates retrying while decreasing the rank of s_w, then under r statement S terminates eventually with s; if S terminates normally with q or exceptionally with r, then S^{ω} terminates likewise.

A fundamental property of weakest preconditions is *conjunctivity*; it allows the weakest precondition of a conjunction of postconditions to be determined in terms of the precondition of each of the postconditions. Let $\mathcal{Q}$ be a non-empty set of triples of predicates. Extending $\wedge$ element-wise to triples, we say that statement S is conjunctive if:

$$wp\,`S\text{'}\,(\wedge\, Q \in \mathcal{Q} \cdot Q) \equiv (\wedge\, Q \in \mathcal{Q} \cdot wp\,`S\text{'}\, Q)$$

All statements above are conjunctive or preserve conjunctivity. A consequence of conjunctivity is *monotonicity*, which states that for predicate triples Q, R:

$$(Q \Rightarrow R) \Rightarrow (wp\,`S\text{'}\, Q \Rightarrow wp\,`S\text{'}\, R)$$

where $\Rightarrow$ is extended element-wise to triples. Hence all statements above are monotonic.

Weakest preconditions allow to define various useful *domains*. The *termination domain* $tr\,`S\text{'}$ characterizes those states in which $S$ will terminate at any exit. The *normal termination domain* $nr\,`S\text{'}$, the *exceptional termination domain* $ex\,`S\text{'}$, and the *retrying termination domain* $rt\,`S\text{'}$ characterize those states in which S is guaranteed to terminate normally, exceptionally, or retrying. The *enabledness domain* $en\,`S\text{'}$ characterizes those states in which S does not block:

$tr\,`S\text{'} \equiv wp\,`S\text{'}\,(\mathit{True}, \mathit{True}, \mathit{True})$

$nr\,`S\text{'} \equiv wp\,`S\text{'}\,(\mathit{True}, \mathit{False}, \mathit{False})$

$ex\,`S\text{'} \equiv wp\,`S\text{'}\,(\mathit{False}, \mathit{True}, \mathit{False})$

$rt\,`S\text{'} \equiv wp\,`S\text{'}\,(\mathit{False}, \mathit{False}, \mathit{True})$

$en\,`S\text{'} \equiv \neg wp\,`S\text{'}\,(\mathit{False}, \mathit{False}, \mathit{False})$

For example **retry** always terminates, never terminates normally or exceptionally, always terminates retrying, and never blocks. We do not go further into the properties of domain.

4   Derived Statements

The assignment $x := E$, where E is now a program expression, terminates normally if E is defined, in which case the value of E is assigned to x, and terminates exceptionally if E is undefined, without changing any variables. The statement **check** B **end** only evaluates B without changing any variables and terminates exceptionally if B is not defined or its value is false. The statements **if** B **then** S **end** and **if** B **then** S **else** T **end** also terminate exceptionally if B is not defined.

$$
\begin{aligned}
x := E \quad &\cong\; [\Delta E, \neg\Delta E, \textit{False}]\,;\, x := \text{`}E\text{'}\\
\textbf{check } B \textbf{ end} \quad &\cong\; [\Delta B \wedge \text{`}B\text{'}, \neg\Delta B \vee \neg\text{`}B\text{'}, \textit{False}]\\
\textbf{if } B \textbf{ then } S \textbf{ end} \quad &\cong\; ([\Delta B \wedge \text{`}B\text{'}, \neg\Delta B, \textit{False}]\,;\, S)\sqcap\\
&\quad\; [\Delta B \wedge \neg\text{`}B\text{'}, \neg\Delta B, \textit{False}]\\
\textbf{if } B \textbf{ then } S \textbf{ else } T \textbf{ end} \quad &\cong\; ([\Delta B \wedge \text{`}B\text{'}, \neg\Delta B, \textit{False}]\,;\, S)\sqcap\\
&\quad\; ([\Delta B \wedge \neg\text{`}B\text{'}, \neg\Delta B, \textit{False}]\,;\, T)
\end{aligned}
$$

Immediately we have that **check** B **end** = **if** B **then skip else raise end** and **if** B **then** S **end** = **if** B **then** S **else skip end** as consequences.

The loop **from** S **until** B **loop** T **end** first executes S and then, as long as B is false, executes T, and repeats that provided T terminates normally. If S or T terminate exceptionally, the whole loop terminates immediately exceptionally. If S or T terminate retrying, the whole loop terminates immediately retrying.

$$
\begin{aligned}
\textbf{from } S \textbf{ until } B \textbf{ loop } T \textbf{ end} \cong\; &S\,;\\
&([\Delta B \wedge \neg\text{`}B\text{'}, \neg\Delta B, \textit{False}]\,;\, T)^{\omega}\,;\\
&[\Delta B \wedge \text{`}B\text{'}, \neg\Delta B, \textit{False}]
\end{aligned}
$$

The rescue statement **do** S **rescue** T **end** starts with S and if S terminates normally, the whole statement terminates normally. If S terminates exceptionally, T is executed. If T terminates normally or exceptionally, the whole statement terminates exceptionally. This is captured by $U = S;_{\mathsf{E}}(T\,;\,\textbf{raise})$. If T terminates retrying, S the whole rescue statement is attempted again. Intuitively $U^{\omega\mathsf{R}} = \textbf{skip}\sqcap U \sqcap (U;_{\mathsf{R}} U)\sqcap(U;_{\mathsf{R}} U;_{\mathsf{R}} U)\ldots$ repeats zero or more times. However, **do** S **rescue** T **end** repeats indefinitely when T terminates retrying and may only terminate normally or retrying. This is captured by $U^{\omega\mathsf{R}};_{\mathsf{R}}\textbf{stop}$, hence:

$$
\textbf{do } S \textbf{ rescue } T \textbf{ end} \cong (S;_{\mathsf{E}}(T\,;\,\textbf{raise}))^{\omega\mathsf{R}};_{\mathsf{R}}\textbf{stop}
$$

This kind of exception handling differs from **try** S **catch** T **end** = $S;_{\mathsf{E}} T$ in two respects: there is no loop structure in a try-catch statement and normal termination of handler T leads to normal termination of the whole statement but to exceptional termination in **do** S **rescue** T **end**. This means that in Eiffel the handler cannot contain an alternative computation to establish the desired postcondition, but must instead direct the body S to attempt that, typically by setting a corresponding variable and retrying.

Eiffel does not allow retry statements in the body S of **do** S **rescue** T **end**. Above definition permits those, with the meaning that the whole statement is attempted again immediately.

5 Correctness Assertions

The *total correctness assertion* $\{p\}\,S\,\{q,r,s\}$ states that under p, statement S terminates normally with q, exceptionally with r, and retrying with s:

$$\{p\}\,S\,\{q,r,s\} \mathrel{\widehat{=}} p \Rightarrow wp\,`S'\,(q,r,s)$$

We start with two universal rules, generalizing analogous ones for single-exit statements. In a correctness assertion, the precondition can be strengthened and any of the three postconditions weakened. Also, correctness assertions of a statement can be conjoined, thus allowing proofs to be split. By convention, predicates listed on separated lines are to be conjoined:

$$
\begin{aligned}
&p' \Rightarrow p \\
&\{p\}\,S\,\{q,r,s\} \\
&(q \Rightarrow q') \wedge (r \Rightarrow r') \wedge (s \Rightarrow s')
\end{aligned}
\qquad \Rightarrow \quad \{p'\}\,S\,\{q',r',s'\} \tag{8}
$$

$$
\begin{aligned}
&\{p\}\,S\,\{q,r,s\} \\
&\{p'\}\,S\,\{q',r',s'\}
\end{aligned}
\qquad \Rightarrow \quad \{p \wedge p'\}\,S\,\{q \wedge q', r \wedge r', s \wedge s'\} \tag{9}
$$

The first of these follows from the monotonicity of $wp\,`S'$ and the second from the conjunctivity of $wp\,`S'$. The correctness rules for Eiffel statements are:

$$
p \Rightarrow s \qquad\qquad\qquad\qquad \equiv \quad \{p\}\ \mathbf{retry}\ \{q,r,s\} \tag{10}
$$

$$
\begin{aligned}
&p \wedge \Delta E \Rightarrow q[x\backslash `E'] \\
&p \wedge \neg\Delta E \Rightarrow r
\end{aligned}
\qquad \equiv \quad \{p\}\ x := E\ \{q,r,s\} \tag{11}
$$

$$
\begin{aligned}
&p \wedge \Delta B \wedge `B' \Rightarrow q \\
&p \wedge \neg\Delta B \Rightarrow r \\
&p \wedge \neg`B' \Rightarrow r
\end{aligned}
\qquad \equiv \quad \{p\}\ \mathbf{check}\ B\ \mathbf{end}\ \{q,r,s\} \tag{12}
$$

$$
\begin{aligned}
&\{p\}\,S\,\{t,r,s\} \\
&\{t\}\,T\,\{q,r,s\}
\end{aligned}
\qquad \Rightarrow \quad \{p\}\,S\,;\,T\,\{q,r,s\} \tag{13}
$$

$$
\begin{aligned}
&\{p \wedge \Delta B \wedge `B'\}\,S\,\{q,r,s\} \\
&p \wedge \Delta B \wedge \neg`B' \Rightarrow r \\
&p \wedge \neg\Delta B \Rightarrow s
\end{aligned}
\qquad \Rightarrow \quad \{p\}\ \mathbf{if}\ B\ \mathbf{then}\ S\ \mathbf{end}\ \{q,r,s\} \tag{14}
$$

$$
\begin{aligned}
&\{p \wedge \Delta B \wedge `B'\}\,S\,\{q,r,s\} \\
&\{p \wedge \Delta B \wedge \neg`B'\}\,T\,\{q,r,s\} \\
&p \wedge \neg\Delta B \Rightarrow s
\end{aligned}
\ \Rightarrow \ \{p\}\ \mathbf{if}\ B\ \mathbf{then}\ S\ \mathbf{else}\ T\ \mathbf{end}\ \{q,r,s\} \tag{15}
$$

For the loop **from** S **until** B **loop** T **end**, we assume that the postconditions are of a particular form: at normal termination, the loop invariant holds, B is defined and true. At exceptional termination, either the exceptional postcondition of S or T holds (in case S or T failed), or the invariant holds and B is not defined (in case the evaluation of B failed). On retrying termination, the retrying postcondition of S or T holds (in case S or T executed **retry**). The role of S is to establish the loop invariant, here q:

$$\frac{\{p\}\,S\,\{q,r,s\}}{\{q_w \wedge \Delta B \wedge \neg 'B'\}\,T\,\{q_{<w},r,s\}}$$

$\Rightarrow$ (16)

$$\{p\}\,\textbf{from}\,S\,\textbf{until}\,B\,\textbf{loop}\,T\,\textbf{end}\,\{q \wedge \Delta B \wedge 'B', r \vee (q \wedge \neg \Delta B), s\}$$

Recall that $q_w = q \wedge v = w$ where q is the invariant, v the variant, and $w \in W$. In Eiffel, variants are integer expressions and the well-founded set W of their values are non-negative integers. For integer variants, we have the following rule, where $w > 0$:

$$\frac{\{p\}\,S\,\{q,r,s\}}{\{q \wedge v = w \wedge \Delta B \wedge \neg 'B'\}\,T\,\{q \wedge v < w, r, s\}}$$

$\Rightarrow$ (17)

$$\{p\}\,\textbf{from}\,S\,\textbf{until}\,B\,\textbf{loop}\,T\,\textbf{end}\,\{q \wedge \Delta B \wedge 'B', r \vee (q \wedge \neg \Delta B), s\}$$

The rule for **do** S **rescue** T **end** requires that progress towards termination is made whenever S or T exits retrying; termination here means normal termination if S terminates normally or exceptional termination if T terminates normally or exceptionally:

$$\frac{\{p_w\}\,S\,\{q,t_w,p_{<w}\}}{\{t_w\}\,T\,\{r,r,p_{<w}\}}$$

$\Rightarrow$ (18)

$$\{p\}\,\textbf{do}\,S\,\textbf{rescue}\,T\,\textbf{end}\,\{q,r,s\}$$

For integer variants, we have following rule, where $w > 0$:

$$\frac{\{p \wedge v = w\}\,S\,\{q, t \wedge v = w, p \wedge v < w\}}{\{t \wedge v = w\}\,T\,\{r,r,p \wedge v < w\}}$$

$\Rightarrow$ (19)

$$\{p\}\,\textbf{do}\,S\,\textbf{rescue}\,T\,\textbf{end}\,\{q,r,s\}$$

Here p is the *retry invariant* and v is the *retry variant*.

6   Method Correctness

In Eiffel, each method is specified by a single precondition and single postcondition only. The normal exit is taken if the desired postcondition is established and the exceptional exit is taken if the desired postcondition cannot be established. Thus the situations under which an exceptional exit is taken is implicit in the method specification and a "defined" outcome is always possible, even in the presence of unanticipated failures. Since methods never terminate retrying, and some statements only terminate normally, we introduce two abbreviations:

$$\{p\} \, S \, \{q, r\} \,\widehat{=}\, \{p\} \, S \, \{q, r, False\}$$
$$\{p\} \, S \, \{q\} \quad \widehat{=}\, \{p\} \, S \, \{q, False\}$$

We propose to restrict the exceptional postcondition in case the specified postcondition cannot be established [20]. Since classes typically have a class invariant, the class invariant should hold even at exceptional termination, as otherwise the program is left in an inconsistent state and a subsequent call to the same object may fail. (As a consequence, if re-establishing the class invariant cannot be guaranteed, the class invariant needs to be weakened appropriately.) More generally, let p be the condition that holds before a call to method m with body **local** $x : X$ **do** S **rescue** T **end**, where p captures the computation that has been made by the whole program up to this point. We then require a call to m either to terminate normally with the desired postcondition q or terminate exceptionally with p:

$$\{p\} \, \textbf{local} \, x : X \, \textbf{do} \, S \, \textbf{rescue} \, T \, \textbf{end} \, \{q, p\}$$

That is, in case of failure, the method may leave the state changed, but has to undo sufficiently such that p holds again. This regime allows then failures to be propagated back over arbitrarily many method calls. From the correctness theorems for statements, we get immediately following rule, where p, q are predicates that may not mention x and p'_w is a collection of ranked predicates.

$$
\begin{aligned}
&p \wedge x = X_0 \Rightarrow p' \\
&\{p'_w\} \, S \, \{q', t_w, p'_{<w}\} \qquad\qquad \{p\} \\
&\{t_w\} \, T \, \{p', p', p'_{<w}\} \quad \Rightarrow \quad \textbf{local} \, x : X \, \textbf{do} \, S \, \textbf{rescue} \, T \, \textbf{end} \qquad (20) \\
&p' \Rightarrow p \qquad\qquad\qquad\qquad\qquad \{q, p\} \\
&q' \Rightarrow q
\end{aligned}
$$

For integer variants, we have following rule, where $w > 0$:

$$
\begin{aligned}
&p \wedge x = X_0 \Rightarrow p' \\
&\{p' \wedge v = w\} \, S \, \{q', t \wedge v = w, p' \wedge v < w\} \qquad \{p\} \\
&\{t \wedge v = w\} \, T \, \{p', p', p' \wedge v < w\} \qquad\qquad \Rightarrow \quad \textbf{local} \, x : X \, \textbf{do} \, S \, \textbf{rescue} \, T \, \textbf{end} \\
&p' \Rightarrow p \qquad\qquad\qquad\qquad\qquad\qquad\qquad\qquad \{q, p\} \\
&q' \Rightarrow q
\end{aligned}
$$

$$(21)$$

7 Example: Binary Search of Square Root

Suppose the task is to compute the approximate non-negative integer square root of n, which is a non-negative integer itself, such that $\textbf{Result}^2 \leq n <$

190   E. Sekerinski and T. Zhang

$(\textbf{Result} +1)^2$ using bounded arithmetic [4]. Assume that the result must be between l and u. The loop

> **from until** $u - l = 1$ **loop**
> $m := l + (u - l) \mathbin{/\!/} 2$
>   **if** $n < m * m$ **then** $u := m$ **else** $l := m$ **end**
> **end**

maintains the invariant $p \equiv 0 \le l < u \land l^2 \le n < u^2$. The statement $m := l + (u - l) \mathbin{/\!/} 2$ will establish $m = (l + u) \mathbin{/\!/} 2$ according to (4) and never fail according to (3). However, the **if** statement will fail if $m * m > \mathit{max\_int}$. Since necessarily $n \le \mathit{max\_int}$, we know that in case of failure $n < m * m$, thus after assigning $u := m$ the loop can continue. We use the abbreviation $\{retry: q\}$ for $\{\mathit{False}, \mathit{False}, q\}$. The full implementation with annotation is as follows:

> $sqrt(n, l, u : INTEGER) : INTEGER$
> $\{p\}$
>   **local**
> $m : INTEGER$
> $\{$retry invariant: $p\}$
> $\{$retry variant: $u - l\}$
>   **do**
> $\{$loop invariant: $p\}$
> $\{$loop variant: $u - l\}$
>   **from until** $u - l = 1$ **loop**
> $m := l + (u - l) \mathbin{/\!/} 2$
> $\{p \land m = (l + u) \mathbin{/\!/} 2\}$
>   **if** $n < m * m$ **then** $u := m$ **else** $l := m$ **end**
> $\{p, p \land m = (l + u) \mathbin{/\!/} 2 \land n < m^2\}$
>   **end**
> $\{p \land u - l = 1\}$
> $\textbf{Result} := l$
>   **rescue**
> $\{p \land m = (l + u) \mathbin{/\!/} 2 \land n < m^2\}$
> $u := m$
> $\{p\}$
>   **retry**
> $\{$retry: $p\}$
>   **end**
> $\{\textbf{Result}^2 \le n < (\textbf{Result} +1)^2\}$

Note that the retry loop only needs to decrease the variant on the retry exit.

---

[4] The Eiffel Standard [1] and Meyer [16] suggest that an arithmetic overflow leads to an exception. SmartEiffel (version 2.3) does raise an exception, but EiffelStudio (version 7) does not. However, the example can be expressed in EiffelStudio by first formulating a class for safe arithmetic, see http://www.cas.mcmaster.ca/~zhangt26/SBMF/

8   Discussion

In this paper we have derived verification rules for the retrying mechanism of Eiffel exceptions. Beside the contribution of total correctness rules, the novel aspects of the derivation are that we started with a weakest exceptional precondition semantics and defined both normal loops and retry loops through strong iteration. All theorems have been checked with Isabelle/HOL.

The statements considered include the **check** statement, but we have not discussed **ensure** and **require** method specifications. Since these are evaluated at run-time in Eiffel, they are restricted to be program expressions (extended with the **old** notation). However, since these are evaluated program expression they have be treated like the **check** statement. It should be straightforward to extend the approach for method correctness (Sec. 6) accordingly.

We have neither considered dynamic objects, therefore no method calls, nor other features of Eiffel like inheritance. While we believe that exception handling is largely independent of other features and the treatment here would carry over to a more general setting, this remains to be shown.

Strong and weak iteration are appealing because of their rich algebraic structure. However, we have not explored the resulting algebraic properties of rescue and retry statements. For example, following theorems can be shown to hold:

$$\textbf{do skip rescue } S \textbf{ end} \quad\quad = \textbf{skip} \tag{22}$$

$$\textbf{do raise rescue retry end} = \textbf{abort} \tag{23}$$

An interesting consequence of our definition of statements is that retry statements can also appear in the main body of a method, not only the exception handler. The proof rule (18) supports this use. With this, the binary search of the square root example can be rewritten without the **from** / **until** loop, using only the retry loop:

$$sqrt2(n, l, u : INTEGER) : INTEGER$$
$$\{p\}$$
local
$$m : INTEGER$$
$$\{\text{retry invariant: } p\}$$
$$\{\text{retry variant: } u - l\}$$
do
$$m := l + (u - l) \;//\; 2$$
$$\{p \wedge m = (l + u) \;//\; 2\}$$
if $n < m * m$ **then** $u := m$ **else** $l := m$ **end**
$$\{p, p \wedge m = (l + u) \;//\; 2 \wedge n < m^2\}$$
if $u - l > 1$ **then retry end**
$$\{p \wedge u - l = 1, \text{retry: } p \wedge u - l > 1\}$$
$$\textbf{Result} := l$$
rescue

$$\{p \wedge m = (l + u) \mathbin{/\!/} 2 \wedge n < m^2\}$$
$$u := m$$
$$\{p\}$$
retry
$$\{\text{retry: } p\}$$
end
$$\{\mathbf{Result}^2 \le n < (\mathbf{Result} + 1)^2\}$$

Nordio et al. propose to replace the retry statement with a retry variable in order to avoid the third exit [17]. Below is their example of safe division, with annotation to show termination of the retry loop; the example shows that the third exit does not cause further complications:

$$safe\_division\ (x, y : INTEGER) : INTEGER$$
  local
    $$z : INTEGER$$
  $\{\text{retry invariant: } (y \ne 0 \wedge z = 0) \vee (y = 0 \wedge (z = 1 \vee z = 0))\}$
  $\{\text{retry variant: } 1 - z\}$
  do
    $$\mathbf{Result} := x \mathbin{/\!/} (y + z)$$
    $\{(y = 0 \Rightarrow \mathbf{Result} = x) \wedge (y \ne 0 \Rightarrow \mathbf{Result} = x \mathbin{/\!/} y), y = 0 \wedge z = 0\}$
  rescue
    $$\{y = 0 \wedge z = 0\}$$
    $$z := 1$$
    $$\{y = 0 \wedge z = 1\}$$
    retry
    $$\{\text{retry: } y = 0 \wedge z = 1\}$$
  end
  $\{(y = 0 \Rightarrow \mathbf{Result} = x) \wedge (y \ne 0 \Rightarrow \mathbf{Result} = x \mathbin{/\!/} y)\}$

Acknowledgement. We are grateful for the helpful comments of the reviewers. In particular, one reviewer suggested theorems (22) and (23).

References

1. Eiffel: Analysis, Design and Programming Language, 2nd edn. Standard ECMA-367. Ecma International (June 2006)
2. Back, R.-J., von Wright, J.: Refinement Calculus: A Systematic Introduction. Springer (1998)
3. Back, R.J.R., von Wright, J.: Reasoning algebraically about loops. Acta Informatica 36(4), 295–334 (1999)
4. Bowen, J., Gordon, M.: A shallow embedding of Z in HOL. Information and Software Technology 37(5-6), 269–276 (1995)
5. Buhr, P.A., Russell Mok, W.Y.: Advanced exception handling mechanisms. IEEE Transactions on Software Engineering 26(9), 820–836 (2000)

6. Cohen, E.: Separation and Reduction. In: Backhouse, R., Oliveira, J.N. (eds.) MPC 2000. LNCS, vol. 1837, pp. 45–59. Springer, Heidelberg (2000)
7. Cristian, F.: Correct and robust programs. IEEE Transactions on Software Engineering 10(2), 163–174 (1984)
8. Gordon, M.J.C.: Mechanizing programming logics in higher order logic. In: Birtwistle, G., Subrahmanyam, P.A. (eds.) Current Trends in Hardware Verification and Automated Theorem Proving, pp. 387–439. Springer, New York (1989)
9. Harrison, J.: HOL Light tutorial (for version 2.20). Technical report, Intel JF1-13 (January 2011)
10. Jacobs, B.: A Formalisation of Java's Exception Mechanism. In: Sands, D. (ed.) ESOP 2001. LNCS, vol. 2028, pp. 284–301. Springer, Heidelberg (2001)
11. King, S., Morgan, C.: Exits in the refinement calculus. Formal Aspects of Computing 7(1), 54–76 (1995)
12. Leavens, G.T., Baker, A.L., Ruby, C.: Preliminary design of JML: a behavioral interface specification language for Java. SIGSOFT Software Engineering Notes 31, 1–38 (2006)
13. Leino, K.R.M., van de Snepscheut, J.L.A.: Semantics of exceptions. In: Olderog, E.-R. (ed.) PROCOMET 1994: Proceedings of the IFIP TC2/WG2.1/WG2.2/WG2.3 Working Conference on Programming Concepts, Methods and Calculi. IFIP Transactions A-56, pp. 447–466. North-Holland Publishing Co., Amsterdam (1994)
14. Rustan, M., Leino, K., Schulte, W.: Exception safety for C#. In: Software Engineering and Formal Methods, SEFM 2004, pp. 218–227. IEEE Computer Society (2004)
15. Liskov, B., Guttag, J.: Program Development in Java: Abstraction, Specification, and Object-Oriented Design. Addison-Wesley Longman Publishing Co., Boston (2000)
16. Meyer, B.: Object-Oriented Software Construction, 2nd edn. Prentice-Hall, Inc., Upper Saddle River (1997)
17. Nordio, M., Calcagno, C., Müller, P., Meyer, B.: A Sound and Complete Program Logic for Eiffel. In: Oriol, M., Meyer, B. (eds.) TOOLS EUROPE 2009. LNBIP, vol. 33, pp. 195–214. Springer, Heidelberg (2009)
18. von Oheimb, D.: Analyzing Java in Isabelle/HOL: Formalization, Type Safety and Hoare Logic. PhD thesis, Technische Universität München (2001)
19. Sekerinski, E.: Exceptions for dependability. In: Petre, L., Sere, K., Troubitsyna, E. (eds.) Dependability and Computer Engineering: Concepts for Software-Intensive Systems—a Handbook on Dependability Research, pp. 11–35. IGI Global (2011)
20. Sekerinski, E., Zhang, T.: Partial correctness for exception handling. In: Bonakdarpour, B., Maibaum, T. (eds.) Proceedings of the 2nd International Workshop on Logical Aspects of Fault-Tolerance, pp. 116–132 (June 2011)
21. Tschannen, J., Furia, C.A., Nordio, M., Meyer, B.: Verifying Eiffel programs with Boogie. In: Rustan, K., Leino, M., Moskal, M. (eds.) First International Workshop on Intermediate Verification Languages: BOOGIE 2011. CADE 23 Workshop, pp. 14–26 (2011)
22. von Wright, J.: Towards a refinement algebra. Science of Computer Programming 51(1-2), 23–45 (2004); Mathematics of Program Construction (MPC 2002)
23. Wildmoser, M., Nipkow, T.: Certifying Machine Code Safety: Shallow Versus Deep Embedding. In: Slind, K., Bunker, A., Gopalakrishnan, G.C. (eds.) TPHOLs 2004. LNCS, vol. 3223, pp. 305–320. Springer, Heidelberg (2004)
24. Yemini, S., Berry, D.M.: A modular verifiable exception handling mechanism. ACM Trans. Program. Lang. Syst. 7(2), 214–243 (1985)

A Sound Reduction of Persistent-Sets for Deadlock Detection in MPI Applications[*]

Subodh Sharma[1],[**], Ganesh Gopalakrishnan[2], and Greg Bronevetsky[3]

[1] University of Oxford
subodh.sharma@cs.ox.ac.uk
[2] University of Utah
ganesh@cs.utah.edu
[3] Lawrence Livermore National Laboratory
bronevetsky1@llnl.gov

Abstract. Formal dynamic analysis of Message Passing Interface (MPI) programs is crucially important in the context of developing HPC applications. Existing dynamic verification tools for MPI programs suffer from exponential schedule explosion, especially when multiple non-deterministic receive statements are issued by a process. In this paper, we focus on detecting *message-orphaning* deadlocks within MPI programs. For this analysis target, we describe a sound heuristic that helps avoid schedule explosion in most practical cases while not missing deadlocks in practice. Our method hinges on initially computing the potential non-deterministic matches as conventional dynamic analyzers do, but then including only the entries which are found *relevant* to cause a refusal deadlock (essentially a macroscopic-view persistent-set reduction technique). Experimental results are encouraging.

1 Introduction

The Message Passing Interface (MPI, [9]) is one of the central APIs used in large-scale high performance computing (HPC) simulations. Most of today's supercomputers and high performance clusters are programmed using MPI, and this trend is expected to continue [6]. There are also embedded system communication standards built around message passing, such as MCAPI [8]. In this paper, we study the problem of adequately testing message passing programs using formal techniques for the purpose of deadlock detection. While our research is conducted with MPI-specific details, with relatively minor modifications our results also apply to other message passing paradigms.

In MPI, message send commands directly address the destination process while message receives are of two types: either directly address the source process (called *deterministic receives*) or the *non-deterministic* (or "wildcard") receives that can receive from any sender that targets the process issuing such a receive. The sends and receives issued by an MPI process that target the same destination or source from the same process are required to match in program order (the "non-overtaking rule of MPI",

---

[*] This research has been supported by NSF OCI 1148127 and EPSRC project EP/G026254/1.
[**] The work was performed when the author was in University of Utah.

R. Gheyi and D. Naumann (Eds.): SBMF 2012, LNCS 7498, pp. 194–209, 2012.
© Springer-Verlag Berlin Heidelberg 2012

Section 3.5 in [9]). The MPI runtime computes the eligible matches for each receive operation. The matching operations are called *match pairs*. At any runtime state of an MPI program, a deterministic receive will always have a single matching send, thus, all concurrent match pairs consisting of deterministic receives and matching sends can *commute* (i.e. match pairs can interleave resulting in the same program state). This is because all such match pairs have non-overlapping destinations/sources. However, non-deterministic receive matches do not, in general, commute. A non-deterministic receive $R(*)$ can have multiple eligible matching senders; an $R(*)$ matching a send S_i results in a system state different from when another send S_j matches the same receive where S_i and S_j are issued from different processes. This is not good news for dynamic partial order reduction (DPOR [3]) methods because in many MPI programs, $R(*)$ calls occur in sequence (typically in a loop). Thus, it seems that any DPOR technique is doomed to examine an exponential number of interleavings—something that does not bode well for our *Exascale* computing aspirations (exascale roadmap [10]) in which several message passing APIs (including MPI) are expected to play an important role. This paper develops a simple but very effective (in practice) heuristic that avoids the afore-mentioned schedule explosion in many cases.

Background and Related Work. It is important to have a balanced portfolio of verification tools in any area—including for MPI. Informal testing approaches for MPI (e.g., based on schedule perturbation [18]) do not guarantee coverage, and are also highly redundant because they will, in practice, generate many equivalent schedules (e.g., permuting deterministic message match pairs). While static analyzers for MPI exist (e.g., [1]), they are known to be unsound (can generate too many false alarms) when used for bug-hunting, due to their overapproximation of possible message matches. Model-checking based methods (e.g., MPI-SPIN [12]) can guarantee coverage, but on *models* of MPI programs; such models are very difficult to create, and become obsolete with each design change.

From a designer's perspective, dynamic formal testing tools are attractive in many ways: (1) they are sound (meaning no false alarms), (2) they can be made complete with respect to non-determinism coverage (meaning no omissions w.r.t. a safety property). Formal dynamic verifiers such as ISP [14,17] and DAMPI [15,16] take an approach that integrates the best features of testing tools (ability to run on user applications) and model checking (message match non-determinism coverage guarantees). They run the MPI program under the control of *verification-oriented scheduling mechanisms* (a central scheduler for ISP and logical clocks for DAMPI). The MPI semantics-aware algorithms of these tools guarantee non-determinism coverage (e.g., all the potential match pairs w.r.t. a non-deterministic receive) while not examining the schedule space with respect to commuting deterministic receive/send match pairs. They have been shown to scale up to 1000 MPI processes for many MPI programs (in the case of DAMPI). The scheduling mechanisms in these tools are robust across all MPI-compliant platforms and computational delays between communication calls. *However, these dynamic verification tools suffer from the aforesaid exponential schedule explosion when a sequence of $R(*)$ commands are issued.* A practical dynamic verification tool that avoids this schedule explosion and provides reasonable coverage is, to the best of our knowledge, currently unavailable. This paper describes such a tool.

Contributions. The specific contributions of this paper are as following:

- Our general focus is on the problem of detecting deadlocks in MPI programs. We define a notion of *orphaning deadlocks* in which an MPI receive is left without a matching send in some MPI program execution state. We modify ISP's dynamic partial order reduction algorithm called POE (standing for Partial Order avoiding Elusive interleavings, [14]) to result in a new algorithm called MSPOE (*Macro-Scopic POE*). MSPOE applies to MPI programs that "do not decode data," i.e., do not employ data dependent control flows, and do not alter their control flows based on *which* sends a non-deterministic receive matches with. It is a reasonable assumption since a large class of SPMD programs are coded in a manner that is consistent with our simplification.
- The formulation of MSPOE relies on a notion of *commuting sends*; this notion results from a macroscopic re-interpretation of the basic tenets of partial order reduction. To this end, we modify and re-state the definition of *independent transitions* in the context of MPI programs.
- We measure the efficacy of MSPOE on *real* examples, and show that MSPOE can dramatically reduce the number of interleavings examined.

MSPOE is, by design, incomplete. In practice, MSPOE has caught all the deadlocks that ISP has discovered on the set of selected realistic benchmarks. A study of any successful large-scale formal software testing or analysis approach (e.g. [5]) shows that rather than aiming for a theoretically complete algorithm, one almost always has to aim for "completeness in practice."[1]

Detailed Look at an Example. Let a call denoted by $S_{i,j}(k)$ be a asynchronous send call from process i sending to process k with the local process program counter (PC) at j. Similarly an asynchronous receive call sourcing from process k which is issued by process i indexed at j is denoted by $R_{i,j}(k)$. A non-deterministic asynchronous receive is represented by $R_{i,j}(*)$. We will use this notation through the rest of the paper. Note that in the notation, the arguments of the call can be suppressed for brevity since each call can also be uniquely identified by the process ID and the PC value. For instance, $R_{i,j}(*)$ can be uniquely identified by $R_{i,j}$. We would use the actual and suppressed notation interchangeably in the paper. Let us examine the example shown in Figure 1. Assume that all the asynchronous calls have their associated *wait calls* (wait is a blocking call to ensure the successful completion of the associated non-blocking send/receive request, Section 3.7.3 in [9]) posted which are not shown in the example for brevity. A scheduler such as ISP will explore 24 interleavings for this example. This is because, the first wildcard receive will have 4 eligible matching sends and the subsequent receive will have 3 eligible matching sends and so forth, leading to a total of 4! schedules. As long as all sends *commute*, such examples cannot have deadlocks and there is no necessity to examine other schedules. In the example under discussion, observe that all sends commute. MSPOE will analyze the program in Figure 1 in the following way: MSPOE will explore the first interleaving and will subsequently discover that the program does not issue any deterministic receive calls and all sends commute. Thus, it will conclude that

---

[1] In practice, it seems one can obtain at most two of the following three attributes: *sound, complete, scalable.*

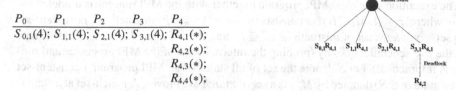

P_0	P_1	P_2	P_3	P_4
$S_{0,1}(4);$	$S_{1,1}(4);$	$S_{2,1}(4);$	$S_{3,1}(4);$	$R_{4,1}(*);$
				$R_{4,2}(*);$
				$R_{4,3}(*);$
				$R_{4,4}(*);$

Fig. 1. Example illustrating explosion in schedule space   **Fig. 2.** Deadlocking match for $R_{4,1}(*)$

every receive must find a match in each interleaving. It will terminate the exploration right after the first run.

Now consider the same example of Figure 1, however, replace $R_{4,2}(*)$ by $R_{4,2}(3)$. The code now has a deadlock. Figure 2 illustrates the various match-pairs possible for the receive $R_{4,1}$. If $R_{4,1}$ were to match $S_{3,1}$ (right-most transition from the initial node), the subsequent deterministic call ($R_{4,2}$) will be orphaned, thus creating a refusal deadlock. ISP and other verification schedulers like DAMPI explore all the matches starting from leftmost choice shown in Figure 2 and then moving right with every new run, generating four interleavings before finding the deadlock. MSPOE, on the other hand, discovers that since there is a deterministic receive $R_{4,2}$, its matching send can get consumed by a prior wildcard receive. Thus, MSPOE prioritizes the schedule in which $S_{3,1}$ is matched with $R_{4,1}$ thus forcing the program to take a schedule where $R_{4,2}$ is orphaned. MSPOE detects the deadlock in two interleavings.

2   Preliminaries

Let P be a concurrent MPI program and P_i is the ith sequential process executing P where $i \in PID$ and $PID = \{0, 1, ..., n\}$. We assume the program is executed with finite many processes. Each P_i is L_i instructions long. Let l denote the program counter (PC) array; thus, $l_i \in l$ denotes the PC value for the ith process. The jth MPI command in the ith process is denoted $p_{i,j}$ where $j = l_i$.

The work presented in this paper can be understood with only a subset of MPI calls which comprises of: non-blocking send, non-blocking receive, wait, and the barrier call. Since providing the whole overview of MPI is beyond the scope of this paper, we will restrict the presentation to the afore-mentioned subset of MPI calls. We have already presented the notations for representing non-blocking send and receive calls. A non-blocking send or receive call returns a "handle" that is waited upon by a later issued *wait* (W) operation. For instance, the wait call for the corresponding $S_{i,j}(k)$ would be represented as $W_{i,l_i}(h_{i,j})$. In our illustrations of examples, we suppress showing the W calls explicitly. We replace them by suitably adding the program order edges. Note that our implementation handles them correctly. A *blocking* send call's effect is obtained by placing wait call immediately after the non-blocking send call. A blocking receive can be obtained in a similar fashion. An MPI Barrier operation by process i is represented as $B_{i,j}$ where j is the l_i for that process. Let Op be the set of MPI operations comprised of $S_{i,j}(k)$, $R_{i,j}(k)$, $R_{i,j}(*)$, $W_{i,j'}(h_{i,j})$ and $B_{i,j}$, for all possible i, j, j', k. Note that an operation belonging to Op is a *visible* operation and all other operations (non MPI) are *invisible*. A visible operation is one that is intercepted by the ISP scheduler.

The execution state of an MPI program together with the MPI runtime is modeled using σ where $\sigma = \langle I, M, C, l \rangle$ that consists of *issued* ($I \subseteq Op$) instructions, *persistent-set* (M) set, *completed* set of instructions ($C \subseteq I$), and the PC array l. This is also the state that the ISP scheduler goes by (probing the internal state of the MPI processes and runtime is impractical). Let S denote the set of all states of an MPI program. Persistent-set M at a state $\sigma \in S$ (denoted by M_σ) is a set of *match-set* moves. A match-set at a state is either a set of matching send and deterministic receive or a set of matching sends and a wildcard receive. Since match-set transitions the system from one state to a subsequent state, we view match-set moves as the *transitions* of the MPI program under the execution of a verification scheduler like ISP. The terms match-sets and transitions in this paper would be used interchangeably. Thus, when a send call $S_{i,l_i}(k)$ matches a receive call $R_{k,l_k}(i)$ at σ, the associated transition $t \in M_\sigma$ is represented by $\langle S_{i,l_i}(k), R_{k,l_k}(i) \rangle$ or just $\langle S_{i,l_i}, R_{k,l_k} \rangle$. We denote the issue set and the completed set at σ by I_σ and C_σ respectively. Let $\mathcal{T}$ denote the set of all transitions of the system. A $t \in \mathcal{T}$ enabled at state σ which when executed results in a unique successor state σ', written as $\sigma \xrightarrow{t} \sigma'$. The successor state is also represented by the following: $\sigma' = t(\sigma)$. We define the whole MPI program as a state transition system $A_G = (S, \mathcal{T}, \sigma_0)$. where σ_0 is the starting state of the system. We now define the transition rules to model MPI program execution as governed by ISP.

2.1   State Transition Rules (MPI/ISP)

Before we present the state transition rules, it is important to understand the *Matches-Before* (MB) ordering among MPI instructions. We define MB ordering among two operations issued from the same process by the operator $<_{lp}$. MPI standard requires instruction pairs $S_{i,j}(k) <_{lp} S_{i,j'}(k)$, $R_{i,j}(k) <_{lp} R_{i,j'}(k)$, and $R_{i,j}(*) <_{lp} R_{i,j'}(k/*)$ where $j < j'$. The standard also enforce the following ordering: $W_{i,j}(-) <_{lp} any_{i,j'}$ and $B_{i,j} <_{lp} any_{i,j'}$ where $any \in Op$ and the symbol "$-$" denotes don't care condition. MPI instructions are allowed to re-order and violate the program order, however, they must always obey the MB ordering.

Our state transition rules employ a precondition *Ready* to model MB ordering restriction based matching of transitions.

$$Ready(\sigma) = \{x \in I_\sigma | \forall y : (y <_{lp} x \Rightarrow \exists \sigma' \in Prev(\sigma) : y \in C_{\sigma'}\}$$

An instruction would be *ready* to be matched in a certain state only when all prior MB ordered operations have matched. $Prev(\sigma)$ returns the set of preceding states where each state upon firing a unique transition (enabled at that state) leads to σ. Function isW tests whether the instruction that is passed as an argument is a wait call. Similarly functions such as isS and isR test whether a given instruction is a send or a receive respectively. The rules called R_S and R_R can be used to model how the state advances upon instruction issue of send and receive calls from the process P_i.

$$R_S, R_R : \frac{\Sigma(\sigma \text{ as } \langle I, M, C, l \rangle), \quad (isS(x_{i,-}) \vee isR(x_{i,-}))}{\Sigma\langle I \cup \{x_{i,-}\}, M, C, l[i \leftarrow (l_i + 1)] \rangle}$$

Here, Σ is the predicate for the set of reachable states from the start state. Similarly, we define the rules for instruction issue of wait and barrier calls:

$$R_W, R_B : \frac{\Sigma(\sigma \ as \ \langle I, M, C, l\rangle), \quad (isW(x_{i,-}) \lor isB(x_{i,-}))}{\Sigma\langle I \cup \{x_{i,-}\}, \ M, \ C, \ l\rangle}$$

The successful return of wait and barrier calls are modeled by the following rules:

$$R_{Wret} : \frac{\Sigma(\sigma \ as \ \langle I, M, C, l\rangle), \quad isW(x_{i,j}(h_{i,j'})), \quad \exists y_{i,j'} : y_{i,j'} \in C}{\Sigma\langle I, \ M, \ C \cup \{x_{i,j}\}, \ l[i \leftarrow l_i + 1]\rangle}$$

$$R_{Bret} : \frac{\Sigma(\sigma \ as \ \langle I, M, C, l\rangle), \ Bars = \{x_{i,-} \in Ready(\sigma) | isB(x_{i,-}), i \in PID\}, \quad |Bars| = PID}{\Sigma\langle I, \ M, \ C \cup Bars, \ (k \in PID, l[k \leftarrow l_k + 1])\rangle}$$

We now define the transition rule for the completion of send and receive instructions:
R_{SRM}:

$$\frac{\Sigma(\sigma \ as \ \langle I, M, C, l\rangle), \quad \{S_{i,j}(k), R_{k,n}(i/*)\} \subseteq Ready(\sigma)}{\Sigma\langle I, \ M \cup \{S_{i,j}(k), R_{k,n}(i)\}, C\}, \ l\rangle}$$

R_{SR}:

$$\frac{\Sigma(\sigma \ as \ \langle I, M, C, l\rangle), \quad \{S_{i,j}(k), R_{k,n}(i)\} \subseteq Ready(\sigma)}{\Sigma\langle I, \ M \setminus \{S_{i,j}(k), R_{k,n}(i)\}, \ C \cup \{S_{i,j}(k), R_{k,n}(i)\}, \ l\rangle}$$

Rule R_{SRM} is responsible for constructing the persistent-set M at each state. In order to define the matching and completion of wildcard receive calls we first introduce the Fnc predicate. Let $\sigma\rightarrow$ denote σ has a next state, $\sigma\rightarrow_{R_{SR}}$ denote that σ has a next state through R_{SR} (i.e., R_{SR} can fire at σ), and $\sigma\nrightarrow_{R_{SR}}$ denote that R_{SR} cannot fire at σ. Similarly, $\sigma\nrightarrow_{R_{SR},R_B}$ denotes that neither R_{SR} nor R_B can fire at σ. Then we define the fence predicate as follows,

$$Fnc(\sigma) = \sigma\nrightarrow_{R_{SR},R_W,R_B,R_{Wret},R_{Bret},R_S,R_R}$$

When fence predicate is true then the only transition that is enabled at *sigma* is the wildcard transition. We can now define R_{SR*} to be:

$$\frac{\Sigma(\sigma \ as \ \langle I, M, C, l\rangle), \quad \{S_{i,j}(k), R_{k,n}(*)\} \subseteq M_\sigma, \quad Fnc(\sigma)}{\Sigma\langle I, \ M \setminus \{S_{i,j}(k), R_{k,n}(i)\}, \ C \cup \{S_{i,j}(k), R_{k,n}(i)\}, \ l\rangle}$$

In particular, we show the dynamic rewriting by changing '*' to i. Readers are encouraged to refer [14] for more details. We have presented only the required rules and details in order to make the paper self-contained.

We finally present the classical notion of *persistent sets* [4] which is crucial in understanding the match-set reductions presented later in the paper.

Definition 1 (Persistent in σ). *A set T of transitions enabled in a state σ is persistent in σ iff, for all non empty sequences of transitions from σ in A_G*

$$\sigma = \sigma_1 \xrightarrow{t_1} \sigma_2 \xrightarrow{t_2} \sigma_3 ... \xrightarrow{t_{n-1}} \sigma_n \xrightarrow{t_n} \sigma_{n+1}$$

and including only transitions $t_i \notin T$, $1 \leq i \leq n$, t_n is independent in σ_n with all transitions in T.

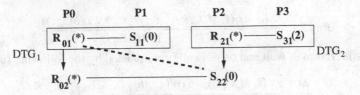

Fig. 3. Dependence among DTG transitions

Informally, this means that when a transition sequence is generated from a state s by choosing only transitions that are independent with transitions in T then the final state reached cannot have a transition that is dependent with any of the transitions in T. The interleavings obtained by only executing the entries in the persistent-set at every state are the *representative* interleavings and result a reduced state graph denoted as A_R.

2.2 Nature of Transitions in a Persistent-Set

A persistent-set at a state can contain multiple transitions. Persistent-sets are constructed in a prioritized manner as discussed in [13] (appropriately summarized in the state transition rules, as needed, in this paper). The only possibility of a persistent-set containing multiple transitions is when there is a wildcard receive involved. When all the potential senders to a wildcard receive $R(*)$ are determined at an execution state, ISP forms a transition involving $R(*)$ and each of the sends. The work in [13] views all resulting entries in the persistent-set of a state as *dependent* and designates the collection of such transitions as *dependence transition group* (**DTG**). For instance, consider the example in Figure 3. This figure shows one trace of the program. Here, the solid un-directed arrows represent the match-sets along which the execution proceeded. The dotted un-directed arrow represents another possible match-set (not realized in the present execution). The solid directed arrows capture the IntraMB ("Intra process matches-before ordering) relation[2]. The *DTG* with respect to the receive $R_{0,1}$ has the following transitions: $t_1 = \langle S_{1,1}, R_{0,1} \rangle$ and $t_2 = \langle S_{2,2}, R_{0,1} \rangle$. We define a function $Dtg(\sigma) \upharpoonright_{R_{i,l}}$ that returns a set of transitions that are enabled at a state σ and belong to the *DTG* w.r.t. to the wildcard receive $R_{i,l}$.

Notice, however, multiple DTGs can co-exist at a state, *and they can influence each other*. The example shown in Figure 3 illustrates such a scenario. Observe that if DTG_2 is fired before the transitions in DTG_1, then $S_{2,2}$ would be co-enabled with $S_{1,1}$, and both these sends can match $R_{0,1}$. In this case, DTG_1 must be augmented.

In our example, DTG_1 is augmented—from containing the transition $\langle S_{1,1}, R_{0,1} \rangle$ to containing two transitions $\langle S_{1,1}, R_{0,1} \rangle$ and $\langle S_{2,2}, R_{0,1} \rangle$. *This is the main source of the exponential explosion alluded to in this paper.*

MSPOE seeks to ameliorate this explosion. The whole exercise of MSPOE is to optimistically treat transitions within a DTG in σ as *independent. This observation is true of MPI programs where application state is independent of the sender that matched the*

---

[2] The edge between $R_{2,1}$ and $S_{2,2}$ indicates that there must be a wait operation W bound to $R_{2,1}$ lying in-between. This W has been suppressed but the effects are appropriately captured in the MB edge shown.

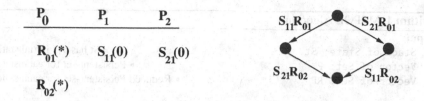

P_0	P_1	P_2
$R_{01}(*)$	$S_{11}(0)$	$S_{21}(0)$
$R_{02}(*)$		

Fig. 4. Commuting example   **Fig. 5.** Transition independence

wildcard receive. MSPOE takes a lazy approach to augmenting DTGs. As mentioned under example explanation on Page 196, as far as orphaning deadlocks are concerned, it is the competition between a wildcard and a deterministic receive for a particular send that must be regarded as the dependency relation *that truly matters*. We shall see that DTG augmentation done precisely at these moments leads to an exploration technique (MSPOE) that *often generates a single interleaving* (implying the absence of deterministic receives). In contrast, POE generate an interleaving blowup. Our results show that orphaning deadlocks are detected by MSPOE in all practical cases, avoiding this explosion.

3 Independent Transitions

In order to define *independent transitions*, we first introduce the notion of *commuting sends* that are part of the transitions within a single DTG.

Definition 2 (Commuting Sends). *Sends* $S_{i,l}(k)$ *and* $S_{j,m}(k)$ *are commuting sends iff the following conditions hold at a state* σ:

- *Exists* $R_{k,n}(*) \in Ready(\sigma)$ *such that* $t_1 = \langle S_{i,l}(k), R_{k,n}(*) \rangle$ *and* $t_2 = \langle S_{j,m}(k), R_{k,n}(*) \rangle$ *and* $t_1, t_2 \in P_\sigma$.
- $S_{j,m}(k) \in t'_2$ *and* $S_{i,l}(k) \in t'_1$ *where* $t'_2 \in P_{t_1(\sigma)}$ *and* $t'_1 \in P_{t_2(\sigma)}$.[3]

Observe that in Definition 2, two sends, $S_{i,l}$ and $S_{j,m}$ can commute only when they are enabled and part of transitions t_1 and t_2 in a state σ and matching one send at σ should not leave the other send *disabled or unmatchable* in the resulting state. Let C be the set of pairs of such commuting sends ("commutes" predicate). Then, we have the following: that $t_1 \equiv_C t'_1$ and $t_2 \equiv_C t'_2$.

We now define the independence relation used by MSPOE as:

Definition 3 (Independent Relation). $Ind \subseteq \mathcal{T} \times \mathcal{T}$ *is an* independence relation *iff for each* $\langle t_1, t_2 \rangle \in Ind$ *the following conditions hold:*

1. **Enabledness:** t_1 *and* $t_2 \in P_\sigma$ *and there exists a* $R_{k,n}(*)$ *such that* $t_1, t_2 \in Dtg(\sigma) \!\upharpoonright_{R_{k,n}}$.
2. **Commutativity:** *If* $S_{i,l}(k) \in t_1$ *and* $S_{j,m}(k) \in t_2$ *then* $(S_{i,l}, S_{j,m}) \in C$.

---

[3] Here, we treat t'_1 and t'_2 as sets; they really are send-receive pairs which model transitions.

Algorithm 1. MSPOE Algorithm

1: **Input:**
2:     Stack of State: St   ▷ St has σ_0; initial state
3:     Vector of Set: P   ▷ Persistent-set for each state
4:     Vector of Set: RP   ▷ Reduced Persistent-set for each state

5: $\sigma \leftarrow First(St)$ ▷ Get bottom of Stack St
6: $St \leftarrow GenerateInterleaving(\sigma)$
7: **while** $\sim Empty(St)$ {   ▷ continue until St becomes empty
8:     $\sigma \leftarrow Top(St)$ ▷ Get top of Stack St
9:     $RP_\sigma \leftarrow RP_\sigma \setminus \{Curr(\sigma)\}$ *   ▷ $Curr(\sigma)$ returns the match-set chosen at state σ
10:     $P_\sigma \leftarrow P_\sigma \setminus \{Curr(\sigma)\}$
11:     **if** $Empty(RP_\sigma)$ { *   ▷ RP_σ was singleton and was explored in the interleaving
12:         $St \leftarrow Pop(St)$ ▷ Remove state σ from St
13:     } **else**
14:         $St \leftarrow GenerateInterleaving(\sigma)$
15:     }
16: }

Thus, with the independent relation, we now can say two transitions t_1 and t_2 are dependent when the send operations in t_1 and t_2 do not commute. Consider the example and its corresponding state graph shown in Figure 4 and Figure 5. The initial state σ_0 has two enabled transitions, namely: $t_1 = \langle S_{1,1}, R_{0,1} \rangle$ and $t_2 = \langle S_{2,1}, R_{0,1} \rangle$. Note that the sends $S_{1,1}$ and $S_{2,1}$ commute. Firing t_1 disables t_2 in the next state, however, the transition enabled at $t_1(s)$ is $t'_2 = \langle S_{2,1}, R_{0,2} \rangle$ and $t_2 \equiv_c t'_2$. Thus, t_1 and t_2 are independent. If the send calls in t_1 and t_2 were not commute (assuming t_1 was fired from σ) then:

- The send from t_2 is disabled at $t_1(\sigma)$.
- The operation available at $t_1(\sigma)$ is not a receive that t_2's send can match with. If the operation enabled at $t_1(\sigma)$ is a receive, then it must be a deterministic receive which is sourcing from a process other than the process that issued t_2's send.

This explanation formulates a detailed summary of our initial observation for the refusal deadlocks. We discuss in detail the ability of MSPOE to compute the independence of transitions in Section 6.

4   Macroscopic Partial Order Elusive (MSPOE) Algorithm

Algorithm 1 presents the MSPOE algorithm in detail (statements tagged with * are additions to POE which help transform POE into MSPOE). In this algorithm, the match-set move (or the transition) selected at a particular state σ in an interleaving is denoted by $Curr(\sigma) \in P_\sigma$ where P_σ is the persistent-set at state σ. RP_σ is the *reduced* persistent-set at state σ which is what MSPOE will accomplish (it trims down persistent-set sizes according to our macroscopic POR independence rules presented in § 3). We also maintain a stack St of states that have been visited but not completely explored. Algorithm 2

Algorithm 2. GenerateInterleaving from state σ

1: **Input:**
2:     State: σ
3:     Stack of State: St
4: **Output:**
5:     Stack of State: St

6: **while** σ is not NULL {   ▷ Continue until next state can't be found
7:     $m \leftarrow Choose(P_\sigma)$ ▷ Choose a match-set to explore from σ
8:     $RP_\sigma \leftarrow RP_\sigma \cup \{m\}$ *
9:     **if** $m = \langle S_{i,l}(j), R_{j,m}(i)\rangle$ { *   ▷ if m has det recv
10:         **for all** σ' from σ until $First(St)$ { *   ▷ Update $RP_{\sigma'}$
11:             **if** $\exists B_{i,-} \in P_{\sigma'} : B_{i,-} \prec_{lp} S_{i,l}$ { *
12:                 **goto** Next_State *
13:             }
14:             **if** $\exists m' \in P_{\sigma'} : m' = \langle S_{i,-}(j), R_{j,-}(*)\rangle \wedge m' \notin RP_{\sigma'}$ { *
15:                 $RP_{\sigma'} \leftarrow RP_{\sigma'} \cup \{m'\}$ *
16:             }
17:         }
18:     }
19:     Next_State: $\sigma \leftarrow Explore(\sigma, m)$ ▷ Get the next state by firing m from σ
20:     $St \leftarrow Push(St, \sigma)$ ▷ Add σ to the Stack
21: }
22: **return** St

Algorithm 3. Choose P_σ

1: **Input:**
2:     State: σ
3: **Output:**
4:     Match-set: m

5: **if** $\exists m \in P_\sigma : m$ contains barrier {
6:     **return** m
7: **else if** $\exists m \in P_\sigma : m$ contains wait {
8:     **return** m
9: **else if** $\exists m \in P_\sigma : m$ contains deterministic recv {
10:     **return** m
11: **else if** $\exists m \in P_\sigma : m$ contains non-deterministic recv {
12:     **return** m
13: }

---

presents ISP scheduler's functioning to generate the interleaving of the program according to POE. Algorithm 3 depicts the prioritized match-set selection policy of POE which remains the same for MSPOE.

MSPOE starts with the initial state σ_0 in the stack. It generates a complete interleaving by calling the function *GenerateInterleaving* (line 6 in Algorithm 1). It repeats the following steps from this point forwards until the state stack (St) becomes empty:

P_0	P_1	P_2
$S_{0,1}(2)$	$S_{1,1}(2)$	$R_{2,1}(*)$
		$R_{2,2}(*)$
$B_{0,2}$	$B_{1,1}$	$B_{2,3}$
	$S_{1,3}(2)$	$R_{2,4}(2)$

Fig. 6. MSPOE with redundant exploration

- Select the last state σ from the trace and remove the match-set entry explored in the trace from P_σ and RP_σ (lines 8-10). If RP_σ becomes empty then pop the state off from the state stack St (lines 11-12).
- If after executing the step the last state has non-empty RP_σ then generate further interleaving from σ (line 14).

Algorithm 2 takes as input a state and generates an interleaving from that state in the following manner:

- From P_σ, choose a match-set m according to POE's prioritized match-set selection procedure (line 7).
- Add m to RP_σ (line 8).
- If m involves a deterministic receive, then search for each state σ' in the stack St and perform the following: (1) If $P_{\sigma'}$ contains a match-set m' involving a send from the same process whose send is a part of m at P_σ then add m' to $RP_{s'}$ (lines 10, 14-15). (2) However, if $P_{s'}$ contains a barrier operation MB ordered with the send that is part of m then terminate (lines 10-12) and move-on to explore the next state in the interleaving (line 19). (3) While generating the new state we fire the state transition rules described in Section 2.1. Consider the example shown in Figure 6. Notice that no matter which interleaving is explored, $S_{1,3}$ can never be enabled and be a potential match for receive calls $R_{2,1}$ and $R_{2,2}$ since such a match is restricted by the presence of barriers. We avoid such unnecessary augmentation of persistent states by adding the barrier check (lines 12-13) to the MSPOE algorithm. This serves as a favorable optimization for MSPOE.
- Repeat all the step until no more states can be explored.

Formal Details. MSPOE is sound, as it explores only feasible interleavings. It is *deliberately incomplete*: our aim is to have a practical alternative to ISP and DAMPI which guarantee completeness (in terms of non-determinism coverage), but suffer from an exponential schedule blow-up. §5 shows that MSPOE is a welcome addition to the practitioners' toolkit.

5   Experimental Results

All the experiments were run on Intel Core i7 quad-core 2.67 GHz with 8 GB of RAM. We set a time limit of 2 hours to verify the benchmarks. We abort the verification process if it did not complete within the time-limit. Example that were deadlock-free and did not finish in 2 hours were independently run on ISP and were verified to be deadlock-free.

Table 1. Interleaving results for deadlock detection

Benchmark	Buffering	# of procs	Deadlocks?	Interleavings		Time(sec)
				ISP	MSPOE	MSPOE
Mat-Multiply	0	4	No	54	1	0.001
		8	No	120	1	0.002
	∞	4	No	54	1	0.3
		8	No	120	1	0.3
2D-Diffusion	0	4	Yes	1	1 √	0.013
	∞	4	No	90	1	0.314
		8	No	> 10, 500	1	0.442
Pi- Monte-Carlo	0	4	No	36	1	0.002
		8	No	5040	1	0.003
	∞	4	No	36	1	0.24
		8	No	5040	1	0.3
Integrate_mw	0	4	No	81	81	20.19
		8	No	2401	2401	1806.738
Madre	0	4	Yes	1	1 √	0.05
	∞	4	No	> 8000	1	1.48
		8	No	> 8000	1	3.09
Parmetis	0	4	No	1	1	128.933
Gaussian Elimination	0	4	No	1	1	0.24
		8	No	1	1	0.276
	∞	4	No	180	1	0.31
		8	No	> 20, 000	1	0.324
Heat Diffusion	0	8	Yes	5041 √	23 √	12.033

$$
\begin{array}{ccc}
P_0 & P_1 & P_2 \\
\hline
R_{0,1}(*) & S_{1,1}(0) & S_{2,1}(0) \\
R_{0,2}(*) & S_{1,2}(0) & S_{2,2}(0) \\
R_{0,3}(*) & & \\
R_{0,4}(*) & & \\
B_{0,5} & B_{1,3} & B_{2,3} \\
S_{0,7}(1) & S_{1,4}(2) & S_{2,4}(0) \\
\cdots & \cdots &
\end{array}
$$

Fig. 7. Communication in 2D-Diff

The results pertaining to the reductions obtained are documented in Table 5. Summary of the tabulated results is that MSPOE explored only one interleaving for almost all benchmarks detecting the same deadlocks that ISP did. The sign √ in the MSPOE column next to the number of interleavings examined illustrates that MSPOE also caught the same deadlock as ISP did.

2D-Diffusion. We tested ISP's POE and MSPOE algorithm on *2D-Diffusion* [2] example. The code has a deadlock when evaluated in *zero buffering mode*. In this mode, the send calls act as synchronous operations. The deadlock was caught by ISP and MSPOE right in the first interleaving. When the same code is run on *infinite buffering mode*, the

```
Worker i: while(1) {
            R(from 0, any-tag); // Recv task
            if(work-tag)
               S(master, result-tag);
            else break;
         }

Master: for(i = 1 to nprocs-1) {
            Send(i, work-tag); // send to each worker the task
            tasks++;
         }
         while(tasks <totalTasks){
            Recv(*, result-tag); // recv result
            S(S.S, work-tag);  // assign more task
            tasks++;
         }
         for(i = 1 to nprocs-1) {
            Recv(i, result-tag); // recv result
            S(i, terminate-tag);  // terminate signal to worker i
         }
```

Fig. 8. High-level Code Pattern of "Integrate"

code becomes deadlock free. The code was modified to run with a single time-step. Its communication pattern is shown in the Figure 7. Note that if sends were treated as synchronous then after barriers each process is blocked on their respective sends causing a deadlock.

Integrate. Integrate_mw [2] is another benchmark that uses heavy non-determinism to compute an integral of sin function over the interval $[0, Pi]$. Integrate has a master-slave pattern where the root process divides the interval in a certain number of tasks. The root process then delegates to each worker process a single task and then waits for results from them by posting wildcard receive calls. Workers that finish early with their work are provided with more tasks until all tasks are distributed (as detailed in the high level code in Figure 8).

This benchmark does not have a deadlock. Notice that MSPOE does not demonstrate any savings over ISP while exploring the schedule space. This is because, the master process finally posts deterministic receive calls targeting each worker before it sends termination signals to each worker. This causes the MSPOE to fully expand the persistent-sets of each prior wildcard receive.

MADRE. MADRE [11], a memory aware data redistribution engine, is a library written in MPI which mainly performs load balancing tasks in an efficient manner. MADRE moves the data blocks across nodes in a distributed system within the bounds of memory available to each of the application's process. We tested MADRE with its *unitBred* algorithm on various data-sets. *unitBred* algorithm is of particular interest to us because it uses MPI_ANY_SOURCE and MPI_ANY_TAGS. MADRE has no bugs provided normal MPI send calls are not treated as blocking calls. We ran ISP's POE and then MSPOE algorithm with sbt9 dataset with unitBred algorithm and the results are documented in the Table 5.

Parmetis. Parmetis [7] is a parallel hypergraph partitioning code-base. Since, Parmetis only uses deterministic calls, ISP and MSPOE complete the verification process in a single interleaving. Parmetis was selected as a benchmark despite the absence of non-determinism because the application issues a lot of MPI calls which served as a basis to evaluate the scalability of the data-structures used in MSPOE. When run on 4 processes, Parmetis issues ~ 55,000 calls.

Heat Diffusion. This is the benchmark obtained from the Supecomputing 2011 tutorial presented by T. Hilbrich, G. Gopalakrishnan and others. The benchmark solves the heat equation on a 2-D grid. ISP discovered the deadlock in 5041st interleaving after running for almost 2.5 hours, however, the same deadlock was discovered by MSPOE in mere 23 interleavings running for approximately 12 seconds.

6   Discussion

As shown, in all our experiments, MSPOE has managed to detect deadlocks whenever POE (supported by the ISP tool) has; and managed to return (by generating) a small number (typically 1) of interleavings in other cases. In the latter cases, MSPOE computes the full persistent sets, but trims it down based on our macroscopic reduction criterion. The real value to a designer is the following (take an example similar to 2D diffusion for discussion): if given 10^3 processes, POE will simply take forever while exploring the persistent sets computed from the initial trace. MSPOE will, on the other hand, examine the initial trace, and perform macroscopic commutation aware persistent set reductions. *This is a search bounding method substantially different from other obvious reduction approaches* (e.g., depth-bounding or bounded mixing [15]), and further this bounding heuristic is *tuned toward detecting orphaning deadlocks*. Further studies are underway to further characterize MSPOE.

An important question pertaining to the working of MSPOE is the following: Does MSPOE precisely compute all the dependent actions in an MPI program? Notice that MSPOE only augments the persistent-set of prior states (at which a wildcard move took place) only when a deterministic receive is witnessed later in the trace. It is by no means a complete criterion to discover all dependent transitions.

Consider, for instance, some patterns that MSPOE cannot handle. In the example shown in Figure 9, if $S_{3,1}$ matched $R_{1,1}$ then $S_{1,2}$ and $S_{2,1}$ would engage in a cyclic wait on each other causing a deadlock. Notice that $S_{1,2}$ can't match unless $S_{2,1}$ successfully completes since $R_{2,2}$ is the only match of $S_{2,1}$ and $S_{2,1}$ is an enabler operation for $R_{2,2}$. Notice that MSPOE will fail to discover such a deadlock. However, a pertinent question that will underscore the usability of MSPOE is the following: how often such coding patterns are employed in applications, if at all? In real MPI codes that we have assessed, we did not witness such a coding style. Typically, a deterministic communication from a process following a wildcard receive is accomplished by *reply channels*. Processes often employ reply channels to perform dynamic load balancing duties by sending data/task to the sender that matched the prior wildcard receive. Thus, in our opinion, it is rare (almost to none) to observe that applications issue hard-wired deterministic receives/sends following a wildcard receive operation. Notice that in Figure 9, if $S_{1,2}(2)$ is re-written as $S_{2,1}(status.Source)$ (indicating a reply-channel) then the deadlock in the code disappears.

Figure 10 is another example where MSPOE will fail to detect a deadlock. In Figure 10, note that the barriers would not discharge if $S_{3,2}$ were to match $R_{1,1}$ thereby

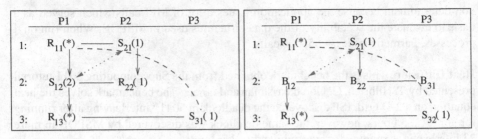

Fig. 9. Deadlock because cyclic dependency between $S_{1,2}$ and $S_{2,1}$

Fig. 10. Deadlock because barriers do not discharge

causing the deadlock. Notice that $S_{3,2}$ is unordered w.r.t. $B_{3,1}$. This can happen only
when $S_{3,2}$ is issued before $B_{3,1}$ however the wait associated with $S_{3,2}$ is issued after
the barrier. Again, such a coding practice is flawed and we have not witnessed any real
MPI program so far that employs such a coding style. Typically, global fence operations (such as barriers) are issued only *after* the local fence operations such as waits are
successfully discharged. If such were to be the programming style then the wait calls
for both $R_{1,3}$ and $S_{3,2}$ should have been issued before the respective process barriers.
In which case, the match-set $\langle B_{1,2}, B_{2,2}, B_{3,1} \rangle$ would be issued only after the completion
of $\langle S_{3,2}, R_{1,3} \rangle$. Even in alternate trace when $S_{3,2}$ pairs-up with $R_{1,1}$, notice that $S_{2,1}$ will
now find a match in $R_{1,3}$. Hence, the deadlock will disappear.

In all our benchmarks, none of above mentioned coding styles were employed except
the deterministic receive calls following a wildcard receive. MSPOE, thus, as a result
of such observations, despite being incomplete works extremely well (in other words,
appears complete) in practice. Constructing a methodology that is complete forms the
basis of our future work.

7   Conclusions

We have presented a novel algorithm MSPOE that demonstrates significant savings in
the exploration space of programs for the purpose of communication deadlock detection. In many cases the reductions were from tens of thousands of interleavings to just
one interleaving. We document the MSPOE reduction results observed over several
benchmarks. We further present evidence on the criticality of the match-set selection in
avoiding redundant explorations and for early detection of bugs.

Future Work. Conditional communication flow pattern is sill not tackled by MSPOE.
However, MSPOE algorithm can be notified of the causal receive calls whose buffers
when decoded would result in a conditional communication flow. Such information can
be statically mined and provided to the dynamic verification scheduler. To gather the
afore-said information, we would require an MPI specific control flow graph (CFG).
Work in [1] presents *pCFG* which is a CFG for MPI programs. Our future work would
therefore lie in modifying the *pCFG* work to handle non-deterministic MPI operations.
Furthermore, we will develop flow-sensitive static analysis methods on top of the improved *pCFG* to analyze conditional communication patterns.

References

1. Bronevetsky, G.: Communication-Sensitive Static Dataflow for Parallel Message Passing Applications. In: CGO: Proceedings of the 7th annual IEEE/ACM International Symposium on Code Generation and Optimization (2009) ISBN: 978-0-7695-3576-0
2. FEVS Benchmark, http://vsl.cis.udel.edu/fevs/index.html
3. Flanagan, C., Godefroid, P.: Dynamic partial-order reduction for model checking software. In: Palsberg, J., Abadi, M. (eds.) POPL, pp. 110–121. ACM (2005)
4. Godefroid, P.: Partial-Order Methods for the Verification of Concurrent Systems - An Approach to the State-Explosion Problem. LNCS, vol. 1032. Springer, Heidelberg (1996)
5. Godefroid, P., Levin, M., Molnar, D.: Whitebox fuzzing for security testing. Communications of the ACM (March 2012)
6. Gopalakrishnan, G., Kirby, R.M., Siegel, S., Thakur, R., Gropp, W., Lusk, E., de Supinski, B.R., Schulz, M., Bronevetsky, G.: Formal analysis of mpi-based parallel programs: Present and future. Communications of the ACM (December 2011)
7. Karypis, G., Kumar, V.: Parallel multilevel k-way partitioning scheme for irregular graphs. In: SuperComputing, SC (1996)
8. http://www.multicore-association.org
9. Message Passing Interface, http://www.mpi-forum.org/docs/mpi-2.2
10. Sarkar, V., Harrod, W., Snavely, A.: Software challenges in extreme scale systems. SciDAC Review Special Issue on Advanced Computing: The Roadmap to Exascale, 60–65 (January 2010)
11. Siegel, S.F.: The MADRE web page (2008), http://vsl.cis.udel.edu/madre
12. Siegel, S.F.: MPI-Spin web page (2008), http://vsl.cis.udel.edu/mpi-spin
13. Vakkalanka, S.: Efficient dynamic verification algorithms for MPI applications. PhD thesis, University of Utah, Salt Lake City, Ut, USA (2010)
14. Vakkalanka, S., Gopalakrishnan, G.C., Kirby, R.M.: Dynamic Verification of MPI Programs with Reductions in Presence of Split Operations and Relaxed Orderings. In: Gupta, A., Malik, S. (eds.) CAV 2008. LNCS, vol. 5123, pp. 66–79. Springer, Heidelberg (2008)
15. Vo, A., Aananthakrishnan, S., Gopalakrishnan, G., de Supinski, B.R., Schulz, M., Bronevetsky, G.: A scalable and distributed dynamic formal verifier for MPI programs. In: Proceedings of the ACM/IEEE International Conference for High Performance Computing, Networking, Storage and Analysis, SC 2010, pp. 1–10. IEEE Computer Society, Washington, DC (2010)
16. Vo, A., Gopalakrishnan, G., Kirby, R.M., de Supinski, B.R., Schulz, M., Bronevetsky, G.: Large Scale Verification of MPI Programs Using Lamport Clocks with Lazy Update. In: PACT, pp. 330–339 (2011), http://doi.ieeecomputersociety.org/10.1109/PACT.2011.64
17. Vo, A., Vakkalanka, S., DeLisi, M., Gopalakrishnan, G., Kirby, R.M., Thakur, R.: Formal verification of practical MPI programs. In: Proceedings of the 14th ACM SIGPLAN Symposium on Principles and Practice of Parallel Programming, PPoPP 2009, pp. 261–270. ACM, New York (2009)
18. Vuduc, R., Schulz, M., Quinlan, D., de Supinski, B., Sornsen, A.: Improving distributed memory applications testing by message perturbation. In: Proceedings of the 2006 Workshop on Parallel and Distributed Systems: Testing and Debugging, PADTAD 2006, pp. 27–36. ACM, New York (2006)

Alternating-Time Temporal Logic
in the Calculus of (Co)Inductive Constructions

Dante Zanarini[1], Carlos Luna[2], and Luis Sierra[2]

[1] CIFASIS, Blvd. 27 de Febrero 210 bis, Rosario, Argentina
dante@fceia.unr.edu.ar
[2] InCo, Facultad de Ingeniería, Universidad de la República, Uruguay
{cluna,sierra}@fing.edu.uy

Abstract. This work presents a complete formalization of Alternating-time Temporal Logic (ATL) and its semantic model, Concurrent Game Structures (CGS), in the Calculus of (Co)Inductive Constructions, using the logical framework Coq. Unlike standard ATL semantics, temporal operators are formalized in terms of inductive and coinductive types, employing a fixpoint characterization of these operators. The formalization is used to model a concurrent system with an unbounded number of players and states, and to verify some properties expressed as ATL formulas. Unlike automatic techniques, our formal model has no restrictions in the size of the CGS, and arbitrary state predicates can be used as atomic propositions of ATL.

1 Introduction

Linear-time and branching-time temporal logics are natural specification languages for reactive systems [8,16]. Alternating-time Temporal Logic (ATL), introduced by Alur, Henzinger and Kupferman [1,2], is a temporal logic suitable for open systems specificiations, where an open system is a system that interacts with its environment and whose behavior depends on the state of the system as well as the behavior of the environment [2].

The logic ATL offers selective quantification over those paths that are possible outcomes of games. For instance, by preceding the temporal operator "eventually" with a selective path quantifier, it is possible to specify that in a game between a reactive system and the environment, the system has a strategy to reach a certain state.

An ATL formula is interpreted over Concurrent Game Structures (CGS) [2]. Every state transition of a CGS results from a simultaneous choice of moves, one for each player. The players represent individual components and the environment of an open system. CGS can capture various forms of synchronous composition for open systems.

In this work we formalize the CGS semantics of ATL in the Calculus of (Co)Inductive Constructions (CIC) [6,15,9], using the logical framework Coq [19,4]. This formalization is divided in two parts: the logic ATL and the CGS semantics for a given game structure S. We show that the proof of the Coq

R. Gheyi and D. Naumann (Eds.): SBMF 2012, LNCS 7498, pp. 210–225, 2012.

proposition φ q guarantees that the CGS S satisfies the ATL formula φ in the state q of S (i.e. $q \models \varphi$). This work uses a general approach to deal with CGS where the number of states is unbounded; this generality is scarcely obtained using standard model checking techniques [3].

There exists previous work in formalizing temporal logic in systems other than Coq. We can mention the axiomatic encoding of Lamport's Temporal Logic of Actions in Isabelle [14]; and formalizations of Linear Temporal Logic (LTL) [16] in PVS [17] and HOL [18].

The choice of the CIC is dictated by its considerable expressive power as well as by the fact that it is supported by a tool of industrial strength, namely the Coq proof assistant. As one example of its applicability, Coq has been used for the development and formal verification of a compiler of a large subset of the C programming language [12]. Furthermore, there are works that formalize temporal logics in the CIC. We can mention the formalization of LTL [7] and Computation Tree Logic (CTL) [13]. LTL assumes implicit universal quantification over all paths that are generated by system moves. CTL [21] allows explicit existential and universal quantification over all paths. ATL introduces a more general variety of temporal logic; offers selective quantification over those paths that are possible outcomes of games. As compared to previous work by the authors [13], the present formalization of ATL is more general and complex.

A detailed description of the formalization is presented in Spanish in [22]. This document, along with the full formalization in Coq may be obtained from http://www.fceia.unr.edu.ar/~dante/.

The rest of the paper is organized as follows. In Section 2 we introduce CGS as well as the syntax and semantics of ATL. In Section 3 are formalized both the logic ATL and CGS including the notions of coalition and strategies. Unlike standard ATL semantics, temporal operators are formalized in terms of inductive and coinductive types, employing a fixpoint characterization of these operators. Then, Section 4 shows a complete list of axioms, theorems and inference rules for ATL according to [10] that have been proved in Coq with our proposal [22,23]. In Section 5 we present the usual train example [2] as a simple (due to space restrictions) case study for the bounded and unbounded cases. Finally, Section 6 concludes with a summary of our contributions and directions for future work.

2   Alternating-Time Temporal Logic

In this section we introduce CGS (Section 2.1) as well as the syntax and the semantics of ATL (Section 2.2) as found in [2].

2.1   Concurrent Game Structures

Definition 1 (CGS). *A CGS is a tuple $S = \langle \Sigma, Q, \Pi, \pi, d, \delta \rangle$ with:*

- *A set $\Sigma = \{1, \ldots, k\}$ of players or agents.*
- *A set Q of states.*

- A finite set Π of atomic propositions.
- For each $q \in Q$, a set $\pi(q) \subseteq \Pi$ of propositions true at q.
- For each player $a \in \Sigma$ and each state $q \in Q$, a natural number $d_a(q) \geq 1$ of moves available at state q to player a. We identify the moves of a at state q with the numbers $1, \ldots, d_a(q)$. For $q \in Q$, a move vector at q is a tuple $\langle j_1, \ldots, j_k \rangle$ such that $1 \leq j_a \leq d_a(q)$ for each player a. We define $D(q)$ as the set of move vectors available at q; function D is called the move function.
- For each state $q \in Q$ and each move vector $\langle j_1, \ldots, j_k \rangle \in D(q)$, a state $\delta(q, j_1, \ldots, j_k) \in Q$ that results from state q if each player $a \in \Sigma$ chooses move j_a. The function δ is called transition function.

For two states q and q', we say that q' is a *successor* of q if there exists a move vector $\langle j_1, \ldots, j_k \rangle$ such that $q' = \delta(q, j_1, \ldots, j_k)$. A *computation* of S is an infinite sequence $\omega = q_0, q_1, q_2, \ldots$ of states such that for all $i \geq 0$, the state q_{i+1} is a successor of q_i. We refer to a computation starting at state q as a *q-computation*. For a computation ω and a position $i \geq 0$, we use $\omega[i]$ and $\omega[0, i]$ to denote the i-th state and the finite prefix $q_0, \ldots, q_i$, respectively.

2.2   ATL Syntax and Semantics

Definition 2 (ATL). *Let Π be a set of atomic propositions, and Σ a set of k players. The set of ATL formulas is inductively defined as follows:*

- *p, for each $p \in \Pi$.*
- *$\neg\varphi$, $\varphi \vee \psi$, $\varphi \wedge \psi$, $\varphi \rightarrow \psi$, where φ, ψ are ATL formulas.*
- *$\langle\!\langle A \rangle\!\rangle \bigcirc \varphi$, $\langle\!\langle A \rangle\!\rangle \square \varphi$, $\langle\!\langle A \rangle\!\rangle \varphi \mathcal{U} \psi$, where φ, ψ are ATL formulas and $A \subseteq \Sigma$.*

The operator $\langle\!\langle \ \rangle\!\rangle$ is a path quantifier; $\bigcirc$ *(next)*, $\square$ *(box) and* $\mathcal{U}$ *(until) are* temporal operators.

ATL can be viewed as a generalization of the branching-time temporal logic CTL where path quantifiers can be parametrized by sets of players. In particular, we obtain a CTL-equivalent logic restricting A to $\emptyset$ or Σ in Def. 2.

Formulas in ATL are interpreted over states of a CGS with the same players and atomic propositions. The concept of *strategy* is introduced in [2] to formalize the semantics.

Definition 3 (Strategy). *Let $S = \langle \Sigma, Q, \Pi, \pi, d, \delta \rangle$ be a CGS and $a \in \Sigma$. A strategy for a is a function $f_a : Q^+ \rightarrow \mathbb{N}$ that maps every nonempty finite state sequence $\alpha \in Q^+$ to a natural number such that if q is the last state of α, then $1 \leq f_a(\alpha) \leq d_a(q)$.*

Given a state $q \in Q$, and $A \subseteq \Sigma$, an A-strategy $F_A = \{f_a \mid a \in A\}$ is a set of strategies, one for each player in A. The *outcomes* of F_A from a state q is the set of traces that players in A can enforce when they follow the strategies in F_A. A computation $\omega = q_0, q_1, \ldots$ belongs to $out(q, F_A)$ if $q_0 = q$ and for all positions i, there is a move vector $\langle j_1, \ldots, j_k \rangle$ such that (1) if $a \in A$, $j_a = f_a(\omega[0, i])$, and (2) $\delta(q_i, j_1, \ldots, j_k) = q_{i+1}$.

Definition 4 (Standard ATL Semantics). *Let S be a CGS and q a state of S. We write $q \models \varphi$ to indicate that the ATL formula φ holds at q. The relation $\models$ is defined inductively as follows:*

- *$q \models p$, for atomic propositions $p \in \Pi$ iff $p \in \pi(q)$.*
- *$q \models \neg\varphi$ iff $q \not\models \varphi$.*
- *$q \models \varphi_1 \vee \varphi_2$ iff $q \models \varphi_1$ or $q \models \varphi_2$.*
- *$q \models \varphi_1 \wedge \varphi_2$ iff $q \models \varphi_1$ and $q \models \varphi_2$.*
- *$q \models \varphi_1 \Rightarrow \varphi_2$ iff $q \models \varphi_2$ given that $q \models \varphi_1$.*
- *$q \models \langle\!\langle A \rangle\!\rangle \bigcirc \varphi$ iff there exists an A-strategy $F_A = \{f_a \mid a \in A\}$, such that for all $\omega \in out(q, F_A)$, we have $\omega[1] \models \varphi$.*
- *$q \models \langle\!\langle A \rangle\!\rangle \square \varphi$ iff there exists an A-strategy $F_A = \{f_a \mid a \in A\}$ such that for all $\omega \in out(q, F_A)$ and all positions $i \geq 0$ we have $\omega[i] \models \varphi$.*
- *$q \models \langle\!\langle A \rangle\!\rangle \varphi_1 \, \mathcal{U} \, \varphi_2$ iff there exists an A-strategy $F_A = \{f_a \mid a \in A\}$, such that for all $\omega \in out(q, F_A)$ there exists a position $i \geq 0$ such that $\omega[i] \models \varphi_2$ and for all positions $0 \leq j < i$ we have $\omega[j] \models \varphi_1$.*

3   Formalizing CGS and ATL

Our formalization is divided in two main parts. Section 3.2 provides a way to represent CGS, coalitions and strategies. In Section 3.3 we proceed to formalize the logic ATL. The formalization of temporal operators follows the axiomatization presented in [10], using fixpoints characterizations for $\langle\!\langle A \rangle\!\rangle \square \varphi$ and $\langle\!\langle A \rangle\!\rangle \varphi \, \mathcal{U} \, \psi$.

We believe that giving semantics to temporal operators using fixpoint definitions by means of inductive and coinductive types has some advantages over the standard semantics from def. 4. The inductive and coinductive principles associated to our definition of temporal operators can be used to construct more elegant and concise proofs for ATL theorems (sect. 4) and for specific propierties of reactive systems (sect. 5).

3.1   The CIC and Coq

The CIC is a type theory, in brief, a higher order logic in which the individuals are classified into a hierarchy of types. The types work very much as in strongly typed functional programming languages which means that there are basic elementary types, types defined by induction, like sequences and trees, and function types. An inductive type is defined by its constructors and its elements are obtained as finite combinations of these constructors. Data types are called "Sets" in the CIC (in Coq). When the requirement of finiteness is removed we obtain the possibility of defining infinite structures, called coinductive types, like infinite sequences. On top of this, a higher-order logic is available which serves to predicate on the various data types. The interpretation of the propositions is constructive, i.e. a proposition is defined by specifying what a proof of it is and a proposition is true if and only if a proof of it has been constructed. The type of propositions is called Prop. We use the usual notation for logical connectives and quantifiers ($\rightarrow$,

$\vee$, $\wedge$, $\neg$, $\forall$, $\exists$). For anonymous functions and predicates, we utilize a notation similar to the Coq specification language. For instance, predicate $pos : \mathbb{N} \to Prop$ is written as $(\lambda n : \mathbb{N} \Rightarrow n > 0)$.

We define a (co)inductive predicate I by giving introduction rules of the form:

$$\frac{P_1 \dots P_m}{I\ x_1 \dots x_n}\ (\text{intro}_i)$$

where free ocurrences of variables are implicitly universally quantified.

In this work we use some inductive types defined in the Coq Standard Library [20]. We employ notation $\{\ \}$ for the empty type, $\{1\}$ for unit type, $A + B$ for disjoint union (sum type). Type $(seq\ A)$ denotes the set of finite sequences of type A. Empty sequence is noted as $\langle \rangle$, and the infix notation $s \frown e$ is used to denote the sequence resulting by appending element e to sequence s. The *Stream* type is used to represent infinite sequences of objects from a fixed type A. Constructor *Cons* adds an element $e : A$ to an infinite sequence ω. Infix notation $e \triangleleft \omega$ is used for $(Cons\ e\ \omega)$. We refer to [19,4] for further details on the CIC and Coq.

3.2   Formalizing CGS

We assume three basic types in sort *Set*: *State*, the set of states; *Player*, the players in the system; and *Move*, the set of moves (or *actions*). These types are specification parameters, and must be instantiated when specifyng a concrete CGS. Observe that we do not imposse any finiteness requirement to these types.

Move Vectors and Transitions. A move vector is a function that assigns a move to each player, $\langle Move \rangle \stackrel{\text{def}}{=} Player \to Move$. The transition function is introduced as a relation $\delta : State \to \langle Move \rangle \to State \to Prop$. We say that the move m is enabled at state q for player a if there exists a move vector mv and a state q' such that mv assigns m to player a and q' is the successor of q when players in Σ chooses the movements in mv. Formally, the relation $enabled : State \to Player \to Move \to Prop$ has one constructor:

$$\frac{mv : \langle Move \rangle \qquad q' : State \qquad mv\ a = m \qquad \delta\ q\ mv\ q'}{enabled\ q\ a\ m}\ (enabled\_intro) \quad (1)$$

A proof of type $(enabled\ q\ a\ m)$ is interpreted as *"player a can choose move m at state q"*. Two expected properties are assumed over δ; the property δ_f guarantees that the relation is indeed a function, while the property δ_d guarantees that for every state q, if you choose a move vector mv such that $(mv\ a)$ is enabled at q for every player a, then you will found an outgoing transition from q labeled with mv.

$$
\begin{aligned}
\delta\_f &: \forall (q, q', q'' : State)(mv : \langle Move \rangle), \delta\ q\ mv\ q' \to \delta\ q\ mv\ q'' \to q' = q'' \\
\delta\_d &: \forall (q : State)(mv : \langle Move \rangle), \\
&\quad (\forall a : Player, enabled\ q\ a\ (mv\ a)) \to \exists (q' : State), \delta\ q\ mv\ q'\ .
\end{aligned}
\quad (2)
$$

Coalitions. A coalition is a set of players $A \subseteq \Sigma$. The Coq Standard Library [20] defines a set over a universe U as an inhabitant of type $U \to Prop$. We say that element x belongs to set X if we can exhibit a proof of proposition $(X\ x)$. In particular, the union of sets X, Y is defined as $Union\ X\ Y \overset{\text{def}}{=} (\lambda x : U \Rightarrow X\ x \lor Y\ x)$. However, this formalization of sets is not satisfactory for our purposes due to its lack of computational content. This computational content is required, for instance, to prove the valid formula $\langle\!\langle A \rangle\!\rangle \bigcirc \varphi \to \langle\!\langle B \rangle\!\rangle \bigcirc \psi \to \langle\!\langle A \cup B \rangle\!\rangle \bigcirc (\varphi \wedge \psi)$, when A and B are disjoint sets. The proof "joins" the strategies for A and B given in the premises to construct a new strategy for the coalition $A \cup B$. For a player $a \in A \cup B$, the new strategy chooses the strategy given by the first premise when $a \in A$, and the strategy given by the second premise when $a \in B$.

As we will introduce strategies as an object with computational content, i.e. an inhabitant of sort *Set*, the election of a strategy cannot be made eliminating an inhabitant in *Prop* [19]. We conclude that proofs of set membership must live in sort *Set*. Therefore, we define a coalition as a term of type *Player* $\to$ *Set*. We say that player a *belongs* to coalition C if we can construct an element in type $(C\ a)$. Coalitions Σ and $\emptyset$, and the union of two coalitions are defined as:

$$\Sigma \overset{\text{def}}{=} \lambda a \Rightarrow \{1\} \qquad \emptyset \overset{\text{def}}{=} \lambda a \Rightarrow \{\ \} \qquad A \uplus B \overset{\text{def}}{=} \lambda a \Rightarrow A\ a + B\ a \qquad (3)$$

Other operators, like coalition complement, can be defined easily. We refer the interested reader to [23].

Strategies. A strategy decides the next move taking into account the complete history of the game:

$$Strategy \overset{\text{def}}{=} seq\ State \to State \to Move \qquad (4)$$

where the first argument is the past sequence of states, and the second the current state of the game. Let A be a coalition. A *strategy for coalition A* is a term of type $(StrategySet\ A)$, where:

$$StrategySet(A : Coalition) \overset{\text{def}}{=} \forall a : Player, A\ a \to Strategy \qquad (5)$$

A term $F_A : (StrategySet\ A)$ gives a strategy for each player a, provided that $a \in A$. We define the notion of F_A-successor state for a coalition strategy F_A. Let q be the current state, and qs the game history. We say that q' is an F_A-successor of $qs \frown q$ if there exists a move vector mv such that: (1) a transition from q to q' labelled with mv exists; and (2) strategy $f_a \in F_A$ for player $a \in A$ is such that $f_a(qs \frown q) = mv(a)$. Formally, relation *suc* is introduced by means of the following definition:

$$suc : \forall A : Coalition, StrategySet\ A \to seq\ State \to State \to State \to Prop$$

$$\frac{mv : \langle Move \rangle \qquad \delta\ q\ mv\ q' \qquad \forall (a : Player)(H : A\ a), F_A\ a\ H\ qs\ q = mv\ a}{suc\ A\ F_A\ qs\ q\ q'} \ (suc\_intro) \qquad (6)$$

In the sequel, we will omit the first argument, since it can be inferred from the second. Also, we write $q' \in suc(qs, q, F_A)$ for a proof of $(suc\ F_A\ qs\ q\ q')$.

Now, we define coinductively the set of traces that a coalition A can enforce by following the strategy F_A. The relation $isOut$ determines if the trace $(q \triangleleft q' \triangleleft \omega)$ is a possible result of the game when players in A follows strategies in F_A and game history is qs:

$$isOut : \forall A : Coalition, StrategySet\ A \to seq\ State \to Trace \to Prop$$

$$\frac{q' \in suc(qs, q, F_A) \qquad isOut\ A\ F_A\ (qs \frown q)\ (q' \triangleleft \omega)}{isOut\ A\ F_A\ qs\ (q \triangleleft q' \triangleleft \omega)}\ (isOut\_intro) \tag{7}$$

where $Trace \stackrel{\text{def}}{=} (Stream\ State)$. The set $out(q, F_A)$ of traces a coalition A can enforce if follows strategies in F_A is defined as:

$$\omega \in out(q, F_A) \stackrel{\text{def}}{=} isOut\ A\ F_A\ \langle\rangle\ (q \triangleleft \omega) \tag{8}$$

3.3   Formalizing ATL

In this section we present a formalization of the syntax and semantics of ATL. Let S be a CGS, an ATL state formula is a term of type $StateForm \stackrel{\text{def}}{=} State \to Prop$. If $q : State$ and $\varphi : StateForm$, a proof (term) of $(\varphi\ q)$ is interpreted as $q \models \varphi$.

Constants and Boolean Connectives. The $\top$ and $\bot$ formulas are easily defined as $\top \stackrel{\text{def}}{=} (\lambda q : State \Rightarrow True)$, and $\bot \stackrel{\text{def}}{=} (\lambda q : State \Rightarrow False)$. We use a standard point-free use of boolean connectives. For example, for state formulas φ, ψ, disjunction is defined as $\varphi \vee \psi \stackrel{\text{def}}{=} (\lambda q : State \Rightarrow \varphi\ q \vee \psi\ q)$.

Temporal Operators. The standard ATL semantics presented in Def. 4 for $\langle\langle A \rangle\rangle \bigcirc \varphi$ uses the notion of execution traces. We present here an alternative (and equivalent) semantics using only the notion of successor state. Let q be the current state of a game. To guarantee that the property φ holds in the next state a coalition A should follow a strategy F_A such that for every possible F_A-successor state q' we have $q' \models \varphi$.

Definition 5 (Next). *Let* $A : Coalition$, $q : State$ *and* $\varphi : StateForm$. *The relation* $Next : Coalition \to StateForm \to StateForm$ *is defined with one constructor as follows:*

$$\frac{F : StrategySet\ A \qquad \forall q', q' \in suc(\langle\rangle, q, F) \to \varphi\ q'}{Next\ A\ \varphi\ q}\ (next) \tag{9}$$

The ATL axiomatization found in [10] establishes that $\langle\langle A \rangle\rangle \Box \varphi$ is the greatest fixed point of equation $X \leftrightarrow \varphi \wedge \langle\langle A \rangle\rangle \bigcirc X$. Following this approach, we introduce a coinductive predicate to model this semantics for formulas of the form $\langle\langle A \rangle\rangle \Box \varphi$.

Definition 6 (Box). *Let A : Coalition, φ : StateForm and q : State. The coinductive predicate Box : Coalition $\rightarrow$ StateForm $\rightarrow$ StateForm is defined as:*

$$\frac{\varphi\, q \qquad F : StrategySet\ A}{\forall q',\ q' \in suc(\langle\rangle, q, F) \rightarrow Box\ A\ \varphi\ q'}{Box\ A\ \varphi\ q} \quad \text{(box)} \tag{10}$$

To construct a proof of $q \models \langle\!\langle A \rangle\!\rangle \Box \varphi$ two conditions must hold: (1) φ must be valid at state q; and (2) we need to find an A-strategy F such that, for all F-successor state q' of q we have $q' \models \langle\!\langle A \rangle\!\rangle \Box \varphi$.

Using the fact that $\langle\!\langle A \rangle\!\rangle \varphi \mathcal{U} \psi$ is the least fixed point of $X \leftrightarrow \psi \vee (\varphi \wedge \langle\!\langle A \rangle\!\rangle \bigcirc X)$ we introduce the semantics of $\langle\!\langle A \rangle\!\rangle \varphi \mathcal{U} \psi$ by an inductive relation.

Definition 7 (Until). *Let A : Coalition, φ, ψ : StateForm and q : State. The inductive relation Until : Coalition $\rightarrow$ StateForm $\rightarrow$ StateForm $\rightarrow$ StateForm is defined with two constructors as follows:*

$$\frac{\psi\, q}{Until\ A\ \varphi\ \psi\ q}\ (\mathcal{U}_1) \qquad \frac{F : StrategySet\ A \qquad \varphi\, q}{\forall q',\ q' \in suc(\langle\rangle, q, F) \rightarrow Until\ A\ \varphi\ \psi\ q'}{Until\ A\ \varphi\ \psi\ q}\ (\mathcal{U}_2) \tag{11}$$

If $q \models \psi$, then $q \models \langle\!\langle A \rangle\!\rangle \varphi \mathcal{U} \psi$ (constructor $\mathcal{U}_1$). To prove $q \models \langle\!\langle A \rangle\!\rangle \varphi \mathcal{U} \psi$ using constructor $\mathcal{U}_2$, we need to prove that $q \models \varphi$ and there exists an A-strategy F such that, if players in A follow this strategy, in all F_A-successor state q' of q we have $q' \models \langle\!\langle A \rangle\!\rangle \varphi \mathcal{U} \psi$.

Derived operators like $\langle\!\langle A \rangle\!\rangle \Diamond \varphi$ (eventually), and $\langle\!\langle A \rangle\!\rangle \overset{\infty}{F} \varphi$ (infinitely often) have been defined. For example, $\langle\!\langle A \rangle\!\rangle \overset{\infty}{F} \varphi \overset{\text{def}}{=} \langle\!\langle A \rangle\!\rangle \Box \langle\!\langle \emptyset \rangle\!\rangle \Diamond \varphi$. For details see [23].

4   A Deductive System for ATL

The formalization presented in Section 3 can be used to reason about properties of ATL and CGS. To prove ATL theorems we often use general properties involving coalitions and strategies.

A complete set of axioms and inference rules for ATL is presented in [10]. We have proved all these results in our formalization. Due to space constraints, proofs are merely outlined; however, all proofs have been formalized in Coq and are available as part of the full specification [23].

Theorem 1. *The following formulas are valid in all states of all CGS:*

($\bot$) $\neg \langle\!\langle A \rangle\!\rangle \bigcirc \bot$.
($\top$) $\langle\!\langle A \rangle\!\rangle \bigcirc \top$.
(Σ) $\neg \langle\!\langle \emptyset \rangle\!\rangle \bigcirc \neg \varphi \rightarrow \langle\!\langle \Sigma \rangle\!\rangle \bigcirc \varphi$.
(**S**) $\langle\!\langle A_1 \rangle\!\rangle \bigcirc \varphi_1 \wedge \langle\!\langle A_2 \rangle\!\rangle \bigcirc \varphi_2 \rightarrow \langle\!\langle A_1 \cup A_2 \rangle\!\rangle \bigcirc (\varphi_1 \wedge \varphi_2)$, if $A_1 \cap A_2 = \emptyset$.
(**FP$_\Box$**) $\langle\!\langle A \rangle\!\rangle \Box \varphi \leftrightarrow \varphi \wedge \langle\!\langle A \rangle\!\rangle \bigcirc \langle\!\langle A \rangle\!\rangle \Box \varphi$.
(**GFP$_\Box$**) $\langle\!\langle \emptyset \rangle\!\rangle \Box (\theta \rightarrow (\varphi \wedge \langle\!\langle A \rangle\!\rangle \bigcirc \theta)) \rightarrow \langle\!\langle \emptyset \rangle\!\rangle \Box (\theta \rightarrow \langle\!\langle A \rangle\!\rangle \Box \varphi)$.

(FP$_\mathcal{U}$) $\langle\!\langle A \rangle\!\rangle \varphi_1 \,\mathcal{U}\, \varphi_2 \leftrightarrow \varphi_2 \vee (\varphi_1 \wedge \langle\!\langle A \rangle\!\rangle \bigcirc \langle\!\langle A \rangle\!\rangle \varphi_1 \,\mathcal{U}\, \varphi_2)$.

(LFP$_\mathcal{U}$) $\langle\!\langle \varnothing \rangle\!\rangle \Box ((\varphi_2 \vee (\varphi_1 \wedge \langle\!\langle A \rangle\!\rangle \bigcirc \theta)) \rightarrow \theta) \rightarrow \langle\!\langle \varnothing \rangle\!\rangle \Box (\langle\!\langle A \rangle\!\rangle \varphi_1 \,\mathcal{U}\, \varphi_2 \rightarrow \theta)$.

Also, the following inference rules preserves validity [1]:

$$\frac{\varphi \rightarrow \psi}{\langle\!\langle A \rangle\!\rangle \bigcirc \varphi \rightarrow \langle\!\langle A \rangle\!\rangle \bigcirc \psi} \text{ (monotonicity)} \qquad \frac{\varphi}{\langle\!\langle \varnothing \rangle\!\rangle \Box \varphi} \text{ (necessitation)}$$

Proof. The proof of **(FP$_\Box$)** in our system is trivial, because we have used this formula as a definition for $\langle\!\langle A \rangle\!\rangle \Box$. Formula **(GFP$_\Box$)** is a consequence of the use of a coinductive type for this operator. A similar consideration can be done about formulas **(FP$_\mathcal{U}$)**, used to define formulas involving $\mathcal{U}$; and **(LFP$_\mathcal{U}$)**, consequence of the inductive definition. Formula (Σ) is valid only in classical logic. In constructive logic we can prove (Σ'): $\neg\langle\!\langle \varnothing \rangle\!\rangle \bigcirc \neg\varphi \rightarrow \neg\neg\langle\!\langle \Sigma \rangle\!\rangle \bigcirc \varphi$. To demonstrate the equivalence $(\Sigma) \leftrightarrow (\Sigma')$ from classical logic in our system, we must add the excluded middle law explicitly. Proof of **(S)** involves reasoning about union of coalitions and strategies, as well as relating the "join" of coalition strategies (collaborative game) and the traces in which each coalition plays regardless the other one (competitive game). These results are properties about game structures, and we have proved them in [23] using definitions introduced in Section 2.1. Rule monotonicity is proved by showing that strategy F_A given by premise $\langle\!\langle A \rangle\!\rangle \bigcirc \varphi$ is an A strategy ensuring ψ in all states $q' \in suc(\langle\rangle, q, F_A)$. We prove necessitation by coinduction, unfolding Def. 6 and using the fact that φ is valid in all states. $\qquad\square$

To show that our formalization can be used as a suitable proof system for ATL, we have proved in [23] an extensive list of ATL theorems taken from [10]. Lemma 1 shows a list with a subset of such formulas.

Lemma 1 (Derived formulas). *The following judges can be proved valid in our formalization:*

(1) *Regularity:* $\vdash \langle\!\langle A \rangle\!\rangle \bigcirc \varphi \rightarrow \neg\langle\!\langle \Sigma \setminus A \rangle\!\rangle \bigcirc \neg\varphi$.

(2) *And monotonicity:* $\vdash \langle\!\langle A \rangle\!\rangle \bigcirc (\varphi \wedge \psi) \rightarrow \langle\!\langle A \rangle\!\rangle \bigcirc \varphi$.

(3) *Coalition monotonicity:* $\vdash \langle\!\langle A \rangle\!\rangle \bigcirc \varphi \rightarrow \langle\!\langle A \uplus B \rangle\!\rangle \bigcirc \varphi$.

(4) *Monotonicity of $\langle\!\langle \ \rangle\!\rangle \Box$:* $(\varphi \rightarrow \psi) \vdash \langle\!\langle A \rangle\!\rangle \Box \varphi \rightarrow \langle\!\langle A \rangle\!\rangle \Box \psi$.

(5) *Monotonicity of $\langle\!\langle \ \rangle\!\rangle \mathcal{U}$:* $(\varphi \rightarrow \varphi'), (\psi \rightarrow \psi') \vdash \langle\!\langle A \rangle\!\rangle \varphi \mathcal{U} \psi \rightarrow \langle\!\langle A \rangle\!\rangle \varphi' \mathcal{U} \psi'$.

(6) *Necessitation of $\langle\!\langle \ \rangle\!\rangle \Box$:* $\varphi \vdash \langle\!\langle A \rangle\!\rangle \Box \varphi$.

(7) *Induction for $\langle\!\langle \ \rangle\!\rangle \Box$:* $(\varphi \rightarrow (\psi \wedge \langle\!\langle A \rangle\!\rangle \bigcirc \varphi)) \vdash \varphi \rightarrow \langle\!\langle A \rangle\!\rangle \Box \psi$.

(8) *Induction for $\langle\!\langle \ \rangle\!\rangle \mathcal{U}$:* $(\psi \vee (\varphi \wedge \langle\!\langle A \rangle\!\rangle \bigcirc \chi) \rightarrow \chi) \vdash \langle\!\langle A \rangle\!\rangle \varphi \mathcal{U} \psi \rightarrow \chi$.

5   A Case Study

The formalization presented in Section 3 has been used in Section 4 to prove general properties over CGS and the logic ATL. In this section, we specify and

---

[1] We omit the modus ponens rule from [10], since this rule is already valid in our meta-logic via the shallow embedding.

verify a simple concrete system which is a good guide to model and analyze many systems. Section 5.1 presents an example taken from [2], describing a control protocol for a train entering a railroad crossing. Section 5.2 presents a generalization of this model where an unknown number of trains compete to enter a gate, and the gate controller must ensure some safety and liveness properties. This example can not be directly analyzed using model checking techniques because it involves an unbounded space of states.

5.1   Controlling a Railroad Crossing

We formalize a protocol for a train entering a railroad crossing with a finite CGS. All components for this CGS are instantiated using definitions presented in Section 3.2, and some properties for the system are specified using ATL formulas as described in Section 3.3.

Example 1. The CGS $S_T = \langle k, Q, \Pi, \pi, d, \delta \rangle$ has the following components:

- $k = 2$. Player 1 represents the train, and player 2 the gate controller.
- $Q = \{q_{out}, q_{req}, q_{gran}, q_{in}\}$.
- $\Pi = \{Out, Request, In\_gate, Grant\}$.
- $\pi(q_{out}) = \{Out\}$, the train is outside the gate; $\pi(q_{req}) = \{Out, Request\}$, the train is still outside the gate, but has requested to enter; $\pi(q_{gran}) = \{Out, Grant\}$, the controller has given the train permission to enter the gate; $\pi(q_{in}) = \{In\_gate\}$, the train is in the gate.

-
  - $d_1(q_{out}) = 2$ and $d_2(q_{out}) = 1$.
    At q_{out}, the train can choose to either stay outside the gate, or request to enter the gate.
  - $d_1(q_{req}) = 1$ and $d_2(q_{req}) = 3$.
    At q_{req}, the controller can choose to either grant the train permission to enter the gate, or deny the train's request, or delay the handling of the request.
  - $d_1(q_{gran}) = 2$ and $d_2(q_{gran}) = 1$.
    At q_{gran}, the train can choose to either enter the gate, or relinquish its permission to enter the gate.
  - $d_1(q_{in}) = 1$ and $d_2(q_{in}) = 2$.
    At q_{in}, the controller can choose to either keep the gate closed, or reopen the gate to new requests.

- The transition function δ is depicted in Figure 1.

A Model Based on CGS. In order to prove properties of the protocol described in Example 1, we proceed to model all the components of S_T following definitions presented in Section 3.2.

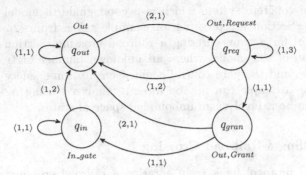

Fig. 1. Graphical representation of Example 1

States, Players and Moves. These sets are introduced as types with one constructor for each element in the set, excepting the sets of moves, where a unique constructor is used to represent an *idle* move.

$$State \quad : Set \stackrel{\text{def}}{=} | \ q_{out} \ | \ q_{req} \ | \ q_{gran} \ | \ q_{in}$$
$$Player : Set \stackrel{\text{def}}{=} | \ Train \ | \ Controller$$
$$Move \quad : Set \stackrel{\text{def}}{=} | \ stayOut \ | \ request \ | \ grant \ | \ delay \ | \ deny \ | \ enter$$
$$| \ relinquish \ | \ keepClosed \ | \ reopen \ | \ idle$$

We use the tuple notation $\langle m_t, m_c \rangle$ to denote the move vector: $\lambda p : Player \Rightarrow (match \ p \ with \ Train \Rightarrow m_t \ | \ Controller \Rightarrow m_c)$.

Transitions. Transitions are introduced with the following predicate [2]:

$$\delta : State \rightarrow \langle Move \rangle \rightarrow State \rightarrow Prop \stackrel{\text{def}}{=}$$

| δ q_{out} $\langle stayOut, idle \rangle$ q_{out} | δ q_{out} $\langle request, idle \rangle$ q_{req}
| δ q_{req} $\langle idle, grant \rangle$ q_{gran} | δ q_{req} $\langle idle, delay \rangle$ q_{req}
| δ q_{req} $\langle idle, deny \rangle$ q_{out} | δ q_{gran} $\langle enter, idle \rangle$ q_{in}
| δ q_{gran} $\langle relinquish, idle \rangle$ q_{out} | δ q_{in} $\langle idle, keepClosed \rangle$ q_{in}
| δ q_{in} $\langle idle, reopen \rangle$ q_{out}

Coalitions. Singleton sets of players $T = \{Train\}$ and $C = \{Controller\}$ are defined as:
$$T \stackrel{\text{def}}{=} \lambda p \Rightarrow match \ p \ with \ Train \Rightarrow \{1\} \ | \ Controller \Rightarrow \{ \ \}$$
$$C \stackrel{\text{def}}{=} \lambda p \Rightarrow match \ p \ with \ Train \Rightarrow \{ \ \} \ | \ Controller \Rightarrow \{1\}$$

Atomic State Formulas. The atomic state formulas are easily introduced using case analysis over the current state. For example, a state formula representing the fact that the train is not in the gate is:

$$OutGate \stackrel{\text{def}}{=} \lambda q \Rightarrow match \ q \ with \ q_{in} \Rightarrow False \ | \ \_ \Rightarrow True$$

. In a similar way, we have defined formulas *Requested*, *Granted* and *InGate* according to Example 1.

---

[2] For the sake of readability, we omit here the name of contructors.

Proving Properties. The following properties, taken from [2], are provable in our system:

1. Whenever the train is out of the gate, the controller cannot force it to enter the gate:

$$\langle\!\langle\varnothing\rangle\!\rangle\square\,(\mathit{OutGate}\to\neg\langle\!\langle C\rangle\!\rangle\Diamond\mathit{InGate})$$

2. Whenever the train is out of the gate, the train and the controller can cooperate so that the train will enter the gate:

$$\langle\!\langle\varnothing\rangle\!\rangle\square\,(\mathit{OutGate}\to\langle\!\langle\Sigma\rangle\!\rangle\Diamond\mathit{InGate})$$

For space constraints, we omit proofs here, and we refer the interested reader to [23].

5.2   Controlling an Unbounded Number of Trains

Suppose there is an unknown number of trains to cross a single gate. The gate controller must ensure some safety (for instance, at most one train is in the gate) and liveness (for instance, a request must be processed) properties.

Formalizing the System Using CGS. We propose an extendend CGS S_∞ as a model of the system described above.

Players. The system components are the controller and the set of trains:

$$Player : Set \stackrel{\text{def}}{=} Train : Id \to Player \mid Controller : Player$$

where $Id \stackrel{\text{def}}{=} \mathbb{N}$. We abbreviate t_n the term $Train\ n$, denoting the n-th train.

States. In each state of the system, we should have information about the trains that have made a request to enter the gate, and which train has obtained such permission. To represent the set of trains that want to enter to the gate, we introduce the type $Petition \stackrel{\text{def}}{=} Id \to Bool$. For a function $f : Petition$, we say that t_n wants to enter the gate if $f\ t_n = true$. The set of states is defined as:

$$State : Set \stackrel{\text{def}}{=}\ \mid q_{out} : State \qquad\qquad\qquad \mid q_{req} : Petition \to State$$
$$\mid q_{gran} : Petition \to Id \to State \mid q_{in} : Petition \to Id \to State$$

The first argument of states q_{req}, q_{gran} and q_{in} is used to represent the set of trains that have made a request. The second argument of state q_{gran} (q_{in}) is the id of the train having permission to enter (has entered) the gate.

Moves and Move Vectors. The set of moves is similar to the finite case. Additional moves are used for communication between components. The set of moves is extended in the following way:

$$Move \stackrel{\text{def}}{=}\ \mid stayOut : Move \mid request : Move \qquad \mid grant : Id \to Move$$
$$\mid delay : Move \quad\ \mid deny : Id \to Move \mid denyAll : Move$$
$$\mid enter : Move \quad\ \mid relinquish : Move \mid keepClosed : Move$$
$$\mid reopen : Move \quad \mid idle : Move$$

In the following moves appear the main difference with the finite example: (*deny n*) represents a move where the controller rejects a request from train t_n, *denyAll* models a situation where controller can reject all requests, and (*grant n*) represents a situation where controller gives permission to t_n.

Let m_c : *Move* be a move of the controller and let m_t : $Id \to Move$ be a function assigning a move to each train, we use the notation $\langle m_t, m_c \rangle$ to represent the move vector defined as $\lambda p \Rightarrow (match\ p\ with\ t_n \Rightarrow m_t\ n \mid Controller \Rightarrow m_c)$.

Transitions. To model the transition relation we use the following auxiliary functions: $=_b$: $Id \to Id \to Bool$, that decides equality in type Id; and an overwrite operator $\oplus$: $Petition \to Id \to Bool \to Petition$, such that $(f \oplus \{n \leftarrow b\})$ applied to m returns b if $m = n$, and $f\ m$ otherwise. The transition relation is defined as follows [3]:

$$\delta \overset{\text{def}}{=} \mid \delta\ q_{out}\ \langle \lambda n \Rightarrow stayOut, idle \rangle\ q_{out}$$
$$\mid \forall f, (\exists n : Id, f\ n = true) \to$$
$$\qquad \delta\ q_{out}\ \langle \lambda n \Rightarrow if\ f\ n\ then\ request\ else\ stayOut, idle \rangle\ (q_{req}\ f)$$
$$\mid \forall f\ n, f\ n = true \to$$
$$\qquad \delta\ (q_{req}\ f)\ \langle \lambda n \Rightarrow idle, grant\ n \rangle\ (q_{gran}\ (f \oplus \{n \leftarrow false\})\ n)$$
$$\mid \forall f, \delta\ (q_{req}\ f)\ \langle \lambda n \Rightarrow idle, delay \rangle\ (q_{req}\ f)$$
$$\mid \forall f\ n, (\exists m : Id, m \neq n \land f\ m = true) \to$$
$$\qquad \delta\ (q_{req}\ f)\ \langle \lambda n \Rightarrow idle, deny\ n \rangle\ (q_{req}\ f \oplus \{n \leftarrow false\})$$
$$\mid \forall f\ n, (\forall m : Id, m \neq n \to f\ m = false) \to$$
$$\qquad \delta\ (q_{req}\ f)\ \langle \lambda n \Rightarrow idle, deny\ n \rangle\ q_{out}$$
$$\mid \forall f, \delta\ (q_{req}\ f)\ \langle \lambda n \Rightarrow idle, denyAll \rangle\ q_{out}$$
$$\mid \forall f\ n, \delta\ (q_{gran}\ f\ n)\ \langle enter_n, idle \rangle\ (q_{in}\ f\ n)$$
$$\mid \forall f\ n, (\forall k : Id, k \neq n \to f\ k = false) \to$$
$$\qquad \delta\ (q_{gran}\ f\ n)\ \langle relinquish_n, idle \rangle\ q_{out}$$
$$\mid \forall f\ n, (\exists k : Id, k \neq n \land f\ k = true) \to$$
$$\qquad \delta\ (q_{gran}\ f\ n)\ \langle relinquish_n, idle \rangle\ (q_{req}\ f)$$
$$\mid \forall f\ n, \delta\ (q_{in}\ f\ n)\ \langle \lambda n \Rightarrow idle, keepClosed \rangle\ (q_{in}\ f\ n)$$
$$\mid \forall f\ n, (\forall m, f\ m = false) \to \delta\ (q_{in}\ f\ n)\ \langle \lambda n \Rightarrow idle, reopen \rangle\ q_{out}$$
$$\mid \forall f\ n, (\exists m, f\ m = true) \to \delta\ (q_{in}\ f\ n)\ \langle \lambda n \Rightarrow idle, reopen \rangle\ (q_{req}\ f)$$

where $enter_n, relinquish_n$: $Id \to Move$ are defined as:

$$enter_n \overset{\text{def}}{=} \lambda m \Rightarrow if\ m =_b n\ then\ enter\ else\ idle$$
$$relinquish_n \overset{\text{def}}{=} \lambda m \Rightarrow if\ m =_b n\ then\ relinquish\ else\ idle$$

The relation δ takes into account the existence of different train requests using the petition function. For instance, when the system is in state q_{out}, there are two possible transitions: (1) no train make a request, then the system stays in q_{out}; and (2) there exists a subset of trains making a request to enter the gate, represented with f; in this case, the system make a transition to state $(q_{req}\ f)$.

---

[3] We have omitted constructors names.

Coalitions. Different coalitions can be defined for this system, depending on the properties to be specified. For example:

$$\{t_n\} \stackrel{\text{def}}{=} \lambda p \Rightarrow match\ p\ with \mid Train\ k \Rightarrow if\ n =_b k\ then\ \{1\}\ else\ \{\ \}$$
$$\mid Controller \Rightarrow \{\ \}$$

State Formulas. State formulas can be defined by pattern matching on states. For example, we define formula *Out*, valid if the current state is q_{out}, and $In(n)$, valid if train t_n is in the gate:

$$Out \stackrel{\text{def}}{=} \lambda q \Rightarrow match\ q\ with \mid q_{out} \quad \Rightarrow True \mid \_ \Rightarrow False$$
$$In(n) \stackrel{\text{def}}{=} \lambda q \Rightarrow match\ q\ with \mid q_{in}\ f\ m \Rightarrow if\ n =_b m\ then\ True\ else\ False$$
$$\mid \_ \quad \Rightarrow False$$

Properties. Some properties proved in S_∞ are:

- Controller and train t_n can cooperate so that this train will enter the gate:

$$\langle\!\langle \varnothing \rangle\!\rangle \Box\,(Out \rightarrow \langle\!\langle \{t_n\} \uplus \{Controller\} \rangle\!\rangle \Diamond In(n)) \qquad (12)$$

- Cooperation is needed in order to ensure progress: Neither the set of trains nor the controller can enforce a trace where state $In(n)$ is reached, for some n:

$$\langle\!\langle \varnothing \rangle\!\rangle \Box\,(Out \rightarrow \neg\,(\langle\!\langle \{Controller\} \rangle\!\rangle \Diamond In(n) \vee \langle\!\langle \{t_1, t_2, \ldots\} \rangle\!\rangle \Diamond In(n))) \qquad (13)$$

Formula (12) express a liveness property. To prove it, we construct a strategy F_A for coalition $A = \{t_n, Controller\}$; then, we proceed to show that, if player in A follows strategy F_A, a state where $In(n)$ is valid will be eventually reached, regardless the behaviour of the other components. To prove the safety property (13), we show that it is not the case that controller (the set of trains) can construct an strategy F such that, if controller (the set of trains) follows F, then state q_{in} will be eventually reached. A detailed proof of these properties can be found in [23], along with the analysis of other safety and liveness properties.

6   Conclusions and Future Work

ATL is a game-theoretic generalization of CTL with applications in the formal verification of multi-agent systems. In this paper we have presented a formalization of ATL and its semantic model CGS. Unlike standard ATL semantics, temporal operators have been interpreted in terms of inductive and coinductive types, using a fixpoint characterization of these operators in the CIC.

The formalization presented here was used to model a concurrent system with an unbounded number of players and states, and we have verified some safety and liveness properties expressed as ATL formulas. Unlike automatic techniques, our formal model has no restriction in the size of the CGS, and arbitrary state predicates can be used as atomic propositions of ATL. We conclude that in systems with an intractable size, our formal model, based on an existent type theory (the CIC) with the proof assistant Coq can be used as a specification and verification tool for open multi-agent systems.

A possible extension of our system would consist of formalizing fair-ATL [2], a logic extending ATL semantics with fairness constraints. These constraints rule out certain infinite computations that ignore enabled moves forever.

The logic ATL is a fragment of a more expressive logic, ATL* [2]. In ATL*, a path quantifier $\langle\langle A\rangle\rangle$ is followed by an arbitrary linear time formula, allowing boolean combination and nesting, over $\bigcirc$, $\square$ and $\mathcal{U}$. Another interesting extension to our work is to formalize this logic in the CIC.

ATL has been used to specify properties in contract signing protocols where n agents exchange signatures [11,5]. The model checker MOCHA [3] has succeeded in verifying these protocols in the case where two agents are involved [5]. However, model checking algorithms fail in case of multi-party protocols $(n > 2)$, since these algorithms can be used only with a fixed (and, in practice, small) value for n.

The formalization presented in this work can be used as basis for a formal verification of such protocols. Thus, a further extension of this work involves the verification of multi-party protocols following an approach similar to the one of Section 5.

References

1. Alur, R., Henzinger, T.A., Kupferman, O.: Alternating-Time Temporal Logic. In: de Roever, W.-P., Langmaack, H., Pnueli, A. (eds.) COMPOS 1997. LNCS, vol. 1536, pp. 23–60. Springer, Heidelberg (1998)
2. Alur, R., Henzinger, T., Kupferman, O.: Alternating-time temporal logic. Journal of the ACM 49, 672–713 (2002)
3. Alur, R., Henzinger, T., Mang, F., Qadeer, S., Rajamani, S., Tasiran, S.: Mocha: Modularity in Model Checking. In: Vardi, M.Y. (ed.) CAV 1998. LNCS, vol. 1427, pp. 521–525. Springer, Heidelberg (1998)
4. Bertot, Y., Castéran, P.: Interactive Theorem Proving and Program Development. Coq'Art: The Calculus of Inductive Constructions. In: Texts in Theoretical Computer Science. Springer (2004)
5. Chadha, R., Kremer, S., Scedrov, A.: Formal analysis of multiparty contract signing. Journal of Automated Reasoning 36(1-2), 39–83 (2006)
6. Coquand, T., Huet, G.: The Calculus of Constructions. In: Information and Computation, vol. 76, pp. 95–120. Academic Press (February/March 1988)
7. Coupet-Grimal, S.: LTL in Coq. Contributions to the Coq system, Laboratoire d'Informatique Fondamentale de Marseille (2002), http://coq.inria.fr/contribs/LTL.tar.gz
8. Emerson, E.: Temporal and modal logic. In: Handbook of Theoretical Computer Science, pp. 995–1072. Elsevier (1995)
9. Giménez, E.: A Calculus of Infinite Constructions and its application to the verification of communicating systems. PhD thesis, Ecole Normale Supérieure de Lyon (1996)

10. Goranko, V., van Drimmelen, G.: Complete axiomatization and decidability of alternating-time temporal logic. Theoretical Computer Science 353(1), 93–117 (2006)
11. Kremer, S., Raskin, J.: A game-based verification of non-repudiation and fair exchange protocols. Journal of Computer Security 11(3), 399–429 (2003)
12. Leroy, X.: Formal verification of a realistic compiler. Communications of the ACM 52(7), 107–115 (2009)
13. Luna, C.: Computation tree logic for reactive systems and timed computation tree logic for real time systems. Contributions to the Coq system, Universidad de la República, Uruguay (2000)
14. Merz, S.: An encoding of TLA in Isabelle. Technical report, Institut für Informatic, Universität München, Germany (1999)
15. Paulin-Mohring, C.: Inductive Definitions in the System Coq - rules and Properties. In: Bezem, M., Groote, J.F. (eds.) TLCA 1993. LNCS, vol. 664, pp. 328–345. Springer, Heidelberg (1993)
16. Pnueli, A.: The temporal logic of programs. In: Proceedings of the 18th Annual Symposium on Foundations of Computer Science, pp. 46–57. IEEE Computer Society, Washington, DC (1977)
17. Pnueli, A., Arons, T.: TLPVS: A PVS-Based LTL Verification System. In: Dershowitz, N. (ed.) Verification: Theory and Practice. LNCS, vol. 2772, pp. 598–625. Springer, Heidelberg (2004)
18. Schneider, K., Hoffmann, D.W.: A HOL Conversion for Translating Linear Time Temporal Logic to ω-Automata. In: Bertot, Y., Dowek, G., Hirschowitz, A., Paulin, C., Théry, L. (eds.) TPHOLs 1999. LNCS, vol. 1690, pp. 255–272. Springer, Heidelberg (1999)
19. The Coq development team. The Coq proof assistant reference manual, version 8.2. LogiCal Project, Distributed electronically (2010), http://coq.inria.fr
20. The Coq development team. The Coq Standard Library. LogiCal Project (2010), http://coq.inria.fr/stdlib/
21. van Leeuwen, J. (ed.): Handbook of Theoretical Computer Science, vol. B: Formal Models and Semantics. Elsevier and MIT Press (1990)
22. Zanarini, D.: Formalización de lógica temporal alternante en el cálculo de construcciones coinductivas. Master's thesis, FCEIA, Universidad Nacional de Rosario, Argentina (2008), http://www.fceia.unr.edu.ar/~dante
23. Zanarini, D.: Formalization of alternating time temporal logic in Coq (2010), http://www.fceia.unr.edu.ar/~dante

Author Index